The Anticolonial Transnational

This volume is the first to explore transnational anticolonialism as a global phenomenon that spanned the entire twentieth century. Its collected essays model both a broadening of the issues under consideration and the collaboration necessary to do justice to the scope of this vibrant field. They showcase new work by scholars who explore the anticolonial transnational in multiple geographical regions, from a variety of perspectives, and at different times across the long twentieth century. Revealing that anticolonial movements everywhere in this period were invariably transnational in terms of their imaginaries, mobilities, and networks, these essays also demonstrate how centering transnational connections changes our understanding of the anticolonial past. The legacies of transnational anticolonial strategies and networks fundamentally shaped the present. Together, these essays present a fresh, kaleidoscopic view of the geographical, chronological, and thematic possibilities of the global anticolonial transnational.

Erez Manela is the Francis Lee Higginson Professor of History at Harvard University.

Heather Streets-Salter is Professor and Director of World History Programs at Northeastern University in Boston, Massachusetts.

T0381720

Global and International History

Series Editors
Erez Manela, *Harvard University*
Heather Streets-Salter, *Northeastern University*

The Global and International History series seeks to highlight and explore the convergences between the new International History and the new World History. Its editors are interested in approaches that mix traditional units of analysis such as civilizations, nations, and states with other concepts such as transnationalism, diasporas, and international institutions.

Titles in the Series

The Anticolonial Transnational

Imaginaries, Mobilities, and Networks in the Struggle against Empire

Edited by

EREZ MANELA

Harvard University

HEATHER STREETS-SALTER

Northeastern University

CAMBRIDGE
UNIVERSITY PRESS

Shaftesbury Road, Cambridge CB2 8EA, United Kingdom

One Liberty Plaza, 20th Floor, New York, NY 10006, USA

477 Williamstown Road, Port Melbourne, VIC 3207, Australia

314–321, 3rd Floor, Plot 3, Splendor Forum, Jasola District Centre,
New Delhi – 110025, India

103 Penang Road, #05-06/07, Visioncrest Commercial, Singapore 238467

Cambridge University Press is part of Cambridge University Press & Assessment,
a department of the University of Cambridge.

We share the University's mission to contribute to society through the pursuit of
education, learning and research at the highest international levels of excellence.

www.cambridge.org
Information on this title: www.cambridge.org/9781009359108

DOI: 10.1017/9781009359115

First published 2023

A catalogue record for this publication is available from the British Library.

Library of Congress Cataloging-in-Publication Data
NAMES: Manela, Erez, editor. | Streets-Salter, Heather, editor.
TITLE: The anticolonial transnational : imaginaries, mobilities, and networks in the struggle
against empire / Edited by Erez Manela, Harvard University, Massachusetts, Heather
Streets-Salter, Northeastern University, Boston.
DESCRIPTION: New York, NY : Cambridge University Press, 2023. |
SERIES: Global and international history | Includes bibliographical references and index.
IDENTIFIERS: LCCN 2023021052 (print) | LCCN 2023021053 (ebook) |
ISBN 9781009359108 (hardback) | ISBN 9781009359092 (paperback) |
ISBN 9781009359115 (epub)
SUBJECTS: LCSH: Transnationalism–History–20th century. | World politics–History–20th
century. | International relations–History–20th century.
CLASSIFICATION: LCC JZ1320 .A58 2023 (print) | LCC JZ1320 (ebook) | DDC 305.8009/
04–dc23/eng/20230520
LC record available at https://lccn.loc.gov/2023021052
LC ebook record available at https://lccn.loc.gov/2023021053

ISBN 978-1-009-35910-8 Hardback
ISBN 978-1-009-35909-2 Paperback

Contents

v

Figures

Contributors

Nicole CuUnjieng Aboitiz is a research fellow at Clare Hall, University of Cambridge

Zaib un Nisa Aziz is Assistant Professor in the History of the Modern British Empire at the University of South Florida, Tampa

Vivien Chang is a postdoctoral fellow in International Security Studies at Yale University's Jackson School of Global Affairs

Ruodi Duan is Assistant Professor of History and East Asian Languages and Cultures at Haverford College

Sarah C. Dunstan is Lecturer in the International History of Modern Human Rights at the University of Glasgow

Cindy Ewing is Assistant Professor of Contemporary International History at the University of Toronto

Michael Goebel is Einstein Professor of Global History at the Free University of Berlin

Michele Louro is Professor of History at Salem State University

Erez Manela is the Francis Lee Higginson Professor of History at Harvard University

Kristin Oberiano is Assistant Professor of History at Wesleyan University

Mark Reeves is Senior Lecturer in History at the University of the West of England (Bristol)

Heather Streets-Salter is Professor of History at Northeastern University

Quito Swan is Professor of African American and African Diaspora Studies at Indiana University Bloomington

Lydia Walker is Assistant Professor and Seth Andre Myers Chair in Global Military History at The Ohio State University

Tony Wood is Assistant Professor of History at the University of Colorado Boulder

Acknowledgments

This book began with a workshop that gathered online in June 2021, in the midst of the Covid-19 pandemic. We are grateful to Cemil Aydin, Durba Ghosh, and Su Lin Lewis, who served as commentators there, and especially to Michael Goebel, who, in addition to commenting also contributed an epilogue to the volume. For funding the workshop, we thank the Weatherhead Center for International Affairs at Harvard University. Thanks also to Lucy Rhymer and Emily Plater at Cambridge University Press, who encouraged this volume and helped bring it to publication, and to the anonymous readers for the press, who helped make it better. Finally, our gratitude goes to the authors who contributed to this book. What a pleasure it has been to work with all of them.

I

Introduction

Erez Manela and Heather Streets-Salter

Perhaps more than any other historical process, the struggle for self-determination by colonized people defined the international history of the twentieth century. That struggle transformed a world governed by a handful of sprawling global empires at the dawn of the century into one of some two hundred independent, sovereign states by its end. For decades, historians responded to this transformation by exploring the multiple stories behind the emergence of these new states. The histories that resulted both took the advent of new nation-states as natural and inevitable, and focused on the mass-based, constitutionalist, nationalist parties that developed in nearly every colony by mid-century.[1] Although the various paths to decolonization differed widely, most histories of this process nevertheless followed a narrative in which anticolonial movements emerged and eventual decolonization occurred within bilateral relationships between imperial metropoles and their colonies, with little reference to external events or issues.

In recent years, scholars have begun to rewrite this narrative in ways that point toward a fundamental reassessment of how and why decolonization occurred.[2] This scholarship has shown that many anticolonial movements drew extensively on extra-national connections and

---

[1] This historiography is particularly large for the Indian and African National Congresses. For example, Amales Tripathi, *Indian National Congress and the Struggle for Freedom, 1885–1947* (Oxford: Oxford University Press, 2014); Sheridan Johns and R. Hunt Davis, Jr., *Mandela, Tambo, and the African National Congress: The Struggle Against Apartheid, 1948–1990, A Documentary Survey* (Oxford: Oxford University Press, 1991).

[2] Historians of the British empire have been particularly active in this regard. See, for example, Antoinette Burton, *The Trouble with Empire: Challenges to Modern British*

organizations to realize their goals or imagined different arrangements for the postcolonial world than the collection of independent nation-states as we now know it. These included communist anticolonial movements that envisioned decolonization as a drive toward a confederation of nations bound together through the Communist International (see chapters by Louro, Aziz, and Wood); movements that imagined the realignment of international society based on visions of common religion or heritage, such as pan-Islamism, pan-Asianism, or pan-Africanism (see chapters by CuUnjieng Aboitiz, Dunstan, and Swan); and movements that sought to drive change from outside the colonial–metropolitan relationship altogether (see chapter by Ewing).[3] Just as important, recent scholarship has consistently demonstrated that even the mass-based nationalist parties (including the Indian National Congress, the African National Congress, and the Nationalist Party of Indonesia, to name only a few) were in fact transnationally oriented from the outset.[4] This scholarship

Imperialism (Oxford: Oxford University Press, 2017), and Priyamvada Gopal, *Insurgent Empire: Anticolonial Resistance and British Dissent* (London: Verso Books, 2019).

[3] For example, Frederik Petersson, "'We Are Neither Visionaries Nor Utopian Dreamers': Willi Münzenberg, the League against Imperialism, and the Comintern, 1925–1933" (Abo Akademi University, 2013); Ali Raza, Franziska Roy, and Benjamin Zachariah, eds., *The Internationalist Moment: South Asia, Worlds, and World Views, 1917–1939* (New Delhi: Sage, 2014); N. K. Barooah, *Chatto: The Life and Times of an Indian Anti-Imperialist in Europe* (New Delhi: Oxford University Press, 2004); Michael Goebel, *Anti-Imperial Metropolis: Interwar Paris and the Seeds of Third World Nationalism* (New York: Cambridge University Press, 2015); Leslie James, *George Padmore and Decolonization from Below: Pan-Africanism, the Cold War, and the End of Empire* (New York: Palgrave Macmillan, 2015); Susan Pennybacker, *From Scottsboro to Munich: Race and Political Culture in 1930s Britain* (Princeton, NJ: Princeton University Press, 2009); Maia Ramnath, *Haj to Utopia: How the Ghadar Movement Charted Global Radicalism and Attempted to Overthrow the British Empire* (Berkeley: University of California Press, 2011); Heather Streets-Salter, *World War One in Southeast Asia* (Cambridge: Cambridge University Press, 2017); Heather Streets-Salter, "The Noulens Affair in East and Southeast Asia: International Communism in the Interwar Period," *Journal of American East-Asian Relations* 21 (2014); Margaret Stevens, *Red International and Black Caribbean: Communists in New York City, Mexico, and the West Indies, 1919–1939* (London: Pluto Press, 2017); Christopher Dietrich, *Oil Revolution: Anticolonial Elites, Sovereign Rights, and the Economic Culture of Decolonization* (Cambridge: Cambridge University Press, 2017); David Featherstone, *Solidarity: Hidden Histories and Geographies of Internationalism* (London: Zed Books, 2012); Seema Sohi, *Echoes of Mutiny: Race, Surveillance, and Indian Anticolonialism in North America* (Oxford: Oxford University Press, 2014).

[4] For example, Michele Louro, *Comrades against Imperialism: Nehru, India, and Interwar Nationalism* (Cambridge: Cambridge University Press, 2018); Glenda Sluga, *Internationalism in the Age of Nationalism* (Philadelphia: University of Pennsylvania Press, 2015); Harald Fischer-Tiné, "Indian Nationalism and the 'World Forces':

has shown how nationalist leaders drew inspiration, developed policy, and formulated plans of action as a result of their contacts with other anticolonial leaders and movements from around the world. Often this was because anticolonial leaders developed personal relationships with their counterparts from other colonies, but it was also aided by the wide, transnational dissemination of news and literature about anticolonialism through this period.[5] As it turns out, anticolonialism in the twentieth century, and even beyond, was almost invariably transnational in both thought and action.

In spite of the recent surge of work exploring the anticolonial transnational, no single volume yet exists that explores it as a general phenomenon that operated in all regions of the world and across the chronological divide of World War II.[6] This volume takes up that challenge, and in doing so seeks to model both a broadening of the conversation and of the collaboration necessary to do justice to the scope of this vibrant field. The essays featured here, then, are designed to showcase the work of scholars who are actively engaged in exploring what we are calling "the anticolonial transnational" in multiple (and sometimes

Transnational and Diasporic Dimensions of the Indian Freedom Movement on the Eve of the First World War," *Journal of Global History* 2:3 (2007); Christopher Goscha, *Thailand and the Southeast Asian Networks of the Vietnamese Revolution, 1885–1954* (Richmond, Surrey: Curzon Press, 1999); Jeffrey James Byrne, *Mecca of Revolution: Algeria, Decolonisation and the Third World Order* (Oxford: Oxford University Press, 2006); Adom Getachew, *Worldmaking after Empire: The Rise and Fall of Self-Determination* (Princeton, NJ: Princeton University Press, 2019); Su Lin Lewis, *Cities in Motion: Urban Life and Cosmopolitanism in Southeast Asia, 1920–1940* (Cambridge: Cambridge University Press, 2016); Jonathan Derrick, *Africa's Agitators: Militant Anti-Colonialism in Africa and the West, 1918–1939* (New York: Columbia University Press, 2008).

[5] Nicholas Owen, "The Soft Heart of the British Empire: Indian Radicals in Edwardian London," *Past & Present*, 220:1 (August 2013); Brent Hayes Edwards, *The Practice of Diaspora: Literature, Translation, and the Rise of Black Internationalism* (Cambridge, MA: Harvard University Press, 2003).

[6] Among those that have attempted a global scope are the following, though these are focused around single institutions or a single historical moment. See Erez Manela, *The Wilsonian Moment: Self-Determination and the International Origins of Anticolonial Nationalism* (Oxford: Oxford University Press, 2007); Michele Louro, Carolien Stolte, Heather Streets-Salter, and Sana Tannoury-Karam, *The League against Imperialism: Lives and Afterlives* (Leiden and Chicago: Leiden University Press, 2020); Christopher J. Lee, ed., *Making a World after Empire: The Bandung Moment and Its Political Afterlives* (Athens, OH: Ohio University Press, 2010); Holger Weiss, *International Communism and Transnational Solidarity: Radical Networks, Mass Movements, and Global Politics, 1919–1939* (Leiden: Brill, 2016).

understudied) geographical regions, from a variety of perspectives, and at many different times across the long twentieth century.

Our intention is that individual essays should be read as part of the greater whole rather than merely as stand-alone pieces. In our desire to move the field forward and to stimulate conversation and collaboration, our process for this volume deliberately created space for both among all of the authors, the editors, and three outside commenters when essays were still in early draft form.[7] Authors read all of the essays, and then participated in an intensive workshop in which the entire group thought together about the structure, themes, and individual contributions they surfaced. Only then did the authors redraft their essays into their final form. The result, we believe, is a series of essays about very different places, times, and people that nevertheless speak to one another and to the wider field as a whole.

Of course, no single volume seeking to explore such a vast issue as the anticolonial transnational writ large can be encyclopedic. Much excellent work on important topics, for reasons of timing or space, could not be included. Some well-known actors or events do not appear in these pages, while lesser-known counterpoints do. Yet the intention was not to be exclusive but rather to offer a kaleidoscopic view of the geographical, chronological, and thematic possibilities offered by attention to the global anticolonial transnational. Taken together, we believe the essays gathered here demonstrate that viewing anticolonialism as a fundamentally transnational phenomenon has deep implications for understanding both the twentieth and the twenty-first centuries. Not least, they highlight the fact that many anticolonial activists and organizations – and not just those on the far-left – understood imperialism as a global challenge that required coordinated strategies and networks of solidarity on a transnational scale. Essays in this volume also demonstrate that centering once-marginalized transnational connections can change our understanding of the anticolonial past more generally, and indeed that the legacies of transnational anticolonial strategies and networks shaped the world we live in today, right up to the present.

The definition of "the anticolonial transnational" we agreed upon for this volume is capacious. If we apprehend the *inter*national as interactions that happened *between* recognized, sovereign states, then *trans*national

---

[7] We were aided in this task by a generous grant from Harvard University's Weatherhead Center, which funded the workshop, and by Michael Goebel, Cemil Aydin, and Durba Ghosh, who served as commenters.

space, by its very nature, existed outside or went beyond such formal spaces, centered instead in networks and connections that were either informal or operated through institutions – such as the League against Imperialism – that existed on the margins of international society.[8] The anticolonial transnational and those who operated within it often intersected with and even crossed into formal international spaces; indeed, this transition was, more often than not, an explicit goal of their efforts. Thus, we see the anticolonial transnational intersecting with formal international institutions in petitions written by still-colonized people to formerly colonized members of the United Nations (Ewing), in the creation of informal anticolonial networks by officials in the US government, or in the corporate world (Walker). We also see its legacies in the tensions between class-based and race-based imaginaries that inflected the relations between the People's Republic of China and post-colonial nations in Africa (Duan).

Transnational anticolonial activities pervaded the interstices of international society, reflected in connections between individuals and organizations who were forced to operate outside the formal spaces of sovereignty or at their margins. Many of the subjects in these essays were barred from participating in formal international networks and thus established their own counter-organizations (Wood and Aziz) or created their own informal networks that transcended racial, colonial, or cultural boundaries (Louro, CuUnjieng Aboitiz, Swan). Different though the context of each essay is, a persistent theme across many of them is the ways the relationships and networks chronicled within them pushed *beyond* national, regional, imperial, social, racial, organizational, or institutional boundaries. Taken together they constituted what we are calling here "the anticolonial transnational."

***

The actors and organizations that made up the anticolonial world throughout the twentieth century were transnational in at least three different ways. First, they were transnational in their imaginaries, that is, in how they thought about the world and imagined its possible futures. Second, they were transnational in their mobilities, in how they moved about the world as they pursued their struggle against colonialism and imperialism. And third, they were transnational in their networks,

---

[8] See Louro et al., *The League against Imperialism.*

meaning in the people they met and the connections they made with them, whether through in-person meetings or through correspondence and other writings. Understanding how each of these aspects of the anticolonial transnational worked and how they intersected has for some time now been at the forefront of new scholarship on anticolonialism. The essays collected in this volume exemplify and probe all of them, extending our understanding and offering fresh perspectives on each aspect separately and on how they interacted across the twentieth century.

Anticolonial *imaginaries* were transnational because, from early on, those who struggled against empire recognized that their struggle was global in scope. The new world order they were seeking to bring into existence, they realized, could not come into being or persist for long solely within individual national, regional, or imperial spaces. Rather, the transition from the imperial to the postcolonial order would necessarily be a transformation of global scope, and it required not simply the withdrawal of colonial rule but the complete reorganization of international society through the delegitimization and elimination of imperialism everywhere. The struggle for self-determination in any one place or context, therefore, was inextricably linked to similar struggles elsewhere across the world. For this reason, the activists who operated in the spaces of the anticolonial transnational were exquisitely attuned to events and developments across the world and to ideas and discourses that circulated transnationally. Sarah Dunstan's essay, for example, shows us how Cheikh Anta Diop's rewriting of African history was fed by multiple scholars across the African diaspora, while Nicole CuUnjieng Aboitiz demonstrates that early Filipino nationalists were inspired by other Asian nationalist movements as well as by Japan's success in keeping the European imperial powers at bay. Writing about a much later period, Kristin Oberiano's chapter illustrates how native Chamorros seeking self-determination on the US-controlled island of Guam were inspired and mobilized by the movements of other Pacific peoples seeking independence.

The anticolonial world was a transnationally *mobile* world, too. This was because many colonial peoples, whether they were self-consciously activists against empire or not, were themselves supremely mobile, sometimes by choice but more often out of necessity. Some moved as students, sometimes to the colonial metropole but elsewhere as well. This was true, for example, of Cheikh Anta Diop and the Filipino nationalist Carlos Romulo. Others, like the Indian communist leader M. N. Roy or the American radical activist Agnes Smedley, moved to escape the reach of colonial authorities, while still others moved as itinerant laborers, merchants, working professionals, or political leaders. Often, a single individual could claim several of these identities, either in succession or at once, donning and doffing them as circumstances required. In the cases of many such individuals, the development of a transnational imaginary grew and was fed by their very mobility. This mobility allowed and indeed required them to view their peoples' experiences with colonialism at a remove, to encounter new realities, new places, and new ideas and, sometimes, afforded them greater freedoms of movement, publishing, and association.[9]

Such mobility also played an important role in constructing the complex, shifting, transnational *networks* that connected anticolonial activists across the world. Indeed, in many cases mobility allowed anticolonial activists the chance to meet and organize with others fighting colonialism in different ways and places. These networks, plotted across global space, often were initially centered on what Michael Goebel has called, in reference to Paris, the "anti-imperial metropolis."[10] In the early years of the twentieth century, perhaps the most notable of these places were imperial metropoles that, in addition to Paris, included London, Berlin, and Tokyo (CuUnjieng Aboitiz). These were soon joined by centers of fervent revolutionary activity, like Mexico City after 1910 (Wood) and Moscow after 1917 (Aziz), with additional ancillary sites in Europe (Geneva) and Asia (Hong Kong, Shanghai, Singapore) emerging in the first half of the twentieth century. In the post–World War II era, however, the centers of activity of these anticolonial networks shifted decisively southward, as cities such as Delhi, Bandung, Dakar, Cairo, Algiers, and Dar es Salaam became major nodes after they transitioned from colonial to postcolonial status.[11]

Yet transnational anticolonial networks did not have to rely on travel and in-person meetings. Just as often, as a number of the chapters in this volume show, they were knitted together through correspondence,

---

[9] This greater freedom of movement was sometimes limited by metropolitan surveillance networks, as Seema Sohi, Daniel Brückenhaus, and Klaas Stutje demonstrate. See Sohi, *Echoes of Mutiny*; Daniel Brückenhaus, *Policing Transnational Protest: Liberal Imperialism and the Surveillance of Anticolonialists in Europe, 1905–1945* (Oxford: Oxford University Press, 2017); and Klaas Stutje, *Campaigning in Europe for a Free Indonesia: Indonesian Nationalists and the Worldwide Anticolonial Movement, 1917–1931* (Copenhagen: NIAS Press, 2019).

[10] Goebel, *Anti-Imperial Metropolis*.

[11] Stephen Legg et al., eds., *Placing Internationalism: International Conferences and the Making of the Modern World* (London: Bloomsbury, 2021).

messages moving through couriers, and the flow of ideas about the purposes of the struggle and the means for carrying it out. Moreover, by the latter part of the twentieth century, these transnational networks increasingly penetrated into the official organizations of international society, such as the United Nations, as more and more postcolonial nations joined that organization (Ewing and Chang), or were shifted into international, state-to-state relations as anticolonial movements became ruling parties (Duan). At the same time, even in a notionally postcolonial era struggles against colonial arrangements, as in Guam (Oberiano), or neocolonial relationships, as in Bermuda (Swan), continued to sustain and redefine the spaces of the anticolonial transnational. Taken together, the essays collected here show the myriad ways in which the imaginaries, mobilities, and networks that together made up the anticolonial transnational shaped the lives of individuals and movements and were, in turn, shaped by them.

* * *

Just as we no longer speak of "internationalism" in the singular but rather, following Glenda Sluga and Patricia Clavin,[12] of internationalisms in the plural, this volume prompts us to consider the existence not of a single anticolonial transnational but of many. To date, perhaps the most widely studied type of anticolonial transnational activity has been the left variety, tracking a strong though not uncomplicated association throughout the century between anti-imperialism and radical left-wing politics. Still, as the essays by Tony Wood and Zaib un Nisa Aziz in this volume demonstrate, left-wing anticolonialism, too, came in several flavors. The radicals of Mexico City in the 1920s, on whom Wood's essay centers, differed in multiple ways from those about whom Aziz writes, seeking as they did proletarian revolution in British India, even if they were both inspired by and sought leadership and aid from the Communist International after 1920 and often intersected with each other along various anticolonial transnational circuits.

In the 1920s, anticolonial activists in Mexico City established the city as a hub of transnational anti-imperialist activism in the western hemisphere. Until the end of the decade – when government authorities in Mexico stopped tolerating such visible leftist radicalism – the metropolis

<hr/>

[12] Glenda Sluga and Patricia Calvin, eds., *Internationalisms: A Twentieth Century History* (Cambridge: Cambridge University Press, 2017).

served as a beacon of solidarity and locus of connection between the colonized people of the world and those in Latin America suffering under US economic imperialism. At the same time, the Bolshevik Revolution and the establishment of the Comintern gave Indian anticolonialists a new language and impetus for rising up against British rule. Yet, as Aziz shows, systematic repression by the colonial authorities compelled Indian communist revolutionaries further into the anticolonial transnational, as they were forced to operate either underground or from exile in Europe, North America, or elsewhere. Meanwhile, the Comintern worked to harness the anticolonial transnational for its own purposes, leading to the establishment in Brussels in 1927 of the League against Imperialism as a counter-organization to the Geneva-based League of Nations, where the major imperial powers held sway.[13]

Throughout the twentieth century many anticolonial circuits, like those just mentioned, were also anticapitalist. In fact, in much of the historical scholarship on anticolonialism there prevails the (sometimes explicit, often implicit) assumption, following Lenin's famous dictum, that this connection is a necessary and intrinsic one. However, several essays in this volume demonstrate that not all anticolonial activists saw themselves in those terms. Some, like the protagonist of Mark Reeves' essay, the Filipino diplomat Carlos Romulo, couched their demands for self-determination in the language of Wilsonian liberalism and saw independence as a path to fuller participation in the capitalist world order rather than to its dismantling.[14] Others, like Winifred Armstrong, the American consultant who is the subject of Lydia Walker's essay, saw support for self-determination and decolonization in the Global South as part of the push to reform, rather than overturn, the machinery of global capitalism. Since Armstrong advised not only politicians but also corporate leaders, Walker's essay also raises the question of how multinational corporations, many of which were long among the major beneficiaries of colonial exploitation, came to support decolonization even as they sought to use transnational advocacy to shape its dynamics in ways that advanced their interests. By interrogating the intersections between anticolonialism and capitalism in the twentieth century, Reeves

---

[13] Louro et al., eds., *The League against Imperialism.*

[14] For another example of a liberal (but not radical left-wing) anticolonialist, see Harald Fischer-Tiné, *Shyamji Krishnavarma: Sanskrit, Sociology and Anti-Imperialism* (London: Taylor & Francis Group, 2014).

and Walker ask us to reconsider the scope and nature of the anticolonial transnational.

If debates over social and economic arrangements – whether anarchist, socialist, communist, or capitalist – were central features of the anticolonial transnational, so were projects centered on commonalities of culture, history, and race. These included, as already mentioned, political projects and connections predicated on a variety of "pan" ideologies, as in the proliferation of pan-Asian, pan-African, pan-Turkic, or pan-Islamic anticolonial networks, each with its own subvariants and groupings (there were different versions of pan-Asian ideologies, for example, that centered on Japan, or China, or India, or on perceived cultural affinities, such as Buddhism). Such projects sometimes served as vehicles to advance the nationalist or imperial agenda of one power or another, most notably with the Japanese promotion of a pan-Asian "co-prosperity sphere" in the 1930s and 1940s.[15] But more often than not such projects were viewed by their promoters and adherents as designed to transcend rather than reinforce narrow nationalisms, as was the case with the advocacy of pan-Asian connections by such figures as the Bengali poet Rabindranath Tagore or the Chinese intellectual Liang Qichao.[16]

Placing oft-ignored Filipino activists and intellectuals at the center of the early development of pan-Asian anticolonial circuits, Nicole CuUnjieng Aboitiz argues that histories of the Philippines' struggle for independence have tended to ignore Filipino imaginaries and networks that tied them to the larger East and Southeast Asian region. She demonstrates how Filipino activists consciously sought to connect the history of the islands with the nearby Malay world, and to draw inspiration – and seek aid – from the Japanese, who provided an example of successful Asian modernization. CuUnjieng Aboitiz's story highlights the intellectual and affective power of pan-Asianism as a means of transcending the isolation of the Filipino struggle, and it also underlines the limitations of this ideological formation and the solidarities it engendered when, for example, the Japanese failed to deliver military aid to Filipino rebels and instead transferred it to fellow Asian anticolonialists in China.

Moving from a pan-Asian context to a pan-African one, Sarah Dunstan brings another fresh perspective to the role of culture, race,

---

[15] See Jeremy Yellen, *The Greater East Asia Co-prosperity Sphere: When Total Empire Met Total War* (Ithaca, NY: Cornell University Press, 2019).

[16] Pankaj Mishra, *From the Ruins of Empire: The Revolt against the West and the Remaking of Asia* (London: Penguin, 2012).

and history in the anticolonial transnational, showing how the work of Senegalese historian Cheikh Anta Diop sought to decolonize African history and recover it from western frameworks that portrayed it as primitive, unchanging, and unworthy of study. Diop was part of a global network of anticolonial and antiracist thinkers who believed that the recovery of a complex, dynamic African past was crucial to the pan-African, anticolonial politics in the present.

Whether operating through ideology or culture, the exchanges and connections that made up the anticolonial transnational both reflected and facilitated expressions of solidarity among colonial peoples fighting for self-determination. Moreover, as Michele Louro's essay about the American radical Agnes Smedley reminds us, anticolonial solidarities were not just performed among institutions or movements, but also between individuals, and could be intimate as well as political. Indeed, Louro traces the way that Smedley's personal choices can be read as deeply political statements about both racial and class solidarities. Smedley's romantic partnership with the Indian revolutionary Virendranath Chattopadhyaya ('Chatto') challenged established racial boundaries and scandalized many of her contemporaries, as did her later choice to live independently in China and associate with Chinese revolutionaries. Similarly, her romantic partnership there with the German journalist and Soviet spy Richard Sorge signaled Smedley's willingness to prioritize class solidarity over national ethos, even in her personal life.

Smedley's life story, along with that of Winifred Armstrong explored in Lydia Walker's chapter, also highlight the roles that women played within the spaces of the anticolonial transnational, an important contribution to a literature that has so far overwhelmingly focused on men and their homosocial institutional worlds.[17] Louro's chapter raises a range of issues about the place of women in transnational anticolonial networks, calling for more attention to the role of women in building and sustaining these networks and in working within them. Winifred Armstrong, who worked behind the scenes to encourage anticolonial policy within the United States government and to undermine apartheid through corporate strategy, seems to fit uncomfortably with Agnes Smedley's radical leftist politics and support for women's rights. Indeed, Armstrong herself seems

---

[17] This is certainly the case in Louro et al., *The League against Imperialism*. Tim Harper's recent *Underground Asia: Global Revolutionaries and the Assault on Empire* (Cambridge, MA: Harvard University Press, 2021) does try to surface women revolutionaries, though it, too, is mostly a story of men.

not to have identified as a feminist and did not see her work in terms of her gender, in spite of the fact that her influence and independence as a woman were unusual for the time. Even so, Armstrong's story invites us to think about the ways other centrist, practical, and even conservative women may also have played roles in the many anticolonial transnationals operating over the course of the twentieth century.

In the post–World War II era, as the acceleration of decolonization gave birth to dozens of newly sovereign, postcolonial states, transnational anticolonial activism began to spill more often from the transnational realm into the international arena, thus giving rise to new mechanisms for solidarity. One such mechanism is illuminated in Cindy Ewing's essay, which focuses on petitions claiming human rights abuses submitted to the United Nations by colonized peoples living in UN trust territories in the 1940s and 1950s. Ewing shows how UN representatives from nations that had only recently gained their independence – initially dubbed the Arab-Asian group – worked in concert to bring international attention to the complaints made in these human rights petitions. Thus, not only did members of the Arab-Asian group work in solidarity with one another, they also used the UN as a platform to foster solidarity with groups who had not yet attained the right to self-determination. While the Arab-Asian group could not always effect the desired outcomes, it did achieve important victories that had real impact on the timeline of decolonization, including, for example, turning the UN against Dutch efforts to reassert colonial control in Indonesia.

If solidarity against imperialism was a main feature, indeed a major purpose, of the anticolonial transnational, several of the essays here also remind us of the limits and contradictions that often complicated such solidarities. Ruodi Duan explores this theme in the context of Chinese–Tanzanian relations in the first half of the 1960s. When Tanzania became independent in 1961, representatives of the People's Republic of China who hoped to gain influence in the new East African state bonded with Tanzanian socialists over a common critique of Indians. For the Tanzanians, Indian merchants in East Africa had been despised collaborators with British imperialism, while the Chinese had just fought a brutal border war with India, and thus solidarity was built over this mutual antipathy. However, when Tanzanian nationalists later targeted Arabs in their midst for similar reasons, this collided with the Chinese view of Arabs and Africans as part of a united, global working class. Thus, the Tanzanian view of Arabs in Zanzibar through a racial lens as exploitive others conflicted with Chinese class-based visions of an anticolonial international rooted in a global working class that encompassed all victims of Euro-American imperialism.

This volume also challenges the typical timeline of anticolonialism and decolonization. According to the common chronology, modern anticolonialism emerged in various places across Asia and Africa in the late nineteenth and early twentieth centuries. It then accelerated in the years that followed the World War I and the transformations it wrought in international society, and finally came to fruition in the decades that followed the World War II. In those years, dozens of overseas colonial possessions of the British, French, Dutch, and finally the Portuguese empires threw off the shackles of colonial rule to become sovereign nation-states, a status that was cemented with the formal recognition represented in their admission to full membership in the United Nations. This timeline is, of course, broadly accurate as far as it goes. But as several of the chapters that follow suggest, it arguably obscures as much as much as it reveals.

First, as Vivien Chang's chapter reminds us, the political sovereignty that was gained with decolonization left many of the promises of anticolonialism unfulfilled, a phenomenon that might be called "arrested decolonization."[18] The disappointment was most notable in the realm of economic development, as colonial era relations of economic exploitation were replaced by what many in the newly independent nations saw as neocolonial dependency. In response, newly independent states in Asia and Africa, joined by many long-independent yet economically underdeveloped Latin American nations, worked in international forums to advance demands for a New International Economic Order (NIEO).[19] The advocates for the NIEO argued that it would help to make up for centuries of colonial exploitation, promote a fairer distribution of resources globally, and bring postcolonial nations closer to their long-deferred goal of economic prosperity and self-determination. But Chang's contribution moves beyond the familiar story of the rise and fall of the NIEO to argue that when the push for a New International Economic Order faltered in the face of resistance led by the United

---

[18] We are grateful to Kristin Oberiano for this phrase. For a similar usage, see Alessandro Iandolo, *Arrested Development: The Soviet Union in Ghana, Guinea, and Mali, 1955–1968* (Ithaca, NY: Cornell University Press, 2022).

[19] See essays in *Humanity* 6:1 (Spring 2015), Special Issue: Toward a History of the New International Economic Order.

States, some Third World nations then turned to a strategy of economic self-reliance as an alternative path toward economic independence.

Another perspective on the persistence of anticolonialism after decolonization emerges from the recognition that for every successful claim for self-determination that led to decolonization and independence there were numerous other, conflicting claims that could not succeed and that therefore remained, and often still remain, unfulfilled. This dynamic often manifested as what Lydia Walker has identified as "states-in-waiting"; that is, separatist ethnic groups living within newly independent states who claim the right to secede from the postcolonial state and often continue to fight toward that goal both on the ground and around the world.[20] Perhaps the bloodiest example of this phenomenon in the post-war era was the short-lived Republic of Biafra, predominantly populated by Igbo people, whose attempt to separate from the postcolonial Nigerian state was suppressed by the central authorities in a brutal civil war that lasted from 1967 to 1970. But there were many others.

Some of the most innovative recent work on the dissemination and deployment of discourses of self-determination has emphasized the ways in which such claims have been used throughout the twentieth century to advocate for something other than the establishment of an independent, internationally recognized sovereign state. In this vein, Kristen Oberiano's chapter in this volume looks at this question from the rarely examined perspective of the Chamorro people, the Indigenous people of the US-ruled Pacific Ocean island of Guam, whose fight for the recognition of their right to self-determination has persisted well into a time which, for most of the world, would count as a postcolonial era.[21] In a context both very different and yet quite similar in its relationship to US empire in the late-twentieth century, Quito Swan's chapter examines the resonance of colonialism and decolonization in the reggae music scene in Bermuda. Taken together, the two chapters show us how, in a postcolonial era, the scope of the anticolonial transnational has simultaneously narrowed and broadened. The first, because many nationalist movements that had previously been forced to operate in the transnational space won recognition and, with it, the right to shift into the international realm. The

---

[20] Lydia Walker, "States-in-Waiting: Nationalism, Internationalism, Decolonization." Doctoral dissertation, Harvard University, 2018.
[21] There is a burgeoning literature on Indigenous struggles for self-determination in transnational contexts. See, e.g., Brad Simpson, "The United States and the Curious History of Self-Determination," *Diplomatic History* 36:4 (2012), pp. 675–694.

second, because those anticolonial claims that remained had to evolve their language and tactics to suit the postcolonial era and to shift the struggle into new realms, including that of popular culture.

The persistence of anticolonial transnational networks in the postcolonial era is a reminder that, beyond the substantial material interests involved in the fight for self-determination, that struggle is also, and in some cases perhaps centrally, a quest for recognition and dignity. Indeed, Charles Taylor's famous notion of the "politics of recognition" was informed and shaped by the struggles of Indigenous peoples in places such as the United States, Canada, Australia, and New Zealand, where the goals have most often not been framed in terms of the attainment of full, international sovereignty but rather defined in terms of the recognition of collective identity and rights by and within an existing polity.[22] Yet the insights suggested by the idea of the politics of recognition also apply to more "traditional" struggles of self-determination; that is, to the struggles that the term "anticolonialism" has traditionally conjured up, and particularly to their relationship to the history of the anticolonial transnational. Anticolonial movements and activists, after all, were compelled to operate in the *transnational* space precisely because they were denied recognition in the *international* arena and their demands were therefore generally excluded from formal international institutions. It is hardly surprising, then, that in many cases such actors retreated from the anticolonial transnational to the extent that they achieved the international recognition and status they demanded and fought for.

Thinking about anticolonialism as a struggle for recognition within international society highlights yet another important theme in this volume: the centrality of questions of inclusion and exclusion as they were understood by anticolonial actors throughout the twentieth century. Nicole CuUnjieng Aboitiz's essay, for example, centers on the Philippine quest for inclusion within emerging ideas of Asia. Sarah Dunstan's chapter shows how Cheikh Anta Diop's struggle for the inclusion, indeed the centering of Africa within world history was crucial to his anticolonial practice. Mark Reeves, meanwhile, borrows the concept of "clubbability" from Mrinalini Sinha's work on British India and applies it to international society to characterize the aspirations of anticolonial activists

---

[22] Charles Taylor, *Multiculturalism and "The Politics of Recognition": An Essay* (Princeton, NJ: Princeton University Press, 1992). Implications of this concept for international politics are explored in Thomas Lindemann and Erik Ringmar, eds., *The International Politics of Recognition* (Boulder, CO: Paradigm, 2012).

such as Carlos Romulo for acceptance and inclusion in international forums – it was not a "family of nations" as much as it was an exclusive club.[23] This was an aspiration that in the post–World War II era became codified in, but was by no means limited to, the formal admission to membership in the United Nations, an organization that displays many of the characteristics of the exclusive clubs that Sinha originally wrote about.

Like the concept of "sociability," which has also recently been applied to international affairs and interactions,[24] the idea of "clubbability" highlights the social and interpersonal aspects of the anticolonial struggle. But it underscores more emphatically the bright line that separates exclusion from the club of sovereign nations from inclusion in it and, therefore, highlights the central significance of making the transition from the former status to the latter. As many of the essays in this volume show, in the course of the twentieth century many of those who operated within one or more anticolonial transnational spaces made that transition to recognition when they were "admitted" into the international realm. Others, however, remained on the outside looking in, explaining the persistence of the anticolonial transnational, *mutatis mutandis*, into the twenty-first century. Our hope is that the essays in this volume, taken together, will help to expand the boundaries of scholarship on anticolonialism, decolonization, and the postcolonial condition in their innovative treatment of some of the complex issues, places, and contexts that have constituted the anticolonial transnational in the twentieth century and beyond.

---

[23] Mrinalini Sinha, "Britishness, Clubbability, and the Colonial Public Sphere: The Genealogy of an Imperial Institution in Colonial India," *Journal of British Studies* 40:4 (October 2001), pp. 489–521.

[24] Deepak Nair, "Sociability in International Politics: Golf and ASEAN's Cold War Diplomacy," *International Political Sociology* 14:2 (2020), pp. 196–214.

PART I

THE MANY ANTICOLONIAL TRANSNATIONALS

2

Philippine Asianist Thought and Pan-Asianist Action at the Turn of the Twentieth Century

Nicole CuUnjieng Aboitiz

The long Philippine Revolution of 1896–1905, which began against Spain and continued against the United States of America, took place against a backdrop of imperial consolidation and local resistance that was truly region-wide. This included: the French conquest of Cambodia, Vietnam, and Laos and creation of French Indochina by 1897; the 1885–1888 Cần Vương movement in Vietnam, a contemporaneous anti-French revolt in Cambodia, and the 1903–1905 activism of the Vietnamese scholar-gentry; the British annexation of Upper Burma following the Third Anglo-Burmese War in 1885; the incorporation of Burma as a province of British India by 1897; and the formation of the Burmese nationalist movement continuing into the 1920s. In archipelagic Southeast Asia, it included: the full extension of direct Dutch colonial rule throughout the Netherlands East Indies from 1872 to 1910 against stiff resistance, especially in Aceh; the centralization of British power in the Federated Malay States from the 1890s to the 1910s. This era also saw the emergence of Japan as a non-Western imperial power after the Meiji Restoration of 1868, the early exertion of its dominance over Korea in 1876 culminating in annexation of Korea in 1910, as well as the Japanese annexation and incorporation of Taiwan beginning in 1895. Yet, this transnational and regional historical setting has barely been incorporated into the locally and Western-oriented historiography of the Philippine Revolution, while our accounts of the anticolonial transnational generally begin in the mid-twentieth century. This chapter seeks to extend our consideration of the anticolonial transnational earlier to the turn of the twentieth century, when the rising power of Japan was redrawing anticolonial geographies of political affinity in Asia and providing a new model of non-Western modernity, and when the anticolonial "periphery" of Asia was redefining what defined Asia, actively envisioning its anticolonial/postcolonial modern future. Crucial to this was a recuperation and reimagination of precolonial Asia itself, a central anticolonial and transnational Asianist strategy that impacted formulations of civilization, universal history, and the anticolonial international within Asia.

In 1875 the Philippine Propaganda Movement, led by the *ilustrado* (educated elite), began publishing arguments for Spanish colonial reform. The Propaganda Movement had established a foundation for a Filipino nation built upon "reclaimed" Asian history and a "reawakened" racial Malay consciousness. This slow work was eventually abandoned as increasingly politicized reformists turned to secret societies (José Rizal's Liga Filipina and Andrés Bonifacio's Katipunan, both established in 1892) and later to violence in the form of the Philippine Revolution. The secret society founded by Andrés Bonifacio first organized in the urban heart of Manila, with the help of his right-hand man Emilio Jacinto. The Katipunan spread to the surrounding eight provinces of Central Luzon,[1] with Cavite province (home of the future First Philippine Republic President Emilio Aguinaldo) as a stronghold. Emilio Aguinaldo was a Filipino revolutionary, military leader, and member of the provincial governing elite.[2] After taking over the leadership of the Philippine Revolution, he would go on to lead the Filipino resistance against the Spanish and then the American forces.

This chapter will trace ilustrado and revolutionary Filipinos' constructions of Asia and of universal civilization at the turn of the twentieth century. In doing so this chapter aims to restore the Asianist intellectual foundations to this early history of transnational anticolonialism, as well as the role of affect in the histories of anticolonial transnational lives and Pan-Asian solidarity. This chapter shows that the revolutionary First Philippine Republic's foreign collaboration represents the first instance of fellow Pan-Asianists lending material aid toward anticolonial revolution against a Western power (rather than overthrow of a domestic dynasty) and harnessing transnational Pan-Asian networks of support, activism, and association toward doing so. This material dimension is

---

[1] Manila, Bulacan, Pampanga, Tarlac, Nueva Ecija, Laguna, Batangas, and Cavite.
[2] For further study of Aguinaldo, see Pedro S. de Achutegui and Miguel A. Bernad, *Aguinaldo and the Revolution of 1896: A documentary history* (Quezon City: Ateneo de Manila University Press, 1972) and Epifanio de los Santos, *The Revolutionists: Aguinaldo, Bonifacio, Jacinto*, trans. and ed. Teodoro A. Agoncillo (Manila: National Historical Commission, 1973).

crucial to understanding the anticolonial transnational solidarity of the colonized Southeast Asian "periphery" of the Pan-Asian movement and to incorporating the periphery into this history. So too is the affective dimension, in which fantasies, imagination, and a certain emotionality formed much of the colonized periphery's engagement with the model of Meiji-era Japan and Asian solidarity.[3] This chapter argues for the importance of both dimensions as lenses through which the transnational Pan-Asianism of the "periphery" can be recognized and made legible to the workings of the East Asian "center," and as lenses through which we may recover such early anticolonial transnational imaginaries, experimentation, and politics.

THE ASIAN PLACE OF THE FILIPINO NATION

Lacking ancient kingdoms or precolonial ruins around which Filipinos could assemble their nationalism, the ilustrados who first theorized the Filipino nation apparently thought it necessary to associate the islands with an older, richer documented civilizational realm. So, they turned to a generalized "Asia" in their anticolonial argumentation and anticolonial nationalist imaginings. Claiming Asia imbued the nation with civilizational importance recognizable even to the Europeans and it conferred a separate existence on the Philippines apart from that of Spain. T. H. Pardo de Tavera's monograph on the Sanskritic origins of the Tagalog language, *El Sanscrito en la lengua Tagalog* (1887), aroused great fervor and admiration among the ilustrados, notably the future Philippine national hero José Rizal. The Propagandists developed a Tagalog orthography, rejecting Spanish missionaries' systematization of the language. Rizal wrote of it excitedly to fellow Propagandist Mariano Ponce on August 18, 1888, as "perfectly in accord with the ancient writing and

---

[3] This chapter is indebted to Caroline S. Hau and Takashi Shiraishi, whose use of network science methodology interprets Pan-Asianism as a "network formed through intellectual, physical, emotional, virtual, institutional, and even sexual contacts, or some combination thereof," and highlights the role of traveling nationalists, transnational associations, and fantasy (Caroline S. Hau and Takashi Shiraishi, "Daydreaming about Rizal and Tetchō: On Asianism as network and fantasy," *Philippine Studies: Historical and ethnographic viewpoints*, 57, 3 [2009]: 362.) This chapter draws from my research published in my book *Asian Place, Filipino Nation: A global intellectual history of the Philippine Revolution, 1887–1912* (New York: Columbia University Press, 2020) and article "Fantasy, Affect, and Pan-Asianism: Mariano Ponce, the First Philippine Republic's Foreign Emissary, 1898–1912," *Philippine Studies: Historical and ethnographic viewpoints*, 67, 3–4 (2019): 489–520.

with the Sanskrit origin of many Tagalog words as I have found out through my research in the British Museum."[4] This act of recovery not only effected a symbolic separation from Spain, but also restored Tagalog to its precolonial Asian world.

An important feature in the construction of Asia through the history of civilization was the premise that there is something like universal civilization, and that it merely passed from one incarnation to another, from East to West and back again. This ephemeral, unitary concept of civilization formed the mechanism by which the civilizational construction of Asia reconciled itself with the history of the rise and fall of great powers and the current state of material inequality between East and West. José Rizal discussed this civilizational tenet in his May 15, 1889, article in the Propagandist mouthpiece *La Solidaridad*, writing: "Religion, civilization, science, laws, and customs came therefore from Egypt, but in traveling along the pleasant shores of the Elaides, they were shorn of their mystic robes and they put on the simple and charming clothes of the sons of Greece." "Science and civilization had been until then the patrimony of the Orient," he underscored, "but following the natural course of the stars, it directed its step to the Occident, and when it got to the heart of the world, it tarried as if to draw all nation and races together."[5] From here he spoke explicitly of the uses of travel and of learning from others, while implicitly working to reassert the East's place in the history of high civilization. These are precisely the theoretical premise and moves that would later characterize wartime President Jose P. Laurel's historical and political thinking, and that grounded his Pan-Asianism in the mid-twentieth century.[6]

From this starting point of universal civilization then flowed *La Solidaridad*'s political work of presenting the historical achievements of the Filipinos as on par with those of other Asian civilizations. The future (and present) Filipino project, however, was not only to master civilization's achievements, but to craft a Filipino aesthetic that could rival and yet be distinct from that of the others – something native that they could

[4] José Rizal, *Rizal's Correspondence with Fellow Reformists* (Manila: National Historical Institute, 1992), p. 197.
[5] Laon Laan, "Los viajes," *La Solidaridad* I, 7 (May 15, 1889). "Laon Laan" was one of Rizal's pen names when writing for *La Solidaridad*. Unless otherwise stated, all translations are mine.
[6] See Nicole CuUnjieng, "Cultures of Empire, Nation, and Universe in Pres. José P. Laurel's Political Thought, 1927–1949," *Philippine Studies: Historical and ethnographic viewpoints*, 65, 1 (March 2017): 3–30.

claim, as the Chinese and Japanese could, in the face of the Europeans who lorded over them culturally. *La Solidaridad* assigned this task to Vicente Francisco, "a futuristic artist, one who feels and understands what is native," and who "could, by forgetting the old formulas of exaggerated classicism, form a Filipino art distinct like those of the Chinese and the Japanese which are well-known in Europe."[7] "The key" to this, the article concluded, "is the study of the natural," with which statement we see the primacy of place.[8] It was only through the natural, through a return to place, they believed, that something uniquely Filipino could issue.

At the end of the nineteenth century, the Propagandists first highlighted Asia, then specified the Malay race and its historical environment within that, and then alluded to the particularities of a more general Philippines – to place. Poetry published in *La Solidaridad* eulogized this place's rivers, to which it imputed an automatic knowledge and affinity on the part of the Filipinos, and its theorizations on race attributed unique developments arising from its climate and environment. "A plant I am, that scarcely grown, / Was torn from out its Eastern bed, / Where all around perfume is shed, / And life but as a dream is known" – these are the opening lines of Rizal's poem "Me Piden Versos" written in Madrid for his mother in 1882. Though Filipinas[9] had barely known its own surroundings and taken root upon the advent of Spanish colonialism, having "scarcely grown," it was located firmly within the cradle of the East – its "Eastern bed." Moreover, there was something seemingly destined and easy to the image of natural development rooted at home in Asia, while uprooting Filipinas from its Eastern bed required work. The bed of perfume and dreams presented itself as not only more natural, but also Edenic. The Katipunan in the lead-up to the Philippine Revolution would eventually take this grounding primacy of place a step further with its allusion to *inang bayan* (mother country) in the poem "Pag-ibig sa tinubuang bayan" (Love of country).[10]

---

[7] "Hauling water," *La Solidaridad* (August 31, 1891).   [8] Ibid.

[9] I use the contemporary name of the Spanish colony when discussing the archipelago prior to the idea of the Filipino nation and when discussing the colony as distinct from the imaginations of that nation.

[10] For a theorization of "place" in the Philippine discursive and political landscape, see Ramon Guillermo, *Translation & Revolution: A study of Jose Rizal's Guillermo Tell* (Honolulu: University of Hawai'i Press, 2009).

BANDS OF RACIAL BROTHERS AND OTHERS

The Philippine archipelago has long been part of the larger Malay world, and it remained so even under the Spanish crown, as well as a participant in trade with Chinese merchants. Yet when did racial consciousness among "Malays" in this area begin and at what points did this optic operate transnationally? The Malay term *Melayu* ("Malay" or "Malaya") appears in the historical record in the fifteenth century during the era of the Sultanate of Melaka (Malacca) from 1400 to 1511, when the sultanate dominated the Straits of Malacca and Malay became the trading language of insular Southeast Asia. Anthony Reid records that the term "Malay" at first referred only to the Malaccan royalty and its subjects (an ethnopolitical category), but in the seventeenth and eighteenth centuries it gradually came to refer to the many Malay-speaking regions of the Malayan peninsula, Sumatra, and surrounding islands, and thus included various ethnicities, including Chinese.[11] Chinese and European writings mirrored this change. During this period, the German pioneer of comparative ethnology Johann Friedrich Blumenbach's 1775 work, *De generis humani varietate*, introduced classification techniques that were pioneered by Carl Linnaeus in the 1730s. Blumenbach paved the way for the development of "race" and "racial science," and featured a division of five races: white Caucasians, yellow Mongoloids, brown Malays, black Ethiopians, and red Americans.[12] Yet, even as thinkers began to talk of racial divisions, the corpus of Western racial thought did not truly acquire a biological sense or hierarchical implications until the nineteenth century, and this timeline is also mirrored outside the West. In the nineteenth century, as thinkers in colonial Malaya interacted with their European counterparts, their vernacular ethnic categories, such as that of Melayu, began to lose their indigenous meanings while at the same time acquiring new racial tones. In this period a word for "race" itself also developed. Anthony Milner records that the word *bangsa*, which once referred to "caste," increasingly began to refer to "race" – moving from usages such as *bangsa syed*

---

[11] Anthony Milner, *The Invention of Politics in Colonial Malaya: Contesting nationalism and the expansion of the public sphere* (New York: Cambridge University Press, 1995), p. 51.

[12] Anthony Reid, *Imperial Alchemy: Nationalism and political identity in Southeast Asia* (New York: Cambridge University Press, 2012), pp. 97–98.

(the caste of the syeds) and *bangsa kechil* (of low birth) to *bangsa India,*
bangsa Bugis,[13] and *bangsa Melayu*.[14]

For the ilustrados in the late nineteenth century, asserting Malayness
was a way to counter the European descriptions of the archipelago as
overrun by an anarchy of tribes and races. Filipino nationalist writings of
the period commonly referred to Filipinos as belonging to the Malay race,
and they used evidence found in European scholarship to argue that
Filipinos were of "Malay civilization." Rizal declared himself to be
"Malayo-Tagalo"[15] and his 1890 annotations to the *Sucesos de las islas*
Filipinas por el Doctor Antonio de Morga (1609) explored hypotheses of
shared racial and civilizational origins for Filipinos with Sumatrans,
Polynesians, and even Japanese. Facing Spanish persecution, Rizal spent
a week in 1892 traveling through Sandakan, Borneo (in Malaya) to seek a
land grant from the British government to establish a Filipino colony
there at home among racial brothers.[16] Prior to that, while still in
Europe, Rizal's Paris-based organization Indios Bravos agreed on a secret
agenda of liberating first the Philippines, then Borneo, Indonesia, and
Malaya.[17]

La Solidaridad reinforced the Filipino connection to the larger Malay
world throughout its issues, casually reporting new "Malay" publications
and studies as part of the Philippines' assumed sphere of interest and
concern. The "Crónica" of June 15, 1890, reported on the findings of a
Dutch professor regarding 111 Malay dialects and alerted readers
to its forthcoming translation into Spanish. The eulogy piece for
"G. A. Wilken" upon the death of the Dutch scholar from the
University of Leiden similarly brought this connection home.[18] *La*
Solidaridad, and in particular Mariano Ponce, also hotly challenged the
charge that the inhabitants of Filipinas were not Malay. Ponce dedicated
an article, "Pag-diwata Barrantes" (To god-like Barrantes) to the Spanish
writer Vicente Barrantes, writing: "His Excellency has the nerve to say

---

[13] An ethnolinguistic group native to Sulawesi.
[14] Milner, *The Invention of Politics in Colonial Malaya*, p. 51.
[15] Besides declaring himself so in *La Solidaridad*, in a letter on January 14, 1899, to
Ferdinand Blumentritt, an Austrian scholar on the Philippines, he referred to himself as
"Malayo-Tagalo," but to Antonio Ma. Regidor as "mestizo Filipino" (John Nery,
Revolutionary Spirit: Jose Rizal in Southeast Asia [Quezon City: Ateneo de Manila
University Press, 2011], p. 107).
[16] "Recuerdos de España," Box 33, Folder 3, T. H. Pardo de Tavera Archives, Ateneo de
Manila University.
[17] Reid, *Imperial Alchemy*, p. 99.
[18] "G. A. Wilken," *La Solidaridad* III, 64 (September 30, 1890).

that the Malay element is not exclusive, not even preponderant in the Philippines. To what race then do the Filipinos belong?"[19] Writing indignantly, Ponce continued, "All ethnographers of the world will be grateful to His Excellency if he were to surprise us with the news that the natives (with the exception of the Negritoes) do not belong to the Malay race. And not only the scholars would be grateful, but even the children of the primary schools of Austria and Germany because they know from their teachers."[20] The deep offense taken at Barrantes' assertion reveals just how much the ilustrados' civilizational and racial pride depended upon their identification with the Malays. This underscores not only the instability of these racial constructions, but also their importance to the ilustrados' nationalism, in which global hierarchies and international perceptions of civilizational achievement were deeply implicated. The easy disavowal here of the "Negritoes," the blanket term of the time for animist tribal peoples in Filipinas, also evidences the implicit workings of an internalized sense of hierarchy. The Negritoes were either a liability to the ilustrados' quest to win political and civilizational recognition for the Filipinos or an easy instrument by which to shore up their own racial superiority – a way to say to Europe: your stereotypes may fit "them" but not "us." These acts to claim Malayness hierarchized the peoples in the same ways as the European sources (from which the ilustrados derived their genealogical, anthropological, and historical evidence). In claiming Malayness, the Malayo-Tagalogs doubly distanced themselves from the pagan tribal peoples in their midst by emphasizing their associations with both "Malayan civilization" and Christianity.

José Rizal asserted that the Spanish government itself also recognized racial similarity and affinity not only between the Filipinos and other Malays, but also with the Japanese. In his famous article "Sobre la indolencia de los Filipinos" (On the indolence of the Filipinos), published serially from July to September 1890 in *La Solidaridad*, he wrote: "fearing to have the Filipinos deal frequently with other individuals of their own race, who were free and independent, as the Borneans, the Siamese, the Cambodians, and the Japanese, people who in their customs and feelings differ greatly from the Chinese, the government acted toward these others with great mistrust and great severity ... until they finally

[19] Mariano Ponce, "Pag-diwata Barrantes," *La Solidaridad* II, 31 (May 15, 1890).
[20] Ibid.

ceased to come to the country."[21] In this interpretation, the Chinese stand apart from the rest of Asia, while the Japanese purportedly stand with Southeast Asians and Filipinos racially and culturally (even though the Japanese were integrated members of the Sinic world). The inclusion of the Japanese but not the Chinese on these terms seems a difficult paradox to reconcile, except through the Propagandists' desire to aggrandize their own race by claiming the Japanese as among their own while holding a status superior to the Chinese immigrants in their midst, in the same manner as the Spanish did. This explains why they would seek to do so, despite the Chinese mestizo ethnicity of the late-nineteenth-century rising ilustrado class itself. Such distancing from the Chinese also sat paradoxically alongside their racial claims to a generalized civilizational Asia, which was a vision of a classical Asia that rested crucially upon ancient Chinese achievements.

Writing from Paris on May 30, 1888, the famous painter and member of the Propaganda Movement Juan Luna wrote to José Rizal, "My dear friend Rizal ... Tell me what happened to you in our country, for you said nothing about it in the card which I received from Hong Kong ... Tell me also about your travel impressions, especially about your stay in Japan whose people is so attractive to me."[22] "I am an enthusiastic admirer of their painting and I think that it is as advanced as that of Greece and Italy," he went on. "We should study more that country whom we resemble so much."[23] Luna was not alone in his admiration for Japan or in his desire to see racial resemblance between the Filipinos and Japanese: while in Japan, Rizal noted that he was taken for a Japanese man.[24] Further, in his contribution to *Trubner's Record* in July 1889, Rizal compared the Tagalog and Japanese versions of the fable of the tortoise and the monkey and suggested a possible Malay origin for the Japanese people.[25] Rizal wrote to Ferdinand Blumentritt, an Austrian scholar on the Philippines and a friend of Rizal, on March 4, 1888 of his admiration for Japan's order and cleanliness and for the trustworthy and industrious Japanese, among whom crime was rare. Yet, in the pages

---

[21] See José Rizal, "Sobre la indolencia de los Filipinos" published serially from July to September 1890 in *La Solidaridad*.

[22] Rizal, Rizal's Correspondence with Fellow Reformists, p. 158.   [23] Ibid., p. 159.

[24] José Rizal, "Appendix C: Letter to Prof. Blumentritt," in *Rizal in Japan*, eds. Caesar Z. Lanuza and Gregorio F. Zaide (Tokyo: The Philippine Reparations Mission, 1961), p. 75.

[25] Resil B. Mojares, "Rizal Reading Pigafetta," in *Waiting for Mariang Makiling: Essays in Philippine cultural history* (Quezon City: Ateneo de Manila University Press, 2002), p. 73.

of *La Solidaridad*, Japan appeared less a kindred "Malay" relative to the Filipinos than a historical alternative – one imagined possible precisely through this resemblance that Luna and Rizal asserted. This resemblance we can assume to be geographical, for the Japanese were largely unlike the Filipinos except through their common location in an Asia beset by Western imperialism and through a geographic construction of an "Asian" race.

The ilustrados employed race as a category and treated races as real, but they argued for an understanding of race through multilinear evolutionism rather than deterministic, orthogenetic Darwinism. This despite the fact that their use of racial categories had its own hierarchizing logic and involved responses to Western practices of ranking that only served to legitimize the framework of that hierarchizing. The Propagandists employed the semiotics (and findings) of science to draw explicit contrast to the subjectivity of the purportedly politicized, self-interested, unscientific position of the Spanish friars who asserted the indios' racial inferiority. This was an appropriation of the methodology of the racial supremacists who equally arrayed the semiotics of science to legitimize their position.

Within their reclamation of Malayness, the ilustrados also carved out a very distinct national space on which a more specific enunciation of "place" would rest and through which Filipino nationalism could also be put in service of broader Pan-Malay and Pan-Asian goals. During the Philippine Revolution, Baldomero Roxas and Gregorio Aguilera, who were active as part of the revolution in Lipa, Batangas, founded a republican organ called *Columnas volantes de la federación Malaya* (1899–1900, Leaflets of the Malay Federation) and declared themselves moved by "noble sentiments that cherish the beautiful idea of seeing the Philippines not only independent but progressing at the head and in union with all the peoples of *Malasia*."[26] A member of General Aguinaldo's troops and of the First Philippine Republic's constitutional convention, Clemente Zulueta published in 1898 during the throes of revolution an illustrated magazine called *La Malasia* that covered topics relating to the Malay race.

The Sino-Japanese War (1894–1895) had stirred the Filipino nationalists' imagination, as it had also done for the Vietnamese and, after the Russo-Japanese War (1904–1905), others in Southeast Asia. The dream

---

[26] Max Bernard, *Columnas volantes de la federación Malaya* (*Contribución a la historia del periodismo Filipino*) ([no pub.], 1928), p. 2.

of acquiring Japanese aid, imitating the successful Japanese model, and entering into the Pan-Asian orbit greatly expanded their perceived political possibilities. Marcelo H. del Pilar wrote: "In the same way that European hegemony does not need to position itself against the rest of the world to maintain its dominance in Europe, the Asian hegemony of Japan can sustain itself without alienating *all* the European powers."[27] There seems here to be a statement of fact, of naturalness, of the inability to alienate the Asian from Asia in such a way that made the dominance of Japan, now that the nation had modernized, into an inevitability. There was something seemingly natural to place, to race, and, thus, to Asianness that would leave room for native leadership. Indeed, the Spanish, too, often noted the "inevitable sympathy" between Japan and Filipinas on these grounds.[28]

The Philippines represents the first case of successful transnationalization of Pan-Asianism as an actual movement, as opposed to the failure in Korea that led to Fukuzawa Yukichi's 1885 editorial advocating that Japan "leave Asia" (Datsu-A Ron).[29] The Asianist politicians, activists, and thinkers that the Filipinos and Vietnamese would encounter in Japan differed from their predecessors. The Meiji state, which emerged during the Meiji Restoration of 1868, had fully established and stabilized itself by the late 1890s and Japan began to experience its first successes in the international sphere. The Asianist support that the Filipinos and Vietnamese found in Japan came from a loose-knit group of liberally inclined Japanese realists and from small political groups on the political

[27] Marcelo H. del Pilar, *La Solidaridad* VII, 143 (January 15, 1895).

[28] See "Peligros y temores," *La Solidaridad* VII, 151 (May 15, 1895).

[29] The program of humanitarian social and economic reforms alongside tutelage that Ôi Kentarô and his "radical liberal" followers advocated in Korea provided the blueprint for later, similar programs focused on the Philippines and Sun Yat-sen's China. They also pushed in Korea radical reforms that had been blocked in Japan, reasoning that success in Korea would have political implications for Japan, as progress elsewhere in Asia would discredit Japan's claim to leadership, thereby forcing the Tokyo government's hand. Unable to find wide bases of support within Japanese society, however, the radical liberal groups became prone to adventurism, which both discredited them and brought them closer to the ultranationalists on the other side of the spectrum. Fukuzawa Yukichi (the famous advocate of Western learning), who tried to influence reforms in Korea and supported Korean reformers, eventually gave up. "After pro-Japanese groups failed in their attempt to take over the direction of government policy in Seoul in 1884, and as the French victory in Indo-China pointed to the further increase of European power in Asia, Fukuzawa turned his back on the idea of providing aid and comfort to reform forces in Asia," Marius B. Jansen records (Marius B. Jansen, *China in the Tokugawa World* [Cambridge, MA: Harvard University Press, 1992], p. 105). Fukuzawa wrote in March 1885 that Japan should "leave Asia" ("Datsu-A Ron") – albeit only temporarily.

right, rather than official aid from the Japanese government, which was careful not to antagonize the West as it sought to end the unequal treaties.

At the close of the nineteenth century, Filipinos were redrawing their geographies of political affinity along a score of colonial repression. Such shared understanding of colonial suffering worked to amplify the role of (Southeast) Asia in the Filipinos' geography of political affinity. Conversely, it also enshrined Asian cities where they could enjoy greater political freedom (such as Hong Kong) into their geography of political revolution. Abutting empires in the region created inadvertent safe havens for the colonized of one empire to operate outside the regime of repression found at home, yet remain just next door. Pan-Asianism as a network operated mainly by means of meeting and movement in and through major cities. When Rizal gave up on the Propaganda Movement and returned to Asia in 1892 – having decided that the appropriate battlefield was at home – it marked the beginning of a new phase to the anticolonial struggle. The Revolution was fully attuned to the modern colonized world and to Asia. As Jim Richardson has similarly argued, the Katipuneros perceived their own battle as "part of a wider, transnational war. They cheered the rebels in Cuba, wanted to establish a presence in Hong Kong, and sought aid from Japan."[30]

Bonifacio and the Katipunan understood Philippine history as Asian history, and they located Filipinas' precolonial condition of independence and autonomy as occurring within the temporal and spatial ambit of Asia. The importance of this original autonomy to the Katipunan then gave Asia, itself, a corollary importance in the Katipunan's political imaginary. The Katipunan's initiation rites included a formulaic, performative recitation of its promulgated interpretation of Tagalog history. "What was the condition of Katagalugan [the Tagalog people] in early times?" the initiator asked. To this, the initiate had been coached to respond that the Filipinos had had their own civilization, alphabet, and religion before the Spaniards arrived; they enjoyed political liberty, used artillery, wore clothes of silk, and maintained diplomatic and commercial relations with their Asian neighbors.[31] The famous revolutionary rallying call attributed to Bonifacio, "Ang dapat mabatid ng mga Tagalog" (What the Tagalogs should know), singled out Japan from among all the Asian neighbors to be historically or potentially linked with the Philippines.

[30] Jim Richardson, *The Light of Liberty: Documents and studies on the Katipunan, 1892–1897* (Quezon City: Ateneo de Manila University Press, 2013), p. xvi.
[31] Ibid., p. 102.

BRINGING ASIA INTO THE PHILIPPINE REVOLUTION

For the colonized, no strategy could afford to be purely transnational nor could it supersede nationalist priorities. Southeast Asian Pan-Asianism's networks, political organizing, and fantasies challenged the so-called pure Pan-Asianism that flowed from the center of uncolonized Japan, which had come to represent "Asian awakening," by featuring the nationalist priorities of the colonized world as central both to Pan-Asianism and to its larger political strategies. Japanese Pan-Asianist organizations such as the Tōa Dōbun-kai (the Society for Asian Solidarity) developed from within the Sinic thread of Pan-Asianism, which emphasized the importance of Chinese–Japanese cooperation in establishing peace in Asia and worked toward preserving Chinese integrity from the rapacious West. This discursive East Asian strain did not concern itself with the Filipino cause, which was taking place outside the Sinic world of China, Japan, and Korea, the heart of the long-standing China-centered tribute-system network. Rather, it was the more inclusive Teaist strain (based on the Asia-as-one thesis) and the muscular imperial Meishuron strain (emphasizing Japanese leadership in Asia) of Pan-Asianism that lent themselves to and involved themselves with the Filipinos. The Kokuryūkai (the Black Dragon Society)[32] was among the organizations that stressed the Meishuron perspective that Japan should not worry about potential Western reaction, and should instead work to establish its position as the leader (*meishu*) of East Asia. They rejected the need to accommodate the Western policies and precepts dominating the international community. In Japan, this Asianist reaction was a response to the Meiji period's effort to harmonize East and West. In the colonized world, however, Asianism drew upon a much deeper sense of oppression and cultural loss.

The Katipunan tried repeatedly to contact the Japanese government and to collaborate with individual Japanese sympathizers to their cause in the lead-up to and immediately after the outbreak of the Philippine Revolution in 1896. Though ultimately official Japanese aid never came, individual Japanese sympathizers were always to be found and did render unofficial aid. Sakamoto Shirō, a nationalist *shishi* (man of spirit), travelled to the Philippines as a civilian and, from there, wrote extensively to

[32] See "The Genyōsha (1881) and premodern roots of Japanese expansionism" and "The Kokuryūkai, 1901–1920" in *Pan-Asianism: A documentary history, volume 1: 1850–1920*, eds. Sven Saaler and Christopher W. A. Szpilman (Lanham: Rowman & Littlefield Publishers, Inc., 2011).

Japan's Taiwan General Staff, reporting on Philippine conditions.[33] According to his biography written by Ozaki Takuya, Sakamoto was invited to and participated in various Katipunan meetings and was nearly caught by the Spanish authorities when they raided a Katipunan meeting house on March 25, 1898.[34] Sakamoto wished Japan to aid the Philippines, and he felt that aid was particularly due to the revolutionaries, given the kinship he recognized between the Japanese and Filipinos. Later, Foreign Minister Okuma obtained permission from the US government on July 27, 1898, for military shishi Captain Tokizawa to accompany US troops in the Philippines as an observer. While there, Tokizawa renewed his prior contacts with Filipino revolutionaries, and even met with Emilio Aguinaldo in mid-July 1898 – a meeting arranged through Teodoro Sandiko, who was assigned by Aguinaldo to negotiate with the Japanese Consulate in Manila and to seek Japan's aid.[35] Aguinaldo reportedly assured Tokizawa that when his forces attacked Manila they would respect any house flying the Japanese Imperial flag.[36] In Cavite, Tokizawa was informed by Aguinaldo's officers of a gift they had received from Japan of two cannons, information that apparently took the captain by surprise.[37] A letter from Sandiko to Aguinaldo on August 9, 1898 shows the depth of information that Tokizawa was freely passing back to the Filipino revolutionaries – including that he was told the Americans would attack Manila three days hence, that the Americans' opinion had turned against the Filipinos, and that the Japanese would be the first to recognize Philippine independence if the United States retained part of the Philippine archipelago but left a portion to the Spanish.[38] Advocating Pan-Asian unity and mutual aid, Tokizawa told Sandiko that he was planning to return to Japan on a secret mission, and would ask his government to provide secret assistance, if it could not for the moment provide it openly.[39]

As Bonifacio's leadership was already being eclipsed by that of General Emilio Aguinaldo at home, the Philippine emissaries in Japan would begin, under Aguinaldo, to see success in securing material aid from the Japanese in a way that they had not under Bonifacio. The Propagandist Mariano Ponce had initially escaped arrest in Barcelona upon the outbreak of the Philippine Revolution, though he was later apprehended and

---

[33] Josefa M. Saniel, *Japan and the Philippines, 1868–1898* (Quezon City: University of the Philippines Press, 1969), p. 227.

[34] Ibid., p. 231.   [35] Ibid., p. 237.   [36] Ibid., p. 238.   [37] Ibid.   [38] Ibid., p. 239.

[39] Ibid., p. 242.

spent a night in jail. Upon his release, Ponce fled to Hong Kong in 1896 and became the Philippine Revolution's official foreign emissary to Japan in June 1898. There, he was charged with discovering Japan's policy toward the Revolution and its various parties, enlisting its aid, and securing and shipping arms and ammunition. The mission ranked fourth out of 28 budget items of the Aguinaldo government between May 1898 and February 1899, with the representative in Japan receiving PhP 20,524.70 out of the total PhP 678,610.42 spent over the period.[40]

Operating principally from Yokohama, Ponce lived in Japan from June 1898 to March 1901. He met Japanese officials and persons of all levels, and joined and attended meetings of various Asianist societies, including: the Shokumin Kyōkai (Colonization Society); the Toho Kyōkai (Oriental Cooperation Society) founded in 1890 by Japanese intellectuals to study the East Asian political landscape and opportunities for the spread of Pan-Asianism; and the Oriental Young Men's Society.[41] The latter included Koreans, Chinese, Japanese, Indians, Siamese, and Filipinos, and gained the patronage and membership of prominent Japanese politicians, for whom the problems of Korea and the Philippines were reportedly active topics of discussion. In Japan, Ponce met the Chinese Confucian scholar Kang Yu-wei, who led the "Hundred Days of Reform," the exiled leaders of the Korean reform movement Prince Park Yeong-hyo, War Minister An Kyong-su, and Home Minister Yu Kil-chun, and Chinese revolutionary and future President of the Republic of China, Sun Yat-sen.[42] Among the Japanese Pan-Asianists, Ponce formed connections with the ultranationalists Hirata Hyobei and Fukushima Yasumasa.[43]

In August 1898 Mariano Ponce began receiving private offers of support from Japanese individuals. That month Ponce secured an offer in Yokohama of 20,000 Maüser rifles at a price of $10 each, according to Ponce's letters. The same seller proposed bayonets for $1.50, artillery belts for $0.80, cartridges for $30 per thousand units.[44] Then in

---

[40] Motoe Terami-Wada, *The Japanese in the Philippines 1880s–1990s* (Manila: National Historical Commission of the Philippines, 2015), p. 22.

[41] Mojares, "Los itinerarios de Mariano Ponce y el imaginario político filipino," p. 42.

[42] Ibid., pp. 42–43.

[43] Fukushima was a colonel, and later general, in the Imperial Army. Hirata had reportedly been in contact with Filipino revolutionary agents as early as 1895 and was rumored to be the intermediary for Prince Konoe Atsumaro.

[44] Translation mine, as are all to follow from this archive. Mariano Ponce, "Carta a D. W. Jones" (1898) in *Cartas sobre la revolución 1897–1900* (Manila: Bureau of Printing, 1932), p. 155.

November Ponce also began fielding offers from individual Japanese supporters to train the Philippine Revolutionary Army. "The Japanese government finds it worthwhile to give us one of the most expert chiefs of the Army Staff, if our government wishes to request it," Ponce counselled Galicano Apacible, chairman of the First Philippine Republic's Hong Kong Committee, on November 28, 1898.[45] According to Aguinaldo's letters, meanwhile, one of the first confirmed Japanese military officers to join the Philippine Republic's army was indeed "Mageno Yoshitora" – likely Nagano Yoshitora – who embarked for the Philippines on February 11, 1899.[46] Another volunteer arrived on February 20 bearing a letter of credence from Apacible to Aguinaldo.[47]

On July 19, 1899, a ship purchased by the Filipinos, an old Mitsui tugboat *Nunobiki Maru*, sailed from Japan with 10,000 Murata rifles, 6 million cartridges, 10 machine guns, and assorted military equipment from Moji bound for the Philippines, via Formosa. But the ship sank in a typhoon near the Saddle Islands two days later.[48] Three Japanese volunteers were on board, bound for the Philippines to provide military training to the Filipinos. Six other Japanese volunteers, among them Hirayama Shu, had departed for Luzon earlier, and though they landed safely and delivered to President Aguinaldo Inukai Tsuyoshi's gift of a Japanese sword and letter of congratulations, the loss of the arms and boat discouraged these volunteers. They ultimately abandoned their mission and fled the Philippines disguised as fishermen.[49] Nakamura Haizan would later face accusations of corruption from Inukai's colleagues. Mariano Ponce was deeply disheartened and offered his resignation as envoy to Japan, but Sun Yat-sen consoled him that this was merely part of the process of revolution.

In January 1900, Ponce attempted to dispatch a second arms shipment through the same intermediaries, but would find himself caught in the transnational logic of the Pan-Asian movement in which he was working.

---

[45] Mariano Ponce, "Carta a Apacible" (1898), in *Cartas sobre la revolución 1897–1900*, p. 241.

[46] According to the James A. Robertson Papers' collected letters from Aguinaldo to Ponce on December 16, 1898, from Ponce to Apacible on January 27, 1899, and from Apacible to Aguinaldo on February 20, 1899 (Luis Camara Dery, *The Army of the First Philippine Republic and Other Historical Essays* [Manila: De La Salle University Press, 1995], p. 93).

[47] Dery, *The Army of the First Philippine Republic and Other Historical Essays*, p. 93.

[48] Mojares, "Los Itinerarios de Mariano Ponce y el imaginario político filipino," p. 44.

[49] Ibid.

While Nakamura Haizan again successfully acquired the munitions, strict government surveillance prevented their movement from the Okura Trading Company storehouse.[50] Aguinaldo was then on the run in the mountains, fleeing the US forces that were hunting him; meanwhile, Sun Yat-sen's uprising successfully broke out on October 8, 1900, in Huichow. Sun argued for the Hong Kong Junta and Ponce to loan the guns to China "since the Philippine effort had failed [and] the weapons were of no further use there." He argued this through horizontal, transnational Pan-Asianism – Miyazaki Tōten quotes Sun as saying: "There is neither first nor last in a single cause of great virtue. If our party seizes the opportunity to launch a revolutionary army, it can realize its long-standing goals. And if we succeed it should also lead to independence for the Philippines."[51] Under this framework, the nationalist Filipino aims had to concede not only to the realities of the Revolution's progress, but to the logic of the Pan-Asianist network through which they had acquired Japanese and Chinese aid.

Ponce's strongest success in Japan was in delivering intelligence to the Hong Kong–based Junta of the Philippine revolutionary government and in shaping foreign Asian opinion on the rightness of the Philippine Revolution. His work *Cuestión Filipina: Una exposición histórico-crítica de hechos relativos a la guerra de la independencia* was serialized in *Keikora Nippo*, published as a book in Tokyo in February 1901, and translated into Chinese and published under the title *Feilubin duli zhanshi* in Shanghai in 1902 and reissued in 1913.[52] Rebecca Karl argues that for Chinese intellectuals it was this piece by Ponce that "first persuasively cast colonialism as a global discursive problem, a characterization that not only facilitated the universalization of the Philippine national experience well beyond its particularities, but one that endured well beyond the duration of the Philippine situation itself."[53] Indeed, Asian leaders as late as Sukarno referenced the Philippine Revolution and Rizal as inspiration.[54] The Hong Kong Committee, meanwhile, was successful in procuring other arms for the First Philippine Republic, and the American government worked tirelessly through its military attaché in Peking to disrupt the Committee's activities.

---

[50] Ibid., pp. 43–44.   [51] Ibid., pp. 44–45.   [52] Ibid., p. 45.
[53] Rebecca E. Karl, *Staging the World: Chinese nationalism at the turn of the twentieth century* (Durham, NC: Duke University Press, 2002), p. 103.
[54] Sukarno, *An Autobiography*, trans. Cindy Adams (Indianapolis: Bobbs-Merrill, 1965), p. 34.

AFFECTIVE ANTICOLONIAL ASIANISM

Pivotal to this Pan-Asianism in action was emotion and affinity. "One cold winter night of 1899, in Tokyo," Mariano Ponce wrote, "I was invited to dine at the house of a prominent Japanese politician, the Hon. Inukai Ki [Tsuyoshi], member of the Imperial Diet, descendant of a samurai, ex-minister of public education, and leader of the Shimpotō [Progressive Party] in Parliament ... Among the guests was Sun Yat-sen."[55] Soon after, Sun Yat-sen asked his Japanese friends and former samurais Miyazaki Tōten and Hirayama Shu to help arrange a purchase of arms for the Philippine Revolution. Miyazaki recorded Sun as asking him in Yokohama in 1899:

> Is there any way you can get guns and ammunition to the Philippines?... There is a representative of the independence army in Yokohama. Since I have planned to go to the Philippines with you, I visited this man and revealed my secret support for him. He was overjoyed, and promptly entrusted me with a great matter: the import of guns. It was our very first meeting, and see how he trusted me! I must do everything within my power for this cause. Moreover, this man's spirit is exactly the same as ours. I want to ask you to use all your strength for these valorous Filipinos.[56]

Here one sees how emotion – "see how he trusted me!" – formed the bonds that underpinned the political ideology of Asian solidarity through fantasy and affection. Indeed, the roles of community and affinity are dimensions of Pan-Asianism that the scholarship tends to miss, as Caroline S. Hau and Takashi Shiraishi have insightfully argued.[57] Miyazaki wrote of his response to Sun, "My heart was instantly aflame. Sun, Hirayama, and I made secret plans, and I resolved to reveal these to Inukai and to tap his wisdom."[58] Indeed, Miyazaki saw himself as "romantically" working for the region of East Asia, which he understood in racial terms. He wrote of himself as "romantically as always, a chivalrous hero working for the colored races of mankind, and not as the servant of his country nor his emperor."[59]

[55] Mariano Ponce, *Sun Yat-sen: The founder of the Republic of China* (Manila: Filipino-Chinese Cultural Foundation, Inc., [1912] 1965), p. 3.
[56] Miyazaki Tōten, *My Thirty-Three Year's Dream*, eds. Marius B. Jansen, et al. (Princeton, NJ: Princeton University Press, [1902] 2014), p. 174.
[57] See Hau and Shiraishi, "Daydreaming about Rizal and Tetchō."   [58] Ibid.
[59] Lorraine Marion Paterson, "Tenacious texts: Vietnam, China, and radical cultural intersections, 1890–1930" (Ph.D. diss., Yale University, 2006), p. 97.

On the state of his fellow Asians, Ponce's prose could at times wax poetic, brimming with affect, for a lost era. In *Sun Yat-sen*, Ponce described his acquaintance with the Korean crown prince who fled to Japan to escape persecution instigated by the Russians:

Poor Prince Pak who was then only 35, roamed the Land of the Rising Sun in the company of his daughter – and of his nostalgia for his tragic land, of his grief over the ruin of his noble house, and his mourning for his dead wife. A poor little princess was his daughter – so pretty, so white, so sweet, with her naughty slanting eyes....[60]

"They lived in a little Japanese house in Kanagawa, they who had been born in a regal palace, amid the luxury that abounds in Oriental palaces," Ponce writes, moved by their turn of fortune; "I could never enter that humble laborer's dwelling without being touched to see the little Princess Pak, that descendant of kings, that royal bud just opening, in a modest kimono, her attractive aristocratic figure contrasting with the vulgar background."[61] He seems to be drawing a parallel to the oppressed state of the various historic Asian civilizations and nations, who have been reduced to vulgar conditions under Western persecution – indeed it is telling that Ponce does not mention Japanese encroachments upon Korea, only Russian meddling. Yet, despite such oppression, the noble Asian figure humbly submits and touchingly adapts, as represented in Princess Pak's "pleasant and enchanting" prattle "half in Japanese, which she spoke very well, and half in English, which she already jabbered fast enough."[62] Here Ponce betrayed a sense of hope in addition to his emotionalized response to what he perceived to be the Asian condition. He was not alone. Apolinario Mabini published an article on September 6, 1899 entitled "Debemos aprovecharnos de las lecciones que la historia guarda para nosotros" (We must make use of history's lessons) in which he declared that the Revolution had as "its sole objective and final goal" the aspiration "to maintain alive and bright in Oceania the torch of liberty and civilization, so that, illuminating the gloomy night in which today the Malay race lies debased and degraded, the Revolution will show the road to its social emancipation."[63] Written by Aguinaldo's closest advisor and the First Philippine Republic's Minister of Foreign Affairs, this is the strongest statement we have on the deeply racial

[60] Ponce, Sun Yat-sen, p. 41.   [61] Ibid.   [62] Ibid.

[63] Translation mine (Record Group 350, Records of the Bureau of Insular Affairs, Personal Name Information File, 1914–45, Box 376, Personal Name File: Mabini, Apolinario, the National Archives and Records Administration at College Park).

interpretive framework and Pan-Malay vision that were operative in the Philippine Revolution.

Mabini's writings echoed the thinking on race, Asia, and universal civilization that the Propagandists had articulated in *La Solidaridad*. In a letter to a friend written on November 3, 1899, Mabini reasoned that God allowed for the existence of avarice because it gave him a tool through which to "extend civilization" and to eventually "humiliate the proud and exult the humble."[64] This explained the existence of unequal progress across civilizations at different points in time, but unified them as existing within a single universal narrative. Universal civilization is carried continuously and housed by many, indifferent to whether it lands East or West. Mabini theorized a role for inequality of progress across cultures – inequality allowed for the inevitable process of creeping decadence and decay not to stifle universal civilization. At the point of decay, a youthful, adapted, different nation would take up the mantle of universal civilization and breathe new life into it. In this way, Mabini's thinking on universal civilization advanced that of the Propagandists. The Propagandists' theorization of universal civilization had turned to history in order to diminish the importance of the Philippines' perceived cultural and racial inferiority (which they now theorized as a temporary, historicized state) as well as to tie the Philippines to a history of past and universal greatness. Mabini then took their theorization of universal civilization, which was oriented toward the past, and built into it a causal process that predicted the Philippines' future greatness. This intellectual move mirrored the one that took place more broadly in the transition from the Propaganda Movement to the Philippine Revolution. The Philippine Revolution took the Propaganda Movement's intellectual armature, which was oriented toward the past, and prescribed a future for it, theorizing and mobilizing the action that would achieve it.

CONCLUSION

Though the Philippine Revolution eventually ended unsuccessfully, Asianism continued to inspire certain pockets of Filipino discourse and world of ideas, albeit from the sidelines. After the First World War, the Bolshevik Revolution and Wilsonian principles undercut the international appeal of Pan-Asianism and Pan-Islamism, as we see in Mark Reeves'

---

[64] Apolinario Mabini, "Letter to Remontado: November 3, 1899," in *The Letters of Apolinario Mabini* (Manila: National Heroes Commission, 1965), p. 231.

chapter in this edited volume. After the Second World War, the suffering caused by Japanese occupation and new exigencies of decolonization and strident domestic nationalisms disenchanted Southeast Asia with the idea of Japanese-led Pan-Asianism. Yet the distinct mode of critique and alternative visions of cosmopolitanism, modernity, and world order that Pan-Asianism represented were neither unimportant nor short-lived in Southeast Asia. Not only did they abet and inform what would become the post-war discourses of Third-Worldism and Pan-Malayism in the Philippines, but they are also embedded in the intellectual, political, and transnational anticolonial foundations of the Filipino nation.

The Filipino Asianists saw themselves as leading the charge toward an anticolonial future within colonized Asia, leading brethren Malay nations toward that shared vision, working alongside the modern leader of Japan. Their Pan-Asian vision involved both the explicitly nationalist goals of the constituent nations as well as the realpolitik, internationalist vision of racial solidarity within a loose regional, transnational, Pan-Asian organization. Indeed, because of the racialized Social Darwinist frame through which they interpreted the international sphere, they believed nationalism and racialized internationalism to be existentially, pragmatically necessary and entangled. This Asianism and Pan-Asianism involved important affective and material dimensions in the formation and sustaining of its network of members, in addition to the intellectual and political organizing dimensions on which the traditional Northeast Asia-centric Pan-Asian literature focuses. What we see in this early moment of anticolonial transnationalism are the particular discourses, logics, priorities, and conditions of power at the turn of the twentieth century in the colonized Southeast Asian "periphery" of Asia that gave Social Darwinism such purchase. In Asia, the world appeared to be arrayed into at least two racialized camps, of East and West, making more complex, dualistic internationalist experimentation seem necessary and natural to Asian anticolonialism and anti-Western/anti-imperial solidarity. Many Filipino thinkers and revolutionaries grounded anticolonial political legitimacy in supposedly inalienable understandings of place and nation, but like their Vietnamese neighbors,[65] among others, they fortified such national groundings within wider racial camps, which were assumed to share

---

[65] Though this chapter did not have the space to do so, my book *Asian Place, Filipino Nation: A global intellectual history of the Philippine Revolution, 1887–1912* (New York: Columbia University Press, 2020) develops this Vietnamese comparison and contemporaneous history.

various interests – if not outright civilizational destinies. Southeast Asian dualistic nationalism was the fruit of the region's racialized geopolitical competition, when the unit of the nation-state seemed insufficient to address an international reality of material inequality ordered along racial lines.

Anticolonial nationalisms formed in the interstices of the colonized's and colonizer's imaginaries; it is no surprise then that while often arguing contra or "subverting" the Western epistemologies that were arrayed against them, the colonized also integrated those very epistemologies into their anticolonial nationalism, particularly with regard to race. European Orientalism's statements of difference between East and West obtained not only as intellectual planks supporting Western imperialism and racism but also then positively *and* defensively as the foundations for Asia's unique role within a shared, universal history of civilization. The Propagandist Filipinos linked race to civilization using a blanket, biological, "objective" race concept to allow them to mount a historicized, subjective claim to civilization. These ilustrados were largely constructing Asia in order for the Filipinos to have an anticolonial place in this diachronic Darwinian staged world through racial association with Asia's past greatness, as well as to level its stagedness by asserting a unitary civilization – in whose history they were now included by virtue of race.

The ilustrados' position toward global imperial power, conceptually, was therefore more nonchalant than that of the corollary early-twentieth-century reformists in China. While the Chinese reformists viewed Japan's rise with alarm, the ilustrados were trying to ride on its coattails, to link themselves to it, and to argue for their own civilizedness and racial rank through enlarged, common racial identification with classical Asia and with a rising Japan. The Filipino revolutionaries' goal to lead the Malay race into an anticolonial future, meanwhile, was a sincere act of anticolonial and Asianist political solidarity toward achieving modernity in Asia. At the same time, their claims to modernity also sought to link the Philippine reform movement, revolution, and nation to the history of modern Western revolutions and to the Meiji Restoration. Such concepts of and claims to civilization and to modernity were vital to their anticolonial argumentation and to their conceptions of anticolonial nationalism, to legitimate self-rule, and to the nation-state more broadly. Due to their racialized interpretive framework, the revolutionaries believed Asian transnational solidarity – brokered materially, affectively, and politically – to be the best, natural ally in achieving such a modern, anticolonial future.

3

All Empires Must Fall: International Proletarian Revolution and the Anticolonial Cause in British India

Zaib un Nisa Aziz

In the spring of 1917, as the world remained in the throes of a cata-strophic global war, a group of socialists gathered in Stockholm, to plan a peace conference. As fatigue and trauma set in, the longing for a cessation of hostilities increased on all sides. Meanwhile, the overthrow of the Tsarist monarchy in Russia in March 1917 further signaled the chance of an end to the war. With this in mind, the Dutch and Scandinavian socialist parties proposed an international socialist conference to discuss possible peace terms. The proposal was met, at least initially, with eager-ness. The international socialist movement represented by the Second International had been devastated by the war, having bitterly split on the question of workers' participation in the war. Now, some of its members believed there could be a chance of reconciliation. In the begin-ning, the socialist parties of Britain, France, Germany as well as neutral powers agreed to send in delegates. Even the Petrograd Soviet initially agreed to send a Russian mission to gather support from their counter-parts in the Entente countries in an effort to reunite the international labor movement.[1]

Under the leadership of Camille Huysmans, the Secretary of the Second International, the "Dutch-Scandinavian Committee" began to meet in the Swedish capital to campaign for a peace conference among the belligerent states.[2] As the meetings began, small contingents of delegates from the colonial world also joined the proceedings. These included political

---

[1] Hildamarie Meynell, "The Stockholm Conference of 1917." *International Review of Social History* 5, no. 2 (1960): 202.
[2] Ibid., p.203.

workers and campaigners from Tunisia, Libya, Morocco, Algeria, Iran, Turkestan, Egypt as well as from India.[3] Many of them had been writing and organizing for years, some had been working within their countries while others had decided to protest abroad. Among the latter were two young revolutionaries, Virendranath Chattopadhyaya and Tirmul Acharya, who came as representatives of the Berlin-based Indian Independence Committee (IIC). They had been active in Europe for a few years now, working toward the overthrow of the British Raj in India.[4] They spoke to the assembly of European socialists about the oppressive nature of British rule in the subcontinent and the legitimacy of the cause of Indian self-determination.[5] A necessary condition to achieve peace, they contended, had to be the resolution of the national question.[6]

However, Chattopadhyaya and his peers were eventually disappointed. Their anticolonial program did not make it onto the conference agenda. Indeed, the meetings never led to a peace conference at all. Despite their enthusiasm to convene, many socialists, including patriotic ones, were prohibited by their governments to actually travel to Stockholm. The demise of the Second International was all but complete. Meanwhile, though, the Zimmerwald socialists – the radical splinter group that had opposed the war and which included Karl Liebknecht, Rosa Luxemburg, and Vladimir Ilych Lenin, grew in stature and importance.[7] Refusing to legitimize the leadership of the Second International, the Zimmerwald group organized its own alternative conference. They vociferously argued that the roots of the world crisis lay in the global imperialist system and that hence there could be no lasting peace without its collapse. This stance resonated with many anticolonialists yearning for a post-imperial future. In October 1917, Lenin led the Bolshevik Party to power and announced Russia as the vanguard of a world revolution. And

[3] Correspondence, Under Secretary of State for Foreign Affairs to Under Secretary of India, October 16, 1917 Stockholm, IOR/L/PS/126/P3449/1917, India Office Records, the British Library, London.

[4] See Nirode K. Barooah, *Chatto, the Life and Times of an Indian Anti-Imperialist in Europe* (New Delhi: Oxford University Press, 2004).

[5] Sitzung des Holländisch-skandinavischen Komitees mit der Delegation aus Indien, July 12, 1917, P/55, HA, Stockholm, N. & C., July 1917.

[6] "Indian and Persian Nationalists at Stockholm," July 16, 1917, IOR/L/PS/126/P3449, India Office Records, the British Library, London.

[7] Hildamarie Meynell, "The Stockholm Conference of 1917." *International Review of Social History* 5, no. 2 (1960): 203–210.

as they saw these events unfold, anticolonialists like Chattopadhyaya found in the young revolutionary state a new ally.

The following pages detail a small and early chapter in a long and complex history of the relationship of international socialism with anticolonial movements in British India. South Asian scholars have long been writing on communism in India. In the 1970s, particularly, many Marxist writers such as Devendra Kaushik, P. C. Joshi, and Gautam Chattopadhyaya, among others, published works on the subcontinent's relationship with the Soviet Union and the Communist International as well as on the state of the communist movement within India.[8] For these scholars writing at the height of the Cold War, many of whom were committed to the socialist cause, writing this history carried certain political significance. For many, the history of the formation and evolution of communism in India was a history of a living and dynamic movement. But after the dissolution of the Soviet Union, this history no longer remained as significant a concern in the field of South Asian history.

More recently, though, a new generation of historians have resuscitated the history of communism in the global south, including and especially in the Indian subcontinent. This scholarship particularly emphasizes the transnational and global aspects of this history as well as its relationship to anticolonialism. For instance, Maia Ramnath has chronicled the cross-continental campaign of the *Ghadar* movement – a revolutionary organization led by Indian exiles in North America that aimed to incite mutiny among the Indian contingent of the British army during the First World War.[9] Ali Raza has written on the transnational networks of workers, migrants, and revolutionaries who were influenced by communist thought and practice in different ways.[10] Others, including Caroline Stolte and Michele Louro, have written on the influence and dynamic

---

[8] See Gautam Chattopadhyaya, Puran Chandra Joshi, and Devendra Kaushik, *Lenin in Contemporary Indian Press* (New Delhi: People's Publishing House, 1970), Attar Chand, *Lenin and India: A Bibliography with Selected Abstracts, 1917–1980* (New Delhi: Sterling Publishers, 1980), Shashi Bairathi, *Communism and Nationalism in India: A Study in Inter-Relationship, 1919–1947* (Noida: Anamika Prakashan, 1987), Ram Shakal Singh and Champa Singh, *Indian Communism, Its Role towards Indian Polity*, 1st ed. (New Delhi: Mittal Publications, 1991).

[9] Maia Ramnath, *Haj to Utopia: How the Ghadar Movement Charted Global Radicalism and Attempted to Overthrow the British Empire* (Berkeley: University of California Press, 2011).

[10] Muhammad Ali Raza, *Revolutionary Pasts: Communist Internationalism in Colonial India* (Cambridge: Cambridge University Press, 2020).

interaction between national movements and international socialism during the interwar period.[11]

The present chapter builds on these new interventions to present a transnational history of radical anticolonialism. It does not constitute an institutional history of communist organizing in the early twentieth century. Instead, it tells a story of the global intellectual interaction that informed and shaped international socialism as well as transnational anticolonialism between 1917 and 1924. It does so by highlighting a few aspects of this history. First, it discusses why radical anticolonialists gravitated toward international communism in the wake of the First World War. Second, it shows how the intersection between Marxist theory and anticolonial thought resulted in a capacious understanding of imperialism – not only as a system of direct colonization but rather as a mode of capitalist production and organization of resources. Anticolonialists were able to use the universalist ethos of the communist revolutionary project and the strategic opportunities it provided as a means to vastly increase their activities. The result was the unprecedented symbiosis of the question of proletarian revolution with resistance to empires. Third, it illustrates how interactions with radical anticolonialists from colonies like India led communists across the industrial world to recognize national revolutionary movements as an integral part of the imminent international revolution. Finally, this chapter will reveal the British colonial state's anxiety about the rise of subversive ideas in the inter-war years and its beleaguered response to this type of transnational anticolonialism.

The scholarly dividend of relating this story is twofold. The study of the intellectual exchange between revolutionary activists and thinkers from India with their contemporaries in Europe recalibrates our understanding of the political and intellectual history of *both* anticolonial nationalism and international socialism. Historians have long written that the "national question" was a key point of contention among leftists from the late nineteenth century onwards but these accounts have been dominated, for the most part, by discussions of Western thinkers debating the

---

[11] *See* Kama Maclean, *A Revolutionary History of Interwar India: Violence, Image, Voice and Text* (Oxford: Oxford University Press, 2015), Michele L. Louro, *Comrades against Imperialism: Nehru, India, and Interwar Internationalism* (Cambridge: Cambridge University Press, 2018) and Michele L. Louro, Caroline Stolte, Heather Streets-Salter, and Sana Tannoury-Karam, eds., *The League against Imperialism: Lives and Afterlives* (Leiden: Leiden University Press, 2020).

future of nations and nationalism as it pertained to Europe.[12] Thus, until recently the question of *anticolonial nationalism*, while contemporaneous, had been largely overlooked in these accounts. Indeed, it was considered, for a long time, a separate story altogether. But as new scholarship is showing, the fact is that at the turn of the century, many radical nationalists from India (and the rest of the colonial world) were engaged in a similar set of debates.[13] Not only did they often inhabit the same physical geographies as European socialists, but they also occupied a common intellectual ground. As we shall see, Indian anticolonialists shared with radical socialists the belief that the problem of the twentieth century was the problem of empire; and they too were imagining routes to a world without the scourge of colonial subjugation. Hence, these groups overlapped, their paths crossed literally and metaphorically, and they developed myriad collaborations, entanglements, and engagements. Through this interaction, they were able to inform and shape each other's political thought and practice. The recognition that the history of political philosophy in the colonial world and in the metropole are not discrete but are inextricably tied is significant. It necessitates the adoption of a *global* lens when telling the history of ideas that shaped the modern world.

This is a particularly opportune time to adopt this perspective. As alluded to earlier, since the early 2000s, historians have attended to global and transnational perspectives in history. Indeed, this present volume is a reflection of the significance of the transnational lens, particularly when it comes to understanding the end of empire. Unburdened by methodological nationalism and equipped with a much broader view, scholars have emphasized that the modern world was far more connected and its actors much more mobile than previously assumed. This has led to a proliferation of studies featuring all sorts of crossovers and networks, of the journeys of itinerant artists and activists, political exiles and campaigners. It has brought to our attention the history of officers and

---

[12] See, for example, Ephraim Nimni, *Marxism and Nationalism: Theoretical Origins of a Political Crisis* (London: Pluto Press, 1994), Georges Haupt, Michael Löwy, and Claudie Weill, *Les Marxistes et la Question Nationale: 1848–1914* (Paris: L'Harmattan, 1997), Robert Stuart, *Marxism and National Identity: Socialism, Nationalism, and National Socialism during the French Fin de Siècle* (Albany: State University of New York Press, 2006).

[13] For example, many historians have written on the intellectual contribution of international revolutionaries like M. N. Roy. See, for example, Kris Manjapra, *M. N. Roy: Marxism and Colonial Cosmopolitanism* (London: Routledge, 2010).

agitators active in revolutionary hubs and urban undergrounds as well as of statesmen, campaigners, and lawyers making their way to the international halls of power.[14] In short, this historiography has shown that the movements for political emancipation were not confined to national boundaries but were unfurling in an integrated world and thus reshaped our understanding of what the age of anticolonialism entailed.

But having reaped the tremendous rewards of a generation of scholarship on transnational politics and internationalism, historians of the anticolonial may find themselves in an intellectual cul-de-sac and looking for new avenues for future research. This leads me to the second contribution of this chapter. I hope to expand the ambit of what is meant by the anticolonial transnational by examining more carefully the discursive dimensions of its history. For me, the term "anticolonial transnational" not only signifies the connection and cosmopolitanism of certain mobile figures or communities but also refers to a long-distance community of diverse figures who debated about and discoursed on a global political future. Seen this way, this concept provides a set of investigative tools to think about the global intellectual history of decolonization and anti-imperialism. Hence, the consideration of the characters in this study is not only meant to show the transnational nature of their lives but to emphasize the global scale of their intellectual engagement and the supranational, at times universal ambition of their politics.

---

[14] The literature on transnational resistance networks is vast. A few significant examples include Jennifer Anne Boittin, *Colonial Metropolis: The Urban Grounds of Anti-Imperialism and Feminism in Interwar Paris* (Lincoln: University of Nebraska Press, 2010), Marc Matera, *Black London: The Imperial Metropolis and Decolonization in the Twentieth Century* (Berkeley: University of California Press, 2015), Michael Goebel, *Anti-Imperial Metropolis: Interwar Paris and the Seeds of Third World Nationalism*, Global and International History (New York: Cambridge University Press, 2015), Ariel Mae Lambe, *No Barrier Can Contain It: Cuban Antifascism and the Spanish Civil War* (Chapel Hill: University of North Carolina Press, 2019), Tim Harper, *Underground Asia: Global Revolutionaries and the Assault on Empire* (Cambridge, MA: Harvard University Press, 2021). The international dimensions of anti-imperial movements have been the subject of many important studies including and especially Erez Manela, *The Wilsonian Moment: Self-Determination and the International Origins of Anticolonial Nationalism* (Oxford; New York: Oxford University Press, 2007), Mark Mazower, *No Enchanted Palace: The End of Empire and the Ideological Origins of the United Nations*, Lawrence Stone Lectures (Princeton, NJ: Princeton University Press, 2009) and Susan Pedersen, *The Guardians: The League of Nations and the Crisis of Empire* (New York: Oxford University Press, 2015).

A WORLDWIDE SEARCH FOR ALLIES

Figures like Chattopadhyaya and Acharya were part of a growing tradition of Indian political resistance in exile in the early twentieth century.[15] Like in other parts of the colonized world, India had witnessed a rise in national consciousness since the late nineteenth century. In the succeeding decades, disaffection with the British government grew significantly owing to a string of unpopular and controversial decisions, especially the decision by Lord Curzon to partition the state of Bengal in 1905. Alongside the demand for dominion status and self-governance put forth by the Indian National Congress during the period, there emerged radical and militant groups seeking the end of the British colonial state and the complete independence of India.

The growth of these political ideas in India also resulted from global and international developments. Japan's victory over Tsarist Russia in 1905 signaled the possibilities of a different political future in colonized Asia. In the same period, Pan-Islamism continued to grow as a potent intellectual and political movement against Western hegemony. News of the militant practices of Russian and Irish revolutionaries impinged on the imagination of young underground activists. The anticolonial ethos of civic and political traditions in the United States attracted Indian intellectuals and activists toward it. Some sought political refuge in the relative safety of the metropole and others actively worked to bargain and collaborate with Great Britain's emergent rivals, particularly with Germany.[16] Thus inspiration, expediency, or some combination thereof, led Indian revolutionaries to seek all sorts of affiliates, allies, and supporters abroad.

---

[15] I have written about this elsewhere. See Zaib un Nisa Aziz, "Passages from India: Indian Anticolonial Activism in Exile, 1905–20." *Historical Research* 90, no. 248 (2017): 404–421. For other literature on Indian exiles including Chattopadhyaya and Acharya, see Śrīkrsna Sarala, *Indian Revolutionaries* (New Delhi: Ocean Books, 1999), Ruth Price, *The Lives of Agnes Smedley* (Oxford: Oxford University Press, 2005), Babli Sinha, *South Asian Transnationalisms: Cultural Exchange in the Twentieth Century* (Hoboken: Taylor & Francis, 2014), Enrico Dal Lago, Róisín Healy, and Gearóid Barry, eds., *1916 in Global Context: An Anti-Imperial Moment* (London: Routledge, 2018).

[16] See Harald Fischer-Tiné, "Indian Nationalism and the 'World Forces': Transnational and Diasporic Dimensions of the Indian Freedom Movement on the Eve of the First World War." *Journal of Global History* 2, no. 3 (2007): 325–344, Kris Manjapra, *Age of Entanglement: German and Indian Intellectuals across Empire* (Cambridge, MA: Harvard University Press, 2014). For a useful discussion on the non-national visions of post-imperial futures see Cemil Aydin, *The Politics of Anti-Westernism in Asia: Visions of World Order in Pan-Islamic and Pan-Asian Thought* (New York: Columbia University Press, 2007).

The advent of the First World War filled many Indian national leaders with new hope, many of whom thought that Indian participation in the war effort would allow them to bargain for more substantive political concessions from the British government. But more radical figures, both at home and abroad, considered this an opportune moment to take advantage of Germany's animosity toward Britain and seek its support. As it was becoming increasingly difficult to carry out anti-imperial propaganda elsewhere many Indian anticolonialists decided to move to Berlin to escape the ire of the police in Entente capitals.[17] In 1914, Chattopadhyaya formed the IIC to coordinate the efforts of these activists. The committee continued to carry out the work of propaganda, publishing nationalist and anticolonial literature in multiple languages.[18]

The committee also worked with the German government on more ambitious programs for destabilizing the British war effort.[19] At this early point, there was in more extremist quarters notable support for the German state. Some militant groups waxed lyrical about Germany in their propaganda at the start of the war and portrayed it as a friend to the cause of Indian independence.[20] For its part, the German government considered supporting anti-British nationalists as strategically useful. The chance of an armed challenge to the British state from within its colonies was an especially desirous outcome. Thus the German state sent an Indo-German Mission to the Amir of Afghanistan to convince him to join the Ottoman Sultan's call for a Holy War against the British Empire, and lead an insurgency in the North West Frontier of the subcontinent.[21] They also aided the activities of the Ghadar movement to incite mutiny among Punjabi soldiers.[22] Another plan was to supply arms and ammunition to

---

[17] These included for example Chempakaraman Pillai from Switzerland, Har Dayal, Lala Lajpat Rai, Bhupendra Nath Dutta from the United States as well as at various points Maulvi Barkatullah, Taranknath Das, and Tirmul Acharya.

[18] Horst Krüger, "The Indian National Committee at Stockholm 1917–1921," 1964, pp.1–3, Krüger Nachlaß Akten A4, Nr. 123–125, Box 22, Zentrum Moderner Orient, Berlin.

[19] Jennifer Jenkins, Heike Liebau, and Larissa Schmid, "Transnationalism and Insurrection: Independence Committees, Anticolonial Networks, and Germany's Global War." *Journal of Global History* 15, no. 1 (2020): 61–79.

[20] "Indische Sozialisten und Bolschewisten," 1921–1926, File R 30615, Politisches Archiv des Auswärtigen Amts, Berlin.

[21] "Telegram from the Imperial Envoy in Switzerland, Freiherr von Romberg, to the Foreign Office," September 8, 1914, File R 21070, Politisches Archiv des Auswärtigen Amts, Berlin.

[22] "Telegram from Freiherr von Wangenheim to the Foreign Office, Constantinople," September 13, 1914, File R 21071, Politisches Archiv des Auswärtigen Amts, Berlin.

Indian militant nationalists through the Chinese revolutionary forces in South China.[23] But one by one these efforts failed. The British imperial state was able to successfully thwart any insurgent efforts. In the wake of these new threats, the colonial government doubled its effort to police, repress, and curb the underground movement both within and without the borders of the subcontinent.[24]

Once it was evident that there was no prospect of an internal rebellion in the British military, which would have put their war effort in serious jeopardy, the German government's desire to support Indian revolutionaries by means of arms and funds also lessened. There was, however, another problem. Germany was, of course, an imperial state fighting to preserve and expand its own empire in Asia and Africa. Increasingly, left-leaning nationalists like Chattopadhyaya grew circumspect of the longevity of an Indo-German alliance. By 1917, this had become a point of debate within the IIC. Some members like Bhupendra Nath Dutta continued to consider relations with the German government an asset. Others, however, felt that the displacement of an Anglophile global order by a German one would not guarantee self-determination for India.[25] It was important for the latter group that the German government make explicit reference to the cause of Indian liberation in its official statements and declarations during the war. But the German Foreign Office did not meet this expectation. Proof of this came when the German government refused to espouse the cause of Indian liberation in official declarations. The IIC recorded an official complaint on one occasion when an official German memorandum to the Entente powers made no mention of the right of self-determination for India. A story appearing in the newsletter *Neu Orient* on January 16, 1917 featured an open letter by "leaders of the Indian National Party" in which they expressed their incredulity:

We do not know what we should be more astonished [about] – the impertinence of the Entente powers or about the fact that the German government [has] incomprehensibly failed to mention India in a memorandum in which rightly Ireland and Northern Africa are quoted as examples of oppressed nations ...

[23] Horst Krüger, "The Indian National Committee at Stockholm 1917–1921," 1964, p.7, Krüger Nachlaß Akten A4, Nr. 123–125, Box 22, Zentrum Orient, Berlin. Heather Streets-Salter, *World War One in Southeast Asia* (Cambridge: Cambridge University Press, 2017).

[24] Criminal Intelligence Department, Government of India, James Campbell, *Political Trouble in India 1907–1917* (Calcutta: Superintendent Government Printing, 1917).

[25] Horst Krüger, "The Indian National Committee at Stockholm 1917–1921," 1964, p.7, Krüger Nachlaß Akten A4, Nr. 123–125, Box 22, Zentrum Moderner Orient, Berlin, p.5.

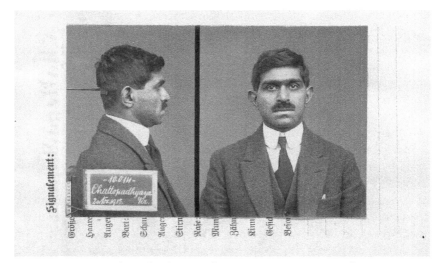

FIGURE 3.1. Virendranath Chattopadhyaya, Deportation Record, 1915, Switzerland. Courtesy Swiss Federal Archives. I am grateful to Gautam Pemmaraju for sharing this image with me.

We do hope that the German government will find ways and means to make good this omission on the first opportunity.[26]

While they continued to remain active in Berlin, Chattopadhyaya, and Acharya, among others, were increasingly cognizant of the need to seek new allies – who shared their ideology as well as their ambition. In the summer of 1917, they traveled to Stockholm, which was a centre for nationalist campaigners during the war. There they established contacts with their counterparts from across the world – from Ireland, Egypt, and Iran as well as with Ukrainian, Polish, and Finnish nationalists. The two were deputed by the IIC to attend the International Socialist Conference being held in the city that July, to elicit the attendees' support for the cause of Indian self-determination. In advance of the 1917 conference, they prepared and published literature about the place of the Indian question in the history of the international socialist movement. For example, one leaflet contained an account of discussions on the state of British colonial rule in India in international socialist conferences in Paris (1900), Amsterdam (1904), Stuttgart (1907), and Copenhagen (1910). It also featured speeches by Indian national leaders on these occasions such

[26] Ibid., p.8.

as an address by the Indian National Congress leader Dadabhai Naoroji in Amsterdam and a speech by the revolutionary organizer Madame B. K. Cama in Paris. Another booklet entitled "Opinions of Leading English Socialists about the English Rule in India" contained statements by figures like Kier Hardie, H. M. Hyndman, and J. R. Macdonald objecting to and bemoaning British colonialism and expressing sympathy toward those who "endeavored to free themselves from this monstrous rule under which they suffer today."[27]

The relation between British socialism and the particular cause of Indian freedom was rather more tenuous and tentative than the account presented by the Indian delegation. However, by citing these historical references, the Indian delegates attempted to create a narrative that wove the question of self-determination with progressive imaginations for a postwar future. This was a means to *internationalize* the question of Indian liberation and to present it as a *sine qua non* for a just peace. "We therefore demand in the interest of all nations that India be liberated from foreign rule and enjoy the benefits of a national government," read a pamphlet distributed to the attendees, "we hope that the International Congress now in session in Stockholm will also this time turn its attention to the Indian Question and will bring into action the entire power of international socialism at the coming peace negotiations in order to insist on the liberation of India."[28]

But the European delegates were less than forthcoming with their support for Indian independence. While some socialist leaders had certainly condemned the brutal excesses of colonial rule, many did not oppose colonialism in principle. On the contrary, there were those among the Second International who believed in the virtue and necessity of the tutelage of the colonized. The Dutch socialist Henri van Kol, for example, was a proponent of a "socialist colonial policy" – one that he believed could have a civilizing effect on "backward" people. Others also expressed their circumspection to the Indian delegates.[29] Huysmans refused the Indian delegation's demand to make the national question part of the conference's official agenda. Since there was no Indian Socialist Party, he explained to Chattopadhyaya, Indian representatives could not officially participate. Moreover, he noted, many assumed Indian revolutionaries to be agents working for the interest of the German government. In his memoirs, Chattopadhyaya recalled how he

---

[27] Ibid., pp.11–12. [28] Ibid., p.13. [29] Ibid., p.14.

protested the charge – telling Huysmans that they "had as little confidence in the Prussian government as they did in the English or Russian governments." Since the start of the war, he explained, Indian anticolonialists had been exiled, arrested, and targeted in Britain, America, and France and expelled even from neutral countries like Switzerland. Germany had become a place of necessary refuge from where they could carry out their political work.[30]

While Huysmans did make sympathetic gestures, in truth, he remained unconvinced. In fact, unbeknownst to Chattopadhyaya, he was in close contact with the British Foreign Office and the British Secret Service. The arrival of anticolonialists from various parts of its empire at Stockholm, perturbed the British Foreign Office. The use of international socialist conferences as a forum for anti-British propaganda was an unhappy development and collaboration by nationalist campaigners with German and Russian representatives presented a sinister possibility. These figures concluded one officer, sought to enlist international sympathy from the attendees for the cause of self-determination and present their own struggle as part of the socialist cause. As Huysmans corresponded with intelligence agents in detail about their activities in Stockholm, he recommended that the British government send in British socialists who could counter and qualify the narrative being propagated by anticolonialists.[31] While the Foreign Office remained recalcitrant about allowing socialists to travel, they did concede to the need for a counter-narrative and eventually sponsored agents to carry out pro-British propaganda in the region.[32]

It was not surprising then when the "Manifesto of the Socialist Parties of the Neutral Countries Represented in Stockholm," published in October 1917, made no mention of India or any other colony. Officially, most parties invited to the International Socialist Congress at Stockholm remained opposed to making self-determination a part of the

---

[30] Ibid., pp.15–16.

[31] Confidential letter from the British Embassy Stockholm to the Secretary Foreign Office, July 25, 1917, IOR/L/PS/126/P3449/1917, India Office Records, the British Library, London.

[32] Later, in April 1918, the Foreign Office sent A. Yusuf Ali on a tour of Scandinavia to give a series of lectures on Indian culture and politics. The support was tacit: Ali did not make public his collaboration with the Foreign Office. In his lectures, he refuted revolutionary claims about the desire for freedom in India and instead argued about the support of the British war effort during the war. His speeches were published in Danish in the book Abdullah Yusuf Ali, *Træk Af Indiens Kultur* (Copenhagen: V. Pios Boghandel/H. Branner, 1918).

peace negotiations. The British Labour Party and Independent Labour Party did not support the dissolution of European empires and neither did the French or Belgian socialists. Later, at the Conference of the Socialist Parties of Allied Powers in 1918 in London, they agreed on the necessity of reform of colonial governance but not on the end of imperial rule.[33]

Meanwhile, the German Social Democratic Party did support the right to self-determination for British and French colonies but did not extend that support to areas under German occupation. The party qualified its stance by demanding the liberation of "formerly independent nations of elevated culture," mentioning Ireland, India, Egypt, Morocco, and Libya. But, crucially the statement did not oppose German plans of expansion toward Russia.

There was little will among the socialists of the Second International to proclaim universal self-determination as an urgent goal, as Chattopadhyaya increasingly realized. In a statement addressed to the Dutch-Scandinavian Committee, the Indian delegates expressed their bitter disappointment. It appeared to them that "for Western-European Socialists, as for all European Imperialists, the word mankind means only Europe ... [and that] they regard all the splendid Asiatic and African lands stretching from Tangier to Peking as the legitimate booty of European wars."[34]

During this time, news of the revolutionary events unfolding in Russia were met with great enthusiasm by Indian nationalists in exile. The Indian delegates had established contacts with radical Russian exiles active in Stockholm, and soon after arriving Chattopadhyaya wrote to his colleagues in Berlin asking them to prepare Russian translations of their political literature. In early September 1917, the IIC sent a telegram of support to the All-Russian Council of Mohammedans in Petrograd:

We Indians welcome the courageous stand of the Russian Mohammedans in favor of the oppressed people of Asia and Africa. They have done a great service to the cause of humanity by demanding from the Provisional Government of free Russia a determined and consistent policy which aims at the recognition of the equal rights of complete national self-determination as well for the peoples of Europe as for the people of Asia and Africa ... The solidarity of all oriental peoples and the support of free Russia which has solemnly abandoned the principle of the Tsarist regime are likely to hasten the renaissance of the Orient ....[35]

---

[33] Krüger, "The Indian National Committee at Stockholm 1917–1921," 1964, p.17, Krüger Nachlaß Akten A4, Nr. 123–125, Box 22, Zentrum Moderner Orient, Berlin.
[34] Ibid., p.23.   [35] Ibid., p.26.

For many anticolonialists, the Russian Revolution was first and foremost a grand and popular defiance of a powerful and long-standing imperial power. The victory of a mass movement over a centuries-old monarchical system signaled the possibility of a similar fate befalling the British Empire. Moreover, revolutionary nationalists were particularly encouraged by Lenin's uncompromising stance on self-determination for all colonial peoples. The IIC, for example, made increasing shows of support to the Workers' and Soldiers' Council in Petrograd, which had a Bolshevik majority and developed contacts with its leaders. In October 1917, Chattopadhyaya, for example, corresponded with K. M. Troyanovsky and the two developed a program for "Indian Work in Russia" on how a new revolutionary government in Russia could support the movement for Indian liberation. "If the leading men in Russia are convinced of the importance of the Indian question, they might take it up as a defensive weapon against the English and even support the Indian nationalist standpoint at the peace negotiations. If Russia takes the initiative in the Indian question, we may (let us hope) obtain support from the Central Powers."[36]

The Stockholm Indians' hope to have ideological supporters take over power in Russia was realized very soon when the Bolshevik Revolution overthrew the Provisional Government and announced the formation of the Soviet Union. After the Bolsheviks came to power and the First World War ended, more Indian radicals gravitated to the new revolutionary state and its ideas. Some were enthused by revolutionary zeal, others saw a chance of strategic collaboration. As these interactions grew, Marxist-Leninist thought increasingly influenced a new generation of Indian revolutionaries.

SOCIALIZING THE NATIONAL QUESTION

The Bolshevik government's international reputation as a champion of the colonized was cemented further as the war concluded.[37]

---

[36] Ibid., p.27. Even at the eve of the Bolshevik Revolution, the Indian Independence Committee had remained neutral toward the multiple socialist groups in Russia. However, its members grew increasingly wary of the Mensheviks when they did not make liberation of the colonized an explicit part of their agenda at international socialist conferences and made no show of support for the demands of self-determination by anticolonial nationalists.

[37] S. A. Smith, "The Russian Revolution, National Self-Determination, and Anti-Imperialism, 1917–1927" in Oleksa Drachewych and Ian McKay, eds., *Left*

The Bolshevik Decree on Peace included an explicit demand for "peace without annexations."[38] This principle was integrated in Bolshevik negotiations with the Central Powers on the Brest-Litovsk agreement. Observers on either side of the imperial divide saw these developments as having profound significance for independence movements worldwide.

Colonial officials across the British Empire and particularly in India expressed deep trepidation about the impact of the Bolshevik Revolution on dissidents and insurgent elements in the colonies. The Bolshevik stance against imperialism, argued many official observers, encouraged radical demands for national independence and liberation from British rule within India. Moreover, they warned, the Bolshevik government had an obvious political interest in destabilizing the British government and would hence actively support its opponents.[39]

This assessment was not without basis. Almost immediately after the October Revolution, emissaries of the various strands of the Indian anticolonial movement started to make their way to the young Soviet state. Certainly, not all those who turned to Moscow were communists – many were still nationalists looking for strategic or tactical support against Britain, such as Raja Mahendra Pratap, who had formed a provisional Indian government in Kabul during the First World War. In 1918, he briefly stayed in Tashkent and Moscow before going to Germany. Some Pan-Islamic campaigners similarly thought that the new revolutionary state could provide a safe haven for their political activity.[40] In 1919, a group of Muslim activists, including Maulana Barkatullah and Maulana Abdul Rab, formed an "Association of Indian Revolutionaries" in Tashkent.[41] They employed socialist rhetoric and idiom to amplify their discourse against British colonialism and to garner Bolshevik support for their political struggle. In a speech in a mosque in Tashkent, Abdul Rab underlined how he and his compatriots shared in the belief that British

Transnationalism: The Communist International and the National, Colonial, and Racial Questions, Rethinking Canada in the World 4 (Montreal: McGill-Queen's University Press, 2019).

[38] "Decree on Peace," Second All-Russia Congress of Soviets of Workers' and Soldiers' Deputies, November 8, 1917, published first in *Izvestiya* No. 208, November 9, 1917.

[39] "Report on the Inter-Departmental Committee on Eastern Unrest," IOR/L/PJ/12/120, India Office Records, the British Library, London.

[40] Devendra Kaushik, "Indian Revolutionaries in Soviet Asia," 1966, Krüger Nachlaß Akten A4, Nr. 123–125, Box 45, Zentrum Moderner Orient, Berlin.

[41] Ibid., pp.3–5. Abdul Rab had been politically active in the North West Frontier and had worked and traveled in Iran; Barkatullah was part of Pratap's provisional government and had been involved with Indian anticolonialists in Japan and the United States.

government was exploiting and oppressing the British working class just as it was oppressing the colonized of India.[42] Similarly, Barkatullah also believed that the Soviet Union was an important anti-imperial force. In a booklet entitled "Bolshevism and the Body Politic" addressed to "Muslim Brethren" across Central and West Asia, he described the British as the "enslavers of the world" and called for Muslim communities to defend the Soviet state against Western imperialism.[43]

But the most enduring impact of the Bolshevik Revolution was, unsurprisingly, on the politics of the left in India. For myriad leftist thinkers and revolutionaries all over the world, the success of a worker-led popular revolution validated their respective political visions and heralded the imminent demise of global capital. In India too, the revolution had a profound impact on socialists, anarchists, and left-wing thinkers and political workers. On October 17, 1920, a group of anticolonialists gathered in Tashkent to officially establish the Communist Party of India. One of its founding members was the Bengali revolutionary, M. N. Roy.[44]

For several years thereafter, Roy was a key part of the communist movement in India though he remained in exile. He was a quintessential representative of a generation of thinkers and political workers who came to recast the national question not only as one of political independence from colonial rule but rather as one of social liberation and economic equality. In so doing, they reconceived what it meant to oppose the British Empire. Concomitantly, communists like Roy also understood internationalism differently. While many nationalists had looked for allies to champion and support the cause of Indian freedom, communists understood the anticolonial movement as necessarily tied to the struggle against oppression worldwide. Writing from Berlin to fellow communists Satish Chakravarty, in Calcutta, Roy underscored this differentiation:

We live in India just like a frog in a well which can never imagine that there is a world bigger than the waters it is living in. So that we too never kept ourselves informed of the world abroad and therefore when we were in India we could never

---

[42] Devendra Kaushik, "Indian Revolutionaries in Soviet Asia," 1966, Krüger Nachlaß Akten A4, Nr. 123–125, Box 45, Zentrum Moderner Orient, Berlin.

[43] "Supplementary History of Maulvi Barkatullah," 1927, IOR/L/PJ/12/213, India Office Records, the British Library, London.

[44] Other founding members included, Evelyn Roy-Trent, Abani Mukherjee, Rosa Fitingov, Mohammad Ali, Mohamad Shafiq, and Tirmul Acharya.

understand that the social and political movements in India are but the inevitable part of the greater ones raging over the whole of the present world.[45]

After the establishment of the Communist International in 1919, Bolshevik strategic and financial support for revolutionary elements in colonial spaces did increase. But, in my view, this type of aid was far less significant than their growing ideological impact. For Roy and his compatriots, Marxist-Leninism provided a heuristic lens for reading history and conceptualizing politics. Their alliance with revolutionary Russia was not an example of an alliance of necessity borne out of political entanglement against a common enemy. Instead, they held a common socialist worldview informed by a dialectical reading of history. "Revolutions, national risings and national movements are all social affairs," underscored Roy repeatedly in his discussions.[46] Hence a political movement that could lead to the liberation of colonialized India had to be based on the principles of history. This political stance explained his deep skepticism of Gandhi. For Roy, Gandhi eschewed historical truth for spiritual explanations, which could be detrimental to the liberation movement. Throughout history, Roy insisted, human societies have been stratified along lines of class and one form of class regime has given way to another. But such hierarchies were not divinely ordained – they were socially constructed and had to be understood as such.

England cannot be driven out of India by prayers or hymns (spiritualism). We must find out why England was able to rule over us as well as over a great Empire. Otherwise, it is impossible to discover the correct method of driving her out. A definite power (which has nothing to do with God) has placed the English in the position of World Rulers. What is that power? I say it is the Commercial Power (Capitalism) . . . which has already out ruled Militarism everywhere.[47]

Hence Roy argued, if there was to be a meaningful revolution in India, it would have to be a workers' revolution. This was why it was necessary for revolutionary forces in India to align themselves with the international proletarian movement. An emerging class of local capitalists in India would not be able to take a stand against British rule, he argued. The Indian bourgeoisie would never take the radical steps needed to liberate India, like economically boycotting the British, because it depended on British capital itself. They had demanded representation, but they had not taken up the

---

[45] Letter Roy to Satish Chakravarty et al., May 29, 1922, Berlin, in Confidential Note. "Indian Communist Party," July 25, 1922, IOR/L/PJ/12/46, India Office Records, the British Library, London.
[46] Ibid. [47] Ibid.

"weapons of revolution," such as boycotting tariffs, demanding economic self-government, or introducing mass public education.[48]

A key point of debate on the national and colonial question in the Third International in 1920 was about the role of national-bourgeois movements in the struggle against empire. Lenin had argued national-bourgeois movements could play a revolutionary role, especially in the colonial world, much of which remained non-industrialized.[49] Roy, however, contended for the necessity of communist organization in colonial countries. If this was not done, he pointed out, the liberation movement would result in the transfer of power to the local industrial and landholding elite. It was important for Roy to take advantage of the rapidly expanding mass movement in India but also necessary to imbue the national movement with a revolutionary spirit.[50] This could be done if more socialists joined the ranks of the national movement. The greatest political achievement of the Indian National Congress was the creation of a mass political party, a phenomenon Roy conceded had never existed before. But he noted that the rapid increase in national and patriotic feeling could not be credited entirely to Gandhi and the leadership of the Congress. On the contrary, the rising power and popularity of the national movement owed to social developments. After the war,

there had come into being an objective force which had not existed before, and this force made it possible that the *Satyagraha* [Non-violence] and Non-Cooperation Movement could have such spectacular success. The morrow of the European War found unrest no longer confined in the small intellectual lower middle class: the masses of the people were affected ... Signs of rebellion were everywhere, and it was not long before actual revolt did break out.[51]

Roy believed that the Congress was able to successfully channel mass disillusionment from British rule and thus expand its role and become a national party. But having done so, it was reaching the end of its political

---

[48] Ibid.

[49] V. I. Lenin, "Theses on National and Colonial Questions for the Second Congress of the Communist International," June 1920, in *Lenin's Collected Works*, Vol. 31 (Moscow: Progress Publishers, 1965), pp.144–151.

[50] M. N. Roy, "Supplementary Thesis on the National and Colonial Questions for the Second Congress of the Communist International," June 1920, in John Riddell, ed. *Workers of the World and Oppressed Peoples, Unite! Proceedings and Documents*, Vol. 2. (London: Pathfinder Press, 1999), pp.313–335.

[51] Letter Roy to Satish Chakravarty et al., Berlin, May 29, 1922 in Confidential Note. "Indian Communist Party," July 25, 1922, IOR/L/PJ/12/46, India Office Records, the British Library, London.

role. Writing to Pulin Das, a long-time member of the militant underground in Bengal, Roy explained the necessity of a revolutionary turn in the national movement. All over the country, he observed, occasions of strikes, boycotts, and industrial action were increasing. The growing discontent of the peasantry in the villages and the workers in the urban centers was proof that there was a conscious desire among the masses of India to improve their economic condition. In rebellions in Uttar Pradesh and Gujarat and in Northern Madras and parts of rural Bengal, peasants had refused to pay rent to landlords. In cities like Bombay, workers had organized regular strikes in protest against low wages and poor working conditions.

The magnificent demonstrations, so many wonderful *hartals* (strikes) could not be organized unless the traditional apathy of the masses of the Indian people is disturbed. Now, when the Congress has proved itself incapable of leading the movement any farther, what is necessary is not to boycott it but to infuse new spirit into it, to bring a certain change in its leadership.[52]

So, Roy believed that national movements played a significant role in the revolution. But once social conditions had evolved and the political movement had matured, communist leaders had to come in to "avail themselves of what had been accomplished and lead it with a new program, with new tactics evolved out of a more realistic political orientation."[53]

At this stage in 1922, Roy thought that communists need not oppose the Congress. On the contrary, he suggested that they should co-opt the party, infiltrating its ranks at the district and village level. "Our party of the revolution should not stay out of the Congress but try to capture it or at least make use of the apparatus created by it."[54] Meanwhile, Roy continued, communists in India had to embark on a parallel program of political education and social uplift. "The economic and consequently political consciousness of the peasantry will thus be developed, not by pedantic and sentimental teachings but in actual struggle in which they will be pitted against their oppressors." Similarly, in the cities, communists had to work with labor organizations. The Congress was, he warned, "coming rigidly under the influence of reactionary and anti-revolutionary reformists, and government agents."[55] Indian communists had to

---

[52] Letter Roy to Pulin Das, Berlin, June 6, 1922, in Confidential Note. "Indian Communist Party," July 25, 1922, IOR/L/PJ/12/46, India Office Records, the British Library, London.
[53] Ibid. [54] Ibid. [55] Ibid.

counteract these efforts by working with the proletariat. Awakening the political consciousness of workers required communist leaders to join with them in their economic struggle against their employers.

These two aspects – the movement of the working class and the political resistance against colonialism – were symbiotically connected for Roy. Mass action of the working class, he argued, was the most effective way of paralyzing the government of the country. Consequently, the proliferation of communist thought and practices would not only strengthen the working class but also shore up resistance against the colonial government. Over the years to come, Roy and his compatriots on the left continued to link economic freedom and social uplift with political liberation for India. Concomitantly, they insisted that the resistance of the masses of peasants and workers in India was organically connected to struggle of workers across the world, thus creating new avenues for solidarity.

THE TROUBLESOME CIRCULATION OF DANGEROUS IDEAS

Colonial authorities viewed the incipient growth of communist ideas after 1919 with increasing anxiety. The government had responded to the growing political agitation in India (and elsewhere) with expanding the repertoire of coercive tactics and increasing the repression of political activity. It is worth noting though that many officers of the India Office and the Intelligence Bureau did not believe that a communist revolution was imminent in India. They were cognizant that communists did not enjoy any mass support and that as a movement communism in India was only in its infancy. Yet, the increasing interest and engagement of a steadily growing audience, especially in urban centers, with revolutionary communist discourse troubled the government. British authorities remained deeply incredulous about the circulation of revolutionary ideas and subversive techniques within the colonies. For one, authorities perceived the colonies as spaces vulnerable to enemy propaganda. They remained convinced that communist forces would, under Moscow's tutelage and instruction, capitalize on the political precariousness in India and spread anti-British sentiment. "Slow to take root in a country where the feudal spirit and hereditary principles are so ingrained as in India, the Bolshevik movement grew no less surely on that account," wrote H. Williamson, Director of the Intelligence Bureau in a later report. "By 1924, its menace to India's peace and prosperity had become sufficiently serious to necessitate the first important Communist Conspiracy Case."[56]

In February 1924, eight Indian communists were charged with "conspiracy to deprive the King-Emperor of the sovereignty of India." In April that year, warrants had been issued for communist leaders in Cawnpore, Bombay, Madras, and Pondicherry. The list included names of leading communist activists including M. N. Roy.[57] The Cawnpore case, officially titled "the Crown vs Bolsheviks," took place in the session court of H. E. Holme, infamous for his punitive judgements against political agitators. Ultimately, the prosecution was able to try and sentence four of the accused – Shaukat Usmani, Muzaffar Ahmad, S. A. Dange, and Nalini Gupta – to four years of imprisonment.[58]

The colonial government imagined that the trial would be swift and severe and would cast an indelible blow to the burgeoning movement. However, the Cawnpore Conspiracy case became an early example of a colonial trial gaining international attention. For communist leaders, the trial was evidence of the authoritarian nature of British colonial rule, robbing the imperial enterprise of any legitimacy. They used the trial as a means to publicize the undemocratic and tyrannical nature of colonial governance with a view to shaming the metropole government and creating a moral impact on the British public. Indian communists immediately noted that while workers in Britain and its dominions were free to organize and join communist organizations, they were punished for doing so in India.[59] In Britain especially, communists like Shapurji Saklatvala, James Maxton, Charles Ashleigh, and George Lansbury among others echoed this argument.[60] For example, a pamphlet published by the CPGB

---

[56] India and Communism: Compiled in the Intelligence Bureau, Home Department, Government of India (Calcutta: Government of India, 1933), p.88, IOR/L/PJ/12/670, India Office Records, the British Library, London.

[57] The government sought to try eight people in sessions court: M. N. Roy, Muzaffar Ahmad, S. A. Dange, Nalini Gupta, Ghulam Hussain, Singaravelu Chettier, Shaukat Usmani, and R. L. Sharma.

[58] Ghulam Hussain made a confessional statement and negotiated his release; Singaravelu was released on grounds of health; R. L. Sharma was in Pondicherry and could not be brought to court; and M. N. Roy was abroad in Germany as well and hence could not be prosecuted.

[59] "Indian Communist Defence Committee: Appeal for Funds," *The Socialist* 2, no. 26, Bombay, July 2, 1924.

[60] Nicolas Owen, "The Alliances from Above and Below: The Failures and Successes of Communist Anti-Imperialism in India, 1920–1934," in Yann Béliard and Neville Kirk, eds., *Workers of the Empire, Unite: Radical and Popular Challenges to British Imperialism, 1910s–1960s* (Liverpool: Liverpool University Press, 2021).

appealed to British workers to show solidarity with their Indian counterparts:

These Communists have been sentenced for carrying on a work within the British Empire which is quite legal and open in Great Britain ... Most active men and women in the Labor Movement will be aware of the terrible conditions under which the workers of that country labor. You will have read repeatedly of the brutal treatment of those workers when they attempt to struggle for better economic conditions ... The Indian Communists who have just been sentenced were engaged in this struggle on behalf of the workers and because British Imperialists in the interest of Capitalism [do] not like it, they have been savagely suppressed.[61]

In the next few months, a series of small protests took place in London, Birmingham, and Manchester in solidarity with the sentenced.[62] Communist literature enumerated the denial of civil and political liberties to the Indian proletariat: workers were denied the vote and kept from organizing; legal trade unions were populated by lawyers and middlemen who "tied the workers to the bosses"; and the police and military wantonly used violence against demonstrators. This treatment of workers, argued these detractors, was evidence of the unrepresentative and undemocratic nature of the colonial government. The situation was more indefensible still, they emphasized, given that a Labour government was in power. "Under a Curzon administration, such a treatment is understandable: under a Labour Government it is a crime against the international solidarity of the working class."[63] The CPGB called on its workers to propagate on behalf of the accused and write about the case to their parliamentarians, to the India Office, and to their local party officials.

Meanwhile in India, the trial brought more notoriety to communists and their cause. By the end of 1924, communists in India decided to extend their work, forming new political organizations while influencing existing ones. Williamson recalled that

the events of the next few years were to make it very clear that Communism had come to stay and that nothing short of the collapse of the Soviet system itself

---

[61] "Letter to Trade Unions and Labour Parties to Central Executive Committee Communist Party of Great Britain, London District Party, May 22nd 1924," IOR/L/PJ/12/185, India Office Records, the British Library, London.

[62] Various Extracts, New Scotland Yard, May–July 1924, IOR/L/PJ/12/180, India Office Records, the British Library, London.

[63] "Points for Propagandists – Indian Communists Sentenced," Communist Party of Great Britain, IOR/L/PJ/12/185, India Office Records, the British Library, London.

would eradicate manifestations of sympathy for that system, at any rate in the urban areas of India. The most that the authorities could hope to do was to mitigate, by constant watchfulness and by judicious and timely action with the narrow limits of the law, the evils and dangers of the preaching of class hatred to those so ill-adapted to receive such doctrines a thoughtful and discriminatory frame of mind.[64]

* * *

At the turn of the century, socialists had been equivocal about anticolonial movements. But in the wake of the Bolshevik Revolution and the formation of the Third International, opposition to empire became increasingly entrenched on the agenda of a global left. At the same time, socialist ideas slowly permeated in India, radicalizing a growing mass movement. Thus, colonial administrators believed that if the British Empire was to survive in the new century, it had to be protected against the plague of insurrectionary ideas. In order to do this, the colonial state decided to employ its full force to impede the spread of pernicious notions. Borders were monitored, speech was sanctioned, movements were controlled, and disloyal elements imprisoned and exiled. As anticolonialists and their allies in the metropole sought to expose the harsh reality of British rule, the imperial government also had to invest in new discursive regimes through which the British Empire could be presented as liberal, lawful, and guarantor of the twin virtues of order and freedom. Yet, despite these efforts, the emissaries of revolution continued to smuggle the invisible baggage of their ideas, eroding the legitimacy of imperial rule and connecting the cause of freedom in India with the liberation of all the oppressed of the world.

---

[64] India and Communism: Compiled in the Intelligence Bureau, Home Department, Government of India (Calcutta: Government of India, 1933), p.90 IOR/L/PJ/12/670, India Office Records, the British Library, London.

4

Indoamerica against Empire: Radical Transnational Politics in Mexico City, 1925–1929

Tony Wood

During the 1920s, Mexico City cemented its role as an "emporium of revolution," as Barry Carr has put it.[1] Already a haven for radicals during the First World War – it notably hosted many North American "slackers" as well as Indian anticolonial activist M. N. Roy – over the following decade it became a magnet for an even broader range of activists, thinkers, writers, and artists from across Latin America and beyond. Amid the political and cultural ferment that followed the Mexican Revolution, and at a moment when repressive regimes held sway in much of the hemisphere, an array of exiles – Cubans, Peruvians, Venezuelans, Colombians – were able to operate in relative freedom there. Radicals from further afield also spent time in the Mexican capital in these years, including leftists from the US such as Bertram Wolfe, Langston Hughes, and the Italian-American photographer Tina Modotti. Mexico City was also a key bridgehead for the Communist International's activities in the Americas. Its envoy established a presence there within months of the organization's founding in March 1919, and in 1921 it dispatched three delegates from Moscow to Mexico, "bestow[ing] upon the Latin American country an importance granted to few others."[2]

In its role as a radical hub, Mexico City was the site of a transnational convergence of different political traditions and outlooks. But it was much more than a passive space of encounter: through an examination

[1] Barry Carr, "Radicals, Revolutionaries, and Exiles: Mexico City in the 1920s," *Berkeley Review of Latin American Studies* (Fall 2010).
[2] Daniela Spenser, *Stumbling Its Way through Mexico: The Early Years of the Communist International* (Tuscaloosa: University of Alabama Press, 2011), 91.

of the Anti-Imperialist League of the Americas (Liga Antimperialista de las Américas, LADLA) and its organ, *El Libertador*, this chapter argues that interactions between Mexican political and social movements and exiled activists, writers, and thinkers generated novel ideas and border-spanning solidarities. Though diverse in their backgrounds and ideologies, these individuals and organizations nonetheless shared a coherent brand of anti-imperialist politics that played a more significant role in the region's interwar political landscape than is commonly acknowledged.

Anti-imperialism was not, to be sure, a novelty in 1920s Latin America. Ever since independence, the countries of the region had proved vulnerable to breaches of their sovereignty by the US and European powers, giving rise to a broad popular awareness of these external threats. The very concept of "Latin" America was forged in the mid-nineteenth century in pan-regional opposition to the looming "Anglo-Saxon" power to the north.[3] In Mexico itself, anti-imperialist sentiments, directed particularly at US corporations and landowners, were a constant presence during the armed phase of the Revolution (1910–1920).[4] But the 1920s iteration of Latin American anti-imperialism was distinctive in being grounded in a newly global sensibility – rooted, that is, in a closer appreciation of parallels between the region's situation and anticolonial struggles around the world. It therefore placed Latin America squarely within the global ferment of the years following the First World War, highlighting the need to integrate Latin American developments more closely into transnational histories of the epoch.[5]

A wave of recent scholarship has addressed transnational radical and anti-imperial networks in the interwar years. Several have focused on imperial metropoles as nodes for oppositional organizing, while others have retraced broader patterns of mobility and their effects on

---

[3] See Michel Gobat, "The Invention of Latin America: A Transnational History of Anti-Imperialism, Democracy, and Race," *American Historical Review*, 118:5 (December 2013), 1345–1375.

[4] There is, however, considerable debate about the degree to which anti-imperial impulses drove the Revolution itself. For the latter argument, see John Mason Hart, *Revolutionary Mexico: The Coming and Process of the Mexican Revolution* (Berkeley, CA: University of California Press, 1987); for a contrasting "internalist" view, see Alan Knight, *The Mexican Revolution*, vols. 1 and 2 (Lincoln, NE: University of Nebraska Press, 1986).

[5] In this respect I seek to build on recent work such as Lara Putnam, *Radical Moves: Caribbean Migrants and the Politics of Race in the Jazz Age* (Chapel Hill, NC: University of North Carolina Press, 2013) and Christy Thornton, *Revolution in Development: Mexico and the Governance of the Global Economy* (Berkeley, CA: University of California Press, 2021).

anticolonial currents.[6] Latin America has tended to occupy an ambiguous position in these discussions: as a region largely composed of sovereign states, it did not share with Asian, African, or Middle Eastern movements the immediate goal of liberation from direct colonial rule, and thus tends not to feature in accounts of the interwar anticolonial ferment. When it does, it is often to underscore its separateness: writing about the 1927 Brussels conference of the League against Imperialism, Michael Goebel has argued that the Latin American delegates – perhaps under the influence of the Comintern's materialist outlook – tended to frame imperialism as above all an economic phenomenon, manifested in the sway of US corporations and banking interests. Goebel sees this as one of the factors inhibiting the construction of a truly global solidarity.[7]

Yet while Goebel's depiction rings true for the Brussels congress, an analysis of anti-imperialist organizing in Latin America itself presents a somewhat different picture. Several cities in the region witnessed a comparable anti-imperial ferment in these years, nourished by similar political, social, and intellectual currents that gave rise to a rich variety of organizations and publications: the Unión Latinoamericana in Buenos Aires, the Universidad Popular José Martí in Havana, *Amauta* in Lima. I focus here on Mexico City's anti-imperialist milieu since it offers an unusually vivid example of how productive and powerful the overlap between transnational networks and domestic actors could be. Drawing on sources from Mexico and from the Comintern archives in Moscow, I show how the Anti-Imperialist League of the Americas (LADLA) helped foster a growing sense of Latin America's commonalities with the wider anticolonial upsurge.

LADLA's trajectory should be of additional interest to scholars of global anticolonialism because of its contradictory relationship with the

---

[6] On the latter point, see notably Tim Harper, *Underground Asia: Global Revolutionaries and the Assault on Empire* (Cambridge, MA: Harvard University Press, 2021). For the role of Paris as an "anti-imperial metropolis," see Michael Goebel, *Anti-Imperial Metropolis: Interwar Paris and the Seeds of Third World Nationalism* (Cambridge: Cambridge University Press, 2015) and Jennifer Boittin, *Colonial Metropolis: The Urban Grounds of Anti-Imperialism and Feminism in Interwar Paris* (Lincoln, NE: University of Nebraska Press, 2010). On New York as a Caribbean hub, see Sandra Pujals, "A 'Soviet Caribbean': The Comintern, New York's Immigrant Community, and the Forging of Caribbean Visions, 1931–1936," *Russian History*, 41 (2014), 255–268.

[7] Michael Goebel, "Forging a Proto-Third World? Latin America and the League against Imperialism," in Michele Louro, Carolien Stolte, Heather Streets-Salter, and Sana Tannoury-Karam, eds., *The League against Imperialism: Lives and Afterlives* (Leiden: Leiden University Press, 2020), 53–78.

League against Imperialism (LAI).[8] LADLA was founded two years earlier than the LAI and anticipated several of its key features – its many strengths but also the weaknesses that ultimately undermined it. Yet the LAI was given much greater priority by the Comintern, and it was one of the mechanisms through which the Comintern sought to rein in the autonomy of organizations such as LADLA in the late 1920s. In that sense the LAI and LADLA illustrate some of the paradoxical hierarchies that were in play amid the forging of anticolonial solidarities.

Communist-affiliated networks played a central role both in LADLA and its publication, and the Comintern's priorities certainly helped shape their agenda as well as their trajectory. Mexico City's anti-imperialist consensus also extended far beyond the Communists' own ranks. By the mid-1920s, a wide range of actors had gathered there – from Mexican peasant leagues to Cuban trade unionists, and from the exiled Peruvians who founded the anti-imperialist American Popular Revolutionary Alliance (APRA) to representatives of the Haitian Patriotic Union – who were all acutely conscious not only of the local and national contexts in which they acted, but also of currents operating far beyond.[9] Principally through links with the Soviet Union, they came into contact with a globe-spanning network that included anticolonial activists from China, Southeast Asia, India, and Africa. This enabled LADLA to develop a capacious anti-imperial politics that extended far beyond a purely econ-omistic framing, highlighting multiple other forms of oppression against which Latin Americans could also stand in solidarity.

At the same time, the newly global sensibility underpinning LADLA made clear the limits of political projects operating solely within the confines of the nation-state. The transnational links through which LADLA emerged at once testified to the accelerating integration wrought

---

[8] For an overview of the LAI, see the editors' introduction to Louro, Stolte, Streets-Salter, and Tannoury-Karam, eds., *The League against Imperialism*, 17–51; see also Fredrik Petersson, "'We Are Neither Visionaries Nor Utopian Dreamers': Willi Münzenberg, the League against Imperialism, and the Comintern, 1925–1933," PhD thesis, Abo Akademi, 2013.

[9] For a rich exploration of the exile milieu in Mexico City at this time, see Sebastián Rivera Mir, *Militantes de la izquierda latinoamericana en México, 1920–1934. Prácticas políticas, redes y conspiraciones* (Mexico City: El Colegio de México, 2018). See also Thomas Lindner, "Transnational Networks of Anti-Imperialism: Mexico City in the 1920s," PhD thesis, Technische Universität, Berlin, 2019. On Communist links between the US, Mexico, and the Caribbean, see Margaret Stevens, *Red International and Black Caribbean: Communists in New York City, Mexico and the West Indies, 1919–1939* (London: Pluto Books, 2017).

by global capitalism and offered tools for those seeking to dismantle it in the name of a socialist world order. In its attempt to foster this internationalism from below, LADLA was a clear forerunner of Third Worldist currents and solidarities forged in the aftermath of the Second World War and in the era of decolonization.[10] In its own time, LADLA produced original insights into Latin America's situation and its place in the world, making a significant contribution to the political and intellectual repertoire of the region's radical left. In what follows, I bring out several of the key issues and themes it took up, including its framings of class, race, and empire, and its opposition to the use of force by US and European colonial powers in Asia, Africa, and Latin America and the Caribbean. I begin, however, by outlining LADLA's origins and overall character.

THE MAKING OF THE LIGA ANTIMPERIALISTA

A man with indigenous features is breaking free of the chains that bind him (see Figure 4.1). He is wearing a worker's overalls and boots and is striding across a map of Central and South America. Above him, where the United States should be, there is cluster of skyscrapers, from whose serried ranks come yet more chains stretching down across Mexico, Cuba, and the rest of Latin America. This image, counterposing indigenous, worker resistance to capitalist domination emanating from the US, adorns the cover of the first issue of *El Libertador*, published in Mexico City in March 1925.[11] The magazine is billed as the "organ of the Liga Anti-Imperialista Panamericana," an organization which, renamed the "Liga Antimperialista de las Américas" only a few weeks later, was to serve as the focal point of anti-imperialist activism in Mexico City for the next several years.[12]

---

[10] See the essays by Cindy Ewing and Ruodi Duan in this volume.
[11] *El Libertador*, No. 1, March 1925, consulted at the New York Public Library. The drawing is signed "Indio," and is probably by the Mexican artist Xavier Guerrero (1896–1974), who was of indigenous descent; a member of the Mexican Communist Party (PCM), Guerrero is also listed as *El Libertador*'s administrator in its first few issues. This same drawing featured in subsequent issues as part of the magazine's masthead.
[12] The definitive study of the Liga, to which the following account is indebted, is Daniel Kersffeld, *Contra el imperio. Historia de la Liga Antimperialista de las Américas* (Mexico City: Siglo XXI, 2012). See also the late Ricardo Melgar Bao's important contribution, "The Anti-imperialist League of the Americas between the East and Latin America," *Latin American Perspectives*, 35:2 (2008), 9–24.

FIGURE 4.1. *El Libertador*, No. 1 (March 1925). Original held at the New York Public Library.

Headquartered in Mexico City's historic center, the Anti-Imperialist League of the Americas broke new political ground in several respects. Firstly, LADLA was ideologically heterogeneous: though founded at the instigation of Communists and dominated organizationally by individuals close to the Mexican Communist Party (PCM), its activities also drew in people from a broad range of political tendencies. Second, and relatedly, it had a cross-class social profile, attracting workers, peasants, middle-class professionals, and members of the bourgeoisie alike. Third, it had a disproportionately strong cultural presence thanks to the involvement of figures from Latin America's artistic and literary vanguard, including the muralists Diego Rivera and David Alfaro Siqueiros, and writers such as the Cuban novelist Alejo Carpentier and the Mexican poet Germán List Arzubide. Fourth, LADLA was a thoroughly transnational entity: its organizational mechanisms and political agenda leapfrogged national frontiers, as did many of its key personnel. Starting in 1925, LADLA sections were set up in one country after another: as well as Mexico, there were branches in Argentina, Colombia, Cuba, Ecuador, El Salvador, Guatemala, Panama, Peru, Puerto Rico, the United States, and Venezuela. In some of these countries, the establishment of LADLA sections accompanied the foundation of Communist parties, or even predated them. At a moment when Communism was still largely a marginal force in Latin America, LADLA figured centrally in its organizational growth across the region.

LADLA's origins are themselves deeply transnational. In June 1920, the Comintern had adopted Lenin's "Theses on National and Colonial Questions," which insisted that "all Communist parties must assist the bourgeois-democratic liberation movement in [colonial] countries."[13] The theses themselves emerged out of debates at the Comintern's Second Congress between Lenin and M. N. Roy, with the latter – freshly arrived from Mexico – urging the organization to give greater priority to struggles in the colonial world. At its Fourth Congress in 1922, the Comintern affirmed this commitment when adopting its "united front" strategy, which called on Communists in colonized territories "to give full support to the national-revolutionary movement against imperialism."[14]

---

[13] V. I. Lenin, "Draft Theses on National and Colonial Questions for the Second Congress of the Communist International" [1920], in *Collected Works*, vol. 31 (Moscow: Progress Publishers, 1966), 149.

[14] Fourth Congress of the Communist International, "Theses on Comintern Tactics," December 5, 1922; available at www.marxists.org/history/international/comintern/4th-congress/tactics.htm.

This new policy was put into action most decisively in China starting in 1923: under instructions from Moscow, the fledgling Chinese Communist Party embedded itself within the much larger nationalist Kuomintang (KMT). This furnished a model the Comintern was keen to see replicated elsewhere, instructing its affiliates to make alliances, in the name of anti-imperialism, with forces that would in other circumstances be deemed class adversaries. These two components of Comintern strategy – hoisting the banner of national liberation, in a bid to lead a cross-class movement – were also present in LADLA from the outset.

The first reference made in Latin America to "anti-imperialist leagues" came in October 1924, concerning their formation in China.[15] The immediate spur for founding an equivalent organization in Mexico was the upcoming congress of the Pan-American Federation of Labor (hereafter referred to by its Spanish acronym, COPA). Due to be held in Mexico City in December 1924, the congress was part of the American Federation of Labor's attempt to extend its influence over Latin America. Prior to the COPA congress, the Mexican Communist newspaper *El Machete* published several articles criticizing the AFL and its leader Samuel Gompers for their support for US interventions in the region.[16] It was in this context that the first iteration of LADLA – the Liga Panamericana Antimperialista – made its appearance, as a signatory to two manifestos, published in *El Machete* just days after the COPA congress opened in December 1924.[17] One is addressed to Chilean and Peruvian workers, urging them to set aside their differences over the disputed territories of Tacna and Arica in the name of anti-imperial solidarity; the second is addressed to COPA delegates, urging them not to re-elect Gompers as COPA head.

The fact that LADLA made its first appearance in *El Machete* reflects its close relationship to that publication, and to the Mexican Communist Party, whose organ the paper became in 1925. Through *El Machete*, the PCM helped publicize LADLA events and publications, and the paper

[15] "Las garras del imperialismo internacional en China," *El Machete*, No. 17, October 16–23, 1924.

[16] "Gompers, agente del imperialismo yanqui," *El Machete*, No. 19, October 30–November 6, 1924 and No. 20, November 6–13, 1924; "Los servicios de Gompers a los trabajadores de la América Latina," *El Machete*, No. 21, November 13–20, 1924; "La oposición comunista en la próxima convención de la Federación Americana del Trabajo," *El Machete*, No. 19, October 30–November 6, 1924; "Manifiesto a los delegados al congreso de la Federación Panamericana del Trabajo," *El Machete*, No. 23, November 27–December 4, 1924.

[17] "Llamamiento a los Trabajadores de Chile y el Perú" and "Samuel Gompers, agente de la Casa Blanca," *El Machete*, No. 24, December 4–11, 1924.

furnished much of the organization's infrastructure. But as we have seen, LADLA's formative matrix extended far beyond the PCM: it included the Comintern's experience in China, Mexican opposition to US dominance of the Americas, as well as Communist attempts to counter the hemispheric labor agenda of the AFL. The decision to rename the organization, made at the PCM's April 1925 congress, stemmed from a desire to take a distance from the adjective "Pan-American," which was commonly associated with the hemispheric integration projects promoted by Washington and its allies in the Latin American elite.[18] The composition of LADLA's original secretariat reflected its transnational blend of concerns: it included Rafael Carrillo, Secretary General of the PCM; the American radicals Bertram and Ella Wolfe, resident in Mexico City from 1923 to 1925 and closely involved in the PCM; and Stanislav Pestkovsky, the Soviet Union's first ambassador to Mexico.[19]

In mid-January 1925, Wolfe wrote to the US Communist Party to announce that the newly formed Liga had "decided to launch the first number of the anti-imperialist bulletin for the Latin-American countries." He made clear its guiding principles: *El Libertador* would be "a bulletin of complete Marxist orientation but we shall ask the collaboration of leading left liberals and socialists ... to give the bulletin a wider circulation and to use it in the building of a mass movement against imperialism."[20] Over the next few years, *El Libertador* was indeed successful in drawing in a range of collaborators. A country-by-country list of contributors printed on the inside front page of the June 1927 issue reads like a *Who's Who* of the anti-imperialist left of the time. It includes the Peruvian Marxist José Carlos Mariátegui; the Argentine socialist Alfredo Palacios; the muralist José Clemente Orozco and the economist and historian Jesús Silva Herzog, both from Mexico; Puerto Rican nationalist leader Pedro Albizu Campos; from the United States, Upton Sinclair, Carleton Beals, Scott Nearing, and Samuel Inman; and European luminaries such as Henri Barbusse, Bertrand Russell, and Anatoly Lunacharsky.[21] But the core of *El Libertador*'s output consisted of

---

[18] Manuel Gómez report on PCM III Congress, April 23, 1925, RGASPI F. 495, op. 108, d. 38, 23.

[19] Kersffeld, *Contra el imperio*, 49. On Pestkovsky, see Daniela Spenser, "Stanislav Pestkovsky: A Soldier of the World Revolution in Mexico," *Journal of Iberian and Latin American Research*, 8:1 (2002), 35–56.

[20] "Copy of letter sent to the American Party," January 14, 1925, Russian State Archive of Social and Political History (hereafter RGASPI), F. 495, op. 108, d. 54: 1.

[21] "Cuerpo internacional de colaboradores," *El Libertador*, No. 12, June 1927.

articles and manifestos by people based in Mexico City, including not only Communists but also Peruvian members of APRA and other Latin American exiles.

Communists and APRA members were two of the most visible currents that converged in LADLA. Both brought something distinctive to the mix. APRA was formed in the mid-1920s by Peruvian exiles scattered across Latin America and Europe, and advocated pan-Latin American unity in the face of US dominance.[22] Former student leader Víctor Raúl Haya de la Torre was its charismatic figurehead and chief ideologue, and in the course of two stays in Mexico in 1923–1924 and 1927–1928 he developed close relationships with officials in the Mexican government, including Secretary of Education José Vasconcelos, and with journalists working for established newspapers such as *Excélsior*. Other *apristas* who lived in Mexico City, including the Peruvians noted above and the poet Magda Portal, similarly connected LADLA to middle-class anti-imperialist sentiment.

The Mexican Communist Party, meanwhile, had been formed in late 1919 by Socialists seeking to join the global struggle now being led by the Comintern. Anticolonialism attended its birth: among its founders was M. N. Roy. (A year after co-founding the PCM, he founded the Indian Communist Party in Tashkent.[23]) Many of the PCM members most closely involved with LADLA were exiles from elsewhere in Latin America: Cuban Communist Julio Antonio Mella and the Venezuelans Gustavo Machado and Salvador de la Plaza, for example, used Mexico as a base to plan their own revolutions. As well as providing LADLA's core staff and publicizing its events, the PCM was also the main link between LADLA and the Comintern, providing a vital conduit for funds and correspondence. Several of those affiliated with LADLA traveled to Moscow to attend Comintern gatherings, where they crossed paths with anticolonial activists from South and East Asia, Africa and the Middle East. It was through the PCM, for example, that future APRA leader Haya de la Torre was invited to Moscow in 1924.[24]

---

[22] On the transnational origins of APRA, see Geneviève Dorais, "Coming of Age in Exile: Víctor Raúl Haya de la Torre and the Genesis of the American Popular Revolutionary Alliance, 1923–1931," *Hispanic American Historical Review*, 97:4 (2017), 651–679.

[23] See Daniel Kent Carrasco, "M. N. Roy en México: cosmopolitismo intelectual y contingencia política en la creación del PCM," in Carlos Illades, ed., *Camaradas: Nueva historia del comunismo en México* (Mexico City: Fondo de Cultura Económica, 2017), 37–71.

[24] Víctor Jeifets and Lazar Jeifets, "Haya de la Torre, la Comintern y el Perú: Acercamientos y desencuentros," *Pacarina del Sur*, 4:16 (2013).

Though the PCM was at this point a small organization with only a few hundred members, it had a notably strong presence among urban artisans and manual workers, enabling LADLA to reach parts of the working class in Mexico City and elsewhere. Perhaps most significant numerically, however, were the links between the PCM, LADLA, and Mexico's peasants. As Barry Carr notes, among Latin American Communist parties the PCM was "the first to develop strong roots within the peasantry."[25] This was largely thanks to the considerable overlap between the PCM and Mexico's radical peasant leagues (*ligas campesinas*), which had emerged in the wake of the Mexican Revolution and by the mid-1920s had 200,000 members between them.[26] The largest and most prominent was the League of Agrarian Communities of the State of Veracruz (LCAEV), founded in March 1923, many of whose leaders were also members of the PCM.[27]

These peasant leagues constituted a further crucial strand in LADLA. The leagues' demographic and geographical reach helped LADLA to establish affiliates across the country, from Nuevo León in the north to Oaxaca in the south. Moreover, peasant leagues also possessed a potent internationalism of their own. Within months of the Veracruz Liga's foundation, for example, its leader, Úrsulo Galván, traveled to the USSR to take part in the congress of the Comintern-affiliated Peasant International or Krestintern, where he shared a platform with Ho Chi Minh and with speakers from China, Mongolia, Indonesia, Japan, the US, France, Bulgaria, Holland, Italy, and Germany.[28] Two years later, in a development that underlines the significance of this peasant internationalism to LADLA, Galván became the first editor of *El Libertador*.

[25] Barry Carr, *Marxism and Communism in Twentieth-Century Mexico* (Lincoln, NE: University of Nebraska Press, 1992), 132.

[26] Victor Jeifets and Irving Reynoso Jaime, "Del Frente Único a clase contra clase: comunistas y agraristas en el México posrevolucionario, 1919–1930," *Izquierdas*, 19 (2014), 15–40. See also Armando Bartra, *Los herederos de Zapata. Movimientos campesinos posrevolucionarios en México 1920–1980* (Mexico City: Ediciones Era, 1985).

[27] Liga de Comunidades Agrarias del Estado de Veracruz (LCAEV), *El agrarismo en México. La cuestión agraria y el problema campesino* (Jalapa: n.p., 1924), 23. On the origins of the Veracruz *liga*, see Heather Fowler-Salamini, *Agrarian Radicalism in Veracruz, 1920–38* (Lincoln, NE: University of Nebraska Press, 1978), 25–47.

[28] Protocols of First Krestintern Congress, October 10, 1923, RGASPI F. 535, op. 1, d. 1: 4–6. Ho was at this point known by a different pseudonym, Nguyen Ai Quoc.

FRAMING IMPERIALISM

From the outset, LADLA adopted a dual framing of imperialism as both a global question and a class issue. "A danger threatens Latin America," warned the editorial that opened the first issue of *El Libertador* in March 1925.[29] Referring to a string of US interventions and occupations in the previous decades, it listed "Cuba, Panama, Haiti, Santo Domingo, Nicaragua, Veracruz" as "successive steps in the agony of a continent." "Uncle Sam," it asserted, "supports autocracies; foments and funds revolutions against 'Bolshevik governments,' and slowly and silently continues on its way to Tierra del Fuego, buying and nullifying, fomenting and destroying; doing as it pleases across two entire continents." Where should Latin America turn for help against such an adversary? *El Libertador* urged its readers to look to "other peoples oppressed by Yankee imperialism, in Russia and China," as well as "in the Orient" and "among the peoples of Europe." But the crucial support would come from "among our own forces that, once united in a single continental anti-imperialist movement, can save us and perhaps also manage to save Europe, Asia, and Africa as well."

Latin America, then, was identified as an integral part of a wider anti-imperialist struggle – and indeed marked out as potentially making a vital contribution to the liberation of other regions of the world. To be sure, the vagueness of its opening editorial's allusion to "the Orient" suggests a limited engagement with the full breadth and variety of anticolonial struggles in Asia and the Middle East – a clear difference from the Third Worldism that emerged in the postwar era. Yet LADLA did make connections between Latin America's situation and that of other peoples across the world subject to imperial domination. *El Libertador* reported on an anti-imperialist resolution passed in 1925 by a meeting of British trade unionists, and ran articles on the combined Spanish–French counter-insurgency against Abd el-Krim in the Rif and on the Filipino struggle for independence, among many other examples.[30] (It even ran a portrait of Abd el-Krim as the cover of its October 1925 issue.)

---

[29] "El Peligro; Las Posibilidades; El Propósito," *El Libertador*, No. 1, March 1925, 1. All quotations in this paragraph from this source.

[30] "Imperialismo de Clase, no de Raza," *El Libertador*, No. 3, June 1925, 15; Haya de la Torre, "El asesinato de un pueblo," No. 7, February 1926; Rafael Carrillo, "La próxima ofensiva en Marruecos," No. 8, April 1926; and "Lucha por la independencia filipina," Nos. 9–10, September–October 1926.

Within LADLA's global frame, one recurrent focus of attention was China. Between July 1925 and August 1927, *El Libertador* devoted several articles to the country, as well as making repeated references to it in articles on other topics.[31] In the mid-1920s, Communists across the world were deeply invested in China's fate, in part thanks to the Comintern's endorsement of the Kuomintang as a standard-bearer for colonial liberation. But China was also a vital battlefront, both literally and metaphorically, for the anti-imperialist left as a whole. While the USSR was often held up as a model for a coming revolutionary transformation of Latin America, China was seen as more directly sharing many of the region's structural characteristics, as a place where a semicolonized population was engaged in radical, often peasant-led revolt against European imperial powers and local elites. Hence *El Machete* had, in 1924, run an article on China subtitled "The[ir] Situation Is Notably Similar to Ours."[32] Haya viewed his own APRA movement as a hemispheric equivalent to Chiang Kai-shek's organization, a comparison he made publicly at an October 1926 event in London attended by representatives of the local KMT branch; thereafter, he would frequently refer to APRA as "a Latin American Kuomintang."[33]

PERSPECTIVES ON CLASS AND RACE

At the same time as they embraced these global connections, *El Libertador*'s editors repeatedly stressed the significance of class solidarities. In 1925, the magazine's opening editorial listed the allies to be found in oppressed colonies and then added another: US workers and poor farmers (*labriegos*). Both they and the peoples of Latin America, it argued, were up against "a monster with two heads" – one named "Imperialism," sowing devastation in Latin America; the other named "Capitalism," besetting workers and small farmers in the US. To counter this two-headed beast, what was needed was a movement spanning the entire hemisphere, to "awaken the somnolent masses of workers and peasants,

---

[31] "El imperialismo en China," *El Libertador*, No. 4, July 1925; "La masacre imperialista en China," No. 7, February 1926; Mella, "El Kuo Min Tang y la revolución china," No. 8, April 1926; Hurwitz, "La esperanza amarilla," No. 12, June 1927; and "Ante una nueva fase de la revolución china," No. 13, August 1927.

[32] "Las garras del imperialismo ..."

[33] See Pedro Planas, *Los orígenes del APRA. El joven Haya* (Lima: Okura Editores, 1986), 60–62.

of indigenous[34] and *mestizos* and whites, groaning under the yoke of imperialism."[35]

While enunciating both a global and a class-inflected view of the struggle against imperialism, LADLA also laid out a suggestively ambiguous approach to the question of race. On the one hand, there was a rejection of the very concept. An item in *El Libertador*'s first issue, titled simply "Enough of 'Races',", argued forcefully against any racialized conception of Latin America's struggle against imperialism.[36] It dismissed the idea of superior and inferior races as part of an "intellectual scaffolding" built by "men of 'science'" in the imperialist countries. A second article by the same pseudonymous author observed that basic information on the indigenous was lacking: "Data: there are none. No statistics either."[37] Racialized pseudo-science should not blind the left to its real adversaries: the enemy was not "the Anglo-Saxon race" but "the North American banker."[38]

On the other hand, there was marked emphasis on both economic uplift and cultural renewal for the indigenous population – a proposition that rested precisely on the identification of the latter as a coherent racial category, and as a collective subject that could be roused to action in much the same way as colonized peoples elsewhere. An item from 1925 insisted that "the Indian" should form the basis of the anti-imperialist movement in Latin America as a whole; otherwise it would remain "a mere literary tendency, a sterile struggle of leaflets and books."[39] The way to secure indigenous support was to organize them in agrarian leagues – the example of Mexico's peasant *ligas* was clearly present in the author's mind – and to abolish peonage and give them land. The author also stressed the need to "re-establish their culture" by

---

[34] The text uses the term *indígena*, rather than *indio*, which was more common at the time. Here and elsewhere, in direct quotations I use the English words "indigenous" and "Indian" to reflect this difference.

[35] "El Peligro. . . ."

[36] "Audifaz," "Basta de 'Razas'," *El Libertador*, No. 1, March 1925, 9–10. According to Ricardo Melgar Bao, "Audifaz" was most likely Bertram Wolfe; this would be consistent with the chronology and frame of reference of the articles. The pseudonym itself is a variant spelling of Audifax, a minor Catholic saint martyred in Rome in 270 CE. Melgar Bao, "The Anti-Imperialist League of the Americas," 16.

[37] "Audifaz," "Apreciaciones falsas y correctas del problema indígena," *El Libertador*, No. 5, August 1925, 3–4.

[38] "Audifaz," "Basta de 'Razas'," 9.

[39] "Audifaz," "El Indio Como Base de la Lucha Anti-Imperialista," *El Libertador*, No. 4, July 1925, 3–4.

educating them in their own languages – a demand that ran directly counter to the strongly assimilationist policies of the Mexican government of the time.

It was also clear to many within the anti-imperialist milieu that the indigenous question needed to be understood within a transnational rather than a national frame. In May 1927, Haya de la Torre wrote to the literary Grupo Resurgimiento in Cuzco arguing that, given the systemic character of their oppression, "the indigenous problem cannot be separated from imperialism."[40] For that reason, the indigenous question was "eminently international."[41]

This understanding was shared by much of Mexico City's radical anti-imperialist milieu: the nation-state was not necessarily the most appropriate unit for liberatory projects, which had to be conceived on a continental or even a global scale. At its Second Congress in 1923, the Veracruz peasant league had called for the formation of a national body, but noted that it would be "incomplete" if it remained "a solely and exclusively national organization": "for it to realize its destiny it is not enough to make it only national, but rather [it must be] International."[42] When the National Peasant League was duly formed in 1926, its founding congress was attended by speakers from Peru, Colombia, Ecuador, and the Netherlands, and the gathering concluded with a rousing rendition of the Internationale.[43]

LADLA AND THE LEAGUE AGAINST IMPERIALISM

Mexico City's anti-imperialists also paid close attention to the Congress against Colonial Oppression and Imperialism held in Brussels in February 1927.[44] *El Libertador* and *El Machete* published advance notices about it, drumming up interest in a gathering that promised to connect disparate realms of anticolonial struggle.[45] Some of the anti-imperialists who had

---

[40] Haya de la Torre, "El problema del indio," in *Obras completas* (Lima: Librería-Editorial Juan Mejía Baca, 1977), vol. 1, 188.

[41] Haya de la Torre, "El problema del indio," 188.

[42] "Tesis sobre relaciones internacionales," December 3, 1924, RGASPI F. 535, op. 2, d. 97: 61.

[43] Liga Nacional Campesina, *Primer congreso de unificación de las organizaciones campesinas de la República* (Puebla: Santiago Loyo, 1927), 28, 43.

[44] For a range of reflections on the Brussels congress and its after-effects, see Louro, Stolte, Streets-Salter, and Tannoury-Karam, eds., *The League against Imperialism*.

[45] See for example *El Libertador*, Nos. 9–10, September–October 1926, 1, 10; and *El Machete*, Nos. 51, September 30, 1926; 52, October 15, 1926; and 55, mid-November 1926.

been attracted to LADLA were also involved in the League's organizing committee, including the Mexican ambassador to Germany, Ramón de Negri.[46]

In Brussels itself, there were just over twenty delegates from the Americas, including five representing Mexican organizations, five doing the same for Puerto Rico, four from the US, and others representing Colombia, Cuba, Peru, and Venezuela.[47] Strikingly, many of the delegates for these Latin American organizations were actually based in Mexico City, underlining its status as an anti-imperial hub. Alongside Julio Antonio Mella as LADLA delegate were representatives of Mexico's National Peasant League, the Mexican Regional Workers' Confederation (CROM), and the Mexican Student Federation. More surprisingly, Mexican delegates also represented organizations with which they seemingly had little connection: former Secretary of Education José Vasconcelos represented the Puerto Rican Nationalist Party, and revolutionary general Juan Andreu Almazán signed the congress's resolutions on behalf of the Haitian League of the Rights of Man and of the Citizen.[48] They likely assumed these roles because of the logistical and financial difficulties delegates from Puerto Rico and Haiti would have faced in getting to Brussels (for similar reasons, a Uruguayan represented the Haitian Union Patriotique). But these apparent incongruities also reflect Mexico's new role on the international stage: as prominent figures from a revolutionary state, Vasconcelos and Almazán clearly felt they could claim to stand for the broader cause of Latin American anti-imperialism.

In June 1927 *El Libertador* devoted almost an entire issue – with a cover drawn by Diego Rivera, who now took over as editor until the end of 1928 – to resolutions from the Brussels congress.[49] This notably included the resolution on Latin America, which referred to "an awakening of national revolutionary consciousness" in the Americas and compared the situation in Latin America to that elsewhere, noting

---

[46] Kersffeld, *Contra el imperio*, 97. De Negri's presence helped burnish the anti-imperialist credentials of the Calles administration, which at the time was locked in disputes with the US over oil companies' prerogatives.

[47] "List of Organizations and Delegates attending the Congress against Colonial Oppression and Imperialism," February 10, 1927, International Institute for Social History, League against Imperialism Archives, ARCH00804 inventory #2.

[48] "Déclaration sur la situation et les nécessités de lutte contre l'imperialisme dans les Amériques," postscript, February 13, 1927, RGASPI F. 542, op. 1, d. 19: 26.

[49] *El Libertador*, No. 12, June 1927, *passim*.

that "all the other peoples who struggle against imperialism: China, India, Egypt, are struggling against our common enemy."[50] *El Libertador* also ran a translation of the Brussels congress's "Resolution on the Black Question," accompanied by a photograph of Senegalese Communist Lamine Senghor, highlighting the depth of racialized oppression in Africa and far beyond.[51]

As noted above, LADLA anticipated many of the distinctive features of the League against Imperialism, and the two organizations had similar origins. Both emerged in accordance with the Comintern's "united front" strategy, and both drew on the example of China. The initial basis for the LAI, indeed, was the "Hands Off China" campaign of mid-1925, coordinated from Berlin by Willi Münzenberg; the success of these solidarity efforts led to the formation of the League against Colonial Oppression in late 1926, renamed the LAI after the Brussels congress.[52]

Once the LAI was formed, it became a point of liaison between LADLA and the Comintern. In the summer of 1927, Münzenberg sent an envoy to Mexico, the Swiss Communist Fritz Sulzbachner (commonly known as Federico Bach), who thereafter served on LADLA's Continental Organizing Committee and took a very active part in setting its priorities.[53] This coincided with an internal reorganization of LADLA, designed to coordinate more effectively the work of its different sections across the region.[54] Yet while the reshuffle and closer contact with the LAI had undoubted benefits, they were also symptomatic of an increasing top-down impulse within the Comintern, and this was also reflected in the relationship between LADLA and the LAI, which was marked by a surprising reassertion of European prerogatives. Rather than drawing on LADLA's experience, both the Comintern and the LAI effectively began to treat it as a branch of the Berlin-based outfit.[55]

---

[50] "Déclaration sur la situation...," 24.

[51] On Senghor see David Murphy, "No More Slaves! Lamine Senghor, Black Internationalism and the League against Imperialism," in Louro et al., eds., *The League against Imperialism*, 211–236.

[52] Petersson, "We Are Neither Visionaries Nor Utopian Dreamers," 53, 90.

[53] On Bach, see Víctor Jeifets and Lazar Jeifets, *América Latina en la Internacional Comunista, 1919–1943: Diccionario biográfico* (Santiago de Chile: Ariadna Ediciones, 2015), 66.

[54] Kersffeld, *Contra el imperio*, 121.

[55] Perhaps unconsciously reflecting this view, in his discussion of the LAI's relationship to Latin America, Fredrik Petersson does not even mention LADLA, which had already existed for two years prior to the LAI's formation: Petersson, "We Are Neither Visionaries Nor Utopian Dreamers," 175–179.

As we will see, however, there was little time for these tensions to play out. Larger strategic disagreements were already looming over Mexico's anti-imperialist milieu, and these were among the factors that contributed to LADLA's downfall. Already in 1927, the rift in China between Nationalists and Communists, bloodily sealed by KMT massacres of Communists in Shanghai that April, had sent tremors through Latin American anti-imperial circles seeking to model their approach on the KMT–Communist alliance.[56] From 1928 onwards, further divergences began to emerge, even as LADLA scored notable successes in its work around another major anti-imperialist reference point: Nicaragua.

"HANDS OFF!"

The central preoccupation of Mexico City's anti-imperialists was US domination of Latin America. LADLA drew attention to different aspects of the workings of imperialism, describing it not only as a systemic economic force but also as a form of direct military domination. With regard to the former, articles in *El Libertador* analyzed Wall Street's dominance of the Caribbean, examined the role of the dollar in cementing US influence, itemized US financial investments in Mexico, and compared US and European shares of global imports and exports.[57] With regard to US imperialism as a military phenomenon, examples were not in short supply. *El Libertador* repeatedly condemned the US occupation of Haiti, under way since 1915. In June 1925, it denounced the occupying authorities' closure of schools and muzzling of the press, while a string of subsequent items assailed US violations of Haitian sovereignty.[58] On at least two occasions, Joseph Jolibois (fils), representing the Haitian Patriotic Union, spoke at LADLA events.[59]

But the overwhelming focus of Latin American anti-imperialists' attention in the second half of the 1920s was Nicaragua. US troops, present in

---

[56] For insights into the Comintern's transnational networks in China after this watershed, see the essay on Agnes Smedley in this volume by Michele Louro.

[57] See Scott Nearing, "Los Bancos Norteamericanos Mandan en el Mar Caribe," and Samuel Inman, "El Tío Sam como Rey Financiero," *El Libertador*, No. 3, June 1925, 11, 12; Enrique Flores Magón, "México es una Colonia Yanqui," and José López, "El balance antimperialista de 1925," *El Libertador*, No. 7, February 1926, 1–4 and 8–9.

[58] Untitled item, *El Libertador*, No. 3, June 1925, 1; "La Desgracia de Haití," No. 7, February 1926, 10; "La ocupación de Haití," No. 15, February 1928, 12; "Aniversario de la Ocupación de Haity [sic]," No. 17, April 1928, 16.

[59] *Excélsior*, January 15, 1928, 1; *El Machete*, No. 109, April 7, 1928, 4.

the country since 1912, had briefly been withdrawn in 1925, only to return a year later. Their redeployment against the rebellion led by Augusto Sandino was quickly condemned across Latin America, and from across a large part of the political spectrum.[60] The speed and breadth of solidarity with Sandino is especially striking when contrasted with Haiti – a sign that Spanish-speaking countries identified much more readily with a rebellion that consciously identified itself as *mestizo* and indeed "Indolatino." In Mexico, pro-Sandino sentiment was strong, and the Calles government's support for the rebels added further strains to already tense diplomatic relations with the US.[61]

For Mexico City's anti-imperialists, Nicaragua became the object of a broad and urgent consensus. Opposition to the US occupation brought a range of organizations together around a clear and morally compelling agenda, providing an immediate focus for solidarity efforts. *El Machete* carried running commentary on events in Nicaragua, publishing dispatches from the frontlines and splashing Sandino's military successes across its front page.[62] It even printed a *corrido* in honor of the Nicaraguan resistance: "This is the story of Nicaragua / the weak and unhappy nation / where the Yankees with their squadrons / have brought crime and dishonor."[63]

Nicaragua featured prominently in events organized by LADLA from 1925 onwards, including public meetings in Mexico City and Veracruz that July and August. A "Grand Anti-Imperialist Rally" was also held in the capital in June 1926, and another that December.[64] *El Libertador*, too, covered Nicaragua from early on.[65] As the occupation ground on, and resistance to it stubbornly continued, the pace of coverage increased, until Nicaragua came to dominate the magazine as a whole: from 1928

---

[60] On Nicaragua solidarity as a whole, see Barry Carr, "Pioneering Transnational Solidarity in the Americas: The Movement in Support of Augusto C. Sandino 1927–1934," *Journal of Iberian and Latin American Research*, 20:2 (2014), 141–152.

[61] Lorenzo Meyer, *México y el mundo. Historia de sus relaciones exteriores, tomo VI: La marca del nacionalismo* (Mexico City: El Colegio de México, 2010), 61–63.

[62] For example "El Heróico Sandino Derrota a las Tropas Americanas," *El Machete*, No. 96, January 7, 1928.

[63] "Esta es la historia de Nicaragua / la infortunada y débil nación / donde los yanquis con sus escuadras / llevan el crimen y el deshonor." See "Los cantos del pueblo: Nicaragua," *El Machete*, No. 99, January 28, 1928.

[64] *El Machete*, No. 40, July 16, 1925; No. 41, August 13, 1925; No. 45, April 8, 1926; and No. 56, early December 1926.

[65] "'Gringolandia y anexos'. La sucursal en Nicaragua," *El Libertador*, No. 3, June 1925; John Kenneth Turner, "Nicaragua, víctima del imperialismo norteamericano," No. 5, August 1925.

onwards, it published more than twenty items about the country in the space of only eight issues. These ranged in genre from reportage to documents to appeals for funds. To cite just a few examples, *El Libertador* translated Carleton Beals's profile of Sandino and ran dispatches from the frontlines – LADLA members Gustavo Machado and Esteban Pavletich both traveled to Nicaragua to join Sandino's forces for a time – as well as publishing Sandino's correspondence with Henri Barbusse.[66]

In January 1928, key LADLA members established the Comité Manos Fuera de Nicaragua – Hands Off Nicaragua Committee, known as Mafuenic – in Mexico City.[67] The crucial impetus seems to have come from Sulzbachner, the LAI envoy, who on January 10 wrote to Münzenberg announcing Mafuenic's foundation earlier that week.[68] As Bach described it, the organization had a dual aim: to gather funds to pay for medical and other supplies for Sandino's army; and to raise awareness of the resistance through public meetings and propaganda work. LADLA hosted Mafuenic at its headquarters, and Mafuenic's Secretary General was the Peruvian *aprista* Jacobo Hurwitz, while Communists such as Mella, Gustavo Machado, and Salvador de la Plaza were also prominently involved, as were members of the peasant leagues.

Among the main reasons for Mafuenic's visibility was the fact that it could draw on the personnel and networks not only of LADLA, the PCM, and the peasant leagues, but also those of several other organizations, from miners' and railway workers' unions to anticlerical organizations and the Mexican branch of the Comintern's International Red Aid. There were also representatives of exile groups such the Haitian Patriotic Union and the Central South American and Antillean Union (UCSAYA).[69]

---

[66] "Desde el campamento de Sandino" and "Carleton Beals con Sandino," *El Libertador*, No. 17, April 1928; Gustavo Machado, "El terror yanqui en Nicaragua," *El Libertador*, No. 18, June 1928; Gustavo Machado, "Con Sandino en las montañas de Nicaragua," *El Libertador*, No. 19, August 1928; Gustavo Machado, "Con Sandino en las montañas de Nicaragua" (continued); and "Desde el campamento de Sandino," *El Libertador*, No. 20, November 1928; "Carta del General Sandino a Barbusse," *El Libertador*, No. 21, May 1929.

[67] *El Machete*, No. 100, February 4, 1928, 1; see also Daniel Kersffeld, "El Comité Manos Fuera de Nicaragua: primera experiencia del sandinismo," *Pacarina del Sur*, 13 (2012).

[68] Bach to Münzenberg, January 10, 1928, RGASPI F. 528, op. 1, d. 28, 1.

[69] Kersffeld, "El Comité Manos Fuera de Nicaragua." UCSAYA was pan-Latin Americanist and anti-imperialist organization set up in Mexico in 1927 by Carlos León, a Venezuelan, and the Argentine Alejandro Maudet. See Ricardo Melgar Bao, "Un neobolivarianismo antimperialista: La Unión Centro Sud Americana y de las Antillas," *Políticas de la memoria*, No. 6/7 (2006–2007).

Most crucially, the Mexican public was from the outset receptive to Mafuenic's message. Pro-Sandino sentiment was widespread, extending far beyond the radical left; but Mafuenic was unusual in coordinating and channeling it on both a national and a local scale, aided by its dense network of allied organizations. By early February, only weeks after Mafuenic's establishment in Mexico City, there was a branch in Jalisco; others soon followed in Monterrey, Puebla, Veracruz, Tampico, Ciudad Victoria, Pachuca, Durango, and Oaxaca.[70] An event held at the Teatro Virginia Fábregas in the capital on April 4, 1928 – only two months after Mafuenic was publicly launched – drew 5,000 people.[71] A string of further events were held in Mexico City, including gatherings on July 4 and 9 at which the Mexican feminist performer Concha Michel sang three revolutionary *corridos*; one was the song dedicated to Nicaragua mentioned above.[72] At the July 9 meeting, the head of the local Mafuenic committee in the working-class Mexico City neighborhood of Colonia Peralvillo read out a poem about the deployment of US troops in Veracruz in 1914 – a reminder that Mexico itself had recently experienced occupation by US forces, testifying to the strong affective basis to feelings of solidarity with Nicaragua.[73]

Outside Mexico City, the peasant leagues provided the organizational infrastructure for Mafuenic, setting up events and hosting speakers. In Veracruz state, such events were held not only in the eponymous city and the state capital, Jalapa, but also in the countryside. Villa Cardel, for example, held a meeting on July 9, 1928, that was addressed by Sandino's brother Sócrates, Rivera, and Gustavo Machado, who had just returned from Nicaragua.[74] Sócrates Sandino and Machado went on to address crowds in the capital and in Guadalajara, where they were the guests of honor at a bullfight on September 4, 1928.[75]

But the most spectacular moment of publicity for Mafuenic came in the Mexican congress on November 26, 1928, when Hernán Laborde, then serving as deputy for the Unified Railway Workers' Party, made a speech denouncing US imperialism. A PCM member, Laborde was also involved in LADLA, and was a contributor to *El Libertador*.[76] While he was

---

[70] *Excélsior*, February 14, 1928, 9; *El Machete*, No. 104, March 3, 1928, 1, 4; see also Kersffeld, "El Comité Manos Fuera de Nicaragua."

[71] *El Machete*, No. 109, April 7, 1928, 1, 4; Kersffeld, "El Comité Manos Fuera de Nicaragua."

[72] *El Machete*, No. 122, July 7, 1928, 1, 4.   [73] *El Machete*, No. 123, July 14, 1928, 1.

[74] *El Machete*, No. 123, July 14, 1928, 4.   [75] *El Informador*, September 4, 1928, 4.

[76] He would be Secretary General of the PCM from 1929 to 1939. See Jeifets and Jeifets, *Diccionario biográfico*, 336–337.

speaking, he proceeded to unfurl an American flag reportedly seized from US Marines by Sandino's forces at El Zapote on May 14, which Sandino had sent to Mafuenic as a token of appreciation for its support. This prompted outrage in the chamber, and several deputies tried to wrest the flag from Laborde.[77] It was an unmistakably physical demonstration of transnational politics in action: a battle prize taken during Nicaragua's struggle for sovereignty was paraded in the Mexican congress by a Communist to highlight the common hemispheric struggle against US imperialism.

The formation and early success of Mafuenic marked a high point for Mexico City's anti-imperialist milieu. The organization's geographical spread across Mexico and its effective use of popular-cultural forms testified to the anti-imperialist left's unusual sociological reach at this time. It demonstrated a capacity to expand the Mexican public's awareness of Nicaragua, giving a specific focus to wider anti-imperialist sentiment and channeling both sympathy and funds toward Sandino's cause.[78] Yet the broad unity on which Mafuenic's success was built proved fragile.

DISINTEGRATION

Even as Mafuenic was making headway, ideological and strategic disagreements within Mexico City's anti-imperialist milieu began to multiply. In early 1928, Communists and *apristas* clashed over Nicaragua, notably over Haya de la Torre's offer to monitor elections the Communists deemed illegitimate. In mid-1928, the Comintern adopted a new strategic orientation at its Sixth Congress which led its affiliates to abandon any attempts at cross-class organizing. Communists and *apristas* now diverged over the question of class alliances: should workers and peasants join with the local bourgeoisie against external domination or, on the contrary, was it now a matter of "class against class," as the Comintern slogan put it?

These fissures widened under the pressure of domestic events in Mexico, especially after the assassination of president-elect Álvaro Obregón in July 1928. Though carried out by a Catholic extremist, it brought a surge in government pressure on the left. While the *apristas*

---

[77] *El Machete*, No. 141, December 1, 1928, 1, 4; the paper had carried a photograph of this same flag on its front page a few weeks earlier: No. 136, October 20, 1928, 1.

[78] While Carr notes that the scale of financial support Mafuenic gave Sandino was "very modest," the contributions would have been a significant sacrifice for the Mexican workers and peasant giving the donations: Carr, "Pioneering Transnational Solidarity," 148.

continued to see post-revolutionary Mexico as an exemplar of anti-imperialism, and the peasant leagues were willing to align with the government to defend the few gains they had made in recent years, the Communists now entered into direct confrontation with the Mexican state. In mid-1929, amid an escalating crackdown in the wake of a failed military revolt, the PCM was formally banned; in January 1930, Mexico broke diplomatic ties with the USSR.[79] Mella had been gunned down in Mexico City in January 1929, and now several key members of the radical exile milieu were deported; peasants aligned with the PCM were harassed or even killed by landlord militias or government forces.

In this altered climate, LADLA quickly disintegrated. What had previously been a broad coalition with a core of Communist organizers was soon pared back, and by early 1929 consisted almost solely of Communists. Even as the Communist movement itself grew increasingly intolerant of ideological differences, thanks in large part to the Comintern's adoption of a more sectarian stance, mounting repression by the Mexican state worked to isolate the PCM and LADLA still further from potential allies. These drastic shifts at the transnational and national levels, then, were mutually reinforcing, and it is their combined effects that explain the speed of LADLA's demise.

By the end of 1929, Mexico City's role as a radical transnational hub had clearly ended. In early November, the PCM wrote to the Comintern describing the shift. Previously Mexico had been the ideal base for anti-imperialist activism because "it was one of the only countries where we enjoyed the legal status necessary to develop, coordinate, and direct continental activities." Added to this was the fact that "the bulk of the Latin American political revolutionary emigration was concentrated in Mexico," which enabled the creation of an anti-imperialist organization that was "broad and with representatives well known by the worker and peasant masses of the continent."[80] Now, however, it had become "almost completely impossible" for LADLA to operate: it could no longer print and circulate materials, and many of its core organizers "have left the country or are preparing to leave, in order to avoid certain deportation by the government."[81] In a crowning irony, the PCM recommended

[79] Daniela Spenser, *The Impossible Triangle: Mexico, Soviet Russia, and the United States in the 1920s* (Durham, NC: Duke University Press, 1999), 162–165.

[80] "Resolución sobre el Comité Continental de la Liga Antimperialista de las Américas," [November] 1929, RGASPI F. 495, op. 108, d. 102: 154.

[81] "Resolución sobre el Comité Continental," 154.

that LADLA's headquarters be moved to where it was easier for people to gather and communications with the rest of the world were faster: to New York City, the belly of the imperial beast.[82] But the move was never completed: LADLA had already fallen apart, its constituent elements taking divergent political paths.

CONCLUSION

LADLA's lifespan was relatively brief: at five years, it lasted half as long as the LAI. In part this reflected the much stronger organizational and financial base on which the LAI was built compared to LADLA; but it also reflected the weaknesses of the Mexican Communists' social base and the divisions between the party and its allies, which made LADLA more vulnerable. Rifts that weakened the LAI, such as those caused by the Comintern's 1928 switch to a strategy of "class against class," all but destroyed LADLA. Yet despite its brevity, LADLA was nonetheless a significant episode in Latin American anti-imperial politics. In this chapter, I have tried to capture the distinctive transnational convergence that gave rise to the organization, and to describe the solidarities it sought to foment. These ranged far beyond Latin America itself; indeed, I have argued that the anti-imperialist agenda LADLA put forward was novel in seeking to understand Latin America's problems through a transnational frame, and in tying the region's attempts to withstand the combined pressures of Washington's guns and Wall Street's dollars to anticolonial struggles elsewhere.

LADLA's anti-imperialism was animated by a constellation of ideas that owed much to the quickened tempo of global politics in the years after the First World War, as well as to the intellectual and artistic ferment unleashed by the Mexican Revolution. A poem written in Mexico in 1927–1928 by Peruvian *aprista* Esteban Pavletich conveys some of its potency: its messianic fervency, its global geographical sweep, its modernist motifs. Opening with an evocation of links between US capitalism and Latin American dictators – "skyscrapers / standard oils / machados gómez leguías" – it then surveys the landscapes of the continent, hearing the "unknown cry of América" in the "pampas of vagabond silences," and finding in the Andes "stone motors / for autochthonous / rebellions." The rivers of the region, meanwhile, would serve as "travelers' paths / for

---

[82] "Resolución sobre el Comité Continental," 155.

our jubilant transoceanic messages." The poem's final lines weave together global and regional anti-imperial causes, binding Andean geography and the concept of a unified mestizo region labeled "Indoamérica" to a wider struggle spanning from Central America to East Asia:

> in Indian souls
> t i t i k a k a s
> on which to splash down the hopes disentangled
> in the violent forests of the KUO MIN TANG
> men of indoamérica
> nicaragua will be our last sadness.[83]

Pavletich's lyricism offers a tantalizing prefiguration of later Latin American solidarities with what became known as the Third World. Indeed, though we should be careful not to draw too direct a line between the 1920s and the moment of decolonization, there are connections between LADLA's activities and, for example, those of the post-revolutionary Cuban state: Raúl Roa, Cuban foreign minister from 1959 to 1976, was in his youth a member of the Havana chapter of LADLA.[84]

Yet LADLA's story could also be read less in a prefigurative than in a cautionary mode. There were sobering limits to what LADLA's radical transnationalism was able to achieve. The organization largely owed its existence to the favorable climate provided by Mexican national politics at the time, and it proved highly vulnerable to changing domestic winds, as well as to sectarian divisions from within. Its ultimate disintegration points to the very real obstacles confronting any anti-imperial project that aspires to meaningful forms of global solidarity. Mexico City's anti-imperial milieu of the 1920s was remarkable in its horizons and aspirations, but for the next several decades, both in Latin America and elsewhere, there remained a painful gap between those hopes and the continued reality of imperial domination.

---

[83] Pavletich, "Alianza Popular Revolucionaria Americana," reproduced in Magda Portal, *El nuevo poema i su orientación hacia una estética económica* (Mexico City: Ediciones APRA, 1928), 22–23.

[84] Raúl Roa, *El fuego de la semilla en el surco* (Havana: Editorial Letras Cubanas, 1982), 131–145, 205–210.

5

Carlos Romulo, Rotary Internationalism, and Conservative Anticolonialism

Mark Reeves

If anyone did, Carlos Romulo lived a transnational life: born in the Philippines in 1899, he crisscrossed the Pacific and circled the globe countless times from 1919 to 1962 in various capacities, as a newspaper editor, ambassador to the United States, and eventually President of the UN General Assembly. Even after his retirement as ambassador in 1962, he returned to the international scene when Ferdinand Marcos tapped him as Foreign Secretary, a post he held from 1969 to 1984. So closely did Romulo tie himself to the Philippines, the United States, and the United Nations that in 1944 he declared before the US Congress that "no longer can we look at the Philippines and say: 'This is Philippine earth, or this American.' It is Fil-America; it is the new world, the El Dorado of all those who throughout history have dreamed of freedom."[1] One of Romulo's famous essays declared that "I am a Filipino," but in his books he also acknowledged his *Mother America* and *My Brother Americans*. And by the end of his life, he was known as "Mr. United Nations."[2]

---

[1] Carlos P. Romulo, "The Jones Act – Foundation Act of Bataan," *Congressional Record*, August 29, 1944, p. 2, in Box 1, Folder 16, Carlos P. Romulo Papers, University Archives and Records Depository, University of the Philippines-Diliman [hereafter CPR Papers, UPD].

[2] Carlos P. Romulo, "I am a Filipino," *Philippines Herald*, August 16, 1941, available on the Philippine presidential website at http://malacanang.gov.ph/75480-i-am-a-filipino-by-carlos-p-romulo/ (accessed April 28, 2021); *Mother America: A Living Story of Democracy* (New York: Doubleday, Doran and Company, 1943); *My Brother Americans* (Garden City, New York: Doubleday, Doran and Company, 1945). Romulo was widely known as "Mr. United Nations" by the 1960s: see "Documentaries Highlight Viewing Schedule on KLRN," *Austin Statesman*, November 9, 1969, T16.

But did Romulo live an *anticolonial* transnational life? As his grand-daughter Liana Romulo said, "he wasn't anti- anything!"[3] Romulo certainly was not anti-American, despite US colonial rule over the Philippines from 1898 to 1946. Rather, he followed the example of his father, Gregorio, and his political mentor, Manuel Quezon, both of whom transitioned from anti-American insurgents to working with the US government while still trying to achieve Philippine independence. Because the United States committed itself to eventual Philippine independence in the Jones Act of 1916, Romulo took Philippine independence to be inevitable, and concerned himself with what that independence would look like. In so doing, he combined an idealistic vision of the United States – as committed to ending its rule in the Philippines – with a pragmatic politics of postcolonialism – trying to position an independent Philippines to survive in a hostile region.

Yet even as Romulo looked at US rule in the Philippines through rose-colored glasses, he condemned colonialism elsewhere. Touring Southeast Asia in the fall of 1941, Romulo contrasted his idealization of a beneficent US policy in the Philippines with perfidious European and Japanese empires, calling the ongoing Second World War a "conflict between rival imperialisms" and a "conflict between these imperialist powers and the one billion colored peoples whom they hold under subjection."[4] Romulo insisted that "imperialism must be destroyed together with [fascism]. Fascism and imperialism are but the two sides of the same coin." Moreover, he saw the Philippines, as a colony poised on the brink of independence, as a vanguard "in the movement to liberate all the colored races in Asia."[5] Since Romulo attributed the Philippines' imminent independence to the goodwill of the United States, he could unite a pro-US stance with anticolonialism, in the Philippines and throughout the world.

This combination of idealism toward a colonial metropole, a commitment to ending colonialism, and a pragmatism about the form anticolonial politics should take presents historians of anticolonialism with a conundrum. What are we to make of figures like Romulo, a leader whose anticolonialism does not fit neatly into a vision of a clean break from the colonial power in every form? Historians have wrestled with this question

---

[3] I spoke to Liana Romulo on January 5, 2017, in Manila.
[4] Carlos P. Romulo, "Billion Orientals Look to America," *Philippines Herald*, September 15, 1941, 1. For "rival imperialisms," see also Carlos P. Romulo, "Brown Democracy," *Philippines Herald*, November 11, 1941, 14.
[5] Carlos P. Romulo, "Indonesians' Struggle for Liberty," *Philippines Herald*, October 29, 1941, 13.

in relation to figures who sought to transform French and British colonial subjects into citizens within global states, such as Annie Besant, Aimé Césaire, and Léopold Senghor.[6] Whereas these leaders sought to preserve a direct institutional link between metropole and colony – creating a British Commonwealth state, departmentalizing the French Antilles, or federating French Africa with the Hexagon – Romulo insisted on Philippine independence, global decolonization, *and* future cooperation with the United States. While Besant, Césaire, and Senghor sought to reform empire through an altered union between metropole and colony, and through the political economy of socialism, Romulo wanted his country to become truly independent from the United States while retaining economic and political friendship, especially through a capitalist political economy.[7]

If Senghor and Césaire relied on federalism and socialism as the modes to transform imperial relationships, Romulo looked to affective ties, ones of fraternity and friendship.[8] As an arena for such affective ties, Romulo turned to the transnational community of the "club," a place where people and even nations – former colonies and former colonizers – could meet as equals. Like Winifred Armstrong, the subject of Lydia Walker's essay in this volume, Romulo believed he could work through existing institutions and build transnational relationships to make incremental anticolonial gains. Thus, for Carlos Romulo, the international club could serve as a place to mobilize for anticolonial purposes, beyond the nation-state. The key, then, was getting into the club.

---

[6] See, for example, Frederick Cooper, *Citizenship between Empire and Nation: Remaking France and French Africa, 1945–1960* (Princeton: Princeton University Press, 2014); Gary Wilder, *Freedom Time: Negritude, Decolonization, and the Future of the World* (Durham, N.C.: Duke University Press, 2015); and Mark R. Frost, "Imperial Citizenship or Else: Liberal Ideals and the Indian Unmaking of Empire, 1890–1919," *Journal of Imperial and Commonwealth History* 46, no. 5 (October 2018), 845–873.

[7] Other recent works on transnational anticolonial activism have privileged the socialist political economy as the arena of focus: Tim Harper, *Underground Asia: Global Revolutionaries and the Assault on Empire* (Cambridge, Mass.: Belknap Press, 2021); Michele L. Louro, *Comrades against Imperialism: Nehru, India, and Interwar Internationalism* (New York: Cambridge University Press, 2018); Jeffrey James Byrne, *Mecca of Revolution: Algeria, Decolonization, and the Third World Order* (New York: Oxford University Press, 2016).

[8] Leela Gandhi, *Affective Communities: Anticolonial Thought, Fin-de-Siècle Radicalism, and the Politics of Friendship* (New Delhi: Permanent Black, 2006), 15 makes the connection that affective ties "confound the manichean logic of colonization by preventing anticolonial nationalism from resolving itself into pure oppositionality."

Not all of Romulo's contemporaries viewed his transnational politics as anticolonial. Jawaharlal Nehru, writing to his sister Vijaya Lakshmi Pandit, dismissed her election as President of the UN General Assembly in 1953 on the grounds that "a place which Romulo has occupied ceases to have value," referring to Romulo's presidency in 1949/50.[9] After the Bandung Conference of 1955, Indian diplomat Subimal Dutt wrote back to Delhi that the Philippine delegation led by Romulo "had completely and unequivocally identified themselves with American policies and attitudes in International affairs."[10]

But to presume that Romulo was not a "genuine" anticolonialist because he did not reject US global leadership or because he did not embrace a broadly radical agenda would be to presume an unchanging, core "anticolonialism." Instead, as historians of anticolonialism, we recognize that the very idea of anticolonialism – like colonialism itself – was a site of contestation by activists across the world throughout the twentieth century. Anticolonialists used different definitions of their projects to explain to themselves and to different audiences how and why they made their decisions.[11]

In this essay I will examine Romulo's non-radical vision of anticolonialism, which he hoped would transform a world of empires into a world of equals meeting in a club. Due to Romulo's embrace of a liberal political economy, privileging business and entrepreneurial freedom, at a time when globally such economics were associated with more conservative politics, I characterize his ideological position as "conservative liberalism," following Lisandro Claudio.[12] This pro-business liberalism led

---

[9] Jawaharlal Nehru to Vijaya Lakshmi Pandit, March 10, 1953, Vijaya Lakshmi Pandit Papers, 1st Installment, Subject File 47, p. 124, Nehru Memorial Museum and Library, New Delhi.

[10] Subimal Dutt to Secretary-General of Ministry of Foreign Affairs, April 25, 1955, p. 3, F.1(37)-AAC/55(S), National Archives of India, New Delhi [hereafter NAI].

[11] For a discussion of anticolonialism as a broad tent, see Frederick Cooper, *Colonialism in Question: Theory, Knowledge, History* (Berkeley: University of California Press, 2005), 28.

[12] I use "conservative liberalism" to acknowledge Romulo's complex position within a global conception of Left and Right politics – conservative in the sense of anti-Communist and anti-socialist, especially later in his career, but liberal in the sense Lisandro Claudio adapts from Ramachandra Guha to characterize anticolonial liberals' combination of hopefulness, patriotism, and attention to mediating institutions: see Lisandro E. Claudio, *Liberalism and the Postcolony: Thinking the State in 20th-Century Philippines* (Singapore: NUS Press, 2017), 7–8. As the attention to mediating institutions attests, the influence of Burke and a global notion of conservatism needs to be acknowledged even in this definition of liberalism, as further indicated by the prominent

Romulo to see the Rotary Club, a US business-based fraternal organization, as a clear expression of his ideal for a world order after empire.

ANTICOLONIAL AMERICANISM?

Carlos Romulo was born in Camiling in central Luzon on January 14,
1899, just nine days before the ongoing Philippine Revolution's leaders
would declare an independent Republic at Malolos.[13] By the end of the
year, the Republic's erstwhile allies in the US government had begun a
bloody war of conquest in the archipelago.[14] During the 1899–1902 war,
Romulo's father fought the Americans as a guerrilla, and Romulo's
grandfather endured torture from US soldiers seeking information.
However, as a child with little memory of these events, Romulo's
American teachers wooed him to embrace the English language, US
ideals, and the occupation.[15] Even his guerrilla father eventually accepted
the occupation, becoming an official within the new colonial apparatus
and a friend to one of the many American couples sent to the Philippines
to inculcate in students just like Romulo the lessons of US benevolence
and greatness.[16] Romulo's birth alongside both an independent
Philippines and its US occupation, his early embrace of the English
language, and an idealized vision of America made him a living representative of the Philippines' complex geopolitical position in the early twentieth century.[17]

Romulo's father, Gregorio, one of the last in Camiling to swear the
oath of allegiance to the United States, became an enthusiastic part of the
US regime, serving as a town councilor, mayor, and eventually the governor of Tarlac province. Supportive of the US establishment of a public

---

role of Burke's notion of "place" in Nicole CuUnjieng Aboitiz, *Asian Place, Filipino
Nation: A Global Intellectual History of the Philippine Revolution, 1897–1912* (New
York: Columbia University Press, 2020), 35–36.

[13] Carlos P. Romulo, *I Walked with Heroes* (New York: Holt, Rinehart and Winston,
1961), 9.

[14] For a useful narrative summary of these complex events and their aftermath, see Michael
H. Hunt and Steven I. Levine, *Arc of Empire: America's Wars in Asia from the
Philippines to Vietnam* (Chapel Hill: University of North Carolina Press, 2012), 10–56.

[15] Romulo, *Heroes*, 30–33, 45, 48, 55, 58.

[16] Sarah Steinbock-Pratt, *Educating the Empire: American Teachers and Contested
Colonization in the Philippines* (New York: Cambridge University Press, 2019), 16–17
on the pedagogical project; 237 on Louis and Winnie Baun's friendship with Gregorio
and Maria Romulo.

[17] For Romulo's self-description of his Malay and Spanish heritage: Romulo, *Heroes*, 13.

education system, he moved his family to Manila to allow his children to attend the new Manila High School, where Carlos excelled as an orator, joining two debate teams, and delivering a prize-winning speech on "My Faith in America."[18] In high school and at the US-established University of the Philippines, Carlos also spent time as a cub reporter for several English-language newspapers. During his reporting he met the former guerrilla Manuel Quezon, now one of the main leaders of the Nacionalista Party pushing for independence under 1916's Jones Act, whereby the Woodrow Wilson administration had committed to an eventual US withdrawal from the Philippines.[19] In July 1918, he led a march of 300 angry students to the offices of a US-owned newspaper in Manila to protest what they saw as a racist editorial. Romulo directly confronted the offending editor, and the students won a retraction of the article.[20] Thus, for Romulo, "faith in America" and pushing against US colonialism went hand in hand.

Romulo extended the many educations he had received in the Philippines by traveling to the mainland United States under the pensionado scheme, whereby US officials hoped to train loyal cadres to run the Philippine state.[21] Romulo attended Columbia University from 1918 to 1922, taking masters' degrees in foreign trade service and comparative literature.[22] In 1920 he joined with several Philippine students in the United States to form the Filipino Students' Federation of America (FSFA), and Romulo served as the editor of the FSFA's journal, *The Philippine Herald*.[23]

Romulo's editorship of the *Herald* from November 1920 to December 1921 provides a concise snapshot of his political thinking in all its

---

[18] Romulo, *Heroes*, 52, 57, 72–74.

[19] On Romulo's budding relationship with Quezon, see Augusto Fauni Espiritu, *Five Faces of Exile: The Nation and Filipino American Intellectuals* (Stanford, Calif.: Stanford University Press, 2005), 12–13. On the Jones Act, see Paul A. Kramer, *The Blood of Government: Race, Empire, the United States, and the Philippines* (Chapel Hill: University of North Carolina Press, 2006), 352–363.

[20] Romulo, *Heroes*, 105–108; Steinbock-Pratt, *Educating the Empire*, 265–268.

[21] For a detailed treatment of the pensionados, see Adrianne Marie Francisco, "From Subjects to Citizens: American Colonial Education and Philippine Nation-Making, 1900–1934" (Ph.D., University of California, Berkeley, 2015), chaps. 4–5.

[22] Espiritu, *Five Faces of Exile*, 9, 206n20.

[23] Romulo participated in a preliminary meeting on February 25, 1920, in New York; the FSFA was formally created during the YMCA's annual convention in Lake Geneva, Wisconsin, in June 1920: "Minutes of Preliminary Meeting: In Re the Proposed Organization of a Filipino Students' Federation in the United States," *PH-FSFA* 1, no. 1 (November 1920): 4.

tensions, many of which would continue throughout his career. Romulo's love for America was evident, expressed as "Americanism," in an inversion of the racialized idiom "one hundred percent Americanism" associated with the ongoing Red Scare and revival of the Ku Klux Klan at the end of Woodrow Wilson's presidency.[24] In the *Herald*, Romulo refused racial definitions of American-ness while still affirming his faith in Americanism. He founded his faith ultimately in the common man and in the country's democratic ideals.[25]

Romulo always decried any attempt to call into question US motives in the Philippines, holding firm to the promises of 1916 that independence was just around the corner: "America does not forget promises made. Washington and Lincoln would indeed turn in their graves if America should fail to redeem the pledge she has given the Filipino people!"[26] In one remarkable passage, he conducts a conversation with the statue of George Washington at Trinity Church in downtown Manhattan, which comes to life to debate with Romulo about US policy. As the statue resolidifies, it leaves Romulo with a promise of US goodwill: "Right and justice you deserve ... And remember – you have – my best – wishes."[27] Augusto Espiritu, the most careful analyst of Carlos Romulo's writings about America, notes that in many of his endorsements of Americanism, "he would begin with a glowing apostrophe to America, then follow this with frank criticism of its present-day policies, and conclude with a reaffirmation of America's benevolence." Since Romulo's Americanism "transcended [America's] immediate historical mistakes," he could always resort to his ideals about the country without ignoring the realities he decried.[28]

---

[24] Though Romulo did not write the article, one piece in an early issue of the FSFA *Philippine Herald* explicitly engaged with Filipinos' relationship to the "One hundred per cent. American"-ism of 1920: Gaudencio Garcia, "Americanism and the Philippine Question," *PH-FSFA* I, no. I (November 1920): 12.

[25] Carlos P. Romulo, "What Constitutes America's True Greatness," *PH-FSFA* I, no. 4 (March 1921): 11. In the same issue, he wrote about "Our Faith in America," and summarized his view of democracy: "democracy in its essence is nothing but a mutual respect for mutual rights and it cannot long survive the disregard of other people's rights and liberties" (15).

[26] "America and the Philippines," in "Editorial Incidence and Reflection," *PH-FSFA* I, no. 2 (December 1920): 33.

[27] Carlos P. Romulo, "Editorial Incidence and Reflection," *PH-FSFA* I, no. 6 (May 1921): 19.

[28] Espiritu, *Five Faces of Exile*, 14. Espiritu makes this observation about an article Romulo published on his return to the Philippines, "The Tragedy of Our Anglo-Saxon Education" (1923).

Woodrow Wilson embodied Romulo's idealized Americanism, and Romulo's time in New York coincided with a Filipino "Wilsonian moment" akin to the global phenomenon described by Erez Manela. After the passage of the Jones Act, and especially due to the sympathy for independence expressed by Wilson's Governor-General in the Philippines, Francis Burton Harrison, Philippine nationalists had high hopes for immediate independence after the Armistice of 1918. The Philippine Congress considered sending a mission to Paris, but instead chose to send its delegates to Washington. Arriving in April 1919, they missed Wilson, who was in Europe, though he did cable them to assure Filipinos that "the Philippine problem was not foreign to the purpose of his trip to Europe." Speaking before Congress in June 1919, Manuel Quezon linked the desires for Philippine independence to the new world order he hoped Wilson would achieve, listing Philippine preferences in order as independence under the League of Nations, or if no League, under guarantee by the great powers; "but if that should not be possible, [we] want independence anyway."[29]

While the 1919 Philippine Independence Mission was soon overshadowed in Congress by the fierce debates over the Treaty of Versailles, Carlos Romulo was enamored by the idea of the League of Nations, and by internationalism generally.[30] After the Senate defeated the Versailles Treaty, Romulo still expressed hope that the United States would join the League. He attached a great deal of importance to the League, in similar language which he would later apply to the United Nations, as "this hope of small nationalities, this flickering star to which the eyes of millions of subject peoples are fixed, this fruition of Tennyson's noble dream." As in 1945, for Romulo in 1921 such a global international institution was needed for survival: "War-worn, battle-scarred Humanity craves for it. It must exist."[31] At the end of Wilson's term in March 1921, Romulo lamented that Wilson "had reaches of imagination and vision far too advanced of his age." In Romulo's eyes, Wilson became a Christ-like figure "upon whom were laid the well-nigh

[29] Bernardita Reyes Churchill, *The Philippine Independence Missions to the United States, 1919–1934* (Manila: National Historical Institute, 1983), 16 and 20; 9–15 on the planning for the delegation.

[30] Romulo followed Rabindranath Tagore's tour of the United States in 1920, and he was particularly fascinated by the Greek statesman Eleftherios Venizelos: see "Editorial Incidence and Reflection," December 1920, 36–38; Romulo, *Heroes*, 254.

[31] Romulo, "Editorial Incidence and Reflection," February 1921, 17.

crushing burdens of an agonized world," emerging from the battle "a broken man," betrayed by his own country.[32]

Romulo would apply the same agonistic and messianic language to the figure who linked his Americanism, Philippine patriotism, and internationalism: José Rizal, the patriot poet and martyr of 1896.[33] Romulo had always celebrated his links to Rizal, who nearly became his cousin by marriage. Romulo even wrote a play in his youth for the celebration of Rizal Day (December 30, the anniversary of Rizal's execution in Manila in 1896) in his hometown of Camiling.[34] Romulo described himself as a Malay and an Asian, as Rizal and the revolutionary generation had, as part of an argument for a Filipino version of pan-Malayism, the unity of the Philippines with Malaya and the Dutch East Indies against European colonialism.[35] Speaking in 1951, Romulo called Rizal a practitioner of "humanist nationalism" and a "constructive nationalist," which Romulo saw as compatible with internationalism.[36] For Romulo, Rizal brought together anticolonialism and internationalism.

But Romulo also linked Rizal to his own Americanism. Romulo highlighted a letter to the editor which described Rizal as a synthesis of American and Filipino liberalism. The writer, Manuel L. Carreon of Minneapolis, claimed that Philippine independence would be due to the policies of "this great country" (the United States), which had "fertilized" the "spirit of liberalism" sown by Rizal, with the current generation "reaping the harvest." In Rizal's exemplary death, the writer found the explanation for "the splendid cooperation between Americans and Filipinos."[37]

---

[32] Carlos P. Romulo, "W.W.," *PH-FSFA* 1, no. 4 (March 1921): 30–31.

[33] For an example of Romulo's tragic view of Rizal, focusing on "his wonderful example of self-sacrifice," see "Editorial Incidence and Reflection," December 1920, 33–34.

[34] Romulo, *Heroes*, 46–47, 64.

[35] Filomeno V. Aguilar Jr., "Tracing Origins: 'Ilustrado' Nationalism and the Racial Science of Migration Waves," *Journal of Asian Studies* 64, no. 3 (August 2005): 605–637; Rommel A. Curaming, "Rizal and the Rethinking of the Analytics of Malayness," *Inter-Asia Cultural Studies* 18, no. 3 (September 2017): 327–328, 331–333. At least in his formulation of pan-Malayism in 1961, Romulo aligned almost exactly with contemporary Malay and Indonesian formulations: Romulo, *Heroes*, 23–24; Joseph Chinyong Liow, *The Politics of Indonesia-Malaysia Relations: One Kin, Two Nations* (New York: RoutledgeCurzon, 2005), 34, 38–40, 45–46, 52, 54–56, 75. For the definitive treatment of the complexities of Asianism in the turn-of-the-century Philippine Revolution, see CuUnjieng Aboitiz, *Asian Place, Filipino Nation*, chaps. 2–3.

[36] Carlos P. Romulo, "Rizal – Asia's First True Nationalist," radio broadcast on December 29, 1951, 1–2, Box 26, Folder 283, CPR Papers, UPD.

[37] "Rizal and America in Philippine Progress," *PH-FSFA* 1, no. 3 (February 1921): 29–30.

While Rizal might not have been so sanguine about the United States as Romulo was, Romulo did share Rizal's passionate anticolonialism. Despite his Americanism, Romulo could be a stringent critic of US policy. In March 1921, Romulo published an editorial on the first page of the *Herald* to decry comments former president Taft made in support of the incoming Harding administration rolling back the Wilson-era expansion of Filipino self-government. More explicitly than elsewhere, Romulo acknowledged the basis of US power in military strength, noting that "she can impose her will even against the consent of the governed," but called for "that much-vaunted American Liberty" which recognized its own limits: "Indeed, 'it is excellent to have a giant's strength, but it is tyrannous to use it like a giant.'" Romulo even darkly foretold a day when Filipinos like himself might be "shorn of our faith in American democracy and American institutions."[38]

In the very same issue, Romulo warned Americans against their own government leading them into imperialism, which he called "war smouldering," "at war with democracy." In addition to overt military and diplomatic pressure, he decried William Howard Taft's "dollar diplomacy," which "leads to economic imperialism. Economic imperialism is the forerunner of force, of conquest, of wars." Even in this critique, Romulo expressed his faith in the American people, since he insisted "Americans hate imperialism," and Americans "spurned" its "violence to some of the soundest fibre and tissue of the American democratic organism." This made US imperialism all the more insidious, though, since its supporters – whom Romulo did not identify – "disguised" it: "Imperialism comes in the form of preparedness," of a standing army and a creditor nation. "Others call it protection of nation trade and interests. But the ugly look of the wound can't be concealed."[39]

Romulo's faith in Americanism, and his belief in its inextricable link to a global anticolonialism as demonstrated in the Philippine case, would provide the narrative he would use throughout his career to simultaneously praise and critique US policy. For Romulo, Americanism and anticolonialism went hand in hand, even when the United States was sometimes the target of his own anticolonialism. Thus, almost as soon as Romulo returned to Manila from New York in 1922, Quezon snapped him up as assistant editor of his Manila-based *Philippines Herald* and

---

[38] Carlos P. Romulo, "May the Day Never Come," *PH-FSFA* 1, no. 4 (March 1921): 1.
[39] Carlos P. Romulo, "America – Imperialist?," *PH-FSFA* 1, no. 4 (March 1921): 17.

brought him back to the United States as part of an Independence Mission lobbying Congress.[40] Romulo continued to return to the United States throughout the 1920s, including on another independence mission in 1924.[41] In addition to working for Quezon, Romulo was a professor of English at his alma mater, the University of the Philippines, and in 1928 he led his student debate team on a US tour, challenging American collegians on the question of Philippine independence.[42]

If Romulo's Americanism tempered his anticolonialism, it was in the direction of a pragmatic recognition of the Philippines' status as a "small country" in the global balance of power. Back in 1921, Romulo had noted that the Philippines needed to develop its own military to prepare for US withdrawal, and urged anticolonial leaders to be frank with the public that "a lot of self-sacrifice and self-denial is the price of national liberty."[43] At that time, Romulo and other Filipino students were calling for an internationalized guarantee of Philippine neutrality, or a US protectorate, to solve the security problem.[44] Romulo was clear-eyed about the limitations this would present, drawing an explicit parallel to the "colonialism by contract" situation produced by the same arrangement in Cuba under the Platt Amendment.[45] Romulo's concern about the independent Philippines' vulnerability to invasion and domination – first by Japan, in the 1930s and 1940s; then by the Soviet Union and the People's Republic of China from 1945 forward – would drive his acceptance of alliance with the United States as the best international situation the Philippines could hope for for almost forty years.[46]

---

[40] For Romulo's membership of the 1922 delegation as its publicity agent, see Churchill, *Philippine Independence Missions*, 429.

[41] Romulo, *Heroes*, 170.

[42] "University of Philippines Sends Debaters to States to Promote Better Relations," *The China Press*, February 26, 1928, 4.

[43] Romulo, "Editorial Incidence and Reflection," February 1921, 15.

[44] "Filipino Students Ask for Independence," *PH-FSFA* 2, no. 1 (November 1921): 5.

[45] Eliseo Quirino, "Cuba's International Status," *PH-FSFA* 1, no. 4 (March 1921): 24–25. Romulo solicited this article to "furnish some illuminating data for serious thought and consideration" amid "the discussion by the Filipino leaders of the kind of independence that the Philippines should seek from the American Government" (25, editor's note). "Colonialism by contract" is from Emily S. Rosenberg, "The Invisible Protectorate: The United States, Liberia, and the Evolution of Neocolonialism, 1909–40," *Diplomatic History* 9, no. 3 (Summer 1985): 191–214.

[46] See, for example, Carlos P. Romulo, "The Philippines Look at Japan," *Foreign Affairs* 14, no. 1 (January 1935): 476–486.

ROTARY ANTICOLONIALISM?

Yet to portray Romulo's Americanism as purely realist would also be too simplistic. As his words on the floor of Congress from 1944 indicate, Romulo saw a deep connection between the United States and the Philippines formed by historical circumstance, even destiny, which could not be ignored. How Romulo framed this connection – as a partnership, characterized by service – places his anticolonialism and Americanism into an even broader category, of an idealized international order based in civic cooperation. That is, for Romulo, if the United States was ushering the Philippines out of a relationship based on empire, and if other countries should follow suit, then the international order which should be ushered in would correspond to a club, or what Mrinalini Sinha has called "clubland." This "'clubland' as a whole served as a common ground where [elites] could meet as members, or as guests of members, of individual clubs," in "an intermediate zone between both metropolitan and indigenous public spheres." The club could begin within the colonial framework, and yet transcend it, because clubs "simultaneously marked the colonizer as uniquely 'clubbable' and recognized the potential clubbability of the colonized."[47]

For Romulo, it was Rotary's particular values – which included racial equality and community service, with community explicitly construed to transcend the nation-state – which made it "clubbable," and a model for relations among different peoples. The Manila Rotary Club was not racially exclusive, unlike the (initially) whites-only social clubs Sinha describes, though Romulo had experienced exclusion from such clubs in the 1910s.[48] (Romulo also saw and was occasionally subjected to color bars during his time in the United States from 1918 to 1922.[49]) In addition to transcending the color bar, Rotary attracted Romulo with its ethos of equality and service among members.

[47] Mrinalini Sinha, "Britishness, Clubbability, and the Colonial Public Sphere: The Genealogy of an Imperial Institution in Colonial India," *Journal of British Studies* 40, no. 4 (October 2001): 489 and 492.

[48] Romulo, *Heroes*, 96–99 and 115–120 for discrimination in Manila. The Manila Club had Filipino leadership along with US businessmen from its beginning, with Alfonzo Sy Cip the inaugural vice-president and Gregorio Nievo an inaugural director: "Rotary in the Philippines," *The Rotarian*, May 1919, 231; "Manila Internationalizes Itself," *The Rotarian*, July 1919, 30.

[49] Romulo, *Heroes*, 132–133, 136–139, 143, 145–148, and 151–154 for Romulo's various encounters with the racialization of himself and others in New York, including William Howard Taft's intervention to break his engagement to a white woman.

Rotary began as a Midwestern US businessmen's club in 1905 with a distinctly internationalist perspective, and it expanded into the Pacific along with US commerce and colonial power.[50] The club began as a rotating (hence "Rotary" and the club's wheel emblem) lunch meeting of local businessmen, establishing an egalitarian ethic, and quickly evolved into an exportable model of local clubs gathering businessmen around the broad ideal of service. From the generic "service," Rotarians focused on four "objects": "club service" through "the development of acquaintance" and "the recognition of the worthiness of all useful occupations as an opportunity to serve society"; "vocational service" through "adopting and encouraging higher ideals and better practices in his profession"; "community service," "by doing his good-sized bit as a neighbor and a citizen"; and finally, "international service," or "the achievement of understanding, good will, and international peace through a world fellowship of business and professional men united in the Rotary ideal of service."[51]

Writing about the Americanization of Europe after the Great War, Antonio Gramsci drew attention to the spread of Rotary Clubs as an extension of an American "ideology" and "civilization," even if this was only "an organic extension and an intensification of European civilization." Gramsci analogized Rotary to "Free Masonry without the petit bourgeois and without the petit-bourgeois mentality."[52] Elsewhere

---

[50] See, for example, the excellent dissertation by Brendan M. Goff, "The Heartland Abroad: The Rotary Club's Mission of Civic Internationalism" (Ph.D., University of Michigan, 2008), which uses the Tokyo Rotary Club as a case study. See also Brendan Goff, "Philanthropy and the 'Perfect Democracy' of Rotary International," in *Globalization, Philanthropy, and Civil Society: Projecting Institutional Logics Abroad*, eds. David C. Hammack and Steven Heydemann (Bloomington: Indiana University Press, 2009), 47–70; Su Lin Lewis, "Rotary International's 'Acid Test': Multi-Ethnic Associational Life in 1930s Southeast Asia," *Journal of Global History* 7, no. 2 (July 2012): 302–324; Su Lin Lewis, *Cities in Motion: Urban Life and Cosmopolitanism in Southeast Asia, 1920–1940* (New York: Cambridge University Press, 2016), 127–137; Vivian Kong, "Exclusivity and Cosmopolitanism: Multiethnic Civil Society in Interwar Hong Kong," *The Historical Journal* 63, no. 5 (December 2020): 1281–1302. On Rotary in Cuba, see Maikel Fariñas Borrego, "District 25: Rotary Clubs and Regional Civic Power in Cuba, 1916–1940," in *State of Ambiguity: Civic Life and Culture in Cuba's First Republic*, eds. Steven Palmer, José Antonio Piqueras, and Amparo Sánchez Cobos (Durham, N.C.: Duke University Press, 2014), 231–250.

[51] Derived from both "World-Wide Rotary," *The Rotarian*, February 1923, cover; and "Four Objects Cover Whole Rotary Field: Service Club Has Four-Fold Work Program," *Austin American*, April 26, 1942, A8.

[52] Antonio Gramsci, "Americanism and Fordism," in *Selections from the Prison Notebooks*, eds. Quintin Hoare and Geoffrey Nowell Smith (New York: International Publishers, 1971), 318 and 286.

Gramsci identified Rotary as "a particular ideology ... born in a highly developed country [which] is disseminated in less developed countries," thus "functioning as international political parties which operate within each nation with the full concentration of the international forces."[53] While Gramsci overstated the operational power of Rotary as an organization, he did perceive the internationalism inherent in its concept and social basis, and in its spirit, which Romulo would often highlight.

American businessmen founded the Manila Rotary Club, the first in Asia, in 1919, while Romulo was in New York.[54] Americans dominated the Club's membership, though Filipinos constituted about one third of the membership.[55] Even though Romulo would not join the Manila club until 1931, during his time in New York he wrote about the importance of club membership, noting that members of a club needed to "discipline ourselves to submerge our 'ego' and develop a spirit of tolerance and mutuality."[56] This submersion of self into mutuality mapped onto Rotarian notions of submerging the national into an international consciousness.

Once Romulo did join the Manila Club in 1931, he used his newspaper, the *Philippines Herald*, to promote the club as a fraternal family. Rotary would build "goodwill and constructive cooperation between and among the peoples of all countries" by the quiet diplomacy of "awakening ... the ideal of service, the attitude of thoughtfulness of and helpfulness to others" and then connecting these awakened souls "into a fellowship, a friendly comradeship," as "a world citizen in the realm of social relations."[57] A past Rotary International vice-president stated one of the group's goals as "to help develop a world-consciousness among men; to broaden their minds and widen their horizon."[58] An accompanying article reprinted from the *London Rotarian* offered a sort of Rotarian credo for internationalism among nations, in which "the dominating purpose of any nation ought to be the service for the common

---

[53] Gramsci, "The Modern Prince," in *Selections*, 182 (main text and footnote).
[54] Lewis, *Cities in Motion*, 128.   [55] Romulo, *Mother America*, 43–44.
[56] Carlos P. Romulo, "Why Filipino Associations Fail," *PH-FSFA* 2, no. 2 (December 1921): 16.
[57] "'World Citizens' of Rotary," *Philippines Herald*, January 10, 1934. Romulo served as the Manila Club's president in 1935, and Rotary International's Third Vice-President in 1937–1938: "Rotary's New Board of Directors," *The Rotarian*, July 1937, 42.
[58] Wm. de Cock Buning, "Rotary's International Task," *Philippines Herald*, January 31, 1934.

good and through the common good of one's own nation the service to the common good of all nations."[59]

This ideal heavily influenced Romulo's conception of the Philippines and its place as a postcolonial state in Asia. Shortly after the passage of the Tydings–McDuffie Act in 1934, providing for the inauguration of a self-governing Philippine Commonwealth to become an independent republic in 1946, Romulo participated in a business goodwill mission to southern China, which a Chinese delegation reciprocated in December 1934.[60] The *Herald* took the opportunity of the Chinese delegation's visit to offer a new vision of Asian relations, through what it called "an Oriental State" bringing together "groups racially at variance ... to work out the wellbeing of a common spirit," grounded in both "the statesmanship of Confucius" and "the Christian ideal of peace and good-will." The editorial looked forward to "permanent peace in the Orient" based on each country recognizing that "there is no predestined master ... among us in the Far East."[61] Only two months later, Rotary International's Pacific clubs held a regional conference in Manila, which the *Herald* likewise took as an opportunity to promote a "mission of amity" to lead East Asia "to come to a truce, to pause in an interlude of cheer and camaraderie, in an effort to reconstruct our commercial circumstances upon new lines of service."[62]

By analogizing states to individual persons, among whom "there is no predestined master," the club could transform from a site of enacted social equality to a model of what Romulo would call "a more enlightened internationalism." Romulo described this new internationalism at the University of Notre Dame in December 1935, when he received an honorary degree along with President Franklin Roosevelt. Romulo used the occasion to describe the perils and opportunities the Philippines would experience as it emerged as an independent but weak member of international society. Romulo rejected a model seeing "the State as a political and economic, rather than a moral, entity," noting that even under an absolutism like Louis XIV's, by declaring "'I am the State,' he at least made the State a responsible person." By seeing the state as a person, Romulo hoped that "the Congress of nations" could govern itself through

---

[59] C. DeLisle Burns, "A New Definition of International Service," *Philippines Herald*, January 31, 1934.
[60] "Elizalde, Campos, Romulo to Shanghai," *Philippines Herald*, June 18, 1934.
[61] "A Vision of the Orient," *Philippines Herald*, December 18, 1934.
[62] "Rededicating Rotary," *Philippines Herald*, February 2, 1935.

morality rather than diplomacy, insisting that "we learn to apply to nations the same principles of morality we apply to individuals," and thereby "that nations, as well as men, are created equal before the law."[63]

Through the language of states as persons, Romulo conjured an internationalism in which states related like individuals in a club – like the Rotary Club. With its ideals of businessmen relating to one another as equals, united in an ideal of service, we can see Romulo's Rotarian internationalism as his picture of postcolonial Asian diplomacy and the impetus behind his enthusiasm for the US-framed Tydings–McDuffie plan. By seeing the postcolonial Philippines as simply another businessman around the Rotary table with the United States, Romulo could imagine the United States as a benevolent equal, operating its policies on a moral rather than a political or diplomatic basis, with both the Philippines and the United States cooperating in a spirit of service rather than domination.

Romulo elaborated on this ideal in a February 1940 speech to a conference of Philippine Rotary clubs. Despite the ongoing Second World War, Romulo insisted that "Rotary has the opportunity and the power to help bring about a genuine era of peace and understanding among all the nations of the world." He noted that the transnational links which Rotary facilitated continued around Asia despite the ongoing Sino-Japanese War, proving that "our organization has served to link countries together that are otherwise separated by enormous bodies of water or by the animosities of war." But, drawing attention to Rotary's relatively small footprint in Asia compared to Europe and North America, Romulo urged his Filipino Rotarian compatriots to "serve as the hub around which the Far Eastern wheel of Rotary must revolve" through complementing their ongoing personal, club, and community service with an international service by drawing other Rotarians' attention to Asia. Rotarian attention to Asia, however, was only a lagging indicator of the fact for Romulo that "the Far East ... will be the next important stage whereon one of the greatest dramas of our time will be enacted." And the curtain had already lifted on this stage: "The spotlight of contemporary history has been focused upon the Far East."[64]

---

[63] Carlos P. Romulo, "The Mind of a New Commonwealth (December 9, 1935)," in *Mother America*, 233.

[64] Carlos P. Romulo, Speech to Second District Conference of the Philippines, February 23, 1940, pp. 2, 3, 5, and 6, Box 59, Folder 548, CPR Papers, UPD.

If in 1940 Romulo thought Rotary clubbability could help to maintain peace when "staging Asia," then when Japan and the United States joined the European and Asian theaters of the Second World War in 1941 and 1942, Rotary served Romulo as a network for wartime internationalism.[65] After General Douglas MacArthur and the US Armed Forces in the Far East evacuated Bataan and Corregidor, Romulo, who had joined as a press officer, went into exile with the Commonwealth government in the United States. Many US Rotarians wrote to Romulo, desperately asking for updates about their sons imprisoned on Bataan, and Romulo spoke to countless Rotary Clubs around the country, drumming up support for the war effort against Japan.[66] One letter writer, whose son was interned by Japan in Manila, wrote to Romulo that "I still retain my membership – an honorary one – in Manila Rotary, and never miss an opportunity of telling Rotarians here that our club was indeed international."[67]

At the end of the War, Romulo returned to his 1940 theme of Rotary as a guiding star for re-establishing international order. At the first meeting of the reconstituted Manila Club, on February 28, 1945, Romulo brought "a consolidated message of consolation and good will from the 466 cities in every state of the Union which he visited," as well as a message for the future: "Rotary must see that the peace that follows this war must be a just peace, a peace of which Rotary may be proud, a peace that will allow our boys who gave their all in Bataan to say 'It has not been all in vain.'"[68] In late 1945, he tied the nomination of a Manila club member for Rotary's international presidency to his longer-term project of shifting US and Rotary attention to Asia, as well as Philippine independence: Romulo described the man he forwarded as "one of those Americans who believe that the Orient is the coming section of the world," and "incidentally, he is a strong believer in the policy of 'Philippines for the Filipinos.'"[69]

---

[65] For an earlier notion of "staging Asia," see Rebecca Karl, *Staging the World: Chinese Nationalism at the Turn of the Twentieth Century* (Durham, N.C.: Duke University Press, 2002).

[66] For instance, Chesley R. Perry, Rotary International's secretary, wrote to Romulo on March 12, 1942, Box 12, Folder 148, CPR Papers, UPD. Romulo described his early talks at Rotary Clubs in Philadelphia and New York in a letter to MacArthur, August 18, 1942, p. 1, Box 1, Folder 1, CPR Papers, UPD.

[67] Fred C. Fisher to Romulo, December 10, 1943, p. 3, Box 1, Folder 2, CPR Papers, UPD.

[68] Theo. L. Hall, minutes of Manila Rotary Club meeting of February 28, 1945, Box 59, Folder 548, CPR Papers, UPD.

[69] Romulo to Gil Puyat, December 7, 1945, Box 59, Folder 548, CPR Papers, UPD.

By 1945, Romulo was no longer just a businessman among other businessmen in the Rotary fold: he was a policymaker, the Philippine representative in the United States and its delegate to the United Nations. However, his model of operating in a "clubbable" manner continued. In his official report on the San Francisco Conference which had drafted the UN Charter, Romulo wrote that "the world today is no more than a single community. What happens in one neighborhood ultimately affects all the other neighborhoods," using a Rotary-friendly analogy to the world of states as a community, a neighborhood, a network of individuals who could gather to sort out their problems.[70]

Romulo remained engaged with Rotary through the decades of his official diplomatic career, continuing to correspond with Rotarians and to make speeches to Rotary Clubs.[71] Writing to a provincial club in 1951, Romulo reiterated his faith that "one of the true and constant principles that is immutable and changeless is the principle of service which is the basis of Rotary throughout the world. 'He profits most who serves best' will remain true and dynamic as long as man retains his humanity."[72] Another Philippine club lauded Romulo during one visit, celebrating him since "his internationalism has become world-wide and his services has been outstandingly recognized, especially in the areas of world peace and freedom, for the small nations of the earth."[73] An American admirer wrote Romulo in 1953 after he published an article in Rotary's *Rotarian* magazine, to share his "opinion that you have already done more to bring about a friendlier relationship and a better understanding of Asia than any twelve men, living or dead, that I have ever heard of."[74]

Amid the rise of the global Cold War, Romulo's version of Rotarian internationalism could remain palatable for American anticommunists, especially since Romulo had impeccable anticommunist credentials dating back to the 1930s.[75] In 1949, the US National Association of

---

[70] Romulo to Sergio Osmeña, July 15, 1945, Box 1, Folder 15, CPR Papers, UPD.

[71] For instance, en route for an official visit to Indonesia, a Singaporean Rotarian invited Romulo to visit the Singapore club: M. R. Anciano to Romulo, May 6, 1950, Box 4, Folder 60, CPR Papers, UPD.

[72] Romulo to Tim L. Robles (Bacolod), May 7, 1951, Box 59, Folder 548, CPR Papers, UPD.

[73] Gab Tabuñar, "The Rotary Club of Iloilo welcomes Secretary Romulo," October 17, 1951, p. 2, Box 59, Folder 548, CPR Papers, UPD.

[74] Foster Kienholz (St. Paul, Minnesota) to Romulo, March 19, 1953, Box 59, Folder 549, CPR Papers, UPD.

[75] For instance, Romulo wrote about the perils of Communism spreading in Cuba after its 1933 revolution, and articulated a liberal anticommunism which recognized the defects of

Manufacturers wrote to Romulo to support his diplomatic efforts at the UN, affirming a Rotarian faith "that the give and take of open genuinely free discussion can deal successfully with the problems of nations as well as being the basis of promoting industrial peace among the industrial segments of each nation."[76] As Romulo explained to a Philippine Congressman, his strategy was of quiet persistence, in a Rotarian style: "there is no cure-all for such problems, but with vision, realism, wise counsel, and forbearance on both sides of the water, they can be solved, each in its appointed time."[77]

CONCLUSION

One way to explain Romulo's political mélange would be to chalk it up to delusion, a utopian dreaming that the Philippines and the United States could ever sit as equals in an international club. Another approach would be to claim he acted in bad faith, seeking to mystify an embrace of US imperialism through the language of anticolonialism. Thus, the Indian diplomatic corps dismissed Romulo and his compatriots at the Bandung Conference for attending "as among the founder members of this Western club," "determined to act as the spearhead of the Western or US point of view in this Asian-African gathering."[78] However, if the aim all along was to join a club – or *the* club – then was this a failure, or a success, of anticolonialism? As Sinha notes, the social club survived the British transfer of power in India, thanks to "the selective appropriation by Indians of the ever-present tension in colonial clubbability: the potential clubbability of the Indians themselves."[79] Why should the same not apply to the international club, or the "Congress of nations," as Romulo called it in 1935?

Rather than presume that anticolonialists who did not embrace economic and political radicalism were deluded or acting in bad faith, if we

---

communism while abhorring the destruction of individual and religious liberties under Communism: "The Red Menace," *Philippines Herald*, September 9, 1933; "Recognizing Soviet Russia," *Philippines Herald*, September 22, 1933; "A Stabilizing Move," *Philippines Herald*, October 22, 1933.

[76] Telegram from National Association of Manufacturers to Romulo, October 26, 1949, Box 67, Folder 602, CPR Papers, UPD.

[77] Romulo to Francisco M. Pajao, April 14, 1952, Box 6, Folder 79, CPR Papers, UPD.

[78] B. F. B. H. Tyabji to Subimal Dutt, "Some Impressions of the Asian-African Conference," April 28, 1955, pp. 2–3, F.1(37)-AAC/55(S), NAI.

[79] Sinha, "Britishness, Clubbability, and the Colonial Public Sphere," 520.

try to see the world from Romulo's perspective, we can begin to understand how anticolonialism could be seen as compatible with capitalism,
Americanism, and Wilsonian liberal internationalism – which, when
coupled with Cold War anticommunism, could help anticolonial and
postcolonial elites explain to themselves and their audiences why they
should align with the US-led political and economic order. That is, if we
can understand Romulo's notion of the international order as a club, and
his belief that one could use that club to dismantle colonialism, we will
understand why so many former colonies sought to join the American
club after 1945 – not just pragmatically, but idealistically.

Romulo exemplifies other conservatives and center-right liberals who
also practiced internationalism aimed at weakening colonial rule around
the world.[80] Without considering this crucial global political formation of
the mid-twentieth century, international historians will fail to understand
how the United States and European empires in transition were able to
find so many countries' leaders open to cooperating with them in the
global Cold War, even to great domestic political risk. We need to
understand leaders like Romulo to grasp how the "anti-Communist
Third World" came to be an enduring international framework in Asia,
Africa, and the Americas.[81]

---

[80] A main example is Charles Malik of Lebanon, who is prominently featured in Roland
Burke, *Decolonization and the Evolution of International Human Rights* (Philadelphia:
University of Pennsylvania Press, 2010) and Glenn Mitoma, *Human Rights and the
Negotiation of American Power* (Philadelphia: University of Pennsylvania Press, 2013).

[81] See Lisandro E. Claudio, "The Anti-Communist Third World: Carlos Romulo and the
Other Bandung," *Southeast Asian Studies* 4, no. 1 (April 2015): 125–156. Claudio's
article focuses on Romulo's activities at Bandung and his books after 1945, while this
chapter takes an earlier timeframe and relies on Romulo's personal papers. Augusto
Espiritu also reads Romulo's writings about Bandung, detecting a potential anticolonialism and antiracism *despite* Romulo's anticommunism, not because of it: Augusto
Espiritu, "'To Carry Water on Both Shoulders': Carlos P. Romulo, American Empire,
and the Meanings of Bandung," *Radical History Review*, no. 95 (Spring 2006): 173–190.

PART II

SOLIDARITIES AND THEIR DISCONTENTS

6

From Wife to Comrade: Agnes Smedley and the Intimacies of Anticolonial Solidarity

Michele Louro

Agnes Smedley was an American writer, journalist, activist, and spy who traveled North America, Europe, and Asia in pursuit of her feminist, anti-imperialist, and communist agendas.[1] Smedley came to sympathize with anticolonialism through her personal and professional relationships with Indian revolutionaries in the United States in the early twentieth century, among them Lajpat Rai and M. N. Roy. Later in Berlin, her common law marriage to Virendranath Chattopadhyaya (known as Chatto) from 1920 to 1925 strengthened her involvement with anti-imperialist and Indian revolutionary movements in Europe. She also worked behind the scenes to launch the League against Imperialism (LAI), an institution that connected anticolonialism with socialism and communism worldwide. By late 1928, Smedley left Berlin and relocated to Shanghai overtly as a correspondent for a German newspaper and covertly as an agent for the Communist International (Comintern). In China, she chronicled the events of the Chinese civil war and the Asian theater of the Second World War. By the onset of the Cold War, Smedley became the target of FBI surveillance for her ties to communists during the interwar period, although she was never formally charged. Smedley died in 1950 in the UK

[1] I want to thank Erez Manela and Heather Streets-Salter for their invitation to contribute to the volume and their ongoing encouragement for this project. This chapter benefits from comments by Durba Ghosh, Cemil Aydin, Michael Goebel, Lydia Walker, Antoinette Burton, and Howard Spodek. Special thanks to archivists and research assistants who made the research for this chapter possible during the pandemic, particularly the Bridge Research Network for materials in Russia and Shannon Walker, archivist at Arizona State University.

after complications due to a medical procedure related to stomach cancer. Her ashes were scattered in Beijing in 1951.

Smedley's transnational life story is simultaneously ordinary and extraordinary for her times. She joins a myriad of women who participated in revolutionary activities across the interwar world. Inspired by socialism, communism, anticolonialism, anti-racism, and feminism, women were critical to shaping a global revolutionary history as writers, activists, politicians, and spies, as well as stenographers, secretaries, and typists.[2] These women published widely, demonstrated in the streets, and served the cause by performing as wives and intellectual partners to their more famous husbands. At the same time, Smedley was uniquely famous in her own right as an influential writer, contributing countless articles to newspapers in the US, China, Germany, India, and Soviet Russia. She authored six books over her lifetime, many of which were globally circulated and translated into multiple languages.[3] Her success as a writer is particularly notable given her background, growing up in extreme poverty in labor mining camps in Colorado and lacking formal education or the social capital that many of her colleagues had.

Yet, Smedley's fame as a writer offers only a partial and incomplete reading of her life as a transnational revolutionary. Publications aside, her most radical acts were her private, intimate, and sexual relationships with Indian and Chinese revolutionaries, as well as Soviet spies. Such acts were political as much as intimate and go a long way in offering what Antoinette Burton has called a "fuller history" of the "global cultures of

---

[2] Women were significant actors in transnational networks of the interwar period. See for examples, Mrinalini Sinha, Donna Guy, and Angela Woollacott, eds. *Feminisms and Internationalism* (Oxford: Blackwell Publishers, 1999); Brigitte Studer, *The Transnational World of the Cominternians* (Houndmills, Basingstoke, Hampshire: Palgrave Macmillan, 2015); Carole Boyce Davies, *Left of Karl Marx: The Political Life of Black Communist Claudia Jones* (Durham, NC: Duke University Press, 2008); Jessica Namakkal, "Decolonizing Marriage and the Family: The Lives and Letters of Ida, Benoy and Indira Sarkar," *Journal of Women's History*, 31, no. 2 (2019), 124–147; and Kumari Jayawardena, *The White Women's Other Burden: Western Women in South Asia during British Colonial Rule* (New York: Routledge, 1995), especially "Part V: Comrades in Arms." Smedley worked closely with many well-known Indian women in Berlin, including Chatto's sister, poetess and nationalist Sarojini Naidu, and another sister, Suhasini Chattopadhyaya, who became a Comintern agent. In Shanghai, Smedley allied with Soong Ching-ling (known as Madame Sun Yat-sen), who was married to Guomindang founder, Sun Yat-sen, and played a prominent role in Chinese revolutionary politics.
[3] Smedley's books include *Daughter of Earth* (1929), *Chinese Destinies* (1933), *China's Red Army Marches* (1934), *China Fights Back* (1938), *Battle Hymn of China* (1943), and *The Great Road* (posthumously, 1956).

revolutionary politics" in the interwar moment. Burton has implored us to consider the lives of transnational revolutionaries and ask: "Whom did they leave behind when they travelled, who served them tea, whom did they love, whom did they hate, whom did they hold hands with, how did they touch, whom did they sleep with?"[4]

Smedley's life history reveals the importance of intimacy, gender, and race in the writing of a "fuller history" of anticolonial transnationalism. She worked "behind the scenes" as a wife or romantic partner to revolutionaries in ways that are often invisible to archives and historical scholarship.[5] I argue that such everyday practices and intimacies were as important as the manifestos and publications produced by revolutionaries and archived in repositories. While recent scholarship on interwar internationalism has complicated the political categories of history and questioned the meaning and interplay of socialism, communism, and nationalism, there has been less focus on the complex social and intimate ties that connected revolutionaries in a transnational world.[6] Women in the anti-imperialist movement had to navigate the fluidity of political categories, as well as social and intimate ones. What constituted a

---

[4] Antoinette Burton, "Afterword: The Zigzag of the Global," in Michele Louro, Heather Streets-Salter, Carolien Stolte, and Sana Tannoury-Karam, eds., *The League against Imperialism: Lives and Afterlives* (Leiden: Leiden University Press, 2020), 402.

[5] See Lydia Walker's chapter in this volume. She makes a critical point about locating histories of anticolonialism and decolonization by tracing individuals who "worked behind the scenes" in ways that are difficult to locate in official archives of colonial and postcolonial states.

[6] Scholarship on the interwar world has been innovative in rethinking political categories, within and beyond the nation. These include although are not limited to Akira Iriye, *Cultural Internationalism and World Order* (Baltimore: Johns Hopkins University Press, 1997); Erez Manela, *The Wilsonian Moment: Self-Determination and the International Origins of Anticolonial Nationalism* (Oxford: Oxford University Press, 2007); Cemil Aydin, *The Politics of Anti-Westernism in Asia: Visions of World Order in Pan-Islamic and Pan-Asian Thought* (New York: Columbia University Press, 2007); Susan Pennybacker, *From Scottsboro to Munich: Race and Political Culture in 1930s Britain* (Princeton: Princeton University Press, 2009); Manu Goswami, "Colonial Internationalisms and Imaginary Futures," *American Historical Review*, 117, no. 5, 2012, 1461–1485; Ali Raza, Franziska Roy, and Benjamin Zachariah, eds. *The Internationalist Moment: South Asia, Worlds, and World Views, 1917–1939* (Los Angeles: SAGE Publications, 2014); Glenda Sluga, *Internationalism in the Age of Nationalism* (Philadelphia: University of Pennsylvania Press, 2015); Michael Goebel, *Anti-Imperial Metropolis: Interwar Paris and the Seeds of Third World Nationalism* (New York: Cambridge University Press, 2015); Michele Louro, *Comrades against Imperialism: Nehru, India, and Interwar Internationalism* (Cambridge: Cambridge University Press, 2018); and Ali Raza, *Revolutionary Pasts* (Cambridge: Cambridge University Press, 2020).

romantic partner or wife without the bond of legal marriage legitimized by state law, and how did these varying relationships with anti-imperialist men interface with their broader political aspirations and affiliations to anti-imperialism, communism, or socialism? To address these concerns is to underscore the significance of anticolonial revolutionaries as individuals who navigated an uneven and fluid transnational terrain of interwar politics, solidarities, and intimacies.

Like other contributions in this volume, such as Mark Reeves' study of Romulo and Lydia Walker's chapter on Armstrong, this chapter underscores the usefulness of life histories as a lens for interpreting the complexities of anticolonial transnationalism. It breaks with the biographical genre, which too often privileges breadth over depth. More significantly, biographies of Smedley have been bracketed from the transnational and gendered milieu that shaped her life and times. Despite her remarkable life, Smedley is the subject of only two biographies. Janice and Stephen MacKinnon recount "just the facts" about her life without being "overly academic" and instead "as plain-spoken as we can."[7] Written later, Ruth Price's biography is rigorously researched, although her primary concern is questioning Smedley's affiliation to the communist party, reflecting Cold War concerns about the contest between communism and anti-communism.[8] This chapter builds on their research, yet it also embeds Smedley's life history within a transnational and gendered framework as a way to reveal the inner workings, intimacies, and tensions in the making of global revolutionary histories.

This chapter offers two snapshots of Smedley's political and intimate commitments to anticolonialism and communism. The first snapshot considers her experiences as an anti-imperialist wife to Chatto and her involvement with Indian revolutionaries in Berlin. As a writer and activist in her own right, Smedley supported the intellectual and organizational work of projects most often credited to Chatto, the Indian Information Bureau and LAI in particular.[9] As a wife, Smedley also participated in

---

[7] Janice and Stephen MacKinnon, *Agnes Smedley: The Life and Times of an American Radical* (Berkeley: University of California Press, 1988), 2.

[8] Ruth Price, *The Lives of Agnes Smedley* (New York: Oxford University Press, 2005). Smedley's history in Berlin, outside her two biographies, is briefly treated in Nirode K. Barooah, *Chatto: The Life and Times of an Anti-Imperialist in Europe* (New Delhi: Oxford University Press, 2004). None situate her life and times within a transnational or global history of revolutionary politics and intimacies.

[9] See, Barooah, *Chatto*. For a comprehensive history on the LAI, see Michele Louro, Heather Streets-Salter, Carolien Stolte, and Sana Tannoury-Karam, eds. *The League*

anticolonialism in gendered ways by cooking and cleaning for Chatto and the many Indian revolutionary men that traveled to Berlin and stayed with the couple. As Ania Loomba argues, revolutionary women's public and private worlds were not exclusive but rather mutually constitutive.[10] Smedley's public role as a journalist and political organizer was intertwined with her more private and domestic labor as anti-imperialist wife. This interconnection between domestic and worldly, and public and private, is significant in addressing gaps in our understanding of revolutionary women like Smedley who saw their domestic and gendered performativity as inseparable from the anticolonial cause.

Smedley's interracial marriage also performed what Jessica Namakkal has called "decolonial living," or the "quiet subversion of performing interracial intimacies."[11] Such intimacies and marriage between Indian revolutionaries and white women threatened colonial hierarchies of racial difference between colonizer and colonized, and, at the same time, ran counter to anticolonial nationalism in India. Increasingly in the twentieth century, as Partha Chatterjee has argued, India's nationalists sought to protect Indian "tradition" in the private sphere from foreign influence and intervention.[12] Western women as wives, however radical and anticolonial they were, threatened this dominant discourse of Indian nationalism because they "polluted" the domestic sphere and therefore the Indian nation.[13] I argue that Smedley's interracial relationship with Chatto was performative in challenging such racial hierarchies embedded in colonial and Indian nationalist worlds. Her marriage was political as much as intimate.

Although radical in her interracial marriage and anti-imperialist writings, Smedley did not break with patriarchal norms in Berlin. In her

against Imperialism: Lives and Afterlives (Leiden: Leiden University Press, 2020). Few women were included in these essays, prompting my interest in writing here about Smedley.

[10] Ania Loomba, *Revolutionary Desires: Women, Communism, and Feminism in India* (New York: Routledge, 2019).

[11] Namakkal, "Decolonizing Marriage," 129.

[12] Partha Chatterjee, *Nation and Its Fragments: Colonial and Postcolonial Histories* (Princeton: Princeton University Press, 1994).

[13] Famous Indian revolutionaries like M. N. Roy intentionally removed their white wives from their autobiographies, while histories of leaders like Benoy Sakar neglect his interracial marriage and family in biographies. On Roy, Kris Manjapra, *M. N. Roy: Marxism and Colonial Cosmopolitanism* (New York: Routledge, 2010); and Michael Goebel, "Geopolitics, Transnational Solidarity or Diaspora Nationalism? The Global Career of M.N. Roy, 1915–1930," *European Review of History: Revue Européenne d'histoire*, 21, no. 4 (July 4, 2014). On Sakar, Namakkal, "Decolonizing Marriage."

everyday life in Berlin, Smedley had to negotiate tensions between her role as woman and wife and as anti-imperialist in a transnational world. She ultimately collaborated with her male counterparts in the Indian revolutionary, anti-imperialist, and communist circles of Berlin, while also criticizing gender boundaries and norms that limited her political horizons. These positions were not always oppositional, and in fact Smedley, like many of her comrades, believed that socialism was inherently better for women than life under capitalism, even if cultural norms and expectations among Indian revolutionaries and communists in Berlin remained highly patriarchal.[14]

In the second snapshot, I trace Smedley's journey from Berlin to Shanghai as she asserted greater autonomy as an anti-imperialist comrade in her own right and left behind marriage. Her evolution from wife to comrade began before she left Berlin, having ended her marriage to Chatto by 1925, although they maintained a very close relationship until she left Berlin. Other factors shaped the possibilities for Smedley to assert greater financial and political independence as a woman, notably her budding journalist career, Comintern informant work, and the success of her first novel, *Daughter of Earth* (1929). In Shanghai, her autonomy led many of her fellow comrades and lovers to describe her as masculine. Famous Soviet spy and her romantic partner, Richard Sorge, once stated that she was an effective informant because she was "like a man."[15]

A history of Smedley's life from wife to comrade reveals the limits imposed on women who destabilized and challenged gender norms even in the most radical and revolutionary circles of transnational communism and anticolonialism. Smedley's departure from Berlin and assertion of autonomy and masculinity was a double-edged sword, at first providing her access to Sorge and communist networks. As time went on, however,

---

[14] For a compelling case for why women benefit more under socialism than capitalism, see the provocative and accessible book by Kristen R. Ghodsee, *Why Women Have Better Sex under Socialism: And Other Arguments for Economic Independence* (New York: Bold Type Books, 2018).

[15] Quoted in Price, *Lives of Agnes Smedley*, 214. Originally printed in *A Partial Documentation of the Sorge Espionage Case* (Washington: US GPO, 1950). Smedley appears prominently in Sorge's testimony before the House Committee of Un-American Activities (1950). Scholarship in English and Russian on Sorge presents Smedley as an ancillary figure in their espionage collaboration, which was not the case. See for examples, Owen Matthews, *Impeccable Spy: Richard Sorge, Stalin's Master Agent* (London: Bloomsbury, 2020); Sergey Golyakov and Mikhail Il'inskiy, *Rikhard Zorge. Podvig i tragediya razvedchika/ Glava "Osobaya rol' Agnes Smedli."* (Moscow: Veche, 2001). (English translation: *Richard Sorge: The Exploit and Tragedy of the Scout.*)

her deviation from conventional gender norms also became the basis for the Comintern to question her loyalty and trustworthiness as a comrade and informant.[16] Revolutionary comrades were men operating in a homosocial milieu of international communism, and even masculine women like Smedley were limited in accessing such a world. Her life history from Berlin to Shanghai ultimately captures a cultural history of global anticolonialism that is attentive to the ways intimacy, race, and gender shaped the making of radicals and revolutionaries in a transnational world.

ANTI-IMPERIALIST WIFE IN BERLIN

In February 1927, the inaugural meeting of the LAI took place in Brussels. In the British Press, Fenner Brockway, British delegate and member of the Independent Labour Party, celebrated the meeting: "As one looked on the sea of black, brown, yellow, and white faces one felt that here at last was something approaching a Parliament of Mankind."[17] The emphasis on racial diversity alongside "mankind" is striking. Women like Agnes Smedley had been instrumental in planning the Congress in Brussels, although she was not present.[18] In fact, only a handful of European women attended, while only men spoke at the official proceedings and plenary sessions. Smedley's absence in Brussels hardly reflects her significance throughout her years in Berlin, from 1920 to 1928, as a critical figure in anti-imperialist and Indian revolutionary networks. She was an anti-imperialist writer, propagandist, activist, and organizer. At the same time, Smedley was an anti-imperialist wife to Chatto, and she saw her conjugal relationship as deeply intertwined with her political commitments that transcended geographic, political, racial, and gender boundaries.

---

[16] Smedley's cadre file in the Comintern Archive is remarkably thin and focuses on statements that prove she was not a party member or affiliated with the party. I argue below in this essay that she was wiped from the Comintern Archive because she broke with party expectations for women comrades. For her cadre file, see 495/261/1533, Comintern Archive, Russian State Archives for Social and Political History (RGASPI), Moscow, Russia. (Hereafter Comintern Archive.)

[17] Fenner Brockway, "The Coloured Peoples' International," *The New Leader*, August 26, 1927. Extract in L/P&J/ 12/267, Indian Political Intelligence Files (Microfilm), London, United Kingdom.

[18] She withdrew from university studies to assist LAI founders, Chatto and German Communist, Willi Muenzenberg. Smedley was not present in Brussels.

Smedley arrived in Berlin after leaving New York in 1919. She secured a job as a stewardess aboard a shipping company to Europe. She planned to sail to the European continent with the intention of subsequently securing passage first to the Soviet Union and then to India. However, after landing, she made her way to Berlin first, where she met Chatto and began an intimate relationship that would radically alter her life. Although she took his name and was known as his wife, the two were never legally married. The relationship was tumultuous and as Smedley noted: "so complex that it tended only to aggravate my sick state of mind."[19] Both reportedly suffered mental breakdowns over the turbulent years of their bond, frequently splitting, reconciling, and parting ways again. The couple lived together until 1924 and split permanently by 1925, although they continued a close relationship until she left for Shanghai in December 1928.

Smedley shared with Chatto a deep commitment to anti-imperialist and revolutionary politics. Chatto was a masterful propagandist and his networks extended from Berlin to Moscow, New York, Delhi, and Shanghai.[20] His home in Berlin was a hub of anti-imperialist, communist, and Indian revolutionary activity in the 1920s, a history recently documented by scholars.[21] During the First World War, the German Foreign Office encouraged and funded anticolonial revolutionary activity within the British and French empires. Chatto was a member of the Berlin India Committee, an arm of the German wartime government that supported Indian exiles and expatriates in schemes to ship weapons to India and foment mutiny among Indian contingents within the British imperial military. After the war, many exiles stayed on in Weimar Germany, although their status as residents was more ambiguous after 1919. Nevertheless, some of the most innovative collaborations and global

---

[19] Smedley included an autobiographical account of her life in her book, *Battle Hymn of China*, originally published in 1943. Citations in this chapter are from a reprint, *Battle Hymn of China* (Beijing, China: Foreign Language Press, 2003), 11.

[20] See Barooah, *Chatto*.

[21] On Berlin as an anti-imperialist hub, see Louro, *Comrades against Imperialism*; Fredrik Petersson, *Willi Münzenberg, the League against Imperialism, and the Comintern, 1925–1933* (Lewiston: Queenston Press, 2013); Kris Manjapra, *Age of Entanglement: Indian and German Intellectuals across Empire* (Cambridge, MA: Harvard University Press, 2014); Daniel Brückenhaus, *Policing Transnational Protest: Liberal Imperialism and the Surveillance of Anticolonialists in Europe, 1905–1945* (Oxford: Oxford University Press, 2017); and Nathanael Kuck, "Anticolonialism in a Post-Imperial Environment: The Case of Berlin, 1914–33," *Journal of Contemporary History*, 49, no. 1 (2014): 134–159.

solidarities against imperialism were formulated in Berlin's milieu including the League against Imperialism.[22]

Smedley recognized that her interracial marriage to Chatto was political as much as intimate. She admired Chatto for his "white-hot passion for liberty" that "seemed never to wane." She added that this passion "bound me to him even in our most unhappy moments and long after our marriage had become a formality."[23] Her attraction to Chatto was politically inspired. She wrote of him: "To me he was not just an individual, but a political principle. For me he embodied the tragedy of a whole race. Had he been born English or American, I thought, his ability would have placed him among the great leaders of his age."[24] Her bond with Chatto emblemized both her commitment to political independence for the "whole race" in India, as well as her nod to the global racism that barred someone with Chatto's organizational skills from a deserved place alongside other "great leaders of his age."

Smedley also reflected on the intimate crossing of racial and class boundaries in their marriage, even if it remained a patriarchal union. Smedley recalled: "When Viren and I began life together, two eras and two cultures met. I was an American working woman, the product of a distorted commercial civilization, he a high-caste Indian with a cultivated labyrinthine Brahmin mind and a British classical education."[25] This union of class and racial difference, according to Smedley, informed the attraction and turbulence in their relationship. Yet, Smedley also recognized the unevenness of this relationship. As anti-imperialist husband, Chatto dictated the cultural, racial, and class norms practiced in their home: "Our way of life was of his choosing, not mine, our home a small edition of that of a great joint family of India."[26] This took a toll on Smedley, forcing her on occasion to seek psychoanalytic therapy to cope with her relationship. Ultimately, she admitted that she would "walk barefoot around the world to help him," but "would not live with him for a day."[27]

Smedley remained acutely aware of her humble origins and the poverty that informed her revolutionary politics, which were different from Chatto's upbringing. She grew up in labor camps in Missouri and Colorado. Her father was an unskilled laborer and her mother died young

[22] Louro, Streets-Salter, Stolte, and Tannoury-Karam, eds., *LAI: Lives and Afterlives.*
[23] Smedley, *Battle Hymn*, 17.   [24] Smedley, *Battle Hymn*, 22.
[25] Smedley, *Battle Hymn*, 15.   [26] Smedley, *Battle Hymn*, 15.
[27] Smedley, *Battle Hymn*, 11.

from untreated appendicitis. She described these experiences as living a "primitive life," filled with "English folk-songs, cowboy songs, and ballads as those in praise of Jesse James." She stressed that she had "long felt that the poverty and ignorance of my youth were the tribute which I, like millions of others, paid to private interests."[28] Smedley was critical of socialists she met early in her life who enjoyed middle-class lifestyles and spoke of the poor without recognizing the realities of poverty that she had experienced.

Both Chatto and Smedley shared a strong commitment to anti-imperialist politics, and their ideas represented a "special blend" of politics reflective of interwar internationalism.[29] Evident in organizations like the LAI, which Smedley helped launch, anti-imperialism brought together disparate political movements into a broad coalition aiming to eradicate colonialism worldwide. Borrowing heavily from Lenin, the LAI argued that the root cause of imperialism and even fascism was the growth of capitalism, and likewise the anti-imperialist and anti-fascist struggle required solidarity with communists to weaken the power of capitalism globally. The LAI called for solidarity among all individuals and institutions that opposed imperialism, fascism, racism, and capitalism. The differences between political parties and factions, especially anticolonial nationalism and communism, were to be set aside for the broader and global aim of eradicating imperialism.[30]

While Smedley never formally joined the communist party, Chatto did and later in life he moved to the Soviet Union when the Nazis came to power in Germany. Even though Chatto became a communist, Smedley noted: "I could never imagine him being regimented by any political party or following 'lines' of thought and action. His mind took the whole world as its province and drew nourishment from every age."[31] She drew a vivid analogy likening Chatto's mind to vibrant Hindu temples in South India. Having grown up in Hyderabad among Muslims and Hindus, Chatto had been educated in both cultures and learned English, German, Hindi, and Persian. Smedley suggested that this upbringing "made his mind and emotional life" like "one of those Hindu temples in South India – a repository of all the cultural movements of the ages."[32] As he gravitated

---

[28] Smedley, *Battle Hymn*, 5.   [29] Louro, *Comrades against Imperialism*.
[30] Louro, Streets-Salter, Stolte, and Tannoury-Karam, eds., *LAI: Lives and Afterlives*.
[31] Smedley, *Battle Hymn*, 14–15.   [32] Smedley, *Battle Hymn*, 13.

to Marxism and communism in Berlin, she "always wondered just what new design was added to the Hindu temple of his mind by this act."[33]

One aspect of Smedley's attachment to Chatto was the connections he made between her and Indian anticolonial leaders. By 1924, she worked for the Indian Information Bureau, which generated propaganda in Europe about Indian anticolonialism. As Chatto's wife, Smedley met high-profile Indians traveling to Berlin and played a role in entertaining them. Among the visitors to Berlin were South Asia's future heads of states, Mohammed Ali Jinnah and Jawaharlal Nehru. She recalled of Jinnah, later Pakistan's first Prime Minister: "Cold, sleek, cruel-faced, Jinnah was a great landlord who had married a Parsi woman, daughter of a millionaire Bombay factory-owner." Smedley noted that Jinnah's wife was a "superficial society woman, whom Jinnah displayed as he would a jeweled shirt-stud."[34] Chatto hoped to entice Jinnah to fund a scholarship program for Indian students to study in Berlin, although Smedley noted that Jinnah and his wife only sought out Chatto for his advice on the best tourist sites and shopping establishments. Smedley's impression of Nehru was only slightly more favorable. "He was a quiet, unspectacular man, totally unlike most Indian leaders. He was so modest and reserved that it was difficult to think of him as a political leader at all; yet he wielded tremendous influence over Indian youth."[35]

Smedley's public life as an anti-imperialist was complemented by her private one as a wife to Chatto. The couple hosted a steady stream of Indian students, expatriates, and exiles in Berlin. Given his prominence in anticolonial networks in Europe, Indian students frequently stopped at the couple's Berlin home as part of a "pilgrimage" to meet Chatto. For Smedley, this meant "endless" hours of cooking for Indian guests in their home, which was "permeated with the odor of curry."[36] Smedley recalled her role in nursing to health the many expatriates and students who fell ill in Berlin, as well as taking in homeless and newly arrived men from India. An influx of Chinese exiles in the context of the civil war, alongside Chatto's commitment to assist all "Asiatic" peoples, also intensified her domestic labor obligations to ensure the welfare of Berlin's Asian immigrant communities.

Smedley's domestic labor in the kitchen was quite radical for Indians and destabilized racial and caste boundaries. As Jessica Namakkal compellingly argues, women like Ida Sakar were barred from the kitchen and

[33] Smedley, *Battle Hymn*, 14.   [34] Smedley, *Battle Hymn*, 16.   [35] *Battle Hymn*, 24.
[36] Smedley, *Battle Hymn*, 16.

given a separate cook for food preparation in India because their "whiteness was equated with impurity and thus untouchability."[37] White women as wives and cooks undermined Indian nationalist protection of the domestic sphere from foreign and colonial influence, thus whiteness was a significant barrier for revolutionary wives who followed their husbands back to India to reside. However much she loathed it, Smedley's performance of cooking in an interracial home and marriage undermined racial and caste difference in ways that her visitors no doubt noticed, even if these responsibilities were highly gendered and patriarchal, relegating women regardless of race to the kitchen and domestic sphere.

Smedley's commitments to the birth control movement also broke with the conventions and gendered politics of Indian fellow travelers. When Smedley was not writing about or organizing anti-imperialism, she was busy connecting with German physicians and feminists for the launch of birth control clinics in Berlin and Frankfurt. Funded by her friend Margaret Sanger in New York, the clinics were eventually established in 1928 after several years of coordinating and negotiating. Smedley was a pivot in the transnational networks of birth control activists, linking Sanger's movement in the US with Germany, India, and later China. Yet, her ideas for birth control clinics were more radical than other activists in Germany and elsewhere. In one example, Smedley rejected collaboration with German feminists and physicians who envisioned the clinic more broadly to include advice on birth control, sex, and motherhood.[38] She believed that only access to birth control should be the basis of the clinic. She also conflicted with communists and socialists in Germany who were dedicated to the birth control project. Writing to Sanger about an exchange with a male doctor, Smedley recalled that he identified as a "Marxist" and argued that "birth control cannot really change conditions; only a new social order can do that."[39] She confronted him by becoming "very orthodox Marxist right on the spot." She called his assumptions "fallacies," and argued the "goal of Marxism is the right of women to control their own bodies, to have children when they wish it only; that birth control does not mean no children; it means that we

---

[37] Namakkal, "Decolonizing Marriage," 135–136.
[38] Correspondence with Margaret Sanger, Smedley-MacKinnon Collection 1911–1986, MSS-123, Box 1, Folder 7, Arizona State University Archive, Tempe, Arizona (hereafter MacKinnon Papers).
[39] Smedley to Sanger, February 14, 1928, MSS-123, Box 1, Folder 7, MacKinnon Papers.

decide when and where and how we shall have children." She added that he was not speaking as a Marxist, but rather "as a man only."[40]

Although she does not write about conflict between her commitment to birth control and Indian anticolonialism, there is much reason to assume this was a contentious point. She frequently wrote about birth control for the Indian press and encouraged Indian women traveling to Berlin to take up the issue at home.[41] The domain of motherhood, reproduction, and domesticity were not open for public debate within Indian nationalist politics.[42] Smedley's anti-imperialist counterparts in Berlin were mainly men from India, and her attempts to bridge the birth control movement with anticolonialism and feminism ran counter to their gendered politics at home in India.

Smedley's radical ideas as a woman and her whiteness in an interracial marriage left her with a sense of isolation in Berlin. She recalled that despite her caretaking, cooking, and cleaning for Indian and Chinese visitors, as well as her earnest study of Indian history and politics, few understood or appreciated her. Instead, "Everyone understood and loved Viren; few understood me. To them I was a queer creature who grew ever more strange."[43] In a letter to a friend in New York, she complained: "I have no associates and no intellectual companionships such as in NY. The Indian work and my illness have prevented my learning German or anything else. The Indians here harbor harsh prejudices against women and against foreigners."[44]

By 1925, Smedley left Chatto. She could no longer participate in anti-imperialism as a wife leading her to equate marriage with slavery. She later wrote: "For women, marriage is at best an economic investment; at its worst, a relic of human slavery."[45] She also began writing about marriage and gender inequality not as a national problem, but rather transnational even in the most radical and progressive societies. She criticized the fact that no women spoke at the tomb of Lenin in the

[40] Smedley to Sanger, February 14, 1928, MSS-123, Box 1, Folder 7, MacKinnon Papers.
[41] Correspondence with Margaret Sanger, MSS-123, Box 1, Folder 7, MacKinnon Papers.
[42] As Durba Ghosh and Ania Loomba have shown recently, revolutionary women in India contested and reshaped these masculine constructions of gender and politics in India. See Ghosh, *Gentlemanly Terrorists: Political Violence and the Colonial State in India* (Cambridge: Cambridge University Press, 2017); and Loomba, *Revolutionary Desires*.
[43] Smedley, *Battle Hymn*, 16.
[44] Smedley to Florence Lennon (New York), June 1, 1922, MSS-123, Box 1, Folder 7, MacKinnon Papers.
[45] Smedley, *Battle Hymn*, 8.

Soviet Union, while a German wife who was beaten by her husband had no legal recourse unless she died from the abuse.[46]

Between their romantic split in 1925 and Smedley's departure from Berlin in late 1928, the couple maintained an intellectual and political relationship. Smedley continued to provide input and organizational labor for Chatto's major projects, the launch of the LAI's forerunner, the League against Colonial Cruelties and Oppression (LACO), as well as the LAI. Chatto was responsible for introducing Smedley to Willi Muenzenberg, founder of the LAI, and other influential Comintern members in Berlin, many of whom would be important contacts that facilitated her move to Shanghai. Smedley became so immersed in the anti-imperialist project in Berlin that she abandoned her studies at the university to support Chatto and Muenzenberg.

Although brief, lasting from 1920 to 1925, her conjugal union with Chatto demonstrates the significance of interracial marriage and intimacy to transnational revolutionary politics in both the everyday experiences of dining and cleaning to the public roles in organizing and writing about global anti-imperialism. In December 1928, she traveled to China via the Soviet Union and settled in Shanghai to work officially as a correspondent for the *Frankfurter Zeitung* and covertly as an agent for the Communist International's espionage arm.[47] In doing so, Smedley freed herself from the constraints of domesticity and intimacy in the service of transnational anti-imperialism. This transformation came with greater autonomy and more vulnerability.

ANTI-IMPERIALIST COMRADESHIP IN SHANGHAI

Shanghai afforded new experiences and opportunities for Smedley beyond the confines of anti-imperialist marriage. This transformation did not preclude intimacy and romantic entanglements with like-minded revolutionaries, most notably a sustained relationship with Richard Sorge, a Soviet spy based in Shanghai. Smedley and Sorge worked together in building an espionage ring to facilitate Soviet policy in China and Japan. Of her involvement with Sorge, Smedley explained that she was "sort of married," but that this was more of a partnership than a marriage. It was "50-50 all along the line and he [is] helping me and I him

---

[46] On the Soviet Union, Smedley, *Battle Hymn*, 8; on German women, ibid., 22.
[47] For details, see Price, *Lives of Agnes Smedley*.

and we [are] working together in every way."[48] She added that their union was not the stuff of "blazing love affairs, bound together or bust," but rather the Smedley–Sorge alliance was "a big, broad, all-sided friendship and *comradeship.*"[49]

In this next sojourn and stage of Smedley's revolutionary life, she gained greater autonomy by eschewing marriage for "friendship and comradeship." Critical to her move was the success of her first novel, *Daughter of the Earth*, a semi-autobiographical story of her life growing up in poverty in the American west and her political work with Indian revolutionaries in New York and Berlin. Reviewed widely and translated into German and Russian, the book became an important contribution to leftist literature. From Shanghai, Smedley began writing her second book, a journalist's perspective on China. She embedded herself in leftist political and literary circles in Shanghai, boasting of intimate relationships with several Chinese scholar-poets that provided unique access for her journalist endeavors as well as her personal ties. By September 1929, she was traveling across China with her romantic partner, Xu Zhimo, who was in her words "China's leading poet," and informing her American friends that she was never returning to Europe or the US. "I'll go down with Asia or rise with it. I certainly feel at home here."[50]

In her writings in this period, Smedley reflected on her family history, and in particular the women in her life, offering a glimpse of her own ideas about the kind of autonomy she sought as a woman in the world. The women she admired most were those who refused to accept their gender roles, and this is clear in her description of her Aunt Mary. Smedley writes that her aunt was a woman who was fiercely independent and the target of town gossip. "Anything could be expected of that big woman, who came from God only knew where and could do anything from curing diseases with herbs to managing a big farm and rearing more than a dozen children! If Aunt Mary had lived in an earlier period, her abilities might have caused her to be burned as a witch." She added that Aunt Mary was known to have been over ninety, speeding around the country in a Ford with her "white hair flying, her pipe in her mouth." She embellished the story by adding that when Aunt Mary died, she was so

[48] Smedley to Florence Lennon, May 28, 1930, Box 1, Folder 7, MacKinnon Papers.
[49] Smedley to Florence Lennon, May 28, 1930, Box 1, Folder 7, MacKinnon Papers. On the significance of friendship and anti-imperialism, see Leela Gandhi, *Affective Communities: Anticolonial Thought, Fin-de-Siècle Radicalism, and the Politics of Friendship* (Durham, NC: Duke University Press, 2006).
[50] Smedley to Florence, September 11, 1929, Box 1, Folder 7, MacKinnon Papers.

tall that a special coffin had to be constructed and she had no doubt it had
to be carried by a "fabulous" number of men.[51] Smedley juxtaposed this
story to her mother, who died from "hard labor, undernourishment, and
a disease which she had no money to cure."[52] Rather sullenly, she wrote:
"It seemed that men could go anywhere, do anything, discover new
worlds, but that women could only trail behind or sit at home having
babies. Such a fate I rejected."[53]

Smedley aspired to "go anywhere, do anything, discover new worlds."
In Shanghai, this meant assuming a more masculine identity as a fellow
comrade, writer, journalist, and spy. Even her partner, Sorge, noted that
Smedley's uniquely masculine qualities made her a valuable comrade.
When he recalled his time in Shanghai, Sorge stressed that most women
were not credible informants, but Smedley was different. As a wife, "her
value was nil," but she had a "brilliant mind and fit in well as a news
reporter ... In short, she was like a man."[54] Her value as a "man"
amplifies the point Smedley already knew well, that men were revolutionaries and had access to the transnational world of anti-imperialist and
communist politics. Like many, Sorge imagined the world of espionage
and revolution as a homosocial one, and Smedley became his chief agent
and informant not because of their intimacy or her potential as a wife, but
rather because she was "like a man."

Much of Smedley's early years in Shanghai have been recounted
through the sources and perspectives of Sorge.[55] Smedley's intimate and
professional partnership with him began in 1930.[56] Like Smedley, Sorge
arrived in China under the cover of being a correspondent for a German
publication, *Soziologische Magazin*, although his official position was in
the Soviet military intelligence's Fourth Bureau of the Red Army General
Staff. His task was to develop an espionage ring for the Soviets in China,
and Smedley willingly assisted in efforts to build his Shanghai and Canton
operations. As the opening of this section demonstrated, her bond or
"comradeship" with Sorge intertwined the political cause with sexual
intimacy, without the restraints of marriage. She wrote of this moment
to her friends in New York: "Never have I known such good days, never
have I known such a healthy life, mentally, physically, psychically."[57]

---

[51] Smedley, *Battle Hymn*, 4.   [52] Smedley, *Battle Hymn*, 6.
[53] Smedley, *Battle Hymn*, 7.   [54] Quoted in Price, *Lives of Agnes Smedley*, 214.
[55] See Richard Sorge, *A Partial Documentation*.
[56] Price, *Lives of Agnes Smedley*, 195–208.
[57] Smedley to Florence Lennon, May 28, 1930, Box 1, Folder 7, MacKinnon Papers.

Smedley's independence extended beyond her romantic and intimate connections, and this made her an asset and ally for many in China and abroad. Indeed, she was the kind of anti-imperialist and communist sympathizer that moved easily across parties and ideological boundaries. She quickly developed strong ties to Chinese leftists and communists, including Madame Sun Yat-sen, widow of the famous nationalist in China. Not burdened by the constraints and conformity required of the communist party, Smedley could transcend boundaries in politics, friendship, and intimacy that were difficult to do for party members who built careers on their demonstrated fidelity and obedience to Moscow. When she moved between her work for the Communist International, the Chinese Communist Party, and the Soviet Russian state, she did so in the belief that all may have differences, but that all revolutionaries were working for the greater cause of liberation from capitalism and imperialism for Asia and the world.

Smedley's independence in Shanghai was a double-edged sword, however, and Smedley quickly became ensnared in a variety of conflicts and controversies that exposed her vulnerability as an independent actor and woman in a patriarchal and transnational world. The clearest threat was the British Secret Service. Already identified as an insurgent for her connections to Berlin's Indian revolutionary circles, Smedley gained notoriety among British intelligence. She noted in a letter to Margaret Sanger that she had been followed by British agents during a brief trip from Berlin to Paris during the summer of 1928, and she felt certain that she would "be put to much trouble" in a place where "one can just disappear."[58] Smedley admitted that her concerns sounded "ridiculous" and made of "detective story nonsense," but she warned American friends like Sanger that such danger was a reality for her and many others.

Her troubles with authorities in China began almost immediately, even before she reached Shanghai. Traveling through Manchuria and then on to Peking and Nanjing, Smedley noted that she had been terribly ill after eating toast and drinking coffee. In a letter to a friend in the US dated February 7, 1929, she contemplated something far more nefarious at work than natural or food-borne illness. Smedley suspected that she was poisoned after becoming aware that the American Consulate was tracking her in the belief that she was "in reality a Russian communist traveling on

---

[58] Smedley (Berlin) to Sanger, October 30, 1928, MSS123, Box 1, File 7, MacKinnon Papers.

an American passport."[59] Smedley suspected the American Consulate was "in cahoots" with the British Secret Service in attempting to poison her. Only the Germans, she added, had been helpful, largely because she was a correspondent for the *Frankfurter Zeitung*.

British and American surveillance of Smedley intensified over time. She regularly complained about the seizure of mail and frequently changed mailing addresses in the period between 1928 and 1933. Her letters to allies like Roger Baldwin of the American Civil Liberties Union pleaded for help in lobbying policy makers in the State Department to instruct the American Consulate to protect her rights as a citizen rather than align themselves with an "army of spies" serving British interests and working within the Shanghai Municipal Police.[60] By 1932, Smedley complained that the British created a blacklist of "undesirable and suspicious foreigners" to be deported from China and shared it with the American Consulate, which had opened a file on Smedley and sent secret reports on her activities to Washington.[61]

Among the most challenging issues confronting Smedley was her status as an American in a fluid and transnational milieu in Shanghai. Her citizenship mattered in this context, and adversaries questioned the legitimacy of her passport to strip her of extraterritorial rights guaranteed for American citizens in Shanghai. The city of Shanghai was diverse and complex, governed primarily by international stakeholders from China, France, and Britain, although inhabitants represented a truly cosmopolitan composition including substantial populations of Russians, British, French, Americans, South Asians, Portuguese, Germans, and Japanese. Americans enjoyed extraterritorial privileges that allowed them to live within Shanghai and still be protected and subjected to US rather than Chinese law. Smedley became the target of moderate and right-wing English publications in Shanghai, all attacking her ties to communism and suggesting that she violated her extraterritorial rights by acting in accordance with Soviet rather than American interests. A series of three editorials were printed by the *Shanghai Evening Post and Mercury* in 1931 raising concerns about her affiliations with Indian revolutionaries, anti-imperialists, and communists.[62] The attacks motivated Smedley to

[59] Smedley to Florence Lennon, February 7, 1929, MSS123, Box 1, File 7, MacKinnon Papers.
[60] Smedley to Roger Baldwin, December 24, 1931, International Committee for Political Prisoners (ICPP), (microfilm), New York Public Library, New York, New York (hereafter ICPP Papers).
[61] Smedley to Baldwin, August 7, 1932, ICPP Papers.   [62] See China files, ICPP papers.

work harder and contribute more to the anti-capitalist and anti-imperialist causes in Shanghai, as well as to strengthen her connections to Americans like Baldwin, whom she called upon for financial and propaganda assistance to counter such attacks on her citizenship and political rights.

While attacks on Smedley's radicalism from imperialists and the right were not surprising, the strong reprimand and criticism of her work by the Comintern was unanticipated. Disorderly and unruly women ran counter to the increasingly rigid framework of international communism by the 1930s, and this left Smedley in a precarious and compromised spot within the revolutionary movement. She increasingly failed to conform to party practices and expectations, and her employers in the Comintern increasingly viewed her rogue autonomy with great suspicion. In her own writing, she contemplated why she never joined the communist party, although she supported the cause. She wrote:

I could never place my mind and life unquestioningly at the disposal of their leaders . . . I could not become a mere instrument in the hands of men who believed that they held the one and only key to truth. Because of this I was often attacked from two sides: believers in capitalism called me a communist, a Red, or an Anarchist; Communists called me an individualist, an idealist, or a bourgeois democrat. One American woman Communist long delighted in dubbing me a "Smedleyite."[63]

The "Smedleyite" approach was shared with many anti-imperialists of the interwar years as they supported or sympathized with the anti-capitalist campaign of communism while seeking to remain autonomous from the rigid conformity required of party members. Yet, as a woman who failed to conform to both gender norms and political directives within the turbulent milieu of Shanghai and without strong affiliation and therefore legal protection of a nation-state given her contentious relationship with the American Consulate, her precarious status within the Comintern amplified her vulnerability. As Stalin asserted power over the USSR and increasingly tied the Comintern to state imperatives, strict loyalty and adherence to party norms and gender expectations were demanded of communists across the world in the 1930s. Communist women were expected to serve the party above all, and this usually meant serving as ancillary and subordinate roles to the men who led the movement. Smedley's individualism came to be seen as a deviation from

---

[63] Smedley, *Battle Hymn*, 10.

collective norms, a deviation worthy of expulsion from the party or death in the purges of the 1930s.

Smedley's radicalism extended beyond party politics as she challenged gender norms and expectations in Shanghai. Nowhere is this clearer than in her response to the Noulens Affair, a bust by British authorities in Shanghai of a covert network of anti-imperialist and communist activities across Asia.[64] The Noulens Affair, named after the alias of the two Comintern ringleaders, Hilaire Noulens and his wife (known to Smedley as Paul and Gertrude Ruegg, although their actual identities were Jakob Rudnik and Tatiana Moissenko),[65] the bust led to the confiscation of documents exposing financial and communication networks of the Comintern in Asia. This was a tremendous windfall for European and American anti-communist efforts, prompting a crisis for international communist operations in Asia and sending agents underground or into prison. The Rueggs were detained and charged by the Chinese authorities in Shanghai, originally sentenced to life in prison although ultimately released in 1937. Smedley, along with Madame Sun Yat-sen, spearheaded a protest campaign against the case, fundraised for their defense committee in Shanghai, and oversaw the couple's affairs following their arrest.[66]

Smedley was at her best as a transnational propagandist for the Noulens Affair, although much more was expected of her as a woman on the ground in Shanghai. As Brigitte Studer has argued, the "new woman" of the Comintern was celebrated as equal to men, yet gendered expectations persisted: "the mother came before the worker, the wife prioritized her husband's political work above her own, and the woman communist acted first of all to defend children and those who could not help themselves."[67] In particular, Smedley and Madame Sun were expected to care for the Rueggs' son, Jimmy, who remained in Shanghai after the parents were imprisoned. Smedley argued that she was never

---

[64] For a history of this event, see Heather Streets-Salter, "The Noulens Affair in East and Southeast Asia: International Communism in the Interwar Period," *Journal of American East Asian Relations*, 21 (2014).

[65] For simplicity, this chapter uses Paul and Gertrude Ruegg, which Smedley would have used to identify the couple.

[66] Copies of Statements of Account for Paul, Gertrude and Jimmy Ruegg found in Smedley correspondence, dated August 1935, in the Correspondence of Jenn Vincent, Paul Ruegg, Agnes Smedley, Soong Ching-ling, Grunfeld Papers: Addendum de Madame Jacqueline Vincent-Zurbrugg (Femme de Vincent), Private Archive. Hereafter Grunfeld Papers. I am grateful to Heather Streets-Salter for sharing these private archival files related to Smedley.

[67] Studer, *Transnational Cominterians*, 58.

made aware of these guardianship arrangements and had only been asked to oversee the defense committee and manage the financial affairs for the boy. When Smedley left China in 1933 for a trip to the Soviet Union and United States on other business, Gertrude Ruegg complained that Smedley had betrayed and abandoned her maternal duty to protect Jimmy. Upon her return, Smedley argued that neither she nor Madame Sun were capable of supporting Jimmy as a mother or guardian. Smedley explained this on several occasions to the Noulens' attorney in Geneva: "We are up to our throats in work. Neither of us can take on such work, nor can it be good for the child. Neither of us know what our own future life will be like."[68] Instead, Smedley and Madame Sun secured guardianship of Jimmy with a German family in Shanghai. Accepting no maternal responsibility or burden imposed on her by Gertrude, Smedley continued to manage the financial support of Jimmy and remitted funds to the German family until 1935 when they sent him to Nazi schools and hung a picture of Hitler in the home.[69]

Smedley criticized Gertrude for prioritzing motherhood and her son above the cause. Smedley disparaged Gertrude for being "ridiculous," because her life has "led her to lay the chief emphasis on her child, and she sees the world purely and simply through him."[70] In contrast, her husband is "very clear and reasonable" about Jimmy.[71] Smedley reminded the couple's attorney that many Chinese women have been imprisoned and their children have died of starvation. "Were Gertrude to compare the care given her child and the lack of care for the children of Chinese comrades, surely she would have no grounds at all for complaint."[72] For Smedley, the anti-imperialist and communist cause trumped individualism as it related to family and motherhood. Yet, paradoxically, she remained individualist or "Smedleyite," willing to eschew party conformity in other areas of her life by operating in the liminal spaces between party and non-party, Soviet Russia, and China, and communist and anti-imperialist.

By 1933, Smedley was marked by many in international communism as suspicious and potentially dangerous. She traveled to Soviet Russia and the United States between 1933 and 1934 to finish her third book, secure a publisher, and develop a plan for an English-language publication in

---

[68] Smedley to Jacqueline, July 19, 1935, Grunfeld Papers.
[69] Smedley, Correspondence regarding accounts of Rueggs, August 1935, Grunfeld Papers.
[70] Smedley to Jacqueline, Shanghai, June 19, 1935, Grunfeld Papers.
[71] Smedley (Shanghai) to Vincent (attorney, Geneva), May 30, 1935, Grunfeld Papers.
[72] Smedley (Shanghai) to Vincent (attorney, Geneva), May 30, 1935, Grunfeld Papers.

Shanghai funded by the Communist Party of the USA. Smedley then was dispatched from Moscow to New York to facilitate connections between the CPUSA's China Bureau and her contacts in Shanghai. In New York, she reconnected with old friends and met frequently with CPUSA members including America's China expert, Earl Browder. Ruth Price's biographical characterization of her interaction with the CPUSA is telling: "Party members who watched Agnes operate in New York did not know what to make of her."[73] None could figure out if she operated as an agent of the CPUSA, Chinese Communist Party, Comintern, or Soviet Union. No doubt her unconventional masculinity for a woman further perplexed her American comrades.

By the time she departed the US for Shanghai in 1934, the Soviet Union had instructed Sorge and his spy ring to avoid Smedley because she was no longer a trusted comrade. Back in Shanghai, Smedley quickly learned that the Comintern also sought to distance her from the organization. On May 5, 1935, the Political Commission of the Comintern met and decided to abandon any plans for Smedley to launch an anti-imperialist publication in Shanghai and to immediately recall her. Citing her failure to conform to instructions from Moscow, the commission saw Smedley as dangerous to the international mission. In addition, the minutes recommended that the Comintern committee also "prosecute those who recommended such a frivolous comrade for work."[74] By 1937, Earl Browder published a statement in the *Daily Worker* asserting that Smedley was an independent journalist in Shanghai and did not work for the communist party in the US or China.[75] This statement appears in the Comintern Archive, while there is no documentation relevant to her Comintern activities in Shanghai between 1928 and 1933 in her personal file. Consequently, she was written out of the Comintern Archive because her subversion of gender norms ran counter to the practices and expectations of even the most radical revolutionaries of the interwar world.

In Shanghai, Smedley sought friendship and comradeship over marriage and motherhood. Early on, her sexual and intimate ties to Sorge offered her deeper political connections without marriage, although even he credited her value as a comrade to her masculinity. Her decision to lead the defense committee and manage the finances of the Rueggs while rejecting maternal responsibility to Jimmy represented a serious deviation

[73] Price, *Lives of Agnes Smedley*, 250.
[74] Minutes of Political Commission, May 5, 1935, 495/4/348, Comintern Archive.
[75] 495/261/1533, Comintern Archive.

from the gendered practices of international communists. These departures from gender expectations compromised her security and made her increasingly vulnerable politically as she became the target of European and American intelligence, the Shanghai local police, the right-wing press, and communists and socialists. In her later years in Shanghai, which fall outside the scope of this chapter, Smedley sought closer affiliation with Chinese communists, embedding herself in the local milieu in Shanghai rather than the transnational networks of anti-imperialism and communism.

** **

Overall, Smedley's failure to comply with gender expectations and norms was critical to a vulnerability that she experienced at the hands of foes and friends alike. Anti-imperialist women who asserted greater autonomy were not celebrated but rather became subject to a dual attack by men on both sides of the imperialist and anti-imperialist, or communist and anti-communist, divide. Smedley's vast range of political alliances with communists and anti-imperialists in Germany, the United States, China, India, and the Soviet Union also complicated her place within an interwar transnationalism that sought to challenge capitalism and imperialism from a diversity of angles and agendas. Shanghai's fluid and shifting terrain provided a space for her to assert greater independence as an anti-imperialist and communist comrade rather than wife, yet it also exposed the very precarious and vulnerable spaces that autonomous political women had to inhabit in the interwar world.

A history of Smedley also reveals the significance of intimacy, marriage, and motherhood to the making and unmaking of transnational solidarities, as well as the duality of private and personal spaces that were intertwined for women who participated in revolutionary causes. In Berlin, her autonomy and affiliation to feminism were curtailed by her conjugal and private expectations as an anti-imperialist wife. Even though Chatto was a radical in relation to his Indian colleagues and communalist norms, he was not willing to challenge patriarchy and gender inequality. Only a life outside anti-imperialist marriage provided Smedley with the freedom she sought, although she faced constant criticism and reprimand for her independence and radicalism particularly in her openly intimate ties with Sorge and her refusal to take on motherly responsibilities for imprisoned comrades. Her intense vulnerability led to several hospitalizations for heart complications and later stomach cancer. She was certain that these ailments were the consequence of her turbulent life as a revolutionary anti-imperialist, although she was willing to make sacrifices for the cause. She once wrote after her arrival in Shanghai: "I've chosen my way for there is no other. I just hope I get shot while I am young. A woman of my kind is impossible when old. There is no place for us."[76] While she was not shot, she died at the youthful age of fifty-eight after what seemed several lifetimes of revolutionary activities that transcended gender, racial, national, and political boundaries in ways that were radical even to her most radical contemporaries.

---

[76] Smedley (Shanghai) to Florence Lennon, September 11, 1929, MSS123, Box 1, File 7, Mackinnon Papers.

7

Cheikh Anta Diop's Recovery of Egypt: African History as Anticolonial Practice

Sarah C. Dunstan

When the Congolese scholar V. Y. Mudimbe argued in 1994 that knowledge of Africa has, since the time of Greek empire, 'been represented in Western scholarships by "fantasies" and "constructs"', he was making a claim that underpinned much of the anticolonial and anti-racist thinking of the twentieth century.[1] Indeed, the very idea that Africa had a history at all had been long refuted in Western historical narratives. Delivering lectures in the 1820s on the philosophy of history, Frederick Hegel casually observed that 'Africa ... is no historical part of the World; it has no movement for development to exhibit. Historical movements in it – that is in its northern part – belong to the Asiatic or European World'.[2] Writing over one hundred and forty years after Hegel, in 1965, the Regius Professor of Modern History at Oxford, Hugh Trevor-Roper, still felt comfortable writing 'Undergraduates, seduced, as always, by the changing breath of journalistic fashion, demand that they should be taught the history of Black Africa. Perhaps, in the future, there will be some African history to teach. But at present there is none, or very little: there is only the history of the Europeans in Africa.'[3]

Throughout the period separating Hegel from Trevor-Roper, the notion of a lack of history was intimately connected to theories of human evolution that were deployed to justify racist hierarchies of imperial

---

[1] V. Y. Mudimbe, *The Idea of Africa* (Oxford: James Currey Ltd, 1994): xv.
[2] Friederich Hegel, *The Philosophy of History*, trans. J. Sibree (Mineola, New York: Dover Publications, Inc., 1956 [1899]), 99.
[3] Hugh Trevor-Roper, *The Rise of Christian Europe* (New York: Harcourt, Brace and World, 1965), 9.

development and unequal access to rights. The self-ordained *mission civilisatrice* of the French Third Republic (1870–1940) rested, like British imperial justifications of humanitarian intervention and development, upon hierarchies of racial order. French anthropologists such as the influential Lucien Lévy-Bruhl wrote about white Europeans in direct contrast to their non-Western counterparts, describing them in terms of a 'primitive mentality' incapable of the abstract thought used by Europeans. In this schema, concepts beyond the concrete and immediate had no place for African peoples, and thus notions of time, and of history, were beyond them.[4] In contrast, European civilizations were part of a teleological progression of time that reflected their so-called superiority. In particular, the Third Republic notion of *la plus grande France*, or an expanded French nation, rested upon the idea that the colonies were an integral part of France, and any historical significance of these regions was contingent upon France's place in history.[5]

Efforts to equate race with stages of human development were, of course, deeply contested by anticolonial and anti-racist scholars and activists from the very beginning. Indeed, despite the confidence of his assertion, Trevor-Roper's perspective was under siege, as his own admission of student demand for the subject of African history demonstrated. By 1965, many of the African peoples who had been ruled by European empires for centuries had won their independence. The reconfiguration of understandings of African history, and specifically African political and intellectual history, had played an important role during the nationalist decolonizing movements leading to this independence.[6] Pre-colonial political organization in Africa took centre stage as a means of asserting the readiness of African peoples for political independence.

It is important to understand that this approach was a direct response to the research that had been conducted in colonial contexts, studies by anthropologists, international relations specialists and the like

---

[4] See Lucien Lévy-Bruhl, *Les fonctions mentales dans les sociétés inférieures* (Paris: Les Presses universitaires de France, 1910); *La mentalité primitive* (Paris: Les Presses universitaires de France. Collection Bibliothèque de philosophie contemporaine, 1922).

[5] On the 'historical reality' of Greater France, see Gary Wilder, *The French Imperial Nation-State: Negritude and Colonial Humanism between the Two World Wars* (Chicago: University of Chicago Press, 2005), 24–42.

[6] William G. Martin, 'Africa and World-Systems Analysis: A Post-Nationalist Project?' in *Writing African History* (Rochester, NY: University of Rochester Press, 2005), 381–402 (esp. 386–390).

who sought to understand African peoples so as to better rule them.[7] Lévy-Bruhl, for example, believed that ethnology was the route to 'more rational and more human modes of colonisation'.[8] The Senegalese historian, physicist and Egyptologist Cheikh Anta Diop flipped the perspective on this approach when he wrote: 'If we are to believe the Western works, it is in vain that one would seek a single civilization ... which is the work of Black peoples. The truth is what serves and, here, what serves colonialism: the goal is ... to make the Black believe that he was never responsible for anything of value'.[9] The challenge of anticolonial thinkers, then, was to dismantle this version of history that so underpinned the machinery of colonial administration.[10] Diop advocated the use of scientific modes of historical enquiry that provided irrefutable evidence in the face of racism. Such evidence could then be used in the service of anticolonialism and anti-racist politics.

A great deal of scholarship has been devoted to teasing out the intricacies of Cheikh Anta Diop's thought and its legacies.[11] My aim in this chapter is to contextualise his intellectual trajectory by showing how

[7] Achille Mbembe, *On the Postcolony* (Berkeley, CA: University of California Press, 2001), 7.

[8] Michel Leiris, *C'est-à-dire. Entretien avec Sally Price and Jean Jamin* (Paris: Jean-Michel Place, 1992), 38.

[9] Cheikh Anta Diop, 'Preface: Edition 1954', *Nations Nègres et Culture: De L'antiquité nègre égyptienne aux problèmes culturels de l'Afrique Noire d'aujourd'hui* (Paris: Présence Africaine, 1979 [1954]), 14. NB Unless otherwise stated, all translations from the original French are my own.

[10] This mode of thinking can be seen in diverse Black anticolonial and anti-racist movements from Kwame Nkrumah's Pan-Africanism in Ghana through to W. E. B. Du Bois' writings: Michael Hanchard, 'Afro-Modernity: Temporality, Politics, and the African Diaspora', *Public Culture* 11:1 (1991): 251.

[11] This is particularly true of debate around Diop's Black Egypt and Two Cradle theses. Amongst many others see Cheikh Mbaké Diop, 'La Renaissance africaine: Enjeux et perspectives culturelles, scientifiques et techniques dans l'œuvre de Cheikh Anta Diop Thierno Diop', *Présence Africaine*, 2007-1er semestre 175/177 (2008): 469–497; 'Cheikh Anta Diop et le matérialisme historique', *Africa Development / Afrique et Développement* 23:1 (1998): 87–111; Troy D. Allen, 'Cheikh Anta Diop's Two Cradle Theory: Revisited', *Journal of Black Studies* 38:6 (July 2008): 813–829; Théophile Obenga, 'Méthode et Conception historiques de Cheikh Anta Diop', *Présence Africaine* 74 (1970): 3–28; James G. Spady, 'Dr. Cheikh Anta Diop and the Background of Scholarship on Black Interest in Egyptology and Nile Valley Civilizations', *Présence Africaine* 149/150 (1989): 303–304; John Henrik Clarke, 'The Historical Legacy of Cheikh Anta Diop : His Contributions to a New Concept of African History', *Présence Africaine* 149/150 (1989): 110–120; Regina Jennings, 'Cheikh Anta Diop, Malcolm X, and Haki Madhubuti: Claiming and Containing Continuity in Black Language and Institutions', *Journal of Black Studies* 33:2 (2002): 126–144.

Diop's efforts to challenge the racial hierarchies embedded in his historical discipline operated in tandem with his anticolonial politics and with the work of other anticolonial and anti-racist thinkers. To show, in short, how, in the decades immediately following the Second World War, the re-writing of history was a central part of what Paul Gilroy has called a Black Atlantic counter-culture of modernity.[12] Doing so is also revealing of the ways that Western institutions shaped the prevailing understandings of history and historical truth.

I begin with a brief description of the context in which Diop made an intervention into Francophone ethnographic understandings of African history: the 1948 special issue of *Le Musée vivant*. From there, I chart Diop's trajectory in relation to other key anticolonial thinkers in the Francophone context in this moment – specifically those attached to the *Présence Africaine* network – before connecting his historical work to the efforts of African American historians and activists making similar claims about the value of history and historical consciousness for defeating racism and colonialism. Finally, I turn to the Diop's triumphant doctoral defence in 1960, and gesture towards the decolonizing efforts of African states to cement a new version of African history in the emerging world order. A key part of this story will be the multiple spaces in which efforts towards anticolonial and anti-racist histories were developed: museums such as the Musée de l'Homme; journals such as the *Le Musée vivant* (the review of the Association populaire des amis des musées); the *Journal of Negro History* and *Présence Africaine*, as well as in initiatives funded the United Nations Educational, Scientific, and Cultural Organization (UNESCO).

ETHNOGRAPHY, BLACK MODERNITY AND *LE MUSÉE VIVANT*

When Cheikh Anta Diop arrived in Paris in 1946 from his home town of Diourbel, Senegal, the 23-year-old found himself in a France that was in the process of re-definition.[13] As the constitution of the French Fourth Republic was drafted, debates raged about the extent to which the colonial peoples of the French empire would be granted political

---

[12] See Paul Gilroy, *The Black Atlantic: Modernity and Double Consciousness* (Cambridge, MA: Harvard University Press, 1994).

[13] Gary Wilder has described this moment as one of 'world historical opening' not just for France and the French empire but for the world more broadly: *Freedom Time: Negritude, Decolonization and the Future of the World* (Durham, NC, and London: Duke University Press, 2015), 1.

representation and belonging. Diop began his research into the African past that same year, cognizant that prevailing myths about Black inferiority rested, in part, upon historical narratives that erased the Black African presence from world history. Within France at this time, two institutions were instrumental in establishing public understandings of African history. Both were part of the colonial project and both were deeply entwined with notions of France's *mission civilisatrice*: the National Museum of African and Oceanic Art and the Musée de l'Homme.[14] The former was opened in 1931 as part of the Colonial Exhibition held that year, whilst the latter was built in 1937 as part of a new era of ethnographic thought. It was a reconfigured version of the older Musée d'Ethnologie du Trocadéro, funded by the Ministry of Colonies and intended as the repository for ethnographic objects collected by the research teams of the Institut d'Ethnologie.[15]

The three founders of the Musée de l'Homme, George Henri-Rivière, Paul Rivet and Jacques Soustelle, were leaders in French ethnography in this period. They were also part of a new generation of ethnographers that saw their academic work as key to the struggle against racism, and who pushed back against some of the racial hierarchies embedded in pro-imperial projects such as the 1931 Colonial Exhibition. As Rivière phrased it in 1932 'we seek to illustrate the history of human endeavours and help to dispel prejudice against the supposedly inferior races'.[16] For Paul Rivet, the new Musée de l'Homme was an opportunity not just to further such research within the field, but to directly engage the French population at large.[17] As Rivet's fellow ethnographer Jacques Soustelle put it 'The museum of tomorrow can be the museum of the people ... through the union of the technicians and the museum-goers.'[18]

Efforts to reach 'museum-goers' were not limited to the museum exhibits themselves. In 1936 Soustelle, Rivet and Rivière also co-founded the Association populaire des amis des musées (APAM) to further the aims of the museum. APAM was charged with cultural programming and

---

[14] On the nuanced history of the Musée de l'Homme, and French traditions of ethnographic research see Alice Conklin, *In the Museum of Man: Race, Anthropology, and Empire in France, 1850–1950* (Ithaca, NY: Cornell University Press, 2013).

[15] Paul Rivet and Georges-Henri Rivière, 'La réorganisation du Musée d'Ethnographie du Trocadéro', *Outre-Mer* 2:2 (June 1930): 138–148.

[16] Georges Henri Rivière to Gaston Monnerville, 22 December 1932.

[17] Conklin, *In the Museum of Man*, 101.

[18] Jacques Soustelle, 'Musée vivants, pour une culture populaire', *Vendredi*, 26 August 1936.

with a new journal, *Le Musée vivant*. Both the museum and APAM were developed under the auspices of the French Popular Front government. Led by Léon Blum, this government sought to establish the spirit of democracy amongst the French people through a series of cultural initiatives including APAM.[19] The men and women who became members of APAM were drawn from the ranks of the Popular Front, and included a number of recognisable figures in the Parisian landscape, from the Popular Front Minister for National Education, Jean Zay, to the poet Tristan Tzara, through the trade unionist Henri Raynaud, and the Martinican poet and politician Aimé Césaire. Although possessing slightly different ideas about the future of France's democracy, these individuals shared a belief that historical knowledge and cultural appreciation could shape the nature of France's democracy.

In the mid-1930s, this desire to reach the wider populace was directly connected to the goal of combatting scientific racism and fascism, especially as it was then manifesting in France and Germany.[20] Soustelle addressed this directly in an interview in *L'Oeuvre*, where he argued that 'We ethnologists, we know that there is no race that has not contributed to the common patrimony of civilization ... Racism depends on a first confusion between the idea of race and culture.'[21] In the minds of the Musée de l'Homme founders and workers, the Second World War only further underlined the urgency of overcoming these misconceptions. This is not to say that thinkers such as Rivet or Soustelle rejected the idea of racial difference. To the contrary, they embraced a humanism that espoused tolerance and begged the appreciation of individual cultures on their own merits.[22]

The November 1948 special issue of *Le Musée vivant* was a product of this kind of anti-racist inclination, dedicated in particular to the 'cultural problems of Black Africa'.[23] It was also published to coincide with the 100-year anniversary of the French abolition of slavery and thus titled '1848 Abolition de l'esclavage – 1948 Evidence de la culture nègre'.

---

[19] On the cultural politics of the Popular Front see P. Ory, *La belle illusion. Culture et politique sous le signe du Front populaire, 1935–1938* (Paris: Plon, 1994).

[20] Conklin, *In the Museum of Man*, 144.

[21] Georges Schneeberger, 'Un quart d'heure avec un jeune: Jacques Soustelle', *L'œuvre*, 20 November 1938.

[22] Conklin, *In the Museum of Man*, 18–27.

[23] Madeleine Rousseau and Cheikh Anta Diop (eds.), '1848 Abolition de l'esclavage – 1948 Evidence de la culture nègre', special issue of *Le Musée vivant* (November 1948): 36–37.

Madeleine Rousseau and Cheikh Anta Diop were the editors. The entire issue was an exercise in temporal dissonance, with articles oscillating between perspectives that suggest Africans are about to enter into modernity to the argument that they were, in fact, already there, they just need to be recognised as such.[24]

At the time, Diop was already working on the manuscript for his ground-breaking 1954 book *Nations, Nègres et Culture* as well as being involved in the Rassemblement Démocratique Africaine (RDA). The latter organization was a Pan-African political *bloc* of French West and Equatorial African delegates elected to the French National Assembly. Primarily socialist in orientation, the group turned into a political movement encompassing many of the African students in Paris, including Diop. In his capacity as the Secretary General of the RDA students' group, Diop understood the struggle for independence in two ways: political freedom from empire, and the problem of 'restoring the collective national African personality'.[25] Colonialism had distorted African understandings of themselves and it was necessary to return to the African past, and to African languages, to re-assert the African personality necessary for independence. He was a strong advocate of basing this return upon a 'scientific' approach rather than 'taking liberties with scientific truth, by unveiling a mythical, embellished past'.[26] In this, Diop was scathing of 'infantile leftists' whose flights of fancy only opened Black peoples up to further ridicule. Diop's own doctoral work, the product of expertise in archaeology, Egyptology, linguistics and physics, stressed the importance of rational, scientific study. In part, this was connected to Diop's desire for African peoples to be taken seriously not just by themselves but by those who had infantilised them through imperialism.

Indeed, Diop's decision to pursue a doctorate in Paris was inextricable from this political project. It was also the result of a rather eclectic pathway to the study of history. When he had first arrived in Paris in 1946, he was enrolled in a mathematics degree although unofficially studying African history in his free time. By 1947 he had switched to studying philosophy under Gaston Bachelard at the Sorbonne whilst

---

[24] Pierre-Philippe Fraiture describes this in terms of 'a redemptory model': *Past Imperfect: Time and African Decolonization, 1945–1960* (Liverpool: Liverpool University Press, 2020), 5.

[25] Diop, 'Preface: The Meaning of Our Work', in Diop, *The African Origin of Civilization: Myth or Reality*, trans. Mercer Cook (New York: Lawrence Hill & Company, 1974 [1955]), xiii.

[26] Ibid., xiii.

simultaneously pursuing a study of the history of the Senegalese languages of Serer and Wolof.[27] From there he continued to pursue multiple disciplines, enrolling in a course of doctoral study titled 'L'avenir culturel de la pensée africaine' under the direction of the philosopher Gaston Bachelard, as well as in two chemistry certifications. It was at this juncture, within the context of this interdisciplinary training and political community, that he was invited to co-edit the special issue with Madeleine Rousseau.

Born in 1895 in Troyes, France, Rousseau was a curator and museologist who had also amassed an extensive personal collection of artefacts from various regions in Africa.[28] She had begun her career as a painter but, as a result of the financial hardships of the Great Depression, had pivoted in the mid-1930s to the study of art history and curation at the Ecole du Louvre.[29] From APAM's launch, she had been the editor of its journal and, by 1938, had also become the general secretary of the organization. When the French Popular Front government fell from power that same year, she was instrumental in keeping the organization going and in shoring up support from Parisian intellectuals. This was partly possible due to her appointment, in 1943, as Professor of Visual Arts at the Institut des hautes études cinématographiques. By the end of the Second World War, she had secured for APAM the support of such prominent names as the poet Paul Éluard, the artist Pablo Picasso, the architect Le Corbusier and sculptor Henri Laurens.

When Rousseau had first begun collecting African and Oceanic art, her interest had been primarily aesthetic. Indeed, many of the artists and patrons attached to APAM were collectors of such art, with little regard for the often violent provenance of works looted from their original creators. In the post-war period, however, Rousseau increasingly subscribed to the Musée de l'Homme aim of revalorizing indigenous cultures that had been stultified by colonialism.[30] In her Latin Quarter apartment, she held gatherings amongst her collections that brought together a sort of who's who of the Parisian artistic landscape. This included Black

[27] Diop, 'Origines de la langue et de la race Valaf', *Présence Africaine* 4 (1948): 672–679.
[28] Elizabeth Harney, 'Constellations and Coordinates: Repositioning Postwar Paris in Stories of African Modernism', in Elizabeth Harney and Ruth B. Phillips (eds.), *Mapping Modernisms: Art, Indigeneity, Colonialism* (Durham, NC: Duke University Press, 2018): 304–334. (esp. 311).
[29] Danielle Maurice, 'L'art et l'éducation populaire: Madeleine Rousseau, une figure singulière des années 1940–1960', *Histoire de l'art* 63 (2008): 111–112.
[30] Maurice, 'L'art et l'education populaire', 117.

intellectuals and activists such as Cheikh Anta Diop; the so-called fathers of the political-cultural movement of *négritude* and elected members of the French Constituent Assembly, Aimé Césaire, Léopold Sédar Senghor and Léon-Gontran Damas; and the Guinean political activist Sékou Touré.

Discussions at these gatherings opened Rousseau's eyes to the political significance of African art and culture. Rousseau began to publish Black writing in *Le Musée vivant* – including a poem of Césaire's – as well as to question the inclusion of contemporary African art in the ethnology collections at the Musée de l'Homme. Ethnographic collections, Rousseau argued, were supposed to be dedicated to 'the most ordinary objects of everyday material life'. Juxtaposing these 'ordinary materials' with the 'works of art created by pre-Columbian America, Africa, Oceania' was to devalue their very real artistic contribution and, in consequence, the peoples who created them.[31] It was increasingly evident to Rousseau that regardless of the anti-racist intentions of the Musée de l'Homme, the reality remained that the new museum's contents were drawn from collections initially used as evidence for the racial inferiority of colonised peoples.[32] Racial difference had become part of modern ways of seeing the world, and the osteological exhibitions in particular perpetuated such classifications of humanity.

Eventually, these realizations provided the impetus for the 1948 special issue dedicated to the centenary since the French abolition of slavery. The idea was to showcase the potential for modernity in African culture, and to therefore disprove racist stereotypes of inherent Black inferiority. The issue included a number of articles by Rousseau, as well as another APAM member, Olivier le Corneur. Contributors also included Michel Leiris, Denise Paulme and Jean Laude, from the Musée de l'Homme; and two anticolonial historians Emile Tersen and Jean Dresch. Whilst a few of the articles, like Tersen's, were dedicated to economic and political questions in Africa, the majority of the issue explored the question of African culture and its role in world history; a role that had predated European occupation but which now included integration into Western civilization.[33] The preface was written by the African American novelist Richard Wright, who had become a French citizen in 1947 and whose

---

[31] M. Rousseau, 'Sur quelques musées et expositions', *Le Musée vivant* 4 (September 1946): 9.
[32] Conklin, *In the Museum of Man*, 147.
[33] Madeleine Rousseau, 'En marge de l'histoire ancienne africaine', *Le Musée vivant* (November 1948): 19–20.

own work was considered to be at the vanguard of contemporary African diasporic culture.

It is evident from one of her contributions to the special issue – 'La Philosophie des nègres' – that Rousseau subscribed in part to an essentialist vision of Blackness that emphasised the artistic imagination and purity of original African cultures.[34] Drawing on Placide Tempel's (in)famous 1945 essay on Bantu Philosophy, Rousseau contended that this creative energy and artistic imagination 'determines Black behaviour in its entirety'.[35] Indeed, Rousseau believed that this descriptor worked for all pre-industrial Black civilizations, from ancient Egypt through to contemporary Black cultures. Such a view effectively flattened Black African history into a static production of culture that did not change (or develop) over time. The value, or authenticity, of African art came from the way that it lay outside of time. In a similar vein, a piece from the Belgian colonial functionary stationed in the Belgian Congo, Auguste Verbeken, framed his appreciation for Congolese oral story telling traditions in terms of the need to protect 'the indigenous style ... against destructive influences'.[36]

Richard Wright's preface similarly demonstrated an atemporal understanding of African culture. He commended the issue for showcasing the 'astounding art of Africa', exemplar of a culture which 'cannot be allowed to perish under the yoke of imperialism' and 'neglect'. He read this turn to Africa very much in terms of the collapse or crisis of European civilization, arguing that 'we must realize that Europe needs Africa perhaps more desperately than African needs Europe, for it is among these pre-industrial millions of people that the impulse to live and be is to be found in all its original purity'.[37] Wright's emphasis on the 'purity' of Africa is nonetheless indicative of the way that even he was thinking about the

---

[34] As Pierre-Phillipe Fraiture has noted, this is not necessarily true of some of her other contributions to the special issue, some of which are less explicitly determinist. It is nonetheless a position that seems to have formed part of her thinking on African art at this time: *Past Imperfect*, 11.

[35] Rousseau, 'La Philosophie des nègres', 9.

[36] Auguste Verbeken, 'La Poésie nègre du Congo', in Madeleine Rousseau and Cheikh Anta Diop (eds.), '1848 Abolition de l'esclavage – 1948 Evidence de la culture nègre', special issue of *Le Musée vivant* (November 1948): 13–18 (17).

[37] Richard Wright, 'Preface', in Madeleine Rousseau and Cheikh Anta Diop (eds.), '1848 Abolition de l'esclavage – 1948 Evidence de la culture nègre', special issue of *Le Musée vivant* (November 1948): 3.

continent in terms of a colonial teleology.[38] That is to say, he thought of it as pre-modern.[39]

A similar approach to the temporal positioning of African peoples can be found in Michel Leiris' contribution to the special issue, 'Message de l'Afrique'. Contemporaneously involved, alongside Claude Lévi-Strauss, and Alfred Métraux, in UNESCO initiatives to combat racism, Leiris was part of a new generation of French ethnographers who espoused theories of cultural relativism that argued against race as a determinant of civilization.[40] In his piece for *Le Musée vivant*, Leiris argued that Africa is 'marching towards its own discovery', towards an entry in modernity.[41] He intended this in the spirit of anticolonialism, contending that this entrance into modernity cannot occur in an imperial relationship. Contrary to the French imperialist discourse of a *mission civilisatrice*, Leiris declared that it is not for 'those whites who, until recently, regarded themselves as the absolute masters [of Africans]' to 'play the role of spiritual guides' for this rediscovery. Like Wright, Leiris was ambivalent about the progress made by Europeans relative to Africa, writing that recent Western progress seemed to have been more in the lines of destruction, oppression and torture, rather than any great civilization. In this context, he declared: 'once they have achieved equality with those who have ceased to believe that they are the designated custodians of the only true culture, Black peoples will have a lesson to impart'.[42]

Cheikh Anta Diop also feared the damage done to Black African cultures by 'European contamination'.[43] He called instead for an African renaissance that would entail the full intellectual decolonization of African peoples. This involved, for Diop, a rejection of European

---

[38] Fraiture has covered similar ground here and also read this as indicative of Wright's ignorance on the subject of sub-Saharan Africa: *Past Imperfect*, 3.

[39] Kevin Gaines makes this point in terms of Wright's failure 'to question his teleology of modernization': 'Revisiting Richard Wright in Ghana: Black Radicalism and the Dialectics of Diaspora', *Social Text* 19:2 (2001): 75–101 (75).

[40] Michel Leiris, *Race and Culture* (Paris: UNESCO, 1951); Claude Lévi-Strauss, *Race and History* (Paris: UNESCO, 1952). See also Elazar Barkan, *The Retreat of Scientific Racism: Changing Concepts of Race in Britain and the United States between the World Wars* (Cambridge: Cambridge University Press, 1992), 341; Conklin, *In the Museum of Man*, 9–27.

[41] 'Message de l'Afrique', in Madeleine Rousseau and Cheikh Anta Diop (eds.), '1848 Abolition de l'esclavage – 1948 Evidence de la culture nègre', special issue of *Le Musée vivant* (November 1948), 5–6 (6).

[42] Ibid.

[43] Cheikh Anta Diop, 'Quand pourra-t-on parler d'une renaissance africaine?' *Le Musée vivant* (1948): 36–37; 57–65 (57).

cultures and a revival of African authenticity. Language was central to these concerns, as Diop was uncertain that African writers using the languages of empire could be considered truly African. He asked, 'Without underestimating the value of these African foreign language writers, do we have the right to consider their writings as the basis of an African culture?'[44] For him the main sticking point here was whether Black peoples could truly express themselves without deploying 'the genius of their own language'.[45]

Language was a key preoccupation of Diop's, a question inextricable from that of history.[46] A few years after the special issue came out, in 1952, Diop was ready to take his thesis of renaissance further, having developed a methodology of linguistic analysis to argue for a direct lineage between Egyptian civilization and present day sub-Saharan Black communities. In the same way that Europeans linked their cultural and political power to greatness of Roman and Greek civilizations, so too could Black peoples look to a Black Egyptian civilization to bolster their confidence in the present day. Diop contended that 'the moral fruit' of Egyptian civilization needed 'to be counted among the assets of the Black', and as a blueprint for a postcolonial world order.[47]

MAKING THE CASE FOR A *PRÉSENCE AFRICAINE*

Diop also spoke on this topic at the 1956 Congress of Black Writers and Artists held at the Sorbonne under the auspices of the journal and publishing house *Présence Africaine*. *Présence Africaine* was the project of a group of students and intellectuals led by the Senegalese senator to the French parliament Alioune Diop.[48] The journal had been launched in 1947 and, by 1948, had expanded to include a publishing house. In his statement of the journal's aims, Alioune Diop explicitly indicated that the journal was 'open to ... all men (white, yellow or black) who can help define African originality and hasten its insertion into the modern

---

[44] Diop, 'Quand pourra-t-on parler d'une renaissance africaine?', 58.   [45] Ibid., 58.

[46] See Sarah C. Dunstan, '"La Langue de nos maîtres": Linguistic Hierarchies, Dialect, and Canon Decolonization during and after the Présence Africaine Congress of 1956', *Journal of Modern History* 93:4 (December 2021): 877–878.

[47] Diop, 'Vers une idéologie politique africaine', *La Voix de l'Afrique noire* (February 1952): 5–24.

[48] On *Présence Africaine* see Sarah C. Dunstan, *Race, Rights and Reform: Black Activism in the French Empire and the United States from World War I to Cold War* (New York: Cambridge University Press, 2021): 207–213; 226–231; 237–278.

world'.[49] In much the same way as Cheikh Anta Diop and Madeleine Rousseau's special issue of *Le Musée vivant* had sought to open dialogue about the problems facing Africa, Alioune Diop created a forum for the grappling with these issues. The question of connecting Africans and African-descended peoples with modernity was at the forefront of these debates. As the Madagascan poet and politician and regular contributor to the *Présence Africaine* journal Jacques Rabemananjara would later put it, the Second World War had entailed 'the defeat of all the Western values that we had learnt under colonization', thereby puncturing historical narratives of European civilizational prowess and linear progress.[50] *Présence Africaine* was an anti-racist exercise in creating new ways of understanding the present in relation to the past.

Cheikh Anta Diop certainly offered a new way of thinking about the Black past in his speech to the Congress. Drawing from research published in his 1954 book *Nations nègres et culture*, he declared 'we have come to discover that the ancient Pharaonic Egyptian civilization was undoubtedly a Negro civilization'.[51] *Nations nègres et culture* was based on a manuscript Diop had originally prepared as a doctoral thesis in 1954. That thesis was the product of both his work under Bachelard, and the work he had done on a secondary thesis question, 'Qu'étaient les Egyptiennes predynastiques?', which he pursued from 1951 under the supervision of the Sorbonne's first Chair of Anthology, the Dogon expert Marcus Griaule. Despite, or perhaps because of, the influential character of both Diop's supervisors, Bachelard and Griaule, Diop was unable to persuade a jury of examiners to pass the manuscript, which was judged 'too aggressive'.[52] Indeed, the argument Diop was making about Egypt as Black civilization was a direct attack upon the thinking of such French luminaries as the aforementioned anthropologist Lévy-Bruhl. 'Nowhere', Diop declared, 'was there a primitive mentality in the sense intended by Lévy-Bruhl'.[53] To the contrary, Black Africans had created the very first civilization on Earth, a civilization that had led to all those that came

[49] Alioune Diop, 'Niam N'goura ou les raisons d'être de Présence Africaine', *Présence Africaine* 1 (November–December 1947): 7.

[50] Jacques Rabemananjara, 'Alioune Diop, le cenobite de la culture noire', in *Hommage à Alioune Diop, Fondateur de Présence Africaine* (Rome: Éditions des amis italiens de présence africaine, 1977), 17.

[51] *Présence Africaine* 8–10 (June–November 1956): 339.

[52] Catherine Coquery-Vidrovitch, 'L'Historiographie africaine en afrique', *Revue Tiers Monde* (October–December 2013): 114.

[53] Diop, *Nations nègres*, 52.

after, including the Roman and Greek civilizations that Europeans claimed as their antecedents.[54] Such an understanding of Egypt was certainly not accepted within the French Egyptological circles, or, indeed, more broadly. To take this argument seriously was, as Diop observed, to undermine the European characterizations of colonialism as 'a human duty ... to raise the African to the level of the rest of humanity'. It argued, to the contrary, that Europeans had been responsible for obliterating African societies and preventing their natural development.[55] This approach appealed, however, to the broader ideological project of *Présence Africaine*, and Alioune Diop organised to have it published as a book.

Writing in 1955, in reaction to Diop's *Nations nègres et culture*, Aimé Césaire described it as 'the most audacious book yet written by a Negro' because it unravelled the white efforts to hide the truth of Black Egypt from Africans.[56] The American sociologist Immanuel Wallerstein perhaps put it more succinctly when he noted that Diop's 'bold hypothesis' essentially inverted Western assumptions of superiority: 'if the Ancient Egyptians were Negroes, then European civilization is but a derivation of African achievement'.[57] Diop's portrait of Egyptian civilization was not, in fact, new. As Wallerstein himself noted, other Black scholars had been similarly refuting Western narratives around Egypt for some time. The eminent African American scholar activist, W. E. B. Du Bois, is one such example. The difference seemed to be, as Wallerstein reluctantly admitted, that Diop's argument was 'not presented without supporting data'.[58] In other words, by all the contemporary standards of rational scientific enquiry, Diop's argument was supported by evidence.

The question of what constituted 'evidence' for the purposes of rational scientific enquiry was highly racialised in this moment. When Wallerstein raised this issue in his review of Diop's work, he was referring to Diop's use of linguistic analysis, his careful reference to ancient sources, and to his analysis of surviving Egyptian art to bolster his argument. Wallerstein's comment gives us an insight into the manner in which challenges to Western historical narratives were received. They had to be couched in a rationalist frame, relying on notions of Western science

[54] Ibid., 54.   [55] Ibid.

[56] Aimé Césaire, *Discourse on Colonialism*, trans. Joan Pinkham (New York: Monthly Review Press, 1972 [1955]), 56.

[57] Immanuel Wallerstein, *Africa: The Politics of Independence* (New York: Vintage Books, 1961), 129–130.

[58] Ibid., 130.

rather than being attacked on the basis of their underlying racism. Diop, reflecting on this issue in 1971, put it this way:

One must, in the first phase, establish scientifically the facts, and in this domain not even the least complacence is permitted. The way in which unbiased scientific truth must be presented depends on the circumstances, because in the order of the human sciences, it is one thing to demonstrate the veracity and it is another to make this accepted right away.

Only once the science was irreproachable was it possible to 'drive out the bad faith of men' who did not want to accept that history did not bear out their ideas of racial hierarchy.[59]

It is perhaps because of this that Wallerstein could dubiously accept Diop's thesis but American academia had hitherto refused the claims of Black historians such as W. E. B. Du Bois, and William Leo Hansberry. Both men had made a similar arguments about Egyptian civilization in their work. In Du Bois' case, he had written on the subject in his 1947 *The World and Africa*, as well as earlier in his 1939 *Black Folk: Then and Now*, and his 1915 *The Negro*.[60] Certainly, Du Bois was not a trained Egyptologist: his PhD from Harvard had focused on more modern history, titled 'The Suppression of the African Slave Trade in the United States of America, 1638–1871'. Nevertheless, as his qualifications make clear, he was a highly trained scholar of piercing intellect. Rather than turning to so-called scientific evidence, however, Du Bois' book was premised on reading the existing scholarship against the grain and taking into account research by Black scholars who had struggled to publish. That is to say, he was taking to task the very practice of Western historical method for its racial biases. Indeed, Du Bois explicitly declared 'I am challenging Authority – even Maspero, Sayce, Reisner, Breasted, and hundreds of other men of highest respectability, who did not attack but studiously ignored the Negro on the Nile and in the world and talked as though black folk were nonexistent or unimportant.'[61]

To make this challenge, Du Bois adopted a Marxist framework and leant on writers more sympathetic to the idea of African civilization and

---

[59] Cheikh Anta Diop to James Spady, 26 April 1971 as cited in James Spady, 'Negritude, PanBanegritude and the Diopian Philosophy of African History', *A Current Bibliography on African Affairs* 5:1 (1972): 26.

[60] In his biography of Du Bois David Levering Lewis describes *The Negro* as 'a large building block in an Afrocentric historiography': *W. E. B. DuBois: Biography of a Race 1868–1919* (New York: Henry Holt, 1993), 461–462.

[61] W. E. B. Du Bois, 'Foreword', *The World and Africa* (New York: Oxford University Press, 2007 [reprint, 1947]), xxxii.

culture such as Leo Frobenius. He also relied on the work of Howard historian and African specialist William Leo Hansberry; journalist J. A. Rogers; activist intellectual George Padmore, and the journalist and peace activist Anna Melissa Graves, as evidence for his claims. None of these last writers had the credentials and institutional affiliations of Western academia, with the exception of Hansberry, who had a Master's degree and had worked at a number of US universities. Like Diop, Hansberry had found himself unable to earn his doctorate due to the nature of his historical interests. Despite decades of study more than equivalent to a doctorate, no contemporary American faculty members or degree-conferring institutions were willing, or indeed had the expertise, to supervise a PhD in the sub-Saharan African history Hansberry sought to pursue.[62] Du Bois had good reason to draw on his work, as well as that of others, and the challenge he mounted to the existing scholarship was rigorous. A contemporary reader's sympathy to it was, however, contingent upon the extent to which they themselves accepted that racism had shaped the work of the reigning authorities on the subject.

The experience of William Leo Hansberry, particularly in comparison to Cheikh Anta Diop, serves as particular illustration of this argument. As an undergraduate at Harvard, Hansberry had mounted the same challenge to Egyptological circles as Diop would in 1954. In a class taught by the celebrated Egyptologist George Andrew Reisner, Hansberry drew on ancient sources such as Herodotus to make the case for Egypt as a Black African civilization. Reisner refused to entertain the idea, on the basis that Black peoples had never developed civilizational greatness themselves. Reisner used Hansberry, the lone African American student in the class, as a case in point, commenting: 'You are a brilliant student Hansberry, but you are a product of our civilization.'[63] The very evidence that suggested Egyptian civilizational sophistication to Reisner and his like-minded contemporaries seemed to them to simultaneously be proof that it could not have been a Black civilization. The a priori assumption of Black inferiority shaped their conclusions. In a similar vein, Black African societies outside of Egypt, in more southern regions of Africa, were considered to be ahistorical. As such, throughout his career, Hansberry

---

[62] Spady, 'Dr. Cheikh Anta Diop', *Présence Africaine* 149/150 (1989): 303–304. On Hansberry's education see also Kwame Wes Alford, 'The Early Intellectual Growth and Development of William Leo Hansberry and the Birth of African Studies', *Journal of Black Studies* 30:3 (January 2000): 269–293.

[63] James Spady, 'Legacy of an African hunter', *Current Bibliography on African Affairs* 3:10 (November–December 1970): 28–29.

not only repeatedly encountered the refrain that Egypt could not have been Black but also 'the popular misconception that the early history of Africa south of the Sahara was a matter unworthy of serious academic concern'.[64]

BLACK HISTORY AS ANTI-RACISM IN THE UNITED STATES

Compounding the sense of Black people's a-historicity within the American historical discipline was the extent to which not only historians of colour were excluded, but the subject of racism was considered a 'political problem' rather than a historical fact. When the Association for the Study of Negro Life and History (ASNLH) was founded in Chicago in 1915, and its journal, the *Journal of Negro History*, launched by Carter G. Woodson the following year, careful language characterised its mission statement. The stated purpose of the *Journal of Negro History* was not 'to drift into discussion of the Negro problem' but rather to 'popularize the movement of unearthing the Negro and his contributions to civilization'.[65] Woodson's white colleagues at the American Historical Association underlined the segregated character of the discipline's professional associations when they explicitly welcomed what they described as the de-politicised nature of the *Journal of Negro History*. They applauded the decision to not discuss 'the [N]egro Problem, but to exhibit the facts of [N]egro history', an incontrovertibly modern phenomenon.[66] Of course, the hypocrisy of this reaction is clear in the fact that the *Journal of Negro History* was important not just for the topics it pursued, but for the opportunity it provided Black historians to publish their work. It was one of the few venues available to them in the United States in the first half of the twentieth century. W. E. B. Du Bois is unusual in that an article of his was actually published in 1910 in the American Historical Association's *American Historical Review*. It was the first by a Black historian to appear in that journal. This was by no means a sign of greater inclusivity: it was seventy years before John Hope Franklin's 1980 article would make him the second Black historian to publish there.[67]

---

[64] W. L. Hansberry, 'W. E. B. Du Bois' Influence on African History', *Freedomways* 5 (Winter 1965): 82.

[65] The Association for the Study of Negro Life and History, 'A Neglected History', *Journal of Negro History* 1:1 (January 1916): n.p.

[66] 'Historical News', *American Historical Review* 21 (April 1916): 643.

[67] W. E. Burghardt Du Bois, 'Reconstruction and Its Benefits', *American Historical Review* 15:4 (July 1910): 781–799. Earl Lewis makes this observation in his 'Turn as on a Pivot:

Woodson, as the *Journal of Negro History*'s early editor as well as founder, may not have explicitly tackled the question of race relations in the United States in the pages of the journal but he did have a political goal in creating the journal. Much like Cheikh Anta Diop some three or so decades later, Woodson wanted to use history, 'the facts' of Black history, to assert Black humanity and to combat racist stereotypes. Indeed, in his own contributions to the *Journal of Negro History*, Woodson emphasised the 'striking evidence that the colored people generally thrive when encouraged by their white neighbors'.[68] Integration was possible, if white America would just allow it. As such, Woodson also published work by white scholars whose views on Black history ran counter to mainstream white journals.

The topics covered in the *Journal of Negro History* tended to skew towards the Black experience in the United States, although most geographical regions were covered at one time or another. This history of the United States was, however, often framed in international terms that reinforced notions of African diaspora and transnational connections between Black peoples. This was also true of history-focused pieces in W. E. B. Du Bois' the *Crisis*, the organ journal of the National Association for the Advancement of Colored People.[69] Indeed, early efforts towards Pan-African anticolonial and anti-racist organizing were premised on a sense of shared historical origins in Africa, from the Trinidadian barrister Henry Sylvester William's London Pan African Conference of 1900 through to W. E. B. Du Bois' congresses of 1919, 1921, 1923 and 1927. These earlier movements tended to be more assimilationist in

---

Writing African Americans into a History of Overlapping Diasporas', *American Historical Review* 100:3 (1995): 765–787. For more on the history of AHA exclusion of Black historians see Jaqueline Goggin, 'Countering White Racist Scholarship: Carter G. Woodson and The Journal of Negro History', *Journal of Negro History* 68:4 (Autumn 1983): 355–375.

[68] Carter G. Woodson, 'The Negroes of Cincinnati Prior to the Civil War', *Journal of Negro History* 1:1 (1916): 1. See also: 'Freedom and Slavery in Appalachian America', 1 (1916): 132–150; 'The Beginnings of the Miscegenation of the Whites and Blacks', 3 (1918): 335–354; 'Ten Years of Collecting and Publishing the Records of the Negro', 10 (1925): 598–606; 'Negro History Week', 11 (1926): 237–242; 'Attitudes of the Iberian Peninsula', 20 (1935): 190–243; and 'Notes on the Bakongo', 30 (1945): 421–431.

[69] James W. Ivy, 'Traditional NAACP Interest in Africa as Reflected in the Pages of the Crisis', in *Africa Seen by American Negro Scholars* (New York: American Society of African Culture, 1963), 229–246.

ideology, challenging the violence of colonialism rather than criticizing it wholesale.[70]

Carter Woodson was concerned not just with academic arenas but with public outreach. Undergirding both the aim of the *Journal of Negro History*, and the ASNLH more broadly, was the assertion that Black people did in fact *have* a history and overcoming racism involved *learning* that history. Woodson commented in a 1925 article that the ASNLH had become 'a free reference bureau for information respecting the Negro . . .. on the early history of the Negro in this country and the past of the race in Africa'.[71] Building on that momentum he launched Negro History Week in 1926. ANSLH branch leaders, often African American women working as teachers, librarians and community activists, brought the initiative to Black schools and libraries throughout the United States.[72] Eleven years later Woodson also founded the *Negro History Bulletin*, with the aim of offering Black communities a sense of their history. He described the rationale for doing so in the following way: 'Not to know what one's race has done in former times is to continue always a child. If a race has no history, if it has no worthwhile tradition, it becomes a negligible factor in the thought of the world, and it stands in danger of being exterminated.'[73]

In part this was about offering a sense of racial pride, a means through which to assert Black humanity against the de-humanizing racism and oppression of the Jim Crow South and second-class citizenship status African Americans suffered. Of course, even these changes within the parallel academy of African American history did not translate immediately to the classroom in the 1930s and 1940s. For example, in his autobiography the African American activist Malcolm X mused 'I remember, we came to the textbook section on Negro History. It was exactly one paragraph long' and when the teacher came to it, they 'laughed through it practically in a single breath'.[74] Much like the refusal to accept that Black

---

[70] See Sarah C. Dunstan, 'Conflicts of Interest: The 1919 Pan-African Congress and the Wilsonian Moment', *Callaloo* 39:1 (Winter 2016): 133–150.

[71] Carter G. Woodson, 'Ten Years of Collecting and Publishing the Records of the Negro', *Journal of Negro History* 10 (October 1925): 605.

[72] Deborah Gray White, 'Introduction', in *Telling Histories, Black Women Historians in the Ivory Tower* (Chapel Hill, NC: University of North Carolina Press, 2008), 10.

[73] Carter G. Woodson, '"Forgotten Negroes": Who Played Major Roles in the Race's March of Progress', *Pittsburgh Courier*, February 24, 1934, 4.

[74] Malcolm X, Alex Haley, *The Autobiography of Malcolm X* (New York: Ballantine Books, 1992 [1965]), 35.

Africa had a history, Black Americans were understood only to have a history relative to their place in the development of a white United States.

Once again, this came back to prevailing notions that Africa had no history. Both Du Bois and Woodson had been cognisant of the importance of establishing African history on its own terms through the publication of textbooks and encyclopedias. Unfortunately, the lack of funding available for such an endeavour left them without the wherewithal to see these plans to fruition. As early as 1908, Du Bois had in mind 'an Encyclopedia Africana covering the chief points on the history and conditions of the Negro race'.[75] This was work he wanted undertaken by 'leading scholars of the race' rather than white historians, whom he nonetheless imagined might have an advisory role. He went so far as to invite over sixty such scholars from the United States, Africa and the West Indies to take part in such an initiative but was ultimately unsuccessful in procuring funding.[76] Other efforts followed, including a Phelps Stokes funded venture in the 1930s for an *Encyclopedia of the Negro* (although this initially did not involve W. E. B. Du Bois, or Carter Woodson).[77] Woodson, who refused to be involved in the primarily white-led Phelps Stokes initiative, was excoriating of this project.[78] He hoped for a separate *Encyclopedia of the Negro* to be published under the auspices of the ANSLH, and kept in the hands of Black historians, for fear that white written histories would always reflect the racial biases built into white academia. Woodson was ultimately proven correct in his suspicions about the Phelps Stokes' project, and funding dried up in 1941. Du Bois persevered with the project even as he lamented 'that no money sufficient for the publication of such an encyclopedia under the leadership of colored scholars and the collaboration of white men can soon be found'.[79]

[75] W. E. B. Du Bois to Edward W. Blyden, 5 April 1909, reprinted in *The Correspondence of W. E. B. Du Bois: Volume 1, Selections, 1877–1934*, ed. Herbert Aptheker (Amherst, MA: University of Massachusetts Press, 1973), 145–146. For a detailed history of this see Jonathan Fenderson, 'Evolving Conceptions of Pan-African Scholarship: W. E. B. Du Bois, Carter G. Woodson, and the "Encyclopedia Africana," 1909–1963', *Journal of African American History* 95:1 (Winter 2010): 71–91.

[76] W. E. B. Du Bois, 'Encyclopedia Africana', in *W. E. B. Du Bois Speaks: Speeches and Addresses, 1920–1963*, ed. Philip Foner (New York: Pathfinder Press, 1970), 322–325.

[77] For more on this history see Fenderson, 'Evolving Conceptions of Pan-African Scholarship', 77–82.

[78] Carter G. Woodson, 'Notes', *Journal of Negro History* 17 (January 1932): 116–118.

[79] W. E. B. Du Bois, *Dusk of Dawn: An Essay Toward an Autobiography of a Race Concept* (repr. New Brunswick, NJ, 1984 [1940]), 323. For more on the politics of the Phelps Stokes funding see: Fenderson, 'Evolving Conceptions of Pan-African Scholarship', 77–82.

AFRICAN FREEDOM AND TRANSNATIONAL SOLIDARITY THROUGH HISTORY

It was in this context that Du Bois' 1947 *The World and Africa* came out, once again railing against the authorities, whose reading of the past was inextricable from their insistence upon Black inferiority. As such Du Bois' intervention was both academic and aimed at a broader audience. In fact, he blamed a deficiency of historical knowledge for what he saw as the lack of solidarity between African Americans and African peoples. Writing in 1955, in an article also published in *Présence Africaine*, he lamented African American ignorance 'of the history and present situation in Africa' and their indifference 'to the fate of African[s]'.[80] The Black community in the United States had lost interest in Africa because of the lamentable state of African American leadership. From the end of the Second World War, 'American Negro Leadership was in the hands of a new Negro bourgeoisie and had left the hands of teachers, writers and social workers. Professional men joined this black bourgeoisie and the Negro began to follow white American display and conspicuous expenditure'.[81] They sought to emulate white models, rather than build an African solidarity that Du Bois believed would better benefit them in the long term.[82]

At the 1959 second Congress of Black Writers and Artists, Alioune Diop underlined the importance of this message when he declared that the task at hand was 'to restore history to its true dimensions' by accepting that the African and those of the African diaspora had just as much to contribute and had, in fact, already contributed a great deal to the modern world.[83] The Burkinabé historian Joseph Ki-Zerbo, another intellectual luminary associated with *Présence Africaine*, shared Diop's sensibilities about the significance of history in shaping African freedom. Ki-Zerbo, like Cheikh Anta Diop, had been trained in Paris at the Sorbonne. He was the first African to become *agrégé d'histoire* in France and had been a student of the renowned *Annales* historian Fernand Braudel.[84] During his time in Paris, he had also been an important figure

---

[80] W. E. B. Du Bois, 'Africa and the American Negro Intelligentsia', *Présence Africaine*, New Series, 5 (December 1955–January 1956): 34.

[81] Du Bois, 'Africa and the American Negro Intelligentsia', 50.   [82] Ibid., 50.

[83] Alioune Diop, 'Discours d'ouverture du 2ème congrès international des écrivains et des artistes noirs à Rome en 1959', *Présence Africaine* 24–25 (February–May 1959): 49.

[84] See F. Pajot, *Joseph Ki-Zerbo: itinéraire d'un intellectuel africain au XXe siècle* (Paris : L'Harmattan, 2007).

in Black Catholic activist circles, working for change in France's colonial administration of Africa.[85] History, and specifically the cultivation of collective history that would lead to political independence, lay at the heart of his urging for a specifically African renaissance. As far as he was concerned, 'communities and peoples are the fruit of their history. History is the memory of nations'.[86] From at least the fifteenth century onwards, African peoples had had their histories 'brutally confiscated' by European imperialists and slave traders. The task of the historian in the era of decolonization was nothing less than the 'recovery of consciousness of the Black-African peoples'.[87] Ki-Zerbo meant this in an academic *and* a political sense, as he strongly believed that part of reclaiming African history was asserting the national character of the Haut Volta region and winning independence. A committed nationalist, Ki-Zerbo co-founded that Mouvement de libération nationale (MLN) or National Liberation Movement in order to campaign against remaining in Charles de Gaulle's French Community in 1958. The Haut Volta territory ultimately voted against leaving the French Fifth Republic and Ki-Zerbo would relocate to Sékou Touré's independent Guinea until it became independent in 1960.

By 1960, Cheikh Anta Diop had honed his argument about the value of the African past into a narrative that placed a Black Egypt alongside Rome and Greece as the origin points of modern human civilization. Under a new thesis question, 'Comparative study of political and social systems of Europe and Africa, from Antiquity to the formation of modern states', he was finally awarded his doctorate. This time, he had a more sympathetic supervisor, the specialist of pre-history André Leroi-Gourhan. Moreover, his examination committee was chaired by the classicist and *Le Musée vivant* patron André Aymard, then dean of the Faculty of Letters. His thesis had a different resonance in the context of 1960, a moment wherein most of France's African territories had gained or were about to gain their independence from empire. They were joining the world order as modern nation states, literally entering into history in a way that hitherto had been denied them. Such political independence did not automatically equate to a less hostile academic environment but the

---

[85] See E. Foster, '"Entirely Christian and Entirely African": Catholic African Students in France in the Era of Independence', *Journal of African History* 56:2 (2015): 253.

[86] Joseph Ki-Zerbo, 'Histoire et conscience nègre', *Présence Africaine*, New Series 16 (October–November 1957): 53–69 (53).

[87] Ibid., 53.

two phenomena certainly had a reciprocal relationship in terms of what was possible for Black scholars such as Diop.

Diop's thesis became two books, both published with *Présence Africaine*: *L'Afrique noire pré-coloniale* and *L'Unité culturelle de l'Afrique noire*. In these works Diop contended that contemporary Black Africa could look back to a contribution at least equivalent to that of Western Europe. The ramifications of this line of thinking are particularly evident in Diop's 1960 comparative study of European and African political organization: *L' Afrique noire pré-coloniale*. Influenced in particular by Gaston Bachelard's notion of 'units of time', Diop formulated an understanding of historical continuity that linked pre-colonial African civilizations to the Black diasporic present by framing the colonial period as one of 'historical dormancy' or 'memory loss'.[88] In so doing, he sought to disrupt hegemonic readings of linear time and thus overcome their implicit teleological characterization of European cultures as both the pinnacle of civilizational achievement and the only entrance into modernity.[89] Understanding history like this was important because it allowed Africans to realise the continuity of their past and personhood as the natural state of being, a state only corrupted because of European intervention.

A NEW WORLD ORDER THROUGH HISTORIOGRAPHICAL REVISION

As we have seen, Diop was far from alone in adopting this position. It transcended the realm of academic argument and took shape in internationalist African political endeavours. Not long after Diop published *L'Afrique noire pré-coloniale*, the Ghanaian President, Kwame Nkrumah, invited Du Bois to Africa to work on an 'Encyclopedia Africana' at the Ghana Academy of Learning. Nkrumah was not just the president of the newly independent Ghana, he was also, as such, the symbol of the successes of Pan-African anticolonialism. Writing for the *Baltimore Afro-American* in 1961, Du Bois declared that this new project would not just be about race, 'but on the peoples inhabiting the content of

---

[88] See Gaston Bachelard, *La dialectique de la durée* (Paris: Les Presses universitaires de France, 1963 [1950]); *L'Intuition de l'instant* (Paris: Editions Gonthier, 1932).

[89] For an in-depth exploration of the challenge to linear understandings of time in the post-war context see Fraiture, *Past Imperfect*.

Africa'.[90] Such a project had only become possible in a political context with 'independent Africans to carry it out'.[91] Du Bois' and Nkrumah's ambitions for the work were lofty: they hoped it would go some way towards eliminating 'the artificial boundaries created on this continent by colonial masters. Designations such as "British Africa," "French Africa," "Black Africa," "Islamic Africa," too often serve to keep alive differences which in large part have been imposed on Africans by outsiders . . . . The encyclopedia is concerned with Africa as a whole'.[92]

It was a mammoth undertaking, and by the time of Du Bois' death in August 1963, the *Encyclopedia* remained unfinished. The impetus to re-write African history in a way that centred African humanity did not, however, die with him. The staff hired to compile the *Encylopedia Africana* under Du Bois' leadership continued to work on it, eventually publishing three volumes of *The Encylopedia Africana: A Dictionary of African Biography* in 1977, 1979 and 1995 respectively.[93] Similarly, Carter Woodson's vision for an encyclopedia ultimately took shape in the United States through the ASNLH production of ten volumes on *The International Library of Negro Life and History*. This series was much narrower than Woodson's original project, focusing solely on 'the cultural and historical backgrounds' of Black Americans rather than on Africa.[94]

In this post-independence period, the *Encylopedia Africana* and the ASNLH projects were not the only such efforts towards asserting Black and African histories. At the 1964 General Conference of UNESCO, newly independent African nations pushed for a strong position on the recovery of African ownership of their past and for control over the production of knowledge around the past. Political independence from European empire was only the first step in the decolonizing process.

[90] W. E. B. Du Bois, 'Encyclopedia Africana', *Baltimore Afro-American*, 7 (October 1961).
[91] 'Encyclopedia Africana', in Foner, *W. E. B. Du Bois Speaks*, 323.   [92] Ibid.
[93] L. H. Ofosu-Appiah and Keith Irvine (eds.), *Encyclopedia Africana: Dictionary of African Biography: Ethiopia and Ghana*, Volume I (Algonic, MI: Encyclopaedia Africana Project, Reference Publications 1977); L. H. Ofosu-Appiah and Keith Irvine (eds.), *Encyclopedia Africana: Dictionary of African Biography: Sierra Leone and Zaire*, Volume II (Algonic, MI: Encyclopaedia Africana Project, Reference Publications 1979); L. H. Ofosu-Appiah (ed.), *Encyclopedia Africana: Dictionary of African Biography: South Africa, Botswana, Lesotho, Swaziland*, Volume III (Algonic, MI: Encyclopaedia Africana Project Reference Publications 1995).
[94] Charles H. Wesley, 'Preface', in Lindsay Patterson (ed.), *The Negro in Music and Art* (New York: Publishers Co (under the auspices of the Association for the Study of Negro Life and History), 1967), vii.

The future, they argued, needed to include control of the past. The result of their lobbying was the decision to sponsor an eight-volume *General History of Africa*. This General History was intended as an opportunity to centre African voices and demonstrate African contributions throughout time to universal civilization. The resulting eight-volume, multi-authored work took thirty-five years to complete.[95] (A length of time not dissimilar to the efforts behind the *Encyclopedia Africana* and *The International Library of Negro Life and History*.)

In the preface to the first UNESCO volume, on *Methodology and African Pre-History* (1981), the first Black UNESCO General-Director, Amadou-Mahtar M'Bow, wrote 'In exercising their right to take the historical initiative, Africans themselves have felt a deep-seated need to re-establish the historical authenticity of their societies on solid foundations.' One of the great sins of colonialism had been the 'refusal to see Africans as the creators of original cultures which flowered and survived over the centuries in patterns of their own making'.[96] Not only did this distort 'even the basic concepts of historiography' but it cemented harmful racial stereotypes that were in turn used to justify the violence of colonialism.[97]

Born in Senegal in 1921, M'Bow himself had grown up under the auspices of Third Republic France, fighting on behalf of the Free French forces during the war before taking a degree in geography at the Sorbonne. Alongside the UNESCO General History project, M'Bow was a staunch advocate of the return of African artefacts from European museums to their respective points of origin.[98] It seemed abhorrent to him that it was not until his studies in Paris that he, like many Africans of his generation, had 'begun to become fully aware of the most significant facts' of his own history.[99] African peoples needed to have access to their history in their home countries. For M'Bow, the function of the UNESCO history project was thus twofold. It was an emancipatory

---

[95] In 2009, a further three volumes were announced to be in preparation.

[96] Amadou-Mahtar M'Bow, 'Preface', in *Methodology and African Pre-History* (UNESCO. International Scientific Committee for the Drafting of a General History of Africa), xvii–xviii.

[97] M'Bow, 'Preface', xvii–xviii.

[98] See Amadou-Mahtar M'Bow, 'Pour le retour, a ceux qui l'ont crée, d'un patrimoine culturel irremplaçable', *Museum* 31:1 (1979): 58.

[99] M'Bow, 'Hommage à Alioune Diop, fondateur de la Société Africaine de Culture et de la revue "Présence Africaine"', *Présence Africaine*, New Series, 174 (September 2006): Volume I: Cérémonies d'ouverture et hommage / Opening Adresses and Tribute, 84–85.

project for African and African-descended people, and an assertion of African humanity in the face of centuries of European imperialist insistence upon white supremacy.

Such positioning was directly related to the way that the international institutions of the League of Nations and the United Nations had based their systems of mandate and trusteeship upon notions of the a-historicity of Black peoples. If the United Nations of the 1960s was to be different, then it needed, as M'Bow indicated, to acknowledge the falsity of these positions. Joseph Ki-Zerbo, who was the editor of the series' first volume, underlined this need, when he began his contribution to the volume with the simple, yet powerful sentence: 'Africa has a history'.[100] As scholars began to accept this, and to make strides towards the rediscovery of this history, so too would understandings of the current political order be transformed. Cheikh Anta Diop would have agreed with Ki-Zerbo's declaration that 'discoveries about Africa, sometimes spectacular ones, call in question the meaning of certain phases in the history of mankind as a whole'.[101]

In the almost five decades between the publication of Diop's 1954 *Nations nègres* and the final UNESCO volume in 1999, African history established itself firmly as a university discipline.[102] Likewise, African American and African diasporic histories, so long marginalized within the Western academy, began in the same period to figure much more prominently in so-called mainstream conceptions of the field of history.[103] It is, as this essay shows, no coincidence that these efforts gained momentum in the post–Second World War period when the European projects of colonialism in Africa became increasingly politically fragile and ultimately broke down. In the United States, these decades also marked watershed moments in the struggles of Black Americans to secure civil rights. In this period of undoing and remaking, the

---

[100] Joseph Ki-Zerbo, 'General Introduction', in Ki-Zerbo (ed.), *General History of Africa, i: Methodology and African Prehistory* (Paris and London: United Nations Educational, Scientific and Cultural Organization and Heineman Educational Books Ltd, 1981), 1.

[101] Ki-Zerbo, 'General Introduction', 2.

[102] B. Jewsiewicki and V. Y. Mudimbe, '"Africans" Memories and Contemporary History of Africa', *History and Theory* 32:4 (1993): 2.

[103] On the movement of African American history into the 'mainstream' see Pero Gaglo Dagbovie, *What Is African American History?* (Malden, MA: Polity Press, 2015), 6–26. See also Claire Parfait, Hélène Le Dantec-Lowry, and Claire Bourhis-Mariotti (eds.), *Writing History from the Margins: African Americans and the Quest for Freedom* (New York: Routledge, 2017).

imagining of decolonial, anti-racist futures required the revalorization of the African past. As the V. Y. Mudimbe quote that opened this chapter reminds us, the terrain of history was, and remains, an important part of efforts to combat racism and to decolonize the ideological infrastructures of the West.

8

The Right to Petition in the Anticolonial Struggle at the United Nations

Cindy Ewing

INTRODUCTION

The celebratory moment conventionally associated with the passage of the Universal Declaration of Human Rights, at the storied midnight hour, contained within it two important though overlooked postscripts. Following the resolution approving the full text of the declaration were shorter addendums indicating the assembly's intention to study two rights that had been initially included but then removed. One resolution dealt with the question of minorities, to be assessed by a special sub-commission. The other recognized that "the right of petition is an essential human right" but crisply stated the assembly's decision "not to take any action on this matter."[1] This exclusion of the right to petition from the UDHR made its passage possible in 1948, but it also highlighted the boundaries set around the recognition and exercise of certain rights at the international level. Not only were individuals, newly granted international legal legitimacy, limited in their freedom to petition their state governments, but they were also constrained from petitioning the United Nations itself. While the 1948 resolution on the right to petition illustrates its ambivalent status in the postwar human rights imagination, it also opens a lens into another reading of the historical moment, in which petitions nevertheless still reached the UN through other channels and became a mechanism of anticolonial resistance to empire, challenging the global order from within its central institutions. In the 1940s and 1950s,

---

[1] United Nations, General Assembly, A/RES/3/217B, December 10, 1948. www.un-documents.net/a3r217b.htm.

petitions were deployed in multiple arenas, contributing to the recognition of other rights not yet defined by the declaration, namely as an expression of the grievances of colonial peoples and the right to national self-determination, which arose in the UN as a controversial innovation of rights discourse and anticolonial activism.

The transnational solidarity of anticolonial movements did not depend on the existence of the United Nations. However, the UN was a crucial site of resistance to empire in the postwar era – one among many – that enabled new configurations, connections, and circulations of anticolonial ideas.[2] Since the founding of the UN, anticolonial nationalists, some of whom came from occupied territories and others from newly independent nation-states, used the UN as a platform to challenge empire and build solidarity with other anticolonial groups in the global South. Within the UN itself, diplomats and political elites from Asia and Africa promoted liberation movements at the General Assembly and across various agencies of the UN system. But they also sought to remake international society in support of a wide range of anticolonial aims, for example by influencing the development of the international human rights regime, insisting upon international oversight over colonial questions, directly mediating disputes between colonial and indigenous groups, and

---

[2] The large literature on decolonization and the United Nations includes classic works such as Yassin El-Ayouty, *The United Nations and Decolonization: The Role of Afro-Asia* (The Hague: Martinus Nijhoff, 1971); David A. Kay, *The New Nations in the United Nations, 1960–1967* (New York: Columbia University Press, 1970); and more recent volumes such as Akira Iriye, *Global Community: The Role of International Organizations in the Making of the Contemporary World* (Berkeley: University of California Press, 2002); Mark Mazower, *No Enchanted Palace: The End of Empire and the Ideological Origins of the United Nations* (Princeton: Princeton University Press, 2009); Mark Mazower, *Governing the World: The Rise and Fall of an Idea* (London: Allen Lane, 2012); Glenda Sluga, *Internationalism in the Age of Nationalism* (Philadelphia: University of Pennsylvania Press, 2013); Jessica Lynne Pearson, *The Colonial Politics of Global Health: France and the United Nations in Postwar Africa* (Cambridge, MA: Harvard University Press, 2018); Simon Jackson and Alanna O'Malley, eds. *The Institution of the International Order: From the League of Nations to the United Nations* (New York: Routledge, 2018); Alanna O'Malley, *The Diplomacy of Decolonisation: America, Britain and the United Nations during the Congo Crisis, 1960–64* (Manchester: Manchester University Press, 2019); A. Dirk Moses, Marco Duranti, and Roland Burke, eds. *Decolonization, Self-Determination, and the Rise of Global Human Rights Politics* (Cambridge: Cambridge University Press, 2020); Mary Ann Heiss, *Fulfilling the Sacred Trust: The UN Campaign for International Accountability for Dependent Territories in the Era of Decolonization* (Ithaca, NY: Cornell University Press, 2020); Eva-Maria Muschik, *Building States: The United Nations, Development and Decolonization, 1945–1965* (New York: Columbia University Press, 2022).

generally altering the focus and purview of UN deliberations over time.[3] Outside of the UN, anticolonial nationalists lobbied state delegations and UN officials from afar; others used the occasion of UN meetings to promote awareness of their struggle and establish connections across continents. The advent of multi-national peacekeeping operations also brought a new generation of UN officials into the global South, further expanding the presence of international institutions and its agents in contested territories. While the primary sites for global revolution and liberation often took place away from formal institutions like the UN, these spaces enabled cooperation among anticolonial movements, brought international publicity to nationalist movements, and, in some instances, expanded the reach of such efforts by becoming the targets of global political struggle.[4] Therefore, while ongoing inquiry into the historical connections between human rights and decolonization may acknowledge the role of the UN as both site and target of political struggle, it may also comprehend international institutions as just one nodal point in a layered and vast transnational network of anticolonial activity, interweaving different internationalisms and projects of reordering and remaking the world at the end of empire.

PETITIONS AS ANTICOLONIAL STRUGGLE

The exertions of late colonialism and, likewise, its resistance, possessed an international character.[5] Representatives of imperial states and anticolonial nationalists alike turned to the UN and used its authority and

---

[3] On the concept of international society see Erez Manela, "International Society as a Historical Subject," *Diplomatic History* 44, no. 2 (2020): 184–209.

[4] There were limits to the kinds of anticolonial aims that could be pursued in institutionalized settings, sometimes revealing cleavages in the wider transnational movement. See Jeffrey Byrne, "From Bandung to Havana: Institutionalizing the Contentions of Postcolonial Internationalism," in *The League against Imperialism: Lives and Afterlives*, eds. Michele Louro, Carolien Stolte, Heather Streets-Salter, and Sana Tannoury-Karam (Dordrecht: Leiden University Press, 2020), 371–396; Simon Jackson and Alanna O'Malley, "Rocking on Its Hinges? The League of Nations, the United Nations and the New History of Internationalism in the Twentieth Century," in *The Institution of the International Order: From the League of Nations to the United Nations*, eds. Simon Jackson and Alanna O'Malley (New York: Routledge, 2018), 6.

[5] Miguel Bandeira Jeronimo and Jose Pedro Monteiro observe that "devolution of power in late colonialism can only be fully apprehended if its international and transnational dimensions are brought into the picture." See Miguel Bandeira Jeronimo and Jose Pedro Monteiro, "Colonial Labour Internationalized: Portugal and the Decolonization Momentum (1945–1975)," *International History Review* 42, no. 3 (2020): 485.

instruments to make claims about their legitimacy. The internationalism of anticolonialism was constantly met with the internationalism of late colonialism, evidenced by the framework and function of the International Trusteeship System, through which European empires managed to maintain control over distant territories. As a principal organ, the Trusteeship Council executed one of the core missions of the UN and granted administration of so-called dependent or non-self-governing territories to UN member-states as caretaker governments, typically without consulting local populations. This international obligation was frequently referred to as a "sacred trust" in the language of the League of Nations Covenant. The same wording was then reproduced in the UN Charter's chapter on non-self-governing territories.[6] Whereas the UDHR did not recognize or allow for petitions, the charter explicitly charged the Trusteeship Council with examining written or oral petitions from trust territories. This provision continued the practice of the League of Nations Permanent Mandates Commission, which received petitions from mandated territories and produced annual reports that recorded and preserved them. Susan Pedersen has shown how even though petitions increased scrutiny on the mandatory powers, as an institution the commission suppressed agitation from below rather than check imperial power; after all, the administering authority was only responsible to the league and not to the indigenous populations living in its territory.[7] Illustrating a commonly held view among League members and officials, the 1923 *Yearbook of the League of Nations* deemed most petitions received by the commission as "trivial."[8] Under the UN, this interwar conception of petition rights persisted in its reinvented form as the International Trusteeship System, accruing only to those populations under an UN-designated trust rather than as a universal right accessible to everyone.

Petitions formalized the encounter between the colonizer and the colonized. In both systems – the League of Nations and the UN – petitions could not be sent anonymously, rendering the colonial authority and

---

[6] Heiss, *Fulfilling the Sacred Trust*, 19.

[7] Susan Pedersen, *The Guardians: The League of Nations and the Crisis of Empire* (Oxford: Oxford University Press, 2015), 91–94. Also see Natasha Wheatley, "The Mandate System as a Style of Reasoning: International Jurisdiction and the Parceling of Imperial Sovereignty in Petitions from Palestine," in *The Routledge Handbook of the History of the Middle East Mandates*, eds. Cyrus Schayegh and Andrew Arsan (London: Routledge, 2015), 106–122.

[8] *Yearbook of the League of Nations*, Vol. 3 (1923), 279.

colonial subject known to one another by name. Therefore, the individual or group sending written complaints against the administering authority assumed significant personal risk and even financial expense to mail their statements, or, less commonly, present them in person in the UN system. In contrast, the administering authority was not responsible for responding to the complainant. Rather, the petition would be acknowledged in a brief and formal letter by a representative of the United Nations Trusteeship Council and any further communication would be confidential. Despite the protections afforded by the Trusteeship Council's procedure, colonial anxieties prevailed about the volume of petitions that the UN received and the growing transnational anticolonial sentiment they represented.[9] Petitions and complaints not only arrived from the trust territories themselves but were also supported by letters from other Asian and African member-states on behalf of the indigenous populations contesting foreign control. During this period, colonial member-states resisted international oversight by the UN and often characterized allegations of conflict in their colonial territories as domestic issues outside of UN's remit as defined by the charter. Despite this obstructionist logic, the arrival of petitions from trusts and dependent territories continued to draw international attention to the condition of colonial peoples and raise questions about the inviolability of imperial sovereignty in an age of decolonization. Even though many petitions went unanswered or received pro forma letters of acknowledgment, they contributed to a growing atmosphere of transnational anticolonial agitation and created opportunities for anticolonial diplomats within the UN to raise colonial questions as part of official debate.

The importance of anticolonial petitions to the history of decolonization remains overlooked because of the bureaucratic design of postwar international organizations; the normal procedure was to seal petitions and correspondence, thus keeping such records and testimonies of human

---

[9] In one notable complaint, Sir Alan Burns, a British representative to the Trusteeship Council, wrote that petitions had become "a national sport in tropical Africa." See Jessica Lynne Pearson,"'Defending Empire at the United Nations: The Politics of International Colonial Oversight in the Era of Decolonisation," *Journal of Imperial and Commonwealth History* 45, no. 3 (2017): 526. For more on human rights and British colonial anxiety, see A. W. B. Simpson, *Human Rights and the End of Empire: Britain and the Genesis of the European Convention* (Oxford: Oxford University Press, 2010); on France, see Marco Duranti, "Decolonizing the United Nations: Anti-colonialism and Human Rights in the French Empire," in *Decolonization, Self-Determination, and the Rise of Global Human Rights Politics*, eds. A. Dirk Moses, Marco Duranti, and Roland Burke (Cambridge: Cambridge University Press, 2020), 54–78.

rights violations restricted or confidential. The structure of the UN therefore made it difficult to organize or agitate using petitions as evidence of abuses by the administering authorities. Postwar international governance was also dominated by the United States and the European colonial powers in every arena; at the UN they were able to dictate the direction of plenary debate while the processing of petitions constituted a largely unseen task handled outside of the assembly by the UN Secretariat's large administrative bureaucracy. However, in the late 1940s, a small group of Asian and Arab delegates began to coordinate their actions at the General Assembly, becoming a new, collective anticolonial voice that drew attention to these areas of UN activity outside of member-state meetings. As postcolonial internationalists, diplomats from non-Western states used the public platform of the UN to promote liberation movements while also providing an organizational hub for anticolonial activity inside the institution.

Over time, as the UN's membership expanded with the addition of newly independent nation-states from Africa, the Arab-Asian group became more commonly referred to as the Afro-Asian group or Afro-Asian bloc. In the UN's earliest years, however, it was the smaller Arab-Asian group, not yet expanded by the addition of African member-states, that acted as informal representatives of non-white peoples and non-Western nations, many still under colonial occupation and only a few very recently decolonized. While little has been written about the Arab-Asian group, since they were not a formal organization or regional group, UN resolutions reveal a steady record of their international cooperation and their gradual expansion as a group, constituting an early form of Afro-Asianism and postcolonial internationalism.[10] Some historians have observed the importance of the Arab-Asian group's concerted effort to mediate without encouraging military action in the UN response to the outbreak of the Korean War in 1950.[11] However, the Arab-Asian group was already active prior to 1950 and originally came together over anticolonial issues in dedicated campaigns for self-government, rather than out of Cold War concerns.

[10] Cindy Ewing, "The 'Fate of Minorities' in the Early Afro-Asian Struggle for Decolonization," *Comparative Studies of South Asia, Africa and the Middle East* 41, no. 3 (2021): 340–346.

[11] Lorenz M. Lüthi, "Non-Alignment, 1946–1965: Its Establishment and Struggle against Afro-Asianism," *Humanity: An International Journal of Human Rights, Humanitarianism, and Development* 7, no. 2 (2016): 201–223.

The twelve member-states in the Arab-Asian group represented the Asian postcolonial states of Burma, India, Pakistan, the Philippines, the Arab League states of Egypt, Iraq, Lebanon, Saudi Arabia, Syria, Yemen, and Afghanistan and Iran. The most notable example of their cooperation followed the 1947 and 1949 Asian Relations Conferences when Arab and Asian diplomats at the UN rallied to demand sovereignty for Indonesia and condemn the Netherlands' police actions to reassert colonial control. Through their support for the unrecognized Indonesian representative standing in for the jailed Indonesian republican cabinet, the Arab-Asian group helped maneuver member votes in favor of direct negotiations between Indonesia and the Netherlands.

By turning many UN General Assembly members against the Netherlands, the Arab-Asian group contributed to the diplomatic pressure that led to the Dutch government's reluctant agreement to monitored negotiations and the eventual relinquishing of statehood to Indonesia. Less well covered during this same period were the Arab-Asian group's interventions on other colonial questions, when their activism altered the balance of power between colonial powers and non-white delegations toward the recognition of nationalist claims. At the Trusteeship Council, members of the Arab-Asian group supported anticolonial petitions that came from trust territories and aided activists seeking an opportunity to speak at the UN. Trust territories in Africa sent hundreds of petitions to the UN every year; according to Meredith Terretta, the highest number of petitions from any trust territory came from the Union des Populations du Cameroun in Cameroon.[12] Such petitions, recording the names of the inhabitants in trust territories, expanded transnational networks of anticolonial solidarity by putting activists and nationalist groups in contact with NGOs and other non-Western states with formal representation at the UN.

THE NATIONAL FUTURES OF SOMALILAND, LIBYA, AND ERITREA

The Arab-Asian group launched internal initiatives within the UN to expand the reach of anticolonial activists by giving an international platform to political groups, transnational movements, or individuals seeking aid through personal pleas. While petitions were communicated

---

[12] Meredith Terretta, "Cameroonian Nationalists Go Global: From Forest Maquis to a Pan-African Accra," *Journal of African History* 51 (2010): 197.

to the trust authority, representatives from the Arab-Asian group raised issues from the Trusteeship Council at the General Assembly. For example, in the 1948–1949 session, the General Assembly held discussions to decide the status of the former Italian colonies in Africa of Somaliland, Libya, and Eritrea. Drawing on petitions opposing the return of colonial rule, the Arab-Asian group sponsored an alternative resolution to the territorial formula developed by British Foreign Secretary Ernest Bevin and Italian Foreign Minister Count Carlo Sforza. The Bevin–Sforza Plan proposed partitioning Libya and creating trusts under British, French, and Italian administrations, which would have the effect of returning Somaliland and Libya to Italian colonial rule. Having rejected a proposal to grant the Arab League trust authority over Libya, the British, French, and Italian representatives at the Trusteeship Council promoted the Bevin–Sforza Plan as the most feasible option to transfer colonial power to the International Trusteeship System. In addition to strong American support, the plan appeared to work out a compromise that was suitable to the Western powers, even offering defined terms such as an incremental ten-year timeline and provisions for continued European military presence, viewed as urgent and necessary in the face of active rioting and public protest.[13]

In opposition to the Bevin–Sforza Plan, the Burmese, Indian, and Pakistani representatives developed their alternative formula in line with the anticolonial tenor of written petitions to the Trusteeship Council. The Arab-Asian group opposed partitioning of any kind and called for Libya's immediate independence. This constituted a direct challenge to all other proposals for trusteeship, a motion that was intensified when the Indian delegate accused the European states of racial discrimination against Africans by supporting the return of Italian control. The Arab-Asian group also promoted and circulated official statements by nationalist groups from these territories. Individuals, political parties, and civic associations mailed petitions and letters to the UN Secretary-General throughout the assembly meetings.

Letters arrived from within the territories and from other African organizations. In April 1949, the Libyan Committee of Nigeria sent a brief cablegram decrying "Italian rule ... absolutely intolerable" and

---

[13] Carol Anderson, "Rethinking Radicalism: African Americans and the Liberation Struggles in Somaliland, Libya, and Eritrea," *Journal of the Historical Society* 11, no. 4 (2011): 416; Pamela Ballinger, "Colonial Twilight: Italian Settlers and the Long Decolonization of Libya," *Journal of Contemporary History* 51, no. 4 (2016): 813–838.

requesting that the UN Secretary-General "consult Libian [sic] representatives from Tripoli now in Lake Success in whom we have complete
confidence."[14] Representing the Cairo-based Committee for Freedom for
North Africa in New York, Abed Bouhafa expressed collective support by
Moroccans, Algerians, and Tunisians for a united Libya, in pursuit of the
group's "main objective ... to secure by peaceful and legitimate means the
enjoyment for the natural rights of self determination [sic] and independence
as laid down in the United Nations Charter."[15] Likewise, the Somali
Women's Association sent a telegram "object[ing] strongly Italian return
as Italian rule ruined us morally, physically, religiously, racially and culturally."[16] The Somali delegation at the UN emphasized the anticolonial
grounds of their opposition. As Carol Anderson argues, the Somali delegation did not voice its opposition to trusteeship but Italian trusteeship in
particular. Casting a wide net, some Somali petitions were directly addressed
to members of the Arab-Asian group or political leaders from Arab-Asian
group nations rather than Secretary-General Trygve Lie alone.[17]

Arab and Asian diplomats rallied around the African nationalists who
came to the UN session. Abdullahi Issa, the Somali nationalist leader and
eventual first Prime Minister, appeared before the General Assembly as
the representative of the Somali Youth League in October 1949.[18] Issa
and other Somali and Libyan representatives had met with and lobbied
delegations at the General Assembly against the British-Italian agreement.
Despite how little attention had previously been paid to Somaliland, Issa
gained the support of civil rights organizations, including the National
Association for the Advancement of Colored People (NAACP), the
Council on African Affairs, and the International League for the Rights
of Man; the NAACP in particular created a large radio and newspaper
publicity campaign to promote Issa in advance of his appearance before
the assembly.[19] Issa also corresponded with Burmese Prime Minister

[14] Petition from Libyan Committee of Nigeria, April 11, 1949, S-0500-0006-14, UNARMS.
[15] Petition from the Committee for Freedom for North Africa, April 6, 1949, S-0500-0006-14, UNARMS.
[16] Petition from Somali Women Association, May 11, 1949, S-0500-0006-14, UNARMS.
[17] Anderson, "Rethinking Radicalism," 415.
[18] On the fluidities of Somali and Ethiopian nationalities, see Namhla Thando Matshanda, "Constructing Citizens and Subjects in Eastern Ethiopia: Identity Formation during the British Military Administration," *Journal of Eastern African Studies* 13, no. 4 (2019): 661–677.
[19] Anderson, "Rethinking Radicalism," 414; Steven Jensen, *The Making of International Human Rights: The 1960s, Decolonization, and the Reconstruction of Global Values* (Cambridge: Cambridge University Press, 2016), 37–38.

U Nu as part of his preparations for New York, thanking him for "the keen interest voiced by the new State of Burma and other Asiatic Powers in defence and protection of the rights of the subject, weak, and poor people like ourselves."[20] The Libyan nationalist leader and head of the National Council for the Liberation of Libya, Mansour Kaddara, had also written "there is no alternative but our independence," a position supported by the Indian and Burmese representatives in the Arab-Asian group.[21] Kaddara also exchanged letters with U Nu after meeting with the Burmese delegation in New York and maintained regular contact with other sympathetic non-Western delegations. Because of the collective dissent of Arab, Asian, and African representatives, and a last-minute conversion of Latin American delegations to their cause, the Bevin–Sforza Plan was defeated at the General Assembly.[22]

UNDOING IMPERIAL SOVEREIGNTY

Throughout the late 1940s and 1950s, petitions arrived from trust and non-self-governing territories in Africa and Oceania, including both Cameroons, New Guinea, Ruanda-Urundi, Tanganyika, Togoland, and the Pacific Islands. In the process of the creation of the trust territory of Somaliland, appointed to Italian administration in 1950, petitions flooded the Trusteeship Council from individuals and groups describing human rights violations. The question of the former Italian colonies drew the attention of political groups and NGOs active at the UN, such as the NAACP, which had supported Issa and the Somali Youth League in the earlier 1949 vote.[23] The United African Nationalist Movement, based in New York, also sent a cablegram to the Secretary-General "demand[ing] immediate arrest member of Italian delegation now asking the United Nations to return African colonies to Italy."[24] Other petitions addressed the question of unifying the Somali territories and claims by the Ethiopian government to borderlands, reflecting the complex geography and fragmentation of Somali nationalism created by colonial divisions.[25]

---

[20] Abdullahi Issa to U Nu, March 8, 1949, Acc. No. 321, National Archives of Myanmar.
[21] Mansour Kaddara to A. W. Cordier, May 11, 1949, S-05000-0006-14, UNARMS.
[22] The vote received widespread news coverage in the United States. For example, "Rebuffed on Ethiopian Colonies, 'White' Nations Lose Face at UN: Smashing Defeat for Western Bloc Backing Italy," *Pittsburgh Courier*, May 28, 1949.
[23] Anderson, "Rethinking Radicalism," 414.
[24] James R. Lawson to A. W. Cordier, April 16, 1949, S-05000-0006-14, UNARMS.
[25] Matshanda, "Constructing Citizens," 669.

Even petitions by Eritreans that showed more openness to a role for a UN observer or UN presence in East Africa "firmly reject[ed] any partition or mutilation [of] its territory."[26] However, when the United Nations established a commission of inquiry on Eritrea in November 1950, its purpose was "to ascertain more fully the wishes and the best means of promoting the welfare of the inhabitants of Eritrea" yet UN officials supported the British demand to "require severe restrictions on public discussions."[27] The British delegation regularly asserted that Eritrea was not "ripe for independence" because of reported violence and riots.[28]

Trust territories produced large numbers of anticolonial petitions. Rather than keeping such communications confidential, other UN representatives from the postcolonial world referenced these letters in their statements and used them to condemn Italian administration. Later petitions demanded national self-determination for the Somali people, while condemning continued violations of human rights. These letters called for independence through unification of the territories formerly under British and Italian control.[29] Petitions tended to emphasize national unity and territorial integrity, most commonly against divided European rule. However, many Eritrean petitions also called for maintaining unity against partition by neighboring Ethiopia. The vision for national self-determination expressed by these petitions did not identify the imagined national government but it made clear that only an internal and indigenous solution, rather than a regional one, would be acceptable. While Muslim groups in Somaliland and Eritrea appealed to a pan-Islamic sentiment in their letters to Pakistan and Arab League member-states, the primary objective of their demands was immediate independence and national elections, with strong opposition to alternative and gradual arrangements that would redraw the map along ethnic, religious, or linguistic lines.

The early 1950s witnessed continued growth in anticolonial solidarity movements at the UN. Despite the defeat of the Bevin–Sforza Plan, Somaliland was returned to Italy and made into a ten-year trust territory

---

[26] Petition from Mohamed Surur, April 9, 1949, S-05000-0006-14, UNARMS.

[27] General Assembly resolution 4/289, *Question of the Disposal of the Former Italian Colonies*, A/RES/289 (November 21, 1949), www.worldlii.org/int/other/UNGA/1949/51.pdf; Petrus J. Schmidt to Trygve Lie, March 7, 1950, S-0002-0001-01 Eritrea I, UNARMS.

[28] Schmidt to Lie, March 7, 1950.

[29] Petition from the Somali National League, United Nations, Trusteeship Council, T/PET.11/L.33 (February 4, 1959), UNARMS.

beginning in 1950 after "having heard spokesmen of organizations representing substantial sections of opinion in the territories concerned."[30] With the return of Italian military forces, the Trust Territory of Somaliland became the first and only trust in the history of the UN to have been granted to the former colonizer.[31] Libya gained immediate independence, keeping all three regions integral with a future constitution and National Assembly under the guidance of a UN commissioner. The General Assembly also passed another resolution on petitions sent during the visiting missions and inquiry committees conducted as part of the trusteeship process. Without acknowledging the large number of petitions sent in the previous year, the resolution permitted the Trusteeship Council to "accelerat[e] the examination and disposal of petitions" in favor of regular reporting by such visiting missions "on the steps taken towards self-government or independence."[32] The brief resolution thus further minimized direct communication from local inhabitants and groups and magnified the role of UN-appointed officials such as the UN commissioner and state-level missions to give reports on the state of affairs in Somaliland. This sanctioned expansion of Italian sovereignty in East Africa galvanized continued action and coordination by anticolonial and postcolonial delegations, who further condemned the International Trusteeship System and raised other colonial questions.

In November 1952, Indonesian Prime Minister Dr. Ali Sastroamidjojo came to the UN to meet with other leaders and speak at the plenary sessions. At the Fourth Committee of the General Assembly, Sastroamidjojo focused his comments on long-standing criticisms of the Trusteeship Council and "called for a re-examination of the Trusteeship Council's approach to the whole Trusteeship problem" because "such nations as Burma, India, Indonesia, Pakistan and the Philippines are in the position of being able to bring to the United Nations the most recent testimony, that colonialism, however, enlightened it may be made to appear today, is no substitute for self-government or independence."[33]

---

[30] General Assembly resolution 4/289.

[31] Pamela Ballinger, *The World Refugees Made: Decolonization and the Foundation of Postwar Italy* (Ithaca: Cornell University Press, 2020), 129.

[32] General Assembly resolution 4/321, *International Trusteeship System: Petitions and Visiting Missions*, A/RES/321 (November 21, 1949), www.worldlii.org/int/other/UNGA/1949/36.pdf.

[33] Report, "Republic of Indonesia: The Eighth Year of a Free Nation: 1952," August 17, 1953, Indonesian Mission to the United Nations File, Inventaris Arsip Lambertus Nicodemus Palar, No.123, National Archives of the Republic of Indonesia.

Sastroamidjojo stressed the point previously raised by the Arab-Asian group that administering authorities continued to avoid producing development plans or timetables for their trust territories.[34] While the Trust Territory of Somaliland had a fixed term of ten years, it was exceptional for its more rigidly defined terms and direct oversight by UN officials compared to other trust territories. The Trusteeship Council, rather than providing an avenue to self-government, had become an obstacle to the achievement of independence and a means of maintaining imperial sovereignty.

Recalling Indonesia's own independence struggle and the role south–south solidarity played in its international petitioning, Sastroamidjojo also situated his critique of the trusteeship system within his overall foreign policy posture of non-alignment and the rejection of bloc politics. This manifestation of Afro-Asian solidarity not only promoted independence for trust territories but also emphasized independence in the wider Cold War landscape. The entangled and enduring relationship between the global Cold War and empire gave rise to criticisms of the UN from its postcolonial members, especially diplomats from neutralist nations in Asia whose independence did not signal disengagement from international diplomacy but rather a continued presence at the UN, that is, until Indonesia became the first UN member-state to withdraw formally from the UN in 1965 because of "the circumstances created by colonial powers in the United Nations so blatantly against our anti-colonial struggle."[35] Thus, the incomplete process of decolonization remained at the forefront of postcolonial action at the UN, showing that anticolonial member-states from the global South were hardly passive or merely subject to Great Power interference.

The work of undoing imperial sovereignty remained a central objective of postcolonial internationalists even after independence; it constituted a linkage between postcolonial delegations and colonial peoples still petitioning for international recognition. In the early postwar years, the Arab-Asian group was one of the central anticolonial coalitions at the UN that advocated for independence. This group expanded with the addition of more postcolonial Asian and African states. Fabian Klose observes that petitions remained a key part of their strategy. The first mass petitions

---

[34] Ibid.
[35] Indonesia resumed its membership later that year. First Deputy Prime Minister and Minister for Foreign Affairs of Indonesia to the UN Secretary-General, S/6157, A/5857 (January 21, 1965), https://digitallibrary.un.org/record/574683?ln=en.

sent to the General Assembly occurred during the Algerian War and were accompanied by additional petitions by Arab-Asian member-states from within the UN.[36] Such petitions were crucial for building international support for anticolonial causes outside of the UN. Within the UN, petitions by official member-states kept colonial questions on the official agenda, helping to retain attention on conditions in colonies and territories. However, not all petitions received the support of this growing postcolonial collective. Emma Kluge shows how petitions from West Papua in the 1960s, demanding the right to self-determination, were denied consideration by Indonesia, illustrating the limits of decolonization and a focus on dismantling the European empires rather than the liberation of all peoples claiming occupation.[37] Moreover, the UN did not recognize a human right to petition until the passage of the International Covenant on Civil and Political Rights in 1966, an instrument that lists the right to self-determination as its first article. Long before the petition's rights were recognized as universal, colonial peoples deployed them to challenge authority and publicize their campaigns for independence.

CONCLUSION

The right to petition, sundered from the burgeoning international human rights system, instead gained purchase in anticolonial circles as a mechanism to challenge empire. Petitions were used to condemn imperialism and to demand recognition of human rights within colonies that had been reconfigured as trust territories in the postwar international order. As an instrument of critique, petitions also created bonds of solidarity between the colonized and decolonized, raised up by postcolonial elites from the Arab-Asian group through their advocacy for the right to national self-determination. As Adom Getachew has argued, rather than reading the postwar as "a moment in which nationalism and the nation-state eclipsed anticolonial internationalism," it is possible to identify threads of connection that linked different anticolonial visions and proposed alternatives to empire even from within the reassertion of imperial control, prior to the

---

[36] See Fabian Klose, "Human Rights for and against Empire – Legal and Public Discourses in the Age of Decolonisation," *Journal of the History of International Law* 18 (2016): 337.

[37] See Emma Kluge, "West Papua and the International History of Decolonization, 1961–69," *The International History Review* 42, no. 6 (2020): 1155–1172.

achievement of nationhood that trust territories embodied.[38] Despite the denial of independence symbolized by the fact of trusteeship, petitions compelled interactions between the colonizer and colonized, albeit limited, while also widening the horizons of the transnational anticolonial. Petitions established a direct connection between rights claims and the ultimate claim to liberation envisioned as the ends of anticolonial struggle, while at the same time capturing how decolonization linked the postcolonial world to peoples still under domination.

---

[38] Adom Getachew, *Worldmaking after Empire: The Rise and Fall of Self-Determination* (Princeton: Princeton University Press, 2019), 207.

9

African Nationalism, Anti-Imperial Lexicons, and the Development of China–Tanzania Relations, 1960–1966

Ruodi Duan

The arc of negotiations for China–Tanzania relations in the early to mid-1960s reflects the haphazard, uneven process in the transposition of socialist concepts onto the networks and imaginaries of anti-imperial transnationalism. In late colonial Tanganyika, the rise of African nationalism responded in part to long-standing British policies that encouraged Indian settlement in East Africa and granted social and political privileges to the Indian minority. After Tanganyikan independence in 1961, local metaphors of exploitation merged with new discourses of nation-building and *ujamaa*, or the Tanzanian vision of socialism, to target Indian merchants and landlords as the barrier to the full realization of African liberation. For representatives of the People's Republic of China (PRC), hopeful about extending political and developmental influences in postcolonial Africa, this popular identification of Indians as the culprit of economic profiteering in Tanganyika dovetailed with their campaign to denounce India as transgressor of the 1962 Sino-Indian Border War, in active collusion with British and US imperial interests. As such, the discourse of anti-imperial transnationalism between China and Tanzania relied on a nominal collapse of race and class categories, drawing from socialist repertoires to demarcate India and its East African diaspora as pernicious conspirators in advancing Western imperialism and neo-colonialism.

But conversely, in Zanzibar – a collection of islands 30 miles off the port of Dar es Salaam, briefly an independent nation before joining with Tanganyika to form the United Republic of Tanzania in April 1964 – Chinese efforts to realize a class-based vision of anticolonial transnationalism clashed with conceptions of African nationalism and Pan-Africanism that similarly conflated race and class, attacking vestiges of Arab economic and political dominance in Zanzibar as the most intractable impediment to national liberation. Chinese officials argued that the "primarily working-class Arabs of the Middle East and North Africa" belonged to same anti-imperialist camp as other Asians and Africans. Meanwhile, African nationalists in Zanzibar insisted on classifying Arabs as "feudalists," their stakes too deep and privileges too numerous in the pre-colonial and colonial past to justly participate in the islands' postcolonial future.

To capture the promises and tensions embedded within socialist articulations of anticolonial transnationalism, this chapter traces the development of China–Tanzania relations across a number of significant events in Tanzanian history: the transition from colonial to independent Tanganyika in December 1961; the January 1964 Zanzibar Revolution, in which collaborators from the African nationalist Afro-Shirazi Party (ASP) and the socialist Umma Party violently deposed the ruling Sultan a mere six weeks after Zanzibar's independence; and the union of Tanganyika and Zanzibar that followed.[1] In addition, it is attuned to the complex role of Pan-Africanism and the ever-tenuous relationship between Zanzibar and the mainland in the establishment of anticolonial solidarities between China and Tanzania.

More specifically, moments of communion and discord in the early 1960s negotiation of China–Tanzania relations indicate the enduring salience of racial cleavages, inherited from or amplified by colonialism, to socialist formations of anti-imperial transnationalism.[2] If racial formation

---

[1] The Zanzibar Revolution sought to overthrow the postcolonial coalition government of the Zanzibar Nationalist Party (ZNP) and the Zanzibar and Pemba People's Party (ZPPP), as a means of upending the racialized social hierarchy inherited from British colonial rule. During the Revolution and in its immediate aftermath, African insurgents, mostly youth, primarily targeted the Arab community on the islands; thousands lost their lives and countless businesses were destroyed, leading to an Arab exodus to the Persian Gulf. See Anthony Clayton, *The Zanzibar Revolution and Its Aftermath* (London: C. Hurst, 1981).

[2] Reflecting trends in the histories of China in Africa more broadly, discussions of China–Tanzania relations, though diverse in their methods and conclusions, have largely abstained from using race and racialization as a primary or overarching framework in their analyses. See, for example, George Yu, *China and Tanzania: A Study in Cooperative Interaction* (Berkeley: University of California Press, 1970); Bruce D. Larkin, *China and Africa: 1949–1970: The Foreign Policy of the People's Republic of China* (Berkeley: University of California Press, 1971); Alaba Ogunsanwo, *China's Policy in Africa 1958–1971* (Cambridge: Cambridge University Press, 1974); George Yu, *China's African Policy: A Study of Tanzania* (New York: Praeger, 1975); Richard Hall and Hugh Peyman, *The Great Uhuru Railway: China's Showpiece in Africa* (London: Victor Gollancz, 1976); Bailey Martin, *Freedom Railway: China and the Tanzania–Zambia Link* (London: Rex Collings, 1976); Kasuka Mutukwa, *Politics of the Tanzania-Zambia Rail*

is understood as fluid and contingent, socially and historically constructed, then the racialization of China in decolonizing and postcolonial Tanzania was refracted by visions of African nationalism that repudiated Indian – and to a lesser extent, Arab – legacies in the region.[3] All in all, these dynamics evince the contradictions and limits of anticolonial transnationalism at the height of the Cold War, underpinned by the malleability of relatively new analytical categories like nation and class.

The Tanganyika African National Union (TANU), the governing party in postcolonial Tanzania, would forge connections with the Communist Party of China (CCP) on joint condemnations of Indians as abetting Western imperial and neo-colonial interests. But at the same time, Pan-Africanist collaboration between TANU and the Afro-Shirazi Party in Zanzibar, the African nationalist party that assumed governance of the islands after the Zanzibar Revolution, created political conundrums in the progression of China–Zanzibari relations as an anti-imperial alliance. This chapter begins with the account of a visit by a small group of TANU representatives, under the leadership of General Administrative Secretary Ali Mwinyi Tambwe, to Beijing in 1962. The first Tanganyikan cultural delegation to arrive in the People's Republic of China, its express purpose for the trip was to convince Chinese leaders to abandon their endorsement of the socialist-leaning but Arab-dominated Zanzibar Nationalist Party (ZNP) in favor of the ASP if they truly wished to support the anti-imperialist cause in decolonizing and postcolonial Africa.

* * *

Project: *A Study of Tanzania–China–Zambia Relations* (Lanham, MD: University Press of America, 1977); Philip Snow, *The Star Raft: China's Encounter with Africa* (Ithaca, NY: Cornell University Press, 1989); Deborah Brautigham, *The Dragon's Gift: The Real Story of China in Africa* (New York: Oxford University Press, 2009); Jamie Monson, *Africa's Freedom Railway: How a Chinese Development Project Changed Lives and Livelihoods in Tanzania* (Bloomington: Indiana University Press, 2009); and Alicia Altorfer-Ong, "Old Comrades and New Brothers: A Historical Re-examination of the Sino-Zanzibari and Sino-Tanzanian Bilateral Relationships in the 1960s" (PhD diss., London School of Economics and Political Science, 2014). One exception is that Jamie Monson has written about the triangulation of African, Chinese, and white Euro-American racial identities in the construction of China–African relations. See Jamie Monson, "Historicizing Difference: Construction of Race Identity in China-Africa Relations," Working Paper of the China-Africa Knowledge Project, Social Science Research Council, September 2014 (https://china-africa.ssrc.org/wp-content/uploads/2015/01/Monson-Final.pdf).

[3] This is in reference to the classic definition of racial formation, as formulated by the sociologists Howard Omi and Michael Winant. See Howard Omi and Michael Winant, *Racial Formation in the United States: Third Edition* (New York: Routledge, 2015), p. 61.

In the years leading up to formal independence in December 1963, Zanzibar witnessed fierce political and ideological dissension as to the racial and social configuration of its postcolonial identity.[4] From 1698 until the establishment of a British Protectorate in 1890, the islands had been governed first as part of the Omani Empire and later as an Islamic state under the Sultan of Zanzibar; in the eighteenth and nineteenth centuries, it served as the capital of the East African Slave Trade, in which Arab traders transported slaves from East Africa to the Arabian Gulf, the Indian Ocean islands, and South Asia. Under British rule, Zanzibar was allowed to retain its pre-colonial social structure, with the Arab and Indian communities receiving greater opportunities for higher education, commerce, and civil service employment to the exclusion of the African majority.

The rise of Arab nationalism in the 1950s was entwined with the campaign for unconditional independence, both of which found expression in the Zanzibar Nationalist Party.[5] On the other hand, early iterations of African nationalism were characterized by disunity between Shirazis, an ambiguous ethnic classification that denoted Persian heritage, and increasing numbers of African migrant workers from the mainland. The ASP of the late 1950s and early 1960s practiced an ideologically nebulous politics that valued African nationalism above all other considerations, including anticolonialism. Its leader Abeid Karume, who would become the first President of Zanzibar, had even expressed willingness to partner with the British in order to defer any form of independence that would likely result in a predominantly Arab government.[6] Meanwhile, Tanganyikan politicians followed the crises on Zanzibar with great interest and sought to intervene. In 1956 and again in 1957, Julius Nyerere, president of a nascent TANU, visited Zanzibar at the invitation of the island's African Association to declare his support for the union of Shirazis and Africans into a singular political party.[7] Subsequently,

---

[4] These years between 1957 and the January 1964 Revolution are also known in Zanzibar as "*zama za siasa*," or the "time of politics," referring to a period when racial animosities dominated political debates over Zanzibari identity, culminating in the wave of anti-Arab and anti-Indian violence that followed the Revolution.

[5] Michael Lofchie, *Zanzibar: Background to Revolution* (Princeton: Princeton University Press, 1965), pp. 127–156.

[6] Issa Shivji, *Pan-Africanism or Pragmatism: Lessons of the Tanganyika-Zanzibar Union* (Dar es Salaam: Mkuki na Nyota Publishers, 2008), pp. 36–39.

[7] Michael Lofchie, "Party Conflict in Zanzibar," *Journal of Modern African Studies* 1 (1963): p. 197.

FIGURE 9.1. Premier Zhou Enlai with Second Vice President Rashidi Kawawa and First Vice President Abeid Karume (Zanzibar, May 1965). From: *The Afro-Shirazi Party Revolution*, 1974.

preceding the 1957 general elections for Zanzibar's Legislative Council, the African Association and the Shirazi Association announced their merging into the Afro-Shirazi Party.

This working relationship between the ASP and TANU, an affirmation of Pan-Africanism, provides context for the contentious September 1962 visit to China of Ali Mwinyi Tambwe, who led a three-member TANU delegation. Tambwe would praise the medical attention he received in China for his prostatitis and joint pain, and arrangements were made for the selection of the first Tanganyikan students to complete technical courses in China. But Tambwe's objectives for the trip were not contained to medical treatment, drug prescriptions, or, as delineated in the records of the Foreign Cultural Liaison Committee (FCLC) in Beijing, reaching a deeper understanding of nation-building and central party operations within China. Rather, his primary goal was to convince Chinese Prime Minister Zhou Enlai and Vice Minister Chen Yi that their endorsement of the ZNP, predominantly Arab in composition but socialist and anti-imperialist in outlook, was misguided and that they should switch support to the ASP instead. It is unsurprising that among the TANU leadership, Tambwe was chosen for this task. He was a Zanzibari native of Comorian descent who relocated to the mainland

and became involved with TANU amidst the 1950s struggle for Tanganyikan independence.

The course of Tambwe's troubled visit suggests that early 1960s Chinese efforts to realize a class-based conception of anti-imperial transnationalism conflicted with an African nationalism that viewed Arab ascendancy or influence in any way as a continuation of colonial domination. Tambwe premised his arguments on the equation of Arabs in Zanzibar with a class of "feudalists" and "exploiters," employing "imperialist" as a racialized category for all non-African encroachments on Tanganyikan and Zanzibari politics. Zhou and Chen, however, took a different view as to the most significant imperial threat in East Africa; they pushed for a distinction between "old" and "new" colonialisms in which the latter, in the form of Eastern Bloc and Western aid, gravely imperiled postcolonial sovereignty. When Zhou took the opportunity to warn that "the Peace Corps is even more shrewd than old-time colonialism at drugging the masses and maintaining the semblance of peace," Tambwe responded that regardless of the presence of Peace Corps volunteers in Tanganyika, it was only of importance for their presence to not interfere with national economy and foreign policy. Disquieted by this answer, Zhou reminded Tambwe that though Tanganyikan leaders may be aware of the true intentions of the Peace Corps, the Tanganyikan people may not be. Deeply upset, Tambwe countered:

Every move of the Peace Corps is monitored. Tanganyika is an independent country. The independence struggle taught the people what imperialism is. Even if they don't have cultural education, they have political education ... It is in these most difficult of circumstances that we ask for help from China [but] you must know, Tanganyika would rather suffer from hunger and malnutrition than to sell her freedom and sovereignty.[8]

Here, Chinese officials expected one thing that Tambwe would not give: the implicit recognition that China monopolized the power to define "old and new" colonialisms.

In Tambwe's appeals for China to withdraw its support for the ZNP, the underlying assumptions and logic, as well as the hesitance with which they were met, departed from Chinese scripts with regards to the lexicons and strategies of anti-imperial solidarities. For Chinese representatives,

---

[8] "周恩来总理接见坦噶尼喀文化代表团谈话记录 [Record of Conversation during Prime Minister Zhou's Reception of the Tanganyikan Cultural Delegation]," October 19, 1962, File No. 108-00276-06, the Foreign Ministry Archives of the People's Republic of China (hereafter: PRC FMA), Beijing, China.

racism existed and engendered popular divisions, but ultimately detracted from transnational class unity. For Tambwe, anti-imperialism was a racial project that had little to do with global economic systems. Following along this line of reasoning promoted by Tambwe, East African decolonization hinged primarily, if not exclusively, on the undoing of colonial racial hierarchies beyond Black and white; it meant the reclaiming of privileges once granted to the Arab and Indian communities, a necessary measure on the road to African ownership of the national destiny.

With regards to the Zanzibar question, Tambwe was persistent. In discussions with Chen Yi, he emphasized the duplicity of the ZNP. Tambwe claimed that it was after ZNP electoral failures that they siphoned members from the ASP to form the socialist Umma Party, for the sole purpose of inhibiting African unity.[9] "Africans in Zanzibar are not educated," he explained, "and their leadership cannot come to China to state their position. But the ZNP can come to China to publicize their beliefs, in a way that befits your tastes and win your support. They are the feudalists." To this, Chen responded with evident displeasure, countering that "The Chinese people are not so easily duped." "The Arabs of North Africa are anti-imperialists," he added, "and I regret that you, as a leader of the ruling party of Tanganyika, would come [to China and] call them imperialists ... The 50,000 Arabs of Zanzibar are not all feudalists and exploiters. Some of them are laborers, a part of the oppressed, and it is critical to draw distinctions."[10] The debate over the role of Arabs as "feudalists" or anti-imperial allies in late colonial Zanzibar reveals the inconsistency at the heart of Chinese efforts to promote a socialist narrative of anticolonial transnationalism. In this exchange with Tambwe, Chen refused to acknowledge race as a stand-alone analytical category. But as the latter part of this chapter suggests, Chinese officials would be more than willing to endorse racialized equations of the Indian diasporic community in mainland Tanzania with a "class" of reactionary exploiters.[11]

---

[9] "陈毅副总理接见坦噶尼喀文化代表团团长坦布维的谈话纪要 [Summary of Conversation from Vice Prime Minister Chen Yi's Reception of Tanganyikan Cultural Delegation Leader Tambwe]," October 9, 1962, File No. 108-00276-07, PRC FMA.

[10] "陈毅副总理接见坦噶尼喀文化代表团团长坦布维的谈话纪要 [Summary of Conversation from Vice Prime Minister Chen Yi's Reception of Tanganyikan Cultural Delegation Leader Tambwe].

[11] Jonathon Glassman, *War of Words, War of Stones: Racial Thought and Violence in Colonial Zanzibar* (Bloomington: Indiana University Press, 2011), p. 168.

In his persuasive campaign, Tambwe leaned heavily on the motif that the African racial majority, rather than the Arab minority, were the true representatives of Africa. In conversations with the FCLC in Beijing, which coordinated the logistics for his reception, Tambwe stated that many Africans he was acquainted with believed China's support for the ZNP stemmed only from their shared racial heritage with Arabs, as they were both "Asians." That Chinese leaders have given this impression, Tambwe tempered, is rooted in misunderstanding rather than malintent; they can rectify this honest mistake by recognizing the ASP, who constituted "the real Africans," instead.[12] Upon Tambwe's return to Tanganyika, the FCLC reported back to the Chinese Consulate in Dar es Salaam that Tambwe tried repeatedly to win assurance from Chen that China would, at the very least, declare neutrality in the 1963 Zanzibar elections. To this direct request, Chen only offered that China did not wish to interfere in the domestic politics of other nations.

From Beijing, Tambwe embarked on a two-day visit to Shanghai, where its municipal branch of the FCLC received on the eve of his arrival a detailed account of his earlier transgressions: Tambwe claimed that he did not oppose Western imperialism so much as the domination of the Arab "class," that the Tanganyikan road to nationhood was most desirable since no blood was shed, and that the Congolese were wrong to demand independence "in a hurry."[13] Moreover, he insisted that the fundamental issue in the Congo was not one of US imperialism per se but of foreign competition over the breakaway Republic of Katanga.[14] In Shanghai, Tambwe continued to voice resistance to Chinese warnings about US imperialism. "The number one imperialists [in Zanzibar] are the Arabs, followed by the British, Germans, and Americans," Tambwe declared to the Vice Mayor of Shanghai, "and the reason Zanzibar is not independent is not [because of] imperialism. It is because there is a small

[12] "国庆外宾接待工作简报 [Reports from Receptions of Foreign Guests on National Day]," Foreign Cultural Liaison Committee Office for the Reception of Foreign Guests on National Day, October 6, 1962, File No. 108-00284-06, PRC FMA.

[13] "对外文联上海联络处接待坦噶尼喀文化友好代表团长的计划与简报 [Plans and Reports of the Foreign Cultural Liaison Committee Regarding the Reception of Tanganyikan Cultural Delegation Team Leader]," File No. C37-2-858, Shanghai Municipal Archives (hereafter: SMA), Shanghai, China.

[14] Under the leadership of Moise Tsombe, Katanga was a breakaway state that announced its independence in 1960 with the support of the Belgian military and mining interests. Disappointed with the reluctance of United Nations to send troops in order to quell the secession, Congolese Prime Minister Patrice Lumumba agreed to accept military aid from the Soviet Union, a decision which drew the ire of the United States.

ruling group preventing its independence." In response to Chinese efforts to impose their reading of political developments in Africa, Tambwe countered, "We are clear-headed about situations in Africa and we have no further need for education."[15]

The Chinese failure to realize a class-based anti-imperialism that mapped onto the political realities of Zanzibari anticolonial nationalism was not a unique chapter in the shortcomings of Afro-Asian solidarity politics to address the complexity of race relations in the postcolonial world. Radio Cairo, a key component of Egyptian President Gamal Abdel Nasser's campaign to extend Egypt's influence in East Africa, launched its Swahili-language programming in 1954. While the anticolonial messaging of the broadcasts facilitated the rise of popular sentiments against British rule, their stance with regards to race and class generated controversy. Radio Cairo pushed "the Bandung spirit" as one premised on an Asian, Arab, and African united front. In doing so, its programming proved palatable for supporters of the ZNP but alienated scores of African nationalists, serving as ammunition that reinforced their antipathy for Arab platitudes about multiracialism.[16] Just as Egyptian propaganda overlooked the deeply felt history of racial hierarchy in Zanzibar and witnessed its Afro-Asian rhetoric ring hollow, so did Chinese officials who disregarded finer cleavages of race and nation within Asia and Africa.

In May 1964, five delegates from the Afro-Shirazi Party Youth League (ASPYL), a subdivision of the now ascendant ASP, arrived in Shanghai.[17] In the aftermath of the visit, the Chinese Communist Youth League warily assessed that the ASPYL representatives had espoused a reductive and inaccurate understanding of imperialism.[18] They concurred with their

[15] "对外文联上海联络处接待坦噶尼喀文化友好代表团团长的计划与简报 [Plans and Reports of the Foreign Cultural Liaison Committee Regarding the Reception of Tanganyikan Cultural Delegation Team Leader]."

[16] James Brennan, "Radio Cairo and the Decolonization of East Africa, 1953–1964," in Christopher Lee ed., *Making a World after Empire: The Bandung Moment and Its Political Afterlives* (Athens: Ohio University Press, 2010), pp. 173–190.

[17] Established in 1959, the ASPYL figured prominently in the planning and execution of the 1964 Zanzibar Revolution, replacing the Sultan of Zanzibar and his predominantly Arab government with an African one under President Abeid Karume. In the aftermath of the Revolution, the ASPYL continued to play a critical role in the political, social, and cultural life of Zanzibar. See Thomas Burgess, "Remembering Youth: Generation in Revolutionary Zanzibar," *Africa Today* 46 (1999): pp. 29–45.

[18] "共青团上海市委员会接待桑给巴尔奔巴非洲色拉子青年联盟代表团的计划，简报，讲话稿，消息报等 [Plans, Reports, Draft Speeches, and News of the Communist Youth

Chinese hosts that Zanzibar under British rule resembled pre-revolutionary China, with racial discrimination codified into law and equal pay withheld for equal work. But when conversation turned to the Zanzibar Revolution earlier that year, Chinese officials observed that their guests remembered the uprising with inappropriate glee, especially when recounting a three-day stint in which they looted Arab and Indian-owned businesses. Disappointed that the ASPYL delegates appeared to orient their anti-imperialism around racial nationalism rather than transnational class solidarity, they wrote:

The delegates from Zanzibar displayed a blindly anti-foreign attitude, and when they saw Europeans come in to the restaurant they would yell that the foreign devils have arrived ... When we tried to explain that Europe was also home to laboring classes who stand with the Asian, African, and Latin American people, their leader responded "... If one snake has bitten you, the others that have not bitten you are also bad. We must always be on heightened alarm because poor people can be bad too."[19]

In the decade that followed, even as Zanzibari nationalists implemented Chinese discourses and practices of development, specifically an emphasis on discipline and frugality, they sought to exclude Arabs and Indians from the nation-building project in a "simultaneous repudiation and embrace of Afro-Asian solidarities," to borrow from the observation of Thomas Burgess.[20] Their conviction in Zanzibar as an "African nation" free from Arab influences stood at odds with Chinese imaginations of an international socialist anti-imperialist front that included the ranks of Arab peasants and laborers. These ruptures bring to light the ends and limits within the process of fusing socialist vocabularies and anticolonial networks, as national representatives bitterly contested the stakes and meanings of national liberation, class, and neo-colonialism amidst formal decolonization. A fundamental disagreement about race and class categorizations as lexicons for anti-imperialism inhibited the reaching of

---

League Shanghai Branch's Reception of the Zanzibar-Pemba Afro-Shirazi Party Youth League Delegation]," File No. C21-2-2357, SMA.

[19] "共青团上海市委员会接待桑给巴尔奔巴非洲色拉子青年联盟代表团的计划，简报，讲话稿，消息报等 [Plans, Reports, Draft Speeches, and News of the Communist Youth League Shanghai Branch's Reception of the Zanzibar-Pemba Afro-Shirazi Party Youth League Delegation]."

[20] G. Thomas Burgess, "Mao in Zanzibar: Nationalism, Discipline, and the (De) Construction of Afro-Asian Solidarities," in Christopher Lee ed., *Making a World after Empire: The Bandung Moment and Its Political Afterlives* (Athens: Ohio University Press, 2010), p. 200.

common ground between the CCP, the ASP, and its allies within TANU. But compatibility on a very similar issue would help to facilitate growing affinities between Chinese and TANU representatives in the same period.

***

For the plurality of African nationalists on the mainland, the realization of *ujamaa* entailed the undoing of exploitation, racially defined as annulling the influence of Indian landlords and capitalists in the country's urban cores. Indian traders had settled in Zanzibar before the advent of European colonialism, but it was in the late nineteenth and early twentieth centuries that Indian merchant networks expanded throughout German East Africa. In British Tanganyika, colonial officers recruited Indian laborers for the work of construction and administration while encouraging other emigrants to invest in land and small-scale businesses.[21] Racial consciousness among Africans in Tanganyika developed in part to challenge these British policies of the 1940s and 1950s, and after the struggle for independence, Indians in Tanzania found themselves targeted as the antithesis of good postcolonial citizens.[22] This analytic would overlap with Maoist condemnations of "the comprador bourgeois," or internal reactionaries who work with foreign imperialists to preserve a system from which they benefit, a concept coined in 1920s

---

[21] See John Iliffe, *A Modern History of Tanganyika* (New York: Cambridge University Press, 1979), pp. 264–268; Eric Burton, "'What Tribe Should We Call Him?' The Indian Diaspora, the State, and the Nation in Tanzania since 1850," *Stichproben: Wiener Zeitschrift für kritische Afrikastudien* 13 (2013): pp. 1–28; Laura Fair, "Drive-In Socialism: Debating Modernities and Development in Dar es Salaam, Tanzania," *The American Historical Review* 118, no. 4 (2013): pp. 1077–1104; Ronald Aminzade, *Race, Nation, and Citizenship in Postcolonial Africa: The Case of Tanzania* (New York: Cambridge University Press, 2015); Ned Bertz, *Diaspora and Nation in the Indian Ocean: Transnational Histories of Race and Urban Space in Tanzania* (Honolulu: University of Hawaii Press, 2015); and Marie-Aude Fouéré, "Indians Are Exploiters and Africans Idlers! The Production of Racial Categories and Socioeconomic Issues in Tanzania," in Michel Adam ed., *Indian Africa: Minorities of Indian-Pakistani Origin in Eastern Africa* (Dar es Salaam: Mkuki na Nyota Publishers, 2015), pp. 359–396. For a comparative perspective, see Sana Aiyar, *Indians in Kenya: The Politics of Diaspora* (Cambridge, MA: Harvard University Press, 2015). For older texts that offer a regional assessment, see Dharam Ghai ed., *Portrait of a Minority: Asians in East Africa* (Nairobi: Oxford University Press, 1965); Agehananda Bharati, *The Asians in East Africa: Jaihind and Uhuru* (Chicago: Nelson-Hall Co., 1972); and Robert Gregory, *Quest for Equality: Asian Politics in East Africa 1900–67* (Hyderabad and London: Orient Longman & Sangham, 1993).

[22] James Brennan, *Taifa: Making Nation and Race in Urban Tanzania* (Athens: Ohio University Press, 2012), pp. 118–158.

China with reference to right-wing members of the Nationalist Party profitably engaged in commerce with Western investors. In the late 1950s and 1960s, Chinese leaders continued to maintain that in a number of postcolonial contexts, "native reactionaries" facilitated "neo-colonialism" in complicity with Western economic and political interests, echoing the conception that many African nationalists held onto of the Indian role in decolonizing and postcolonial East Africa.[23]

Even before the outbreak of the Sino-Indian Border War in 1962, the negotiation of Chinese relations with Zanzibar took place with the history of the Indian diaspora in the region as a foil. Abdulrahman Mohamed (A. M.) Babu, a Zanzibari nationalist leader and committed Marxist, would become instrumental to forging Cold War connections between Tanzania and China, successfully securing Chinese support in 1965 for construction of the Tanzam Railway that linked landlocked Zambia to the port city of Dar es Salaam. In public speeches and private writings, Babu distanced himself from any conception of Zanzibari nationalism that privileged race over class analysis. Reactionary elements in the ZNP and ASP, he contended, employed the rhetoric of race to conceal the realities of class-based exploitation in Zanzibar. As such, he intended his founding of the socialist Umma Party in 1963 as a salve for the bitter bifurcation of African and Arab nationalism on the islands.[24]

But over the course of a January 1960 visit to Shanghai, during which Babu negotiated for the dispatching of the first Swahili broadcast workers to China for Radio Peking, he voiced to Vice Mayor Jin Zhonghua his suspicions about the outsized influences that Indians commanded in East Africa. "Indians can be very bad ... In many parts of East and Central Africa, the economy is controlled by Indians. In the past, Indians supported African liberation movements," Babu confided to Jin, "but now they are with the imperialists."[25] At this moment, sensing the opening to

---

[23] Anton Harder, "Compradors, Neo-colonialism, and Transnational Class Struggle: PRC relations with Algeria and India, 1953–1965," *Modern Asian Studies* (Published online in August 2020): p. 40. See also Yang Kuisong, "The Theory and Implementation of the People's Republic of China's Revolutionary Diplomacy," *Modern Chinese History* 3 (2009): pp. 127–145.

[24] A. M. Babu, "The 1964 Revolution: Lumpen or Vanguard?" in Abdul Sheriff and Ed Ferguson eds., *Zanzibar Under Colonial Rule* (London: James Currey Ltd, 1991), pp. 239–240.

[25] This belief that Indians participated in African liberation movements only to turn their backs on solidarity soon after is a reductive reading of a tenuous alliance. In the 1940s and 1950s, as African nationalism took shape in Tanganyika, Indian financiers helped support the activities of the African Association and its successor TANU, while TANU

gesture to a common opposition, Liu Liangmo – a member of Shanghai's Political Consultative Conference, who traveled throughout the United States in the 1940s and collaborated with African American singer and activist Paul Robeson to produce Robeson's 1942 Chinese-language album *Chee Lai: Songs of New China* – inserted himself into the conversation.[26] Liu inquired if Babu had received news about the border dispute between China and India from within Zanzibar. "Yes," Babu responded, "but only from India, and it is all a one-sided tale."[27] With this revelation, Liu immediately began to present the Chinese interpretation of events: that Indian Prime Minister Jawaharlal Nehru's pro-capitalist and anti-Chinese essence had provoked undue conflict.

In the ensuing years, Babu's publication *Zanews* in Zanzibar generously promoted this Chinese explanation of the conflict with India, with headlines such as "China's Ceasefire Statement Becomes Focus of Attention in Asia, Africa," which emphasized China's desire for peace in contrast to India's recalcitrance.[28] Perhaps more significantly, *Zanews* attributed popular anti-imperialist consensus within the Afro-Asian world to the question of China–India conflict. In November 1962, *Zanews* ran an editorial proclaiming that the Chinese proposal for ceasefire "is widely acclaimed by world public opinion, and in particular by Afro-Asian peoples and various organizations, and has surprisingly confounded all the reactionaries in the world."[29] Conversely, Nehru was depicted as inspiring the support only of Western leaders like Queen Elizabeth, with

operated as a racially exclusive organization until 1962, relying on racialized rhetoric about economic development and nationhood. See James Brennan, *Taifa: Making Nation and Race in Urban Tanzania*, pp. 143–153.

[26] For biographical information on Liu Liangmo and his collaboration with Paul Robeson, see Richard Jean So, *Transpacific Community: America, China, and the Rise and Fall of a Cultural Network* (New York: Columbia University Press, 2016), pp. 83–121.

[27] "中国人民保卫世界和平委员会上海市分会关于接待桑给巴尔民族主义党总书记穆罕默德及夫人的计划，日程安排，情况简报 [Plans, Itineraries, and Reports of the Chinese People's Committee for World Peace Shanghai Branch Regarding the Reception of ZNP General Secretary A. M. Babu and Wife]," File No. C36-2-105, SMA.

[28] "China's Ceasefire Statement Becomes Focus of Attention in Asia, Africa," *Zanews* (No. 510), November 28, 1962, Folder 4, Box 9, Michael Lofchie Collection, Charles E. Young Research Library, University of California, Los Angeles (UCLA).

[29] "For Peaceful Settlement of the Sino-Indian Boundary Question," *Zanews* (No. 509), November 27, 1962. See also, for example, "Nkrumah Objects to MacMillan's Support for India's Aggression," *Zanews* (No. 492), November 7, 1962; "India Occupies Chinese Territory, Says Pakistani Paper," *Zanews* (No. 492), November 7, 1962; "Cairo Papers Welcome Chinese Government Statement," *Zanews* (No. 509), November 27, 1962; and "Asian, African, and Latin American Press Feature Chinese Statement," *Zanews* (No. 509), November 27, 1962.

the British government pondering a "lend-lease act" for the provision of weapons to India.[30] At the same time, according to *Zanews*, Indians lamented their country's inability to win over allies in Asia and Africa.[31]

Paradoxically, anti-Indian sentiments in East Africa, framed by these new discourses of class and anti-imperialism, mounted in spite of the Indian state's prominent role in Afro-Asian international organizations, from their inception in the late 1940s into the 1960s. India had been an original convener of the 1955 Asian-African Conference in Bandung and an active participant in the anticolonial networks that preceded it.[32] Beyond interstate diplomacy, Indian writers and artists promoted Asian-African political and cultural collaboration in forums ranging from the Afro-Asian People's Solidarity Organization (AAPSO), headquartered in Cairo, to the Afro-Asian Writers' Conferences. On the other hand, Black intellectuals and activists working toward Pan-African liberation often looked to postcolonial India as a model of socialist development.[33] In a sense then, the exigencies of the Cold War both fostered and limited

[30] "British Queen Supports India's Invasion of China," *Zanews* (No. 492), November 7, 1962.

[31] "Indian Papers Continue to Deplore Lack of Afro-Asian Support," *Zanews* (No. 496), November 12, 1962. The Sino-Indian Border War did bring to light for the Indian government that many of its relationships in Africa had frayed and inspired efforts to remedy it, primarily through new forums for economic cooperation and assistance. See Gerard McCann, "From Diaspora to Third Worldism and the United Nations: India and the Politics of Decolonizing Africa," *Past and Present* 218 (2013): pp. 274–276. India's popularity in sub-Saharan Africa was at its height in the decades prior, when Mahatma Gandhi's concept of non-violent resistance influenced a generation of African anticolonial nationalists. See Ali Mazrui, "Africa between Gandhi and Nehru: An Afro-Asian Interaction," *African and Asian Studies* 16 (2017): pp. 14–30.

[32] For India's role at Bandung, see Itty Abraham, "From Bandung to NAM: Non-alignment and Indian Foreign Policy, 1947–65," *Commonwealth & Comparative Politics* 46 (2008): pp. 195–219. For the prelude, see Katharine McGregor and Vanessa Hearman, "Challenging the Lifeline of Imperialism: Reassessing Afro-Asian Solidarity and Related Activism in the Decade 1955–65," in Luis Eslava, Michael Fakhri, and Vasuki Nesiah eds., *Bandung, Global History, and International Law: Critical Pasts and Pending Futures* (New York: Cambridge University Press, 2017), pp. 161–176; Cindy Ewing, "The Colombo Power: Crafting Diplomacy in the Third World and Launching Afro-Asia at Bandung," *Cold War History* 19 (2019): pp. 1–19; Rachel Leow, "Asian Lessons in the Cold War Classroom: Trade Union Networks and the Multidirectional Pedagogies of the Cold War in Asia," *Journal of Social History* 53 (2019): pp. 429–453; and Carolien Stolte, "'The People's Bandung': Local Anti-Imperialists on an Afro-Asian Stage," *Journal of World History* 30 (2019): pp. 125–156.

[33] George Padmore, for example, maintained a close working relationship with Nehru. Leslie James, *George Padmore and Decolonization from Below: Pan-Africanism, the Cold War, and the End of Empire* (Basingstoke: Palgrave MacMillan, 2015): pp. 174–176.

real-time applications of Afro-Asianism and "the Bandung spirit": just as spaces for anticolonial advocacy opened up across national and continental borders, a class-oriented rhetoric of anti-imperial transnationalism worked to contain it.

Absent an enthusiastic proponent of Maoist theory in the vein of A. M. Babu, mainland Tanganyika's progression of relations with the People's Republic of China in the early 1960s was far more uncertain. In the period following Tanganyikan independence in December 1961, Chinese diplomats assessed that in contrast to more explicitly socialist-leaning African countries like the Somali Republic and Mali, Tanganyikan nationalists tended to possess neither an ironclad commitment to anti-imperialism nor any awareness of Chinese history and politics. When a seven-member delegation of the Chinese Commission for Foreign Cultural Relations (CFCR) returned from a visit to Dar es Salaam in March 1963, they negatively contrasted Tanganyika with the Somali Republic, where they had witnessed a deeper commitment to "cultural propaganda work" and received a more eager reception. On the other hand, they noted that Tanganyikans displayed "strong feelings of nationalism . . . [It is good that] they are full of resentment towards old-style colonialism, anger towards the 'middle-man' exploitation of the Indian merchants, and general friendliness towards us, but most people still lack knowledge about [China]. The official [from TANU] who accompanied us did not know Mao Zedong. Another official asked if China still had an emperor."[34] At a time when the future of China–Tanganyika relations was precarious, the CFCR named the positive aspects of Tanganyikan politics as local sentiments against not only the past and present of Western imperialism, but also the Indian role in a profoundly unjust colonial and postcolonial economy. This description of Indian contributions – or lack thereof – to the cause of Tanganyikan liberation, on the part of Babu as well as the CFCR, recalled the "comprador" figure of Maoism, or the native class of managers and contractors in service of colonial or neo-colonial interests.

During their visits to China in the 1960s, Tanganyikan nationalists openly expressed anti-Indian prejudices. Despite the official "non-racialist" outlook of TANU and Nyerere's pledge to a culturally pluralist vision

---

[34] "访问非洲五国总结报告 [Concluding Report from Visit of Five African Countries]," Chinese Commission for Foreign Cultural Relations, March 12, 1963, File No. 108-00955-02, PRC FMA.

of *ujamaa*, racial animosities heightened in this period.[35] Postcolonial discourses of nation-building and socialist development targeted Indian merchants and landlords as the barrier to African liberation, with the Swahili word *unyonyagi*, or "sucking," used as shorthand for non-African exploitation of the country. By 1971, the Building Acquisitions Act, which nationalized the majority of Indian-owned properties in Tanzania, had propelled a mass Indian exodus out of the country. As James Brennan concludes, "For many *ujamaa* supporters ... removing exploitation meant removing the enemies of African socialism, enemies whose qualities blurred economic and racial characteristics."[36] This conception of nation-making in postcolonial Tanzania mapped on to the blueprint for Afro-Asian internationalism advanced by Chinese officials, one which pivoted around the vilification of India in context of geopolitical conflict between China and India.

Chinese and Tanzanian representatives shared many moments of affinity over racial generalizations about Indians; these are meticulously captured in the records of the municipal Chinese associations charged with receiving foreign guests. In May 1965, Otini Kambona, younger brother of Tanzanian Foreign Minister Oscar Kambona, landed in Beijing for a six-city tour. During his time in Shanghai, Kambona delighted his hosts with his comments on topics ranging from the Vietnam War to the necessity for every hotel room to display a portrait of Mao. When the discussion turned to Soviet support for India during the Sino-Indian Border War, Kambona responded: "Indians are the reactionaries of the reactionaries. In Africa, there are many Indians. They brutally exploit Africans. We don't like them at all."[37] In a similar vein, during the visit of a Tanzanian soccer team to Shanghai in June 1966, team leader J. M. Mwongosi offered, "[President Nyerere] says Tanzania should learn from China because the Chinese people are sincere, not false or wicked, but even though Indians pay lip service to the right things, they are bad at heart. The Europeans taught them to be selfish and do bad things."[38]

---

35 Julius Nyerere, "Socialism Is Not Racialism," *The Nationalist*, February 14, 1967.
36 James Brennan, *Taifa: Making Nation and Race in Urban Tanzania*, pp. 4–5.
37 "中国人民对外文化友好协会上海市分会关于接待坦桑尼亚外长之弟奥蒂尼 - 埃博纳的文件 [Documents from the Shanghai Branch of the Chinese People's Association for Cultural Friendship with Foreign Countries Regarding the Reception of Otini Kambona, Younger Brother of the Tanzanian Foreign Minister]," File No. C37-2-1185, SMA.
38 "上海市体育运动委员会1966年接待阿联男子体操队, 马里, 刚果（布）, 坦桑尼亚足球队来沪访问比赛有关文件 [Documents from the Shanghai Athletics Association's

In this manner, unfavorable readings of the Indian diaspora in East Africa were proactively inferred and positively received. They figured critically into Chinese-Tanzanian constructions of friendship, whereby Indians became the stand-in for an Afro-Asian relationship that was unequal, undesirable, or neo-colonial in nature.

Chinese officials arranged for Tanzanian delegations visiting China in the 1960s to watch documentary films about the Sino-Indian Border War, an experience which additionally evoked for some guests their long-held resentment for Indians. Throughout the June 1963 stay in Shanghai of two representatives from the National Union of Tanganyika Workers (NUTA) – whose illicit photographs with Czech women from an earlier visit to Prague had been discovered by Chinese hotel staff, much to the chagrin of their hosts – they expressed a steady series of antagonistic notions about the position that Indians occupied in the Tanganyikan economy. "Tanganyikan Indians like commerce, even more than the British," the team leader explained, "and while the Americans set up their companies, they don't engage in commercial activities. Indians are exceptionally good at business and at speculation; they are the most cunning and dangerous."[39] In this instance, Indians were deemed even more pernicious than Westerners. Chinese representatives, explicitly charged with the mission of promoting the Chinese line with regards to the conflict with India, welcomed these sentiments of distrust.

When these two NUTA delegates watched a documentary about the Sino-Indian Border War, they quickly concurred with their hosts that "the Indians are indeed very bad." In response to a scene depicting the Chinese army victoriously withdrawing from China's claim lines and releasing Indian prisoners-of-war, one of the delegates expressed his awe with the combination of Chinese military prowess and compassion for the Indian soldiers who "provoked" needless conflict, such that the captives "had much to eat and much to laugh about, so grateful for their treatment that they teared up."[40] After the film, Zhang Qi, a representative of the Shanghai Municipal All-Workers Union, reiterated again that Nehru's "capitalist nature" instigated the war in the first place, an explanation

1966 Reception of the United Arab Emirates Men's Gymnastics Team and the Mali, Republic of Congo, and Tanzania Soccer Teams]," File No. B126-1-956, SMA.

[39] "接待坦噶尼喀劳工联合会代表团的计划, 日程, 情况汇报 [Plans, Itineraries, and Reports from the Reception of the National Union of Tanganyika Workers Delegation], File No. C1-2-178-4324, SMA.

[40] "接待坦噶尼喀劳工联合会代表团的计划, 日程, 情况汇报 [Plans, Itineraries, and Reports from the Reception of the National Union of Tanganyika Workers Delegation]."

that the two guests found very satisfying. This interplay of Chinese didactic efforts with Tanganyikan pre-conceptions about Indians actually allowed for these NUTA delegates to be assessed in an affirmative light in the Chinese record in spite of their other infractions, however egregious, including attempts to solicit sexual services from two Polish women staying across the hallway from their hotel rooms.

As trade volume between China and Tanzania grew in the early to mid-1960s, Tanzanian reporting about the increased availability of Chinese goods also took place with reference to the negative backdrop of Indian business practices. In July 1964, a Chinese trade fair held at the Mnazi Mmoja Grounds in Dar es Salaam proved enormously popular with local residents. The displays included both "heavy industry," like cigarette-packing machines, and "light industry," like cotton products, bicycles, watches, wood carvings, cameras, and other electronics. As reported in *The Nationalist*, TANU's official English-language newspaper, lines of expectant customers snaked down Nkrumah Street as many customers expressed their approval for the items sold at the fair, especially as the "prices at the retail counter were far lower than those in the local Asian shops for the same kind and quality." The article proceeded to quote a satisfied man who cried "Just imagine a thermos flask costing five shillings and a drinking glass fifty cents!"[41] Here, the implied foil of Indian shopkeepers charging unfair prices for lower-quality merchandise attested to the desirability of Chinese goods.

To present a contrast to legacies of Western intervention and conquest in Africa, Chinese officials, in speeches and informal conversations with Tanzanian visitors, alluded to the shared history of anticolonial resistance between China and Africa. At the welcome reception for a TANU youth delegation held in Shanghai in June 1965, Pan Wenjing, a representative of the Chinese Communist Youth League, declared, "You have arrived from an anti-imperialist, revolutionary Africa that is in struggle, to an anti-imperialist, revolutionary Asia that is in struggle. On your side are the brave Congolese people. On our side are the brave Vietnamese people." This mapping of anti-imperial confederation, in which China and Tanzania figured as two significant nodes in a greater landscape of revolutionary solidarity, has its own alternative history of anticolonial transnationalism. As Pan elaborated, "The good relationship between our two countries was in place even 900 years ago. The Maji Maji Uprising of

---

[41] Nsa Kaisi, "A Rush in Dar to Buy Chinese Goods," *The Nationalist*, July 24, 1964.

1905 dealt a shock to imperial governance in East Africa, inspiring the Chinese anti-imperialist struggle of the time."[42]

These narratives regarded China–Tanzania relations as singular – a departure from patterns of Western colonialism, Eastern bloc engagements, and continued Indian economic dominance in the region. On the third point, Chinese officials discovered common ground with their Tanzanian counterparts even as they clashed with African nationalists, like Ali Mwinyi Tambwe, on whether race or class should serve as the primary lens for understanding the dynamics of colonial and neo-colonial domination. Taken together, these moments of conflict and communion suggest that postcolonial, Cold War projects of anti-imperial solidarities were profoundly affected by the racial histories of colonialism and decolonization. They called for unity, but equally important were the ways in which they played into long-established lines of friction and animosity within formerly colonized societies.

---

[42] "共青团上海市委迎坦桑尼亚坦噶尼喀非洲民族联盟青年代表团讲话稿 [Draft Speech of the Communist Youth League Shanghai Branch's Reception of TANU Youth League Delegation]," File No. C21-2-2583, SMA.

PART III

ANTICOLONIALISM IN A POSTCOLONIAL AGE

10

The Unexpected Anticolonialist: Winifred Armstrong, American Empire, and African Decolonization

Lydia Walker

INTRODUCTION

If you want to get people to understand a process, sometimes you can't use the word most commonly used.

This opening statement incapsulated elements of the theory and tactics of Winifred Armstrong in her own words.[1] Armstrong was an early African affairs consultant for Senator John F. Kennedy and political economist for the American Metal Climax mining company (AMAX). She used this phrase when discussing how she worked with her colleagues to consider the needs and ramifications of anticolonial issues on the African continent. Born in 1930 in New York City and raised in suburban Pelham, New York, in a white, middle-class family, Armstrong was educated in the Pelham public school system and at Swarthmore College. She benefited from a substantial degree of early exposure to global perspectives and issues of race and inequality within the United States: she first learned about the world and the many peoples it contained from a first grade elementary school teacher, who had her class read about children and their lives in China, Africa, the Middle East, and elsewhere.[2] At college, Armstrong joined the race relations club at Swarthmore, where she helped draft and circulate a poll of local businesses to bridge town–gown divides on issues of segregation.[3] Armstrong's global interests and consistent curiosity were influenced in these formative years by the 'one-world' internationalism of the Second World

---

[1] Armstrong Interview, December 11, 2020. [2] Armstrong Interview, October 2, 2020.
[3] Armstrong Interview, October 9, 2020.

War and early postwar era, before the Cold War modified the horizon of political possibility for many liberal internationalist thinkers and actors.[4]

As a college freshman in 1947, Armstrong met Bayard Rustin, the US Civil Rights activist, who came to give a talk at Swarthmore focused on active pacifism.[5] After his speech, she and her dormmates spent half the night discussing choices of violence and non-violence for their own society and for anticolonial nationalist liberation movements. In the shadow of Gandhi's recent success generating Indian independence – was violence necessary? Can ends justify means? And does violence beget more violence rather than build the just societies Rustin and now a young Armstrong sought? From her university days, Armstrong was persistent and proactive in her pursuit of political change, questioning and consensus-driven in her methods, as well as active in seeking out and developing friendships and connections.

After working and saving her earnings for several years after university, at twenty-six Armstrong carried out a self-funded, self-instigated, two-year trip up and down each coast of the African continent; she had purchased a round-trip plane ticket from Europe to Cape Town that allowed unlimited stops. Between Ghana's Independence Day celebrations in March 1957 and Christmas 1958, she traveled to fourteen countries: Ghana, Senegal, Togo(land), Dahomey (now Benin), Nigeria, (Belgian) Congo, South Africa, the Rhodesias (now Zambia and Zimbabwe), Tanganyika (now Tanzania), Kenya, Uganda, Sudan, and Egypt. There, she "visited and stayed with African and European families, at universities, schools, hospitals, and missions; and met political and educational leaders, [and those] concerned with community development, business and industry, religion, and labor."[6] In West Africa, she drove herself 22,000 miles in a Volkswagen Beetle car with her own camp bed. When she returned to the United States nearly two years later at the end of 1958, she had established connections with nationalist leaders and future heads of state, as well as scholars, teachers, labor union leaders, local

---

[4] Referring to 1940 US Presidential Candidate Wendell Wilkie's *One World* (Simon & Schuster, 1943), articulated in Erez Manela, "Visions of One World," in Brook Blower and Andrew Preston (eds.), *Cambridge History of America and the World*, Vol. III (Cambridge University Press, 2022) pp. 702–722. On Cold War liberalism as a theoretical orientation, see Jan Werner Müller, "Fear and Freedom: On 'Cold War Liberalism.'" *European Journal of Political Theory* Vol. 7, No. 1 (2008) pp. 45–64.

[5] Armstrong Interview, February 4, 2018.

[6] Armstrong CV, Correspondence 1960 File, Box 2. Winifred Armstrong Papers, John F. Kennedy Library.

businesspeople, and White and Black government officials in much of sub-Saharan Africa. Therefore, she had more recent, broad-based familiarity with the continent than almost anyone else in the United States, as there were few other Americans with similar experience.

In this way, Armstrong became an 'Africa expert' because there were so few in the United States before the 1960s with her experience and connections. The US Department of State established its first Bureau of African Affairs only in 1958. Instead, the US government received much of its information from its British, Belgian, French, and Portuguese colonial allies.[7] This organizational absence shaped American governmental understanding of African decolonization during this period along imperial lines. Then Massachusetts Democratic Senator John Kennedy, who chaired the newly created US Senate Subcommittee on African Affairs, wanted to learn more about anticolonial nationalism on the continent. To do so, he chose to find his information from a variety of non-official as well as official sources. His staff solicited and discussed memos and speech drafts from a network of interested individuals and civil society organizations who had African expertise.[8] As part of this process, in the spring of 1959, Kennedy hired Winifred Armstrong in an unofficial capacity as a special consultant. An initial six-week job turned into nearly two years of work for Kennedy.[9]

Before her Africa trip, Armstrong had worked for the National Council for Christians and Jews, where she met Ernest Lefever, then a staffer for the National Council of Churches, and subsequently a staffer for Senator Hubert Humphrey. Lefever introduced Armstrong to Ted Sorenson, chief of Kennedy's small Senate staff, who brought her onboard the Kennedy team.[10] The presence of Lefever within Armstrong's network, a man whose future nomination for a post in the US Department of State under Ronald Reagan would be denied by the Senate Foreign Relations Committee on the grounds that he was too right-wing and did not support Human Rights, showed her pattern of forging friendships that did not adhere to specific camps across the political spectrum even as her own political orientation remained staunchly supportive of

---

[7] Armstrong, recorded interview by Stephen Plotkin, July 8, 2008, p. 4. John F. Kennedy Library, Boston.

[8] Armstrong Interview, June 21, 2015.

[9] Armstrong Interview, February 4, 2018. Her work during this period included helping to set up the Peace Corps as well as a focus on the housing discrimination in Washington DC that severely impacted representatives from newly independent African countries.

[10] Armstrong Interview, December 18, 2020.

anticolonialism and anti-apartheid. People's politics and roles evolved over time; Armstrong and Lefever did not stay in touch.

Armstrong's comment that opens this chapter, that "if you want to get people to understand a process, sometimes you can't use the word most commonly used," articulated her pragmatic approach, operating behind the scenes with non-traditional methods to make political transformation happen collaboratively, and, at times, incrementally. She eschewed radical change and embraced the possible over the ideal. She focused on individuals rather than systems, though she would point out that no entity is completely an individual, people are embedded within their communities. She also worked through networks of fellow intermediaries, and preferred not to use terms such as 'capitalism,' 'communism,' 'under' development, and even 'anticolonialism' because she felt they led to knee-jerk reaction rather than analysis and considered steps toward change.[11]

As articulated throughout this volume, there were many 'anticolonial transnationals' that spanned the political spectrum – leftist, socialist, liberal, right-wing, among others. The trajectories of individual anticolonialists, from national leaders such as Carlos Romulo in Mark Reeves' work to well-known activists such as Agnes Smedley in Michele Louro's chapter, illuminate the complexities within these categories. Understanding anticolonialism at the level of the individual in addition to the movement can help navigate seeming contradictions with sensitivity: an individual may be anticolonial within a metropolitan context and sincerely critical of imperial power, at the same time that they assumed a degree of prestige and the ability to influence anticolonial spaces because of their membership within 'imperial' or 'neocolonial' entities such as governments or corporations. In turn, that membership shaped how their actions have fit into larger global narratives of anticolonial nationalism.

Focus on an individual also allows research to investigate the gap between how people may (or may not) self-identify, and how their actions may be construed from the outside, with the benefit of time and the weakness of subsequent narrative construction. The gap between self-identification and external construction at the individual level mirrored that between self-determination and international recognition at the movement level. Investigating this gap showcases the messiness of anticolonialism – a term that, with its connotations of anti-imperialism and

[11] Armstrong Interview, October 24, 2020.

celebration of national liberation, can (as in Armstrong's opening words) preclude understanding the transformative processes subsumed within the label.

Over time, some narratives and the individuals they center gain prominence over others because they reflect how dominant nationalist movements and state governments would prefer that their histories get told. Which individuals and issues lack visibility and for what reasons? Usually those that do not fit neatly into dominant narratives, because they unsettle those narratives' influence. This dynamic becomes particularly significant for individuals who were not national leaders such as Romulo or famous activists such as Smedley, but who worked behind the scenes to create political change like Winifred Armstrong.

From her arrival in Ghana to celebrate the country's independence in March 1957 until she left her position as a political economist focused on Southern Africa for AMAX in 1975, Armstrong operated inside organs of American empire – a contemporary term neither she, nor her colleagues, would have used. At times, she served implicitly or explicitly as an advocate for nationalist claimants as well as a conduit for 'western,' i.e., American-oriented civil society, government, and corporate interests – spheres that did not neatly align, but also did not necessarily contradict each other as much as it might appear from outside, public presentation.

This chapter explores two specific episodes that frame two decades of Armstrong's career as an Africa expert and advocate – though she would not describe herself with those terms. For its source base, it draws upon information from nearly thirty interviews with Armstrong from 2015 to 2021, with most of them occurring between October 2020 and April 2021, while Armstrong was ninety-one. These thematically oriented conversations focused upon particular episodes in Armstrong's long career, two of which unfold in the subsequent pages. Due to their organization around Armstrong's many professional projects, these interviews have reproduced some of the parameters of these projects. At the same time, they draw on strands of common thematic elements across Armstrong's work, filling some of the interstitial spaces between projects and organizations, rather as Armstrong herself did in her role as an intermediary.

Longform oral history sits upon tricky methodological terrain: there are memory gaps, current perceptions of past events that may conflict with documented accounts (which may not always be available or possible to access), and an ongoing connection between historical subject and researcher that allowed for the interviews and exchanges to take place and shaped the history that gets written, as the subject becomes an interlocutor in the process and production of research.[12] Instead of seeking to mitigate these challenges, this chapter utilizes them to explore the types of intersections and affinities that may not be officially documented and therefore cannot be easily explored in other ways, but which shaped how two powerful entities – the US government and AMAX mining company – navigated the process of decolonization on the African continent, and the role that an individual without official power can play in processes of global transformation.

EPISODE 1: SÉKOU TOURÉ COMES TO DISNEYLAND, OCTOBER 1959

Popular histories of Disneyland and tourism include the meeting between John F. Kennedy and Ahmed Sékou Touré in October 1959 as a fascinating factoid, since it was also Kennedy's only visit to the theme park in Anaheim, California.[13] While it is an intriguing juxtaposition – two young, charismatic political figures meeting in an unusual location that symbolized American cultural promotion and influence – the circumstances of the meeting open up several questions: How and why did Touré and Kennedy meet at Disneyland, and what were the meeting's ramifications? Armstrong herself conceived and set up the meeting as she was working for Kennedy at the time.

During the late 1950s and early 1960s, the foreign policy explorations of John F. Kennedy – as senator, presidential candidate, president-elect, and eventually president – were viewed as an element of American support for anticolonial nationalism.[14] Kennedy and the small team that worked with him provided certain anticolonial nationalists and their allies with inspiration as well as avenues of access to political decision-making. Before becoming president, Kennedy served as the chairman of the newly created US Senate Subcommittee on African Affairs, which was why his team hired Armstrong, to help plan prospective trips and draft speeches particularly on issues pertaining to African decolonization. Since

---

[12] On the epistemological relationship between oral history (or life history) and political activism, see Daniel James, *Doña María's Story: Life History, Memory, and Political Identity* (Duke University Press, 2001).

[13] For example, https://disneyparks.disney.go.com/blog/2009/11/disneyland-resort-remembers/ and www.themeparktourist.com/features/20161008/32230/timeline-each-instance-when-disney-closed-early (both accessed May 3, 2021).

[14] Matthew Connelly, *A Diplomatic Revolution: Algeria's Fight for Independence and the Origins of the Post-Cold War Era* (Oxford University Press, 2002).

the US government lacked an Africa office in its Department of State until 1958, Kennedy sourced his own information network.

For his soaring speeches, such as that on the Algerian War in 1957 (before Armstrong joined his team), Kennedy would solicit ideas and briefing notes from a range of outside experts, weigh in himself to combine these drafts and closely revise the speech's content and messaging, before the speech would receive the skillful transformation at the hands of advisor and official speech writer Ted Sorensen.[15] This procedure articulated the private collaboration that occurred within Kennedy's "intellectual blood bank."[16] It also demonstrated the internal dynamics of the Kennedy team's interaction with individuals and groups connected to the newly postcolonial world that made Kennedy as president an important, global figure during decolonization outside of direct US power projection.[17]

When Armstrong heard that Touré would be in Los Angeles for a state visit in October 1959, overlapping in time and place with Kennedy, who was campaigning for president in Orange County, California, she thought that it would be in the interests of both men to meet.[18] However, they each had full itineraries that would barely overlap. Placing their printed itineraries against each other alongside a map of the greater Los Angeles region, Armstrong realized that the easiest place where their routes intersected (and that was a location that could be secured) was Disneyland. She called Walt Disney's secretary, and asked if the park would host such a meeting. The secretary made the arrangements for the use of a conference room in one of their office blocks. The meeting was a brief, pleasant affair, where there is no evidence that any political commitments were made, though pictures from the meeting were often circulated as evidence for Kennedy's sympathy for African anticolonial nationalism. Indeed, even in such a short exchange Touré and Kennedy made positive impressions upon each other. This association had important consequences as Touré's perception of Kennedy's goodwill meant that he did not adhere so

---

[15] Ibid.; John F. Kennedy, "Algeria Speech," July 2, 1957, Pre-Presidential Papers. Senate Files, Box 784," John F. Kennedy Presidential Library, Boston.

[16] Term used by Kennedy to describe Ted Sorensen, Jurek Martin, "Intellectual Blood Bank of JFK," *The Financial Times*, November 6, 2000.

[17] Cyrus Scheyragh (ed.), *Globalizing the US Presidency: Postcolonial Views of John F. Kennedy* (Bloomsbury, 2020).

[18] Account of this meeting and its arrangements in Armstrong Interview, December 18, 2020. Armstrong's papers at the John F. Kennedy Library in Boston also include a description of the events surrounding this meeting.

closely to the Soviet side of Cold War and development politics while Kennedy was president.[19] Both Touré and Kennedy were on record about how early contact made them each appreciative of the other's political considerations and personal sympathy.[20] Armstrong's role in instigating and facilitating their meeting, however, is not part of the meeting's public narrative.

The Touré–Kennedy Disneyland encounter illustrated how Armstrong operated: behind the scenes, through personal connections, in unorthodox ways to enable discussions that might not otherwise have taken place. While Armstrong never held an official government job, politicians liked working with her. Representative Frances Bolton, a key member of the House Foreign Affairs Committee's subcommittee on Africa,[21] who helped set up the State Department's Bureau of African Affairs, took Armstrong's phone calls and considered her 'good value'.[22] Armstrong had a pattern of setting up private discussions between eminent Black and White Africans and Americans, not necessarily because participants asked for an introduction, but because she herself thought they would find each other's perspectives useful. Her initiatives facilitated these meetings, and the meetings themselves established links between individuals who might not otherwise be connected, expanding networks of influence and communication. The Touré–Kennedy Disneyland meeting demonstrated Armstrong in action. A mundane though symbolic meeting – whose public site featured so strongly in American cultural imagination (and in its exportation)[23] – was practical and personal, with political ramifications wider than its initial circumstances. The images from this meeting became an emblem for Kennedy's perceived sympathy with anticolonial nationalism, an issue he used to draw a contrast between his own prospective foreign policy and that of the then-in-power Eisenhower administration.[24]

[19] Philip Muhlenbeck, *Betting on the Africans: John F. Kennedy's Courting of African Nationalist Leaders* (Oxford University Press, 2012) pp. 59–72.

[20] *Public Papers of the Presidents of the United States: John F. Kennedy, 1962* (US Government Printing Office, 1963) pp. 752–753.

[21] Andrew DeRoche, "Frances Bolton and Africa, 1955–58," *The Newsletter of the Society for Historians of American Foreign Relations*, Vol. 40, No. 3 (2010) pp. 34–37.

[22] Armstrong Interview, December 18, 2020.

[23] Sabrina Mittermeier, *A Cultural History of Disneyland Theme Parks* (University of Chicago Press, 2021).

[24] This distinction was perhaps most strongly articulated with regards to Kennedy's support of Algerian nationalists during the Algerian War, see Connelly, *A Diplomatic Revolution*.

Armstrong herself was never central to the story. She felt that to be written into the narrative would be irrelevant and even potentially a counterproductive distraction to her more important purpose.[25] She was part of a sphere of transnational advocates that helped particular anticolonial nationalists gain access to spheres of power and governance.[26] While Touré was a head of state when he was introduced to Kennedy, it is unlikely that the two would have met before Kennedy became president without Armstrong's intervention. Politicians such as Kennedy and Bolton found Armstrong useful, but neither invited her permanently on staff. The personal connections and contacts with anticolonial nationalists that made Armstrong 'good value,' also made her a bit of an outsider. When Kennedy became president, some government insiders were apprehensive that informed 'outsiders' had too many such contacts, and Armstrong did not take up a government post.

As a senator and presidential candidate, Kennedy made use of the unofficial, transnational connections that had brought Armstrong into his orbit and facilitated his meeting with Touré. Later on, as president with his own Department of State that now had an established Africa office and with increased needs for sensitivity and secrecy, the Kennedy team found these informal contacts less necessary and possibly even destabilizing, as they had the potential to implicitly commit the US government to particular political positions. It is important to note that the Kennedy–Touré impromptu Disneyland meeting could most probably not have happened in the manner it did after Kennedy became president, and that a more formal, orchestrated meeting might not have had a similar personal impact on its key participants.

After her time with the Kennedy team, Armstrong shifted to the private economic research organization of the National Planning Association, continued her Africa research, and co-wrote a report on African private enterprise that included biographical sketches of African entrepreneurs, highlighting her attention to individual agency when describing structural, political, and economic questions.[27] Following her time at the

---

[25] Armstrong Interview, November 13, 2020.

[26] On other elements of this transnational network, see Walker, "Decolonization in the 1960s: On Legitimate and Illegitimate Nationalist Claims-making," *Past & Present*, Vol. 242, No. 1 (2019) pp. 227–264. For the conceptual framework of the transnational advocacy network, see Margaret E. Keck and Kathryn Sikkink, *Activists Beyond Borders: Advocacy Networks in International Politics* (Cornell University Press, 1998) p. 8.

[27] Theodore Geiger and Winifred Armstrong, *The Development of African Private Enterprise* (National Planning Association, 1964).

National Planning Association, the American Metal Climax mining company (AMAX) hired Armstrong in 1966 for the same reason that Kennedy had hired her in 1959: her knowledge of and connections to Africa's anticolonial nationalist leaders and her understanding of the political, social, and economic circumstances of new postcolonial states.

EPISODE 2: LEVERAGING CRITIQUE AGAINST APARTHEID, C. 1971

AMAX – as well as British South Africa Company, Anglo American, Union Minière, Rhodesian Selection Trust (RST, later Roan Selection Trust), and Tanganyika Concessions – was a core actor in the transition between imperial, settler colonial rule and national independence in Southern Africa.[28] Many of these corporations shared shareholders and held financial interests in mines that each other operated.[29] The Southern African Copperbelt stretched from the secessionist Congolese province of Katanga (which had triggered the 1960 Congo Crisis and its subsequent UN intervention), through Northern Rhodesia (independent Zambia as of 1964), and Southern Rhodesia (a settler colonial bastion until 1980), to the northern portion of Namibia (administered as South West Africa by South Africa from 1915 until 1990), where AMAX was a shareholder of Tsumeb mine.[30] While AMAX's interests in Katanga are subject to

---

[28] AMAX, since it was not the majority shareholder and was not the operating company in its regional investments, would not have regarded itself as a core actor in African decolonization. The company had investments in a variety of mining operations across the world, with managerial responsibility in some, mostly in the US. AMAX had a strong Africa interest, particularly in the Rhodesias, because of the personal concern and attitude of then AMAX chairman, Harold K. Hochschild, and his strong friendship and connection with Ronald Prain, chairman of RST, as RST had managerial responsibility for several copper mines in Northern Rhodesia (now Zambia). Part of Armstrong's work at AMAX was to show the company that knowingly and unknowingly it could not and should not hide from the possible responsibility of its role. Armstrong Conversation, August 27, 2022.

[29] On these corporations' shared shareholders, see UN Special Committee on the situation with regard to the implementation of the declaration on the granting of independence to colonial countries and peoples, verbatim record of the hundred and third meeting, September 7, 1962. Allard Kenneth Lowenstein Papers, Subseries 2.11. University of North Carolina at Chapel Hill, Wilson Library.

[30] Tsumeb mine/Tsumeb Corporation Limited was 30 percent owned by AMAX, 30 percent owned by Newmont Mining company, and operated by Newmont (of the final 40 percent, 14 percent was held by Rhodesian/Roan Selection Trust, and the rest was divided between multiple investors). Raymond Mikesell, *The World Cooper Industry: Structure and Economic Analysis* (RFF Press, 2013) Appendix 1-1, Profiles of Selected Major

A Visit to African Copper Mines

Workers Advance in Responsibility in Countries Where AMAX Has Interests

By WINIFRED ARMSTRONG

Location of AMAX Interests in Africa

The author, international economist at AMAX Headquarters in New York, spent two months last summer in Africa.

My first visit to the mines in Zambia (then Northern Rhodesia) was in 1958, eight years before I joined AMAX. The advancement program for African miners was just under way. The training staff were pleased and proud of their imaginative and extensive effort to reorganize job functions so that relatively inexperienced men could be advanced. But they were still uncertain of how successful the program ultimately would be. During my visit last summer, it was obvious that, for all practical purposes, the experiment was over and the success was great. Zambians now work at almost every level of skilled, technical, and professional jobs—though there is still much to be done. Training was started later in the other countries where AMAX has investments, but progress is considerable. *(Continued on next page.)*

THE AUTHOR on her way to visit a mine.

FIGURE 10.1. Excerpted from *AMAX Journal*, Vol. 9, No. 3, 1971. Winifred Armstrong Personal Papers, New York City. The journal issue is also housed in Armstrong's Collections at the Hoover Institution.

debate,[31] the company's chairmen Harold K. and Walter Hochschild, alongside RST's chairman Ronald Prain – which operated the Northern Rhodesian mines in which AMAX invested – made a decision in 1962 to back Kenneth Kaunda and the prospect of an independent Zambia.[32] RST had been working on upgrading the skills of its Black labor force in

Private Copper Producing Companies. Descriptions of the financials of Tsumeb mine in Dennis McCarthy, *International Business History: A Contextual and Case Approach* (Praeger Press, 1994) pp. 184–185.

[31] While Armstrong's AMAX records at the Hoover Institution do not show any AMAX mining interests in Katanga, scholars and activists with deep experience on the issue such as Elizabeth Schmidt and William Minter believe otherwise. (Conversation with Schmidt, June 25, 2015.) Schmidt, *Foreign Intervention in Africa: From the Cold War to the War on Terror* (Cambridge University Press 2013) pp. 60–69 and Minter, *King Solomon's Mines Revisited: Western Interests and the Burdened History of Southern Africa* (Basic Books, 1984) pp. 47–50 cover American mining interests in Katanga without naming AMAX specifically (as Minter does in Namibia).

[32] AMAX unauthored report, "Evolution of the Recent Attacks on Mining Companies Operating in Southern Africa," December 1962, Winifred Armstrong Papers, Hoover Institution, Box 25. Hereafter WA Hoover Papers. Armstrong had not yet started working at AMAX at this time, so she herself did not write or have input on this report.

Northern Rhodesia since the 1950s,[33] in part to keep wages low,[34] in part because of the anti-racist politics of Harold K. Hochschild and Prain.[35]

After he stepped down as chairman of AMAX in 1957 and was replaced by his brother Walter, Harold K. Hochschild then chaired the board of the African-American Institute (which changed its name to the Africa-America Institute in 1997), an American civil society advocacy organization that provided scholarships, training programs, and visa assistance for African students, including chosen African anticolonial nationalists. According to Brenda Gayle Plummer, the Institute was a "paragovernmental organization" (it had been founded with US governmental support) "with little actual Black American representation."[36] At the same time, Black Americans who led and worked at the Institute – Horace Mann Bond,[37] William Leo Hansberry, Evelyn Jones Rich,[38] and others – were not simply showpieces. One of Armstrong's many responsibilities at AMAX was to keep track of activities between the corporation and the Institute, as AMAX contributed to some of the Institute's projects, which were part of a growing sphere of African scholarship and advocacy in the United States.[39] This brew of Africa interests stretched far beyond AMAX. Armstrong was known within intersecting circles of anticolonial nationalists and western advocacy organizations as a knowledgeable, sympathetic interlocutor.

At AMAX, she reported directly to F. Taylor Ostrander, the Assistant to the Chairman. Ostrander had worked on New Deal development projects in the Roosevelt administration, and postwar European planning under Truman before coming to AMAX in 1953, articulating an example

---

[33] L. K. Butler, "Business and British Decolonisation: Sir Ronald Prain, the Mining Industry and the Central African Federation," *The Journal of Imperial and Commonwealth History*, Vol. 35, No. 3 (2007) p. 465.

[34] Duncan Money, "The World of European Labor on the Northern Rhodesian Copperbelt," *International Review of Social History*," Vol. 20 (2015) p. 238.

[35] Harold K. Hochschild to Ronald Prain, September 6, 1955, Prain Papers, cited in Butler, "Business and British Decolonisation," p. 465.

[36] Brenda Gayle Plummer, *In Search of Power: African Americans in the Era of Decolonization, 1956–1974* (Cambridge University Press, 2012) p. 85.

[37] Horace Mann Bond Papers, University of Massachusetts Amherst, Special Collections and University Archives, Boxes 25–27.

[38] Evelyn Jones Rich Papers, Bryn Mawr College Library, Series xv: African American Institute.

[39] On the wider intersections between international relations, regional studies, and decolonization especially at the level of foundation and funding support within this milieu, see Robert Vitals, *White World Order, Black Power Politics: The Birth of American International Relations* (Cornell University Press, 2015).

of the personal linkages between government and corporate spheres of action. Due to her accessibility, placement within the company, and network of African colleagues and contacts, critics of AMAX's continued investment in Namibia, at Tsumeb mine, often found their way to Armstrong's office and home.

International divestment campaigns against South Africa's apartheid system began in the 1950s but were not implemented until the 1980s. However, in the decade prior, large organizations that critiqued the regime began to think about how they might be indirectly financially supporting it.[40] In 1969, the World Council of Churches launched a Programme to Combat Racism three days after the keynote speaker for one of their global workshops, Mozambiquan anticolonial nationalist Eduardo Mondlane, was assassinated.[41]

The following year, the programme started giving funding grants to particular Southern African anticolonial nationalist movements, and the US National Council of Churches began to think critically about their pension scheme investment portfolios, which had investments in American companies with holdings in South Africa and Namibia. In 1969, three US churches that belonged to the National Council sent two recent Duke graduates, Tami Hultman and Reed Kramer, to work with South African churches on social issues in southern Africa.[42]

During their fifteen months in the region, Kramer and Hultman visited and interviewed senior managers at factories, mines, and corporate head-quarters of US-owned companies, including Tsumeb. Interestingly, in the wake of the South African government's anger at the World Council of Churches' grants to 'liberation movements,' it was Hultman and Kramer's church work that got them expelled from South Africa in March 1971, rather than the twenty-seven interviews they had carried

---

[40] Simon Stevens, "Boycotts and Sanctions against South Africa: An International History, 1947–1970" (Columbia University, Department of History, Ph.D. dissertation, 2016).

[41] World Council of Churches Programme to Combat Racism Collections, available through aluka.org. On the broader framework of the global activism of ecumenical protestant organizations, see Udi Greenberg, "The Rise of the Global South and the Protestant Peace with Socialism," *Contemporary European History*, Vol. 29, No. 2 (2020) pp. 202–219.

[42] This episode draws upon material from a shared interview carried out between Armstrong, Tami Hultman, and Reed Kramer, January 23, 2021. After their trip to Southern Africa, Kramer and Hultman founded and ran the publication *Africa News* and then founded and currently run allafrica.com, a daily digital news service on Africa. They had the opportunity to read and comment on a draft of this chapter.

out with South African subsidiaries of US companies, such as automakers in the Eastern Cape that provided vehicles for the South African police.

As the clock ran down on their banning order, Hultman and Kramer rushed to complete interviews, flying from a Johannesburg interview at an IBM facility, which provided technology for such uses as registrations for the 'passbooks' that controlled Black life under apartheid, to Namibia. They drove north to Tsumeb mine, where they interviewed the manager, J. P. Ratledge, and four other officials. The report they published on Tsumeb two years later is particularly notable because it includes specific figures on labor and wages.[43] Hultman and Kramer received those numbers from Armstrong, who had in turn checked in with her AMAX colleagues who agreed to release the numbers.

Armstrong was familiar with earlier work by Hultman and Kramer that she considered to be rigorous and substantive. She was not in the habit of sharing information that she felt might be misused, and she was able to persuade her colleagues at AMAX that it would be more effective to take a proactive role providing information and perspective on the company's investment in Tsumeb to both shareholders and the public, rather than remain either in a defensive position responding to outside critics, or silent by ignoring them. She pushed for organizational transparency between AMAX and Newmont (Tsumeb's operating company) regarding issues such as wages, training opportunities, and working conditions – such transparency had rarely occurred in the past.[44]

By 1970, some of AMAX's shareholders were beginning to ask questions about labor conditions under apartheid. In the early 1960s (before Armstrong was employed), leadership at both AMAX and RST (in which AMAX invested and which was the operating company for the Zambian mines) had noted the differences in the conditions of the employed Black African laborers at Tsumeb in contrast to the mines in the Northern Rhodesian Copperbelt, which they considered an example for how training and development programs might create a highly skilled Black African labor force. AMAX ascribed the difference between their Zambian and Namibian holdings to the difficulties of dealing with the South African apartheid regime, though there were also significant

---

[43] Hultman and Kramer, *Tsumeb: A Profile of United States Contribution to Underdevelopment in Namibia* (1973), African Activist Archive, Michigan State University.

[44] Information in the previous four paragraphs was clarified through email exchanges with Armstrong, Hultman, and Kramer, August 26, 2022.

differences between the operating companies within each region – RST in Zambia, Newmont in Namibia.[45] Apartheid built a system of labor that controlled the wages, role, training, and mobility of people based on race and ethnicity. AMAX believed that apartheid labor laws got in the way of the most effective (and profitable) way to extract copper at Tsumeb.[46]

Since they were not Tsumeb's operating company, and since they were working within the constraints of apartheid's labor laws, AMAX had felt that there was little they could do (short of selling their shares, which they were not willing to accomplish at this time) to raise wages and train Black South West Africans for higher-skilled positions. When Hultman and Kramer approached Armstrong in New York seeking information about Tsumeb, Armstrong saw an opportunity for creating leverage to push for such changes. She was able to persuade her colleagues that it was in AMAX's best interest to give Hultman and Kramer real information, which they then published in their report. Ostrander remained Armstrong's direct manager during this period, but AMAX had a new chairman since Walter Hochschild's retirement in 1966, Ian McGregor, who was less interested in anticolonial nationalism than had been either of the Hochschild brothers. (McGregor is most famous as the subsequent head of British Steel and the UK National Coal Board under Margaret Thatcher and the opponent of Arthur Scargill during the 1984–1985 UK Miner's Strike.) However, Armstrong and McGregor got on well, and she maintained the same degree of respect within the company, allowing her the scope to raise the question of providing Hultman and Kramer with hard numbers.

The publication of Hultman and Kramer's 1973 report by the National Council of Churches contributed to a cascade of political force: It provided ammunition for those of AMAX's shareholders who were already critical of apartheid, to push the corporation to acknowledge its role and responsibility in South West Africa. The report also gave momentum for AMAX to pressure Newmont (Tsumeb's operating company), to push the South West Africa Authority to allow the mine to raise wages and increase training opportunities. This flow of action meant that it was *not* AMAX criticizing apartheid labor practices, but a reputable

---

[45] AMAX, "Evolution of the Recent Attacks on Mining Companies Operating in Southern Africa," unlisted author, December 1962, Armstrong Papers, Box 25, the Hoover Institution, Stanford University.

[46] Stephanie Quinn, "Infrastructure, Ethnicity, and Political Mobilization in Namibia, 1946–87," *Journal of Southern African History*, Vol. 61, No. 1 (2020) pp. 45–66.

non-governmental organization (the National Council of Churches) who worked with the corporations' shareholders to pressure the regime to allow the adoption of such a policy. Armstrong's process worked, and Tsumeb mine raised wages and increased training. This pressure occurred in an environment of increased regional labor mobilization. A widespread strike in South West Africa in 1971–1972 that included mineworkers also led to greater internal corporate and public international attention to the conditions of work and life in Namibia.[47]

During this period of heightened interest, Armstrong learned that a group of Namibian students studying in the US were planning a demonstration in front of AMAX's New York office. She contacted the students in advance to suggest to them a set of tactics: First, that they come with a single page list of demands, making sure that several could be considered feasible by the company – i.e., to include a demand for raising wages alongside that for independence. And second, that they appoint a small delegation that would come inside the office and present their demands in person to AMAX representatives. She then arranged with then AMAX chair Ian MacGregor to meet the student delegation. The demonstration took place, the students arrived with a single page of demands, and a small delegation met with MacGregor in his office. Neither side expected or intended that the meeting would provide a venue for substantial negotiation, but for AMAX it was an important moment of recognition: by providing a venue to actively listen to Namibian nationalist and labor demands, AMAX was acknowledging its own responsibility as an actor in the region, a role it had not previously accepted.[48] The background to this meeting demonstrated how Armstrong worked – pragmatically, behind the scenes, and as a connection between spheres of political and economic action that did not often intersect because they were antagonistic.

The publication of Hultman and Kramer's report and the facilitation of the student meeting showed how Armstrong fed a chain of pressure against the apartheid labor system and got results – Tsumeb mine raised its wages and advanced Black African worker training. She forged a mutually beneficial connection with Hultman and Kramer that lasts to this day, resulting in the shared interview and exchanges that outlined the

---

[47] Saima Nakuti Ashipala, "Technical and Vocational Education and the Place of Indigenous Labour in the Mining Industry of Namibia, 1970–1990," *Journal of Southern African Studies*, Vol. 47, No. 1 (2021) pp. 127–142.

[48] Description of the planning behind the meeting between Namibian students and MacGregor from email exchange with Armstrong, August 29, 2022.

process of how advocacy can leverage activism to achieve a concrete outcome. Their work made a large, powerful organization do something some within it already wanted to do. This strategy mirrored Franklin Delano Roosevelt's most likely apocryphal quote of 'I agree with you, I want to do it, now make me do it,' allegedly made to either union or Civil Rights activists when they lobbied for federal support.[49] The Rooseveltian trope of the relationship between activism and policy is comfortable for leaders of powerful organizations (or governments) because it allows them to demonstrate affinity for more radical political positions while shifting the need to generate and spend political capital on those positions to activist movements. Armstrong's use of such leverage exhibited both the tool's possibilities and its limitations.

By the 1970s, particularly after the demise of Portuguese imperial rule and the independence of Angola and Mozambique in 1975, anticolonialism appeared to have firmly beaten empire. There remained crucial Southern African exceptions – apartheid ruled South Africa and Namibia, the ongoing guerilla war in Rhodesia/Zimbabwe between White settler colonialists and Black African anticolonial nationalists. These were symptoms of arrested decolonization. They were postimperial conflicts surrounding racial hierarchy, land ownership, enfranchisement, and population mobility, born from colonialism, but fighting entrenched settler governments rather than a distant metropole. Issues of arrested decolonization (which also included the New International Economic Order's critique of the Bretton Woods system of economic organization and development) retooled anticolonialism for an era after formal empire. These issues updated transnational anticolonial networks for a postcolonial world, showing that the work of anticolonialism stretched beyond that of specific anticolonial nationalist movements.

The idea of arrested decolonization also highlighted the role of American power and influence in the decolonizing world, especially when it did not bear the name of empire or when it did not operate through the conduits of the US government's official foreign relations. Armstrong's story corresponded with how implicit or naturalized American power projection often functioned during global decolonization – filtered through organizations that bridged the divide between spheres of state

---

[49] There are several unsubstantiated instances of Roosevelt allegedly saying these words to either A. Philips Randolph or Sidney Hillman, or both. The attributed quote reached mainstream attention when Barack Obama used it on the campaign trail in 2008, becoming a political trope rather than fact.

and civil society, such as AMAX mining company and the National Council of Churches. These entities may have operated within the remit of American empire, but they were not simply agents of it. They had their own interests both moral and economic that often stood in conflict with official US government policy, which supported apartheid South Africa with varying degrees of ambivalence.[50]

CONCLUSION: DEFINING TERMS, DETERMINING THE SELF

Armstrong first came to the African continent in 1957 to understand and eventually aid the political, economic, and social transformation that was underway in the transition from empire to independence. On her trip, she grew skeptical of aspects of the development paradigm as a framework for supporting that transformation. "Development, whether [the project of] a missionary or an economist was [often, perhaps inevitably,] I want you to be like us."[51] Some 'developers' could stretch enough to understand the value of local approaches, such as communal land use versus individual land ownership, but they were few and far between, tended to leave their jobs, and were usually not the decision-makers at large organizations.[52] Paraphrased from her colleague, the economist Barbara Ward, 'developers' came with what they knew.[53]

For Armstrong, 'under-development,' 'capitalism,' and 'socialism' were words that often got in the way of the concepts themselves and the discussions that need to happen about them. "Those terms have felt inadequate since McCarthyism. What are the incentives for people within each system? These systems' supposed goals were often undermined by the people within them."[54] At a personal level, Armstrong's commitment to African issues had no connection to the Cold War, which she considered an external trap for structuring politics on the continent that had little resemblance to, and did not actually address, people's needs for self-government and increased standards of living.[55] At the same time, how

---

[50] Ryan Irwin, *Gordian Knot: Apartheid and the Unmaking of the Liberal World Order* (Oxford University Press, 2012); Thomas Borstelmann, *Apartheid's Reluctant Uncle: The United States and Southern Africa in the Early Cold War* (Oxford University Press, 1993); Prexy Nesbitt, *Apartheid in Our Living Rooms: US Foreign Policy and South Africa* (Midwest Research, Inc.: 1986). Nesbitt has been a friend and colleague of Armstrong's.

[51] Armstrong Interview, October 24, 2020.   [52] Ibid.   [53] Ibid.   [54] Ibid.

[55] Armstrong, "Colonial Legacies to Future Crisis," undated position paper, probably December 1961 (based on content of recommendations). Armstrong John F. Kennedy Library papers, Africa and the UN File 2, Box 1.

her presence was construed by many of her African interlocutors could not escape the Cold War frame that structured much of American engagement on the African continent, especially corporate investment. Armstrong's positioning attempted to defy the categories made available to her in ways that demonstrated both the problems within those categories' ideological foundations and their pervasiveness. For example, her work for AMAX demonstrated that a corporation could have certain anticolonialist policies, because it was in the company's interest to do so, a reality that broadens categories of anticolonial and interest beyond liberatory versus imperial binaries.

One lens of analysis that Armstrong did not choose to use for understanding her work is that of gender. It was not the norm for women to do what she chose to do, to travel solo across a continent and work for a mining company. In addition, how she operated professionally – behind the scenes, through personal connections, not needing (or wanting) to be the 'front man,' and working in unofficial capacities – are modes that are often thought of as traditionally female ways of welding influence.[56] Yet as with development, capitalism, socialism, or the Cold War, for Armstrong, gender was another restrictive or even reductive frame for understanding her work.

Stylistically, Armstrong preferred action to words, working behind the scenes to the public eye, and pragmatism to idealism. She has organized her papers according to theme/project, with collections held at number of different archives, attempting to shift the researcher's focus away from herself as an individual toward the subjects upon which she worked.[57] She also would have preferred that her collections be listed by subject, not under her own name, even as she has been assiduous in making sure that they are preserved for future research, and in regular conversation with archivists who manage her collections to add materials and revise their organization.[58] She is deeply invested in how the histories in which she participated get told, though how she has organized her own records can make it challenging for that narrative to feature her as a leading actor.

---

[56] Glenda Sluga and Carolyn James (eds.), *Women, Diplomacy and International Politics since 1500* (Routledge, 2015).

[57] Armstrong has collections at the Schomburg Center for Research in Black Culture (New York City), the Hoover Institution (Palo Alto, CA), the John F. Kennedy Library (Boston), Pace University (White Plains, NY), and New York University's Tamiment Library (New York City).

[58] Armstrong Interview, March 5, 2021.

There is danger in approaching international history biographically – in adopting the world views of its own actors. At the same time, it is an avenue to access the descriptions of phone calls to secretaries that did not become memoranda, the impact of meetings and the conversations that inform how people make decisions.[59] This intermediary layer of information, of intelligence that did not come from intelligence agencies, can be difficult to find in government or organizational archives, which are predicated upon framing and containing official narratives that are structured by hierarchies and institutionalized bureaucratic divisions. By definition, that which falls outside them tends to be excluded from what they contain.

Armstrong's role as an intermediary between proponents of African national liberation and organizations that could be considered neocolonial fits awkwardly with White savior narratives, though her attempts to decenter herself from her own story works to sidestep that dynamic. In Armstrong's career, this intermediary role extended to an intermediary approach to polarizing divisions between empire and national liberation as well as divestment campaigns and corporate investment enterprises. This approach, as well as the intermediaries themselves, were both useful and often publicly obscured. They could be criticized as accommodationist, minimalist, even as window dressing for empire, but they worked in tandem with more radical methods, and perhaps even created access for them. That was Armstrong's intention, where being an anticolonialist was a set of actions, rather than an ideology where polarization could yield paralysis rather than transformation. Calling her an 'unexpected anticolonialist' challenges expectations of who is anticolonialist and categories of what is anticolonial.

---

[59] On the relationship between oral history and gender in these behind the scenes activities in a different region and class dynamic, see James, "'Tales Told Out on the Borderlands': Doña Maria's Story, Oral History, and Issues of Gender," in John D. French and Daniel James (eds.), *The Gendered Worlds of Latin American Women Workers: From Household and Factory to the Union Hall and Ballot Box* (Duke University Press, 1997).

11

Beyond the NIEO: Self-Reliance as an Alternative Vision of Postcolonial Development

Vivien Chang

In June 1972, the United Nations Conference on the Environment in Stockholm catapulted environmental concerns into the limelight. For the first time, the international community debated pollution management, economic growth, and the rights and responsibilities of the citizens of all nations.[1] If the resulting Stockholm declaration suggested consensus across the board on environmental problems and possibilities for international cooperation, the gathering of African representatives in Dakar that spring indicated the emergence of a diverging set of views – a "joint African stand" – that questioned the assumptions of the developed countries' "doctrine" on environmental questions.[2] While the latter viewed environmental degradation strictly in terms of "industrial pollution" – a consequence of "uncontrolled development" – the former emphasized such problems as poor sanitation and housing shortage caused by *under*-development.[3] In light of this development gap, chief among the principles the Dakar group of experts highlighted was the right to "full compensation and reparations" for the exploitation of African nations

---

[1] Report of the United Nations Conference on the Human Environment, June 5–16, 1972, United Nations Digital Library, https://digitallibrary.un.org/record/523249?ln=en.

[2] "Intelligence Note REC – 11 Prepared by the Bureau of Intelligence and Research," May 31, 1972, *Foreign Relations of the United States* (hereafter *FRUS*), 1969–1976, vol. E-1, Documents on Global Issues, 1969–1972, eds. Susan K. Holly and William B. McAllister (Washington: United States Government Printing Office, 2005), doc. 322, 2–4.

[3] Report of the First All-African Seminar on the Human Environment, jointly sponsored by the Economic Commission for Africa and the United Nations Secretariat, August 23–28, 1971, Economic Commission for Africa Repository (hereafter ECA Repository), https://repository.uneca.org/handle/10855/11153, 5.

by (neo)colonial powers.[4] In the eyes of the Dakar group, environmental protection was closely entwined with improving the human condition and cannot therefore be divorced from the challenges of Third World development.

It was precisely this focus on the characteristics and experiences unique to Africa that both characterized the Dakar group and differentiated it from other strands of development thinking at the time, including the New International Economic Order (NIEO). Under the auspices of the African Institute for Economic Development and Planning (IDEP) and the leadership of Egyptian economist Samir Amin, the Dakar group advocated a self-centered development model "designed to serve the interests of Africa's population."[5] This was noteworthy, as preparations for the Stockholm conference took place at a moment when the NIEO emerged as the centerpiece of development thinking in the late 1960s and early 1970s. Disenchanted by the inadequacy of the ad hoc measures of the past decade – the First Development Decade – in narrowing the development gap between the Global North and Global South, a coalition of developing nations demanded a redistribution of wealth and power from the economically advanced countries to their underdeveloped counterparts.

In parallel with growing interest in human rights, globalization, neoliberalism, and the Global South among international historians, the New International Economic Order has resurfaced as a popular avenue of inquiry in recent years following decades of dormancy. Recent scholarship on international development, the 1970s oil crisis, Black internationalism, the rise of neoconservatism, and other topics has excavated the diverse origins and evolution of the NIEO as well as the global negotiations between North and South that followed.[6] Yet they have tended to posit the NIEO as the apotheosis of Third World activism in

---

[4] Quoted in Marvine Howe, "Ecological Reparations Asked by African Group," *The New York Times*, April 14, 1972, 2.

[5] Quoted in "Intelligence Note REC – 11 Prepared by the Bureau of Intelligence and Research," 3.

[6] Christopher Dietrich, *Oil Revolution: Anticolonial Elites, Sovereign Rights, and the Economic Culture of Decolonization* (Cambridge: Cambridge University Press, 2017); Christy Thornton, *Revolution in Development: Mexico and the Governance of the Global Economy* (Berkeley: University of California Press, 2021); Adom Getachew, *Worldmaking after Empire: The Rise and Fall of Self-Determination* (Princeton: Princeton University Press, 2019); Michael Franczak, *Global Inequality and American Foreign Policy in the 1970s* (Ithaca: Cornell University Press, 2022).

the United Nations. This emphasis on the NIEO as *the* alternative to market-oriented solutions to global inequality at times obscures the other possibilities Third World actors – within and beyond sub-Saharan Africa – conceived of and contemplated at the time.

Indeed, the integrationist impulses which animated the United Nations Conference on Trade and Development (UNCTAD) and the NIEO were only one of a myriad of development imaginaries that emanated from the Global South. To sub-Saharan African elites, UNCTAD's – and later the NIEO's – focus on transnational corporate regulation, technology and resource transfer, and non-reciprocal trade preferences in favor of the countries of the Global South were of limited applicability to their societies, which were among the least economically developed in the world. This chapter recovers how intellectuals and technocrats affiliated with the UN Economic Commission for Africa (ECA) and the IDEP in particular were producing their own novel conceptions of self-reliant development, which were by turns analogous to and distinct from the paradigm advanced by UNCTAD. Writing sub-Saharan Africa – the poorest region within the Third World bloc – into the movement for a new international economic order illuminates the perceived inadequacy of *the* NIEO in the eyes of the continent's decision-makers for resolving the region's most deep-seated issues of poverty and inequality.

* * *

The quest for a new international economic order was the most ambitious – and visible – effort of the diverse and often conflicting communities who identified with the Third World movement, whose political birth traced back to the conference of nonaligned nations in Bandung, Indonesia in 1955.[7] The Afro-Asian–Latin American coalition gained further momentum when, in December 1960, the United Nations General Assembly adopted the Declaration on the Granting of Independence to Colonial Countries and Peoples (Resolution 1514) with almost unanimous support from the plenary. In the context of decolonization and the Cold War, which had produced a majority voting coalition in the General Assembly that aligned with neither the United States nor the Soviet Union, the resolution identified a broader political and ideological

---

[7] Asian-African Conference, "Final Communiqué of the Asian-African Conference of Bandung," *Asia-Africa Speaks from Bandung* (Jakarta: Ministry of Foreign Affairs, Republic of Indonesia, 1955), 161–169.

struggle between the North and South that superseded the East–West conflict. The conception of the global economic system's relationship to decolonization and development implicit in Resolution 1514 – that Third World underdevelopment was a legacy of formal colonialism (rather than embedded in broader structures of inequality and exploitation) and that economic development and integration would follow decolonization as a matter of course – informed a series of follow-on projects: Resolution 1515, which upheld "the sovereign right of every state to dispose of its wealth and its natural resources"; Resolution 1707, which identified "international trade as the primary instrument for economic development"; the 1974 New International Economic Order; the Charter of Economic Rights and Duties of States; and UNCTAD.[8] Collectively, these legislative bodies and acts wrote economic self-determination into international public law and in consequence the myriad processes of decolonization.

Despite the optimism and cohesion Third World representatives channeled into the United Nations in this period, it is important to note that their efforts were uneven, not least in relation to the countries of sub-Saharan Africa. In the lead-up to the first UNCTAD conference in early 1964, for instance, Raul Prebisch, the Argentine economist and dependency theorist who served as executive secretary of the United Nations Economic Commission for Latin America and the Caribbean (ECLAC) from 1950 to 1963, traveled extensively throughout capital cities in the Global South but only visited Cairo insofar as African cities were concerned. His relative lack of familiarity with the continent and its inhabitants was apparent when he met with the IMF's managing director Pierre-Paul Schweitzer and Jorge Del Canto, the head of the Western Hemisphere Department, in January. The conversation revolved around the question of regional payments agreements, which was central to UNCTAD's efforts to expand financial capital to the developing world.[9] In this context, Del Canto was no doubt surprised to learn that Prebisch

[8] International Trade as the Primary Instrument for Economic Development, adopted at the 1084th plenary meeting, December 19, 1961, United Nations Digital Library, https://digitallibrary.un.org/record/204606?ln=en; Declaration on the Establishment of a New International Economic Order, adopted at the 2229th plenary meeting, May 1, 1974, UN Digital Library, https://digitallibrary.un.org/record/218450?ln=en.

[9] On regional payments agreements, see Joanna Bockman, "Socialist Globalization against Capitalist Neocolonialism: The Economic Ideas Behind the New International Economic Order," *Humanity: An International Journal of Human Rights, Humanitarianism, and Development* 6, no. 1 (Spring 2015), 115–116.

"did not seem to be familiar with similar arrangements in other parts of the world [outside of Latin America]."[10] Similarly, in early 1966, Tanzania diplomat Waldo Waldron-Ramsay accused Prebisch of "being unfair to Africans in the distribution of secretarial posts," noting that only 125 Africans held appointments in the Secretariat, a mere twenty-three of whom were in the higher-salary brackets.[11]

For African delegates, therefore, UN activism unfolded alongside efforts to organize their regional economies. The first All-African People's Conference (AAPC) in 1958 and the Conferences of Independent African States (CIAS) in Addis Ababa and Accra in 1958 and 1960, respectively, helped to consolidate a uniquely African point of view – what Ghana's Kwame Nkrumah dubbed the "African Personality." Anchored by self-determination, anticolonialism, and antiracism, this worldview held out African decolonization as a collective expression of independence and unity on the international stage.[12]

Nkrumah's ideas about African unity stemmed from broader political and intellectual debates about the constitutional contingencies of continental decolonization in the 1950s and 1960s. While the 1957 transfer of power in Ghana helped inspire other popular nationalist movements in the region – Nkrumah memorably declared that Ghana's independence was "meaningless unless it is linked up with the total liberation of Africa" – the emergence of dozens of new sovereign nation-states on the continent was by no means a given at this juncture.[13] As Frederick Cooper has contended, anticolonial elites in the 1940s and 1950s often envisioned federal and confederal polities rather than territorial autonomy as the endpoint of decolonization.[14] Cognizant that "Ghana alone is too small to make [a] sufficient impact" and embittered by the perceived impotence of Africa in both the political and economic arenas, in 1962 Nkrumah began advocating in earnest for a continental union: "I

---

[10] Meeting with Prebisch, January 30, 1964, 101713, "UN Conference on Trade and Development," Central Files: International Organizations, IMF Archives. I would like to thank Raphaël Orange-Leroy for sharing this source with me.

[11] In response to the complaint, the United Nations dispatched a mission to twenty countries in Africa and returned with eight applications. "Denying Any Bias, U.N. Reports a Rise in Africans on Staff," Special to *The New York Times*, February 16, 1966, L7.

[12] Alex Quaison-Sackey, *Africa Unbound: Reflections of an African Statesman* (New York: Frederick A. Praeger, 1963), 35–58.

[13] "Ghana is Free Forever," March 6, 1957, BBC World Service www.bbc.co.uk/worldservice/focusonafrica/news/story/2007/02/070129_ghana50_independence_speech.shtml.

[14] Frederick Cooper, *Citizenship between Empire and Nation: Remaking France and French Africa, 1945–1960* (Princeton: Princeton University Press, 2014).

see the wider horizon of the immense possibilities open to Africans – the only guarantee, in fact, for our survival – in a total continental political union of Africa."[15] Likewise, in 1960 – on the eve of Tanganyika's own transition from a United Nations trust territory to a sovereign nation-state – Julius Nyerere expressed qualms about the viability of an East African federation project in the face of separate sovereignties and suggested that the British government delay independence until after its neighboring territories had "reached the same kind of constitutional change" in order to federate before independence.[16]

Sub-Saharan Africa's developmental aspirations went hand in hand with the imperative to decolonize in the late 1950s and early 1960s. While Nyerere and Nkrumah disagreed about the tactics by which to foster African unity, they shared similar motivations. They both recognized the relative weakness of African states in the international economy and, relatedly, the disjunction between the continent's vast resources and its low standards of living. "Our continent is probably the richest in the world for minerals and industrial and agricultural primary materials" Nkrumah rhapsodized at the Organization of African Unity's (OAU) inaugural conference in 1963. Yet African states were also plagued by living standards among "the lowest in the world ... crumbling economies, empty treasuries, and nonviable states bearing no possibility of independent and genuine development."[17] Only by means of unified economic planning and "the proper utilisation of all our resources" could African governments transform the existing structures "from poverty to that of wealth, from inequality to the satisfaction of popular needs."[18]

* * *

While UNCTAD and ECLAC loomed large in Third World economic diplomacy by virtue of their roles in promulgating the ideas of *dependencia* theorists like Prebisch and Fernando Cardoso, the ECA

---

[15] "A New Leader in Africa," March 21, 1957, CO 936/576, the National Archives of the United Kingdom (hereafter TNA). Kwame Nkrumah, *Towards Colonial Freedom* (London: Heinemann, 1962), x–xi.

[16] Julius Nyerere, "Freedom and Unity," *Transition*, no. 14 (1964), Indiana University Press on behalf of the Hutchins Center for African and African American Research at Harvard University, 41.

[17] Kwame Nkrumah, *Revolutionary Path* (New York: International Publishers, 1973), 236–237.

[18] Kwame Nkrumah's Speech at First OAU Summit, Kwame Nkrumah Papers, Moorland-Springarn Research Center, Howard University.

was a showcase for how to operationalize economic self-reliance on a continental scale and disseminate the uniquely African perspective(s) Nkrumah, Nyerere, and others had waxed poetic about. By dint of the organization's "dual character" as both an African institution and a United Nations body, African elites regarded the ECA as more important than UNCTAD, as they tended to view the continent's development problems as primarily "a task for African peoples and governments."[19] That is not to say that the ECA did not operate without contention in its early years. Established in 1958, the ECA counted the United Kingdom, France, Portugal, and South Africa, as well as independent African states, among its early members. Although less controversial than the ill-fated Commission for Technical Cooperation in Africa, in the eyes of the continent's elites ECA's ties to former colonial powers and white minority regimes initially rendered it less "African" than as well as subsidiary to the OAU's similar Economic and Social Commission. At the Economic and Social Commission's first session in December 1963, a resolution urged the ECA to "generally [limit itself] to technical and advisory functions" and "pay particular attention to the study of the problems foreseen in the Programme of Work and Priorities of the Economic and Social Commission" so as to attain "close co-operation on a complementary basis" with the commission.[20] An additional resolution the Economic and Social Commission adopted at its second session in January 1965 called for "an agreement or convention which would define in a precise manner the framework of co-operation between the Economic and Social Commission of the OAU ... and the [ECA]. ..." ECA member states were similarly concerned about clarifying the respective roles of the ECA vis-à-vis its OAU counterpart, emphasizing "specialization and division of labour [rather] than lack of co-operation or of competition."[21] Short of absorbing the ECA within the OAU framework, which was unfeasible for legal and political reasons, they were adamant that the OAU's objectives and aspirations trump the non-political nature of the ECA.[22]

[19] "A Venture in Self-Reliance: Ten Years of ECA," 1968, Economic Commission for Africa, United Nations, ECA Repository, https://hdl.handle.net/10855/3173.
[20] ECOS/17/RES/3 (I), December 13, 1963, quoted in Immanuel Wallerstein, "The Early Years of the OAU: The Search for Organizational Preeminence," *International Organization*, Vol. 20, no. 4, (Autumn 1966) 774–787, especially 779.
[21] Economic Commission for Africa Annual Report, March 3, 1964–February 23, 1965, Economic and Social Council, Official Records: Thirty-Ninth Session, Supplement no. 10, 53–54, ECA Repository, https://repository.uneca.org/handle/10855/17810.
[22] Ibid.

By the second half of the 1960s, however, the OAU's inaction in the face of a series of crises in the Congo, Rhodesia, and Nigeria sidelined the organization in the efforts of regional political elites to safeguard their countries' newfound sovereignty. Considering the limited progress toward African unity – the OAU's *raison d'être* – member states chose to explore other avenues of liberation, and economic self-reliance eclipsed continental unity as the primary means of collective action. While the relationships between the ECA, the OAU, and the UN Economic and Social Council (ECOSOC) remained uncertain, the apolitical nature of the ECA – previously deemed a pitfall – reemerged mostly as an advantage for the organization as postcolonial optimism gave way to disillusionment. Given the instability of postcolonial African governments, many of the continent's trained economists and statisticians opted to join the ECA rather than their home governments. The ECA Secretariat – made up of civil servants and technocrats appointed by the United Nations – thus ensured the institutional continuity and technical expertise the OAU Economic and Social Commission sorely lacked.[23]

The ECA's purpose, according to a 1968 report, was to serve as "a promotional and developmental effort to improve material well-being" – less so in the realm of individual projects than "the growth in ideas, outlook, institutions, skills and activities."[24] According to Robert Gardiner, the ECA's first executive secretary, economic empowerment would necessitate moving beyond rhetorical proclamations: "The recognition of need and appreciation of advantages are not … the same thing as the patient evolution of studies, policies and institutions designed to satisfy the need and achieve the advantages; and it is here that I feel ECA can take most credit."[25] In seeking to achieve meaningful, albeit gradual, change, the ECA's most notable accomplishment in its first decade was the training of African personnel in economics and statistics.[26] Between 1961 and 1968, the ECA organized seventeen workshops and seminars and forty courses in public administration, community development, and trade promotion, among other fields.[27] To further meet the demand for national planning staff among new states, in 1964 the ECA established

---

[23] OAU appointees, by contrast, were named (and frequently replaced) by the home governments of four nations selected by all participating heads of state. Wallerstein, "The Early Years of the OAU," 779–780.

[24] "A Venture in Self-Reliance: Ten Years of ECA," 1968, United Nations, iii.   [25] Ibid.

[26] Gardiner's gradualist approach played an important role in shaping the ECA's identity in its early years. James S. Magee, "What Role for E.C.A.? Or Pan-Africanism Revisited," *Journal of Modern African Studies* 9, no. 1 (May 1971), 73–89, especially 82–84.

[27] "A Venture in Self-Reliance: Ten Years of ECA," 1968, United Nations, 148–153.

the IDEP. Through teaching, research, and advisory services, the IDEP sought to address "the special nature of the development problems facing the African continent, which will entail original research for their solution, as Africa cannot be content with slavishly copying the techniques and experience of the other continents."[28]

The ECA under Gardiner constituted an institutional home for the ideas Nkrumah espoused (now from his new perch in Guinea) even as their tactics diverged and after the latter's brand of Pan-Africanism lost its luster among the continent's elites. This was an unexpected development, given the two's often icy relationship throughout their decades-long acquaintance. A descendent of teachers, civil servants, and Methodist preachers from the Ashanti region, Gardiner studied at Oxford University before traveling to the United States in 1942 to visit American universities in anticipation of a teaching post at Sierra Leone's Fourah Bay College.[29] It was there that he first encountered Nkrumah, who was then president of the African Students Association of America and a graduate student at Lincoln University. Upon the Gold Coast's independence in 1957, Gardiner served as the Convention People's Party's (CPP) first head of the Ghana Civil Service.

Gardiner was drawn to the prospect of impending independence in his native country, but he and Nkrumah would soon clash. This was inevitable, as the development economists James Pickett and Hans Singer have observed, for the two were "men of very different vision and temperament. The insistence of the one on rigour and realism was bound to conflict with the untrammelled vision of the other...."[30] An incident in mid-1959 was telling. Gardiner had dismissed a senior nurse for having overstayed a leave of absence. That she was his sister did not deter him: "I had no choice. Her action was clearly contrary to the regulations." Recounting the episode three years later, he remarked wryly that "she has since been reinstated" by Nkrumah.[31] Indeed, it was Nkrumah's

---

[28] "Working Paper on the Proposed Establishment of an African Development and Planning Institute," Economic Commission for Africa, Fourth Session, February–March 1962, 3–5, ECA Repository, https://repository.uneca.org/handle/10855/41312.

[29] Marika Sherwood, "Robert Kweku Atta Gardiner (1914–1994): An Unrecognised Ghanaian Pan-Africanist Par-Excellence," *Contemporary Journal of African Studies* 2, no. 1 (2014), 32–36.

[30] James Pickett and Hans Singer, "Robert Kweku Atta Gardiner: An Appreciation on His Seventy-Fifth Birthday," *Towards Economic Recovery in Sub-Saharan Africa: Essays in Honour of Robert Gardiner*, eds. Pickett and Singer (London: Routledge, 1990), 6.

[31] Quoted in "Firm U.N. Mediator: Robert Kweku Atta Gardiner," August 25, 1962, *The New York Times*, 3.

repeated exhortations that Gardiner provide "jobs for the boys" and Gardiner's immovable refusal that ultimately soured the relationship between the president and Ghana's most senior technocrat and prompted the latter to leave Ghana for the UN Economic Commission for Africa.[32] Gardiner's insistence that the civil service be kept free of politics alienated his CCP colleagues but endeared him to his fellow UN bureaucrats, who applauded him for being "the only African official at the U.N. whose 'we' means the United Nations, not Africa."[33]

While Gardiner – cautious, technocratic, and pro-Western – and Nkrumah – a larger-than-life statesman with messianic tendencies – made strange bedfellows, the ECA Secretariat in fact drew heavily on Nkrumah's insights about neocolonialism to formulate its own prescriptions for African development. Nkrumah's warnings about the dangers of "balkanization" – the division of Africa into small, weak states with limited economic power – especially preoccupied Gardiner, who sought to promote multilateral cooperation and redefine the ECA as the locus of economic planning.[34] According to Gardiner, the formation of larger economic groupings would not only strengthen African countries' foreign exchange position but create a more favorable investment climate for foreign investors. At the 1967 ECA Conference of Industrialists and Financiers, Gardiner sought to foster "mutually advantageous cooperation" between African governments and potential investors from Europe, Asia, and North America through multinational or sub-regional investment promotion centers and a consultative council for industrial development staffed by senior officials from such organizations as the African American Chamber of Commerce and the Confederation of British Industries. "[T]he smaller countries in Africa cannot hope in isolation to achieve the economies of scale which are necessary to ensure real economic growth," Gardiner explained. "There is a minimum size for many of the essential tools of modern production; and that minimum is

---

[32] Russell Warren Howe, "U.N.'s Gardiner Puts New Life Into Congo," February 11, 1962, *Washington Post*, E1. Patronage, favoritism, and petty rivalries were rampant in Nkrumah's Ghana, as Jeffrey Ahlman, Kevin Gaines, Frank Gerits, and Gerardo Serra have shown. Ahlman, *Living with Nkrumahism: Nation, State, and Pan-Africanism in Ghana* (Athens, OH: Ohio University Press, 2017), chapter 5; Gaines, *American Africans in Ghana: Black Expatriates in the Civil Rights Era* (Chapel Hill: University of North Carolina Press, 2006), 211–212; Serra and Gerits, "The Politics of Socialist Education in Ghana: The Kwame Nkrumah Ideological Institute, 1961–6," *Journal of African History* 60, no. 3 (2019), 407–428.

[33] "U.N.'s Gardiner Puts New Life Into Congo," *Washington Post*.

[34] Magee, "What Role for E.C.A.? Or Pan-Africanism Revisited," 73–89.

frequently larger than the size of most national markets in Africa."[35] For Gardiner, the amalgamation of the market strength of independent African nations provided the most realistic path toward rapid economic advancement.

The ECA was thus an ideal vehicle for Gardiner to institutionalize African development without what he viewed as the burdens of meddlesome politicians. According to A. F. Ewing, who chaired the ECA's Division of Economic and Social Development, the ECA program was "for the most part resolutions professionally drafted, mainly by the secretariat, with little trace of genuine involvement on the part of African governments."[36] But divorcing development from politics would also harbor deleterious effects on the efficacy of ECA proposals. While "a sense of agreement" was reached at the Conference of Industrialists and Financiers, for instance, the non-participation of government officials rendered the meeting – like many others – mostly toothless with no binding conventions or resolutions ratified.[37]

Nonetheless, the recognition of the uniqueness of Pan-African perspectives as propagated by the ECA prompted African elites to adopt an attitude of skepticism toward UNCTAD. While UNCTAD was "undoubtedly the best institution the developing countries have got," an ECA report observed in 1966, "[the] proper attitude of Africans states toward UNCTAD is probably one of sympathetic criticism."[38] Nyerere, speaking at the second OAU meeting in Cairo the following year, was equally restrained in his evaluation of the embryonic organization. UNCTAD, he noted, "may result in some change in this state of affairs [the development gap]. At least we hope so."[39] The more pertinent question – for ECA officials as well as Nyerere – was: "[Is] this policy or proposal better calculated than any alternative to promote growth?"[40]

[35] Robert K. A. Gardiner, "U.N.E.C.A. Conference of Industrialists and Financiers," *Journal of Modern African Studies* 5, no. 1 (May 1967), 134–140.

[36] A. F. Ewing, "Reflections from Afar on the Ninth Session of the U.N. Economic Commission for Africa, *Journal of Modern African Studies* 7, no. 2 (July 1969), 330–334.

[37] Gardiner, "U.N.E.C.A. Conference of Industrialists and Financiers," 135.

[38] "The Relevance of UNCTAD to Africa's Trade Problems," Joint Meeting of ECA Working Party on Intra-African Trade and OAU ad hoc Committee of Fourteen on Trade and Development, Addis Ababa, March 28–April 2, 1966, ECA Repository, 43–44.

[39] Julius K. Nyerere, *Freedom and Unity: Uhuru Na Umoja: A Selection From Writings and Speeches, 1952–65* (London, Nairobi: Oxford University Press, 1967), 300–305.

[40] "The Relevance of UNCTAD to Africa's Trade Problems," 44.

Here, the ECA concluded that Africa's development problems remained above all "a task for African peoples and governments." This was echoed by Nyerere, who urged his fellow representatives to "trade between ourselves" so as to capitalize on the continent's market.[41]

For African elites, then, UNCTAD and its economic repertoire represented auspicious first steps to a truly postcolonial global order but were far from ends in themselves. They were cognizant that Africa – especially Black Africa – was the least developed industrially among regions in the periphery and therefore necessitated a radically different trajectory vis-à-vis their Latin American and Asian counterparts.[42] Their primary aim, as the IDEP laid out in 1964, was not just the ability to dictate the terms of their trade with the industrial core but "the development of a self-centred and self-reliant system": "The liberation, or disengagement, of the Third World from the existing unequal international division of labour and its consequences is a *sine qua non* for bringing about real national and autonomous development geared to satisfying the needs of the broad masses."[43]

The IDEP was conceived to train "younger African economists in the problems and methods of economic planning."[44] Yet it was unclear from the start just who was ultimately in charge of the inchoate organization: the ECA, the UN Development Programme (which funded the IDEP), or the UN Secretariat in New York.[45] Based in Dakar, Senegal, the IDEP was made up of a who's who of a cosmopolitan collective of economic powerhouses, including Egypt's Samir Amin, Ghana's Rowland Amoa, and Nigeria's Fatumata Diarra, as well as Jagdish Saigal from India, and

---

[41] Nyerere, *Freedom and Unity*, 303.

[42] For instance, sixteen of the twenty-five least developed countries in the world in 1975 were in Africa. UN Economic and Social Council, *Survey of Economic Conditions in Africa, 1974*, E/5682 (May 13, 1975), 5, quoted in Hugh Arnold, "Africa and the New International Economic Order," *Third World Quarterly* 2, no. 2 (April 1980), 295.

[43] Jagdish C. Saigal, "World Economic Order and Liberation of the Third World (Challenges Facing Newly Emerging Nations)," African Institute for Economic Development and Planning, UN Economic Commission for Africa, ECA Repository, https://repository.uneca.org/handle/10855/42590, 6, 17–18.

[44] "Establishment of an African Institute for Economic Development and Planning," Resolution 58 (IV) adopted by the Commission at its 76th Plenary Meeting, March 1, 1962, Economic Commission for Africa, ECA Repository, https://repository.uneca.org/handle/10855/21919.

[45] Samir Amin, *A Life Looking Forward: Memoirs of an Independent Marxist* (London: Zed Books, 2007), 156.

Norman Girvan from Jamaica.[46] Amin, who would become a trusted adviser to both Nyerere and Burkina Faso's Thomas Sankara in the late 1960s and 1970s, took a circuitous route to IDEP leadership. Originally hired as a professor of economics in 1963, Amin taught at the IDEP for four years – during which he frequently lamented the language barriers between French and English speakers, the rapid turnover of directors, and the uneven educational levels of his students – before ceremoniously resigning.[47] He became the director of IDEP in 1970 when the UN Economic and Social Council under Philippe de Seynes sought to reinvigorate the IDEP and sharpen its focus on analyzing development strategies on the continent.

In the 1970s, Amin – eager to tackle some of the problems he had discerned as a faculty member years earlier – sought to remake the IDEP into "a front-ranking centre for African theory and reflection" and "to take away from foreign 'technical assistance' or 'cooperation' agencies the monopoly of thinking about Africa."[48] To this end, he organized seminar courses, consulted for African regional institutions and the G-77, and hosted two major Third World conferences in Dakar and Antananarivo, Madagascar, in 1972 and 1974 respectively for intellectuals from Asia, Africa, and Latin America.[49] Amin was especially averse to "submit[ting] national-development strategy to the imperatives of 'globalization.'"[50] Short of attaining "socialism on a world scale" through a supranational framework, globalization served to exacerbate rather than attenuate international inequality in Amin's eyes.[51] He thus viewed the type of development economics associated with Prebisch and practiced within UNCTAD – especially its focus on integrating into the capitalist world economy rather than increasing agricultural output and prioritizing the

---

[46] Mogens Boserup, "The African Institute for Economic Development and Planning, Dakar," *Journal of Modern African Studies* 2, no. 4 (December 1964), 573–575; "Establishment of an African Institute for Economic Development and Planning," ECA Repository.

[47] Amin, *A Life Looking Forward*, 153–160. In a letter of resignation Amin sent to the UN Secretary General U Thant, he faulted the IDEP for being "run like a technical college … and not doing its proper job, which was to serve as a place for serious discussion on issues of African development and develop theories relevant for African development." Amiya Kumar Bagchi, "Samir Amin: A Short Intellectual Portrait," *Agrarian South: Journal of Political Economy* 9, no. 1 (2020), 50–62, especially 55.

[48] Amin, *A Life Looking Forward*, 201–202.   [49] Ibid., 202–205.

[50] Samir Amin, "A Note on the Concept of Delinking," *Review* (Fernand Braudel Center) 10, no. 3 (Winter 1987), 435–444, especially 435.

[51] Amin, *A Life Looking Forward*, 213.

basic needs of the masses (especially peasants) – as ultimately counter-revolutionary.[52] If Gardiner was a UN bureaucrat first and African second, then Amin's Pan-Africanist and Third Worldist preoccupations decidedly trumped his uncertain allegiances to the United Nations, whose logic he deemed subordinate to the interests of the developed world and in particular the United States. By the same token, Amin was unapologetically political – a stark contrast to both Gardiner's distaste for politics and claims to neutrality.

* * *

In *Accumulation on a World Scale*, published the same year that the international community passed the NIEO and halfway through his tenure at the IDEP, Amin called upon Third World nations for a "break with the international economy and world market" in their strategy of economic development.[53] In positing "self-centred" development as an alternative to a market-oriented economy, Amin drew on "structuralist" development economists like Andre Gunder Frank's assertion that the unequal relationship between center – the advanced capitalist countries – and periphery was an intrinsic and distinguishing feature of global capitalism. Contrary to Prebisch's belief that unequal terms of trade were obstacles to be overcome through international trade agreements, Amin understood the underdevelopment of the periphery as integral to the wealth North America, Europe, and Japan enjoyed. UNCTAD's popular slogan of "trade, not aid" was therefore not the panacea it was portrayed to be.

According to Amin, the global accumulation of capital was defined by two distinct patterns. Development in the "self-centred economies" – Europe, North America, and Japan – was aimed toward fulfilling a "social contract" with the masses and consumer needs, while peripheral systems were characterized by the production of exports and luxury goods at the expense of developing internal mass markets. Since export sectors in the periphery were created with the "impulse[s] from the centre" in mind, they existed at odds with the rest of the country, in particular its productive forces: "As regards the level of development of the productive forces, it will in this case be heterogenous ... advanced

---

[52] Samir Amin, *Eurocentrism* (New York: Monthly Reviews Press, 1969).
[53] Samir Amin, *Accumulation on a World Scale: A Critique of the Theory of Underdevelopment* (New York: Monthly Review Press, 1974), 9.

(and sometimes very advanced) in the export sector and backward in 'the rest of the economy.'"[54] This phenomenon was deliberately perpetuated by the system in order to maintain a steady supply of cheap labor: "[t]he wage rate in the export sector will ... be as low as the economic, social and *political* conditions allow it to be."[55] The ruling elites within developing countries were compelled to adopt "'European' patterns of consumption," Amin argued, precisely because integrating into the global economy – and the attendant "marginalisation of the masses" – ensured "increasing income for this minority."[56]

What Amin meant by delinking was not the equivalent of national autarky or isolation but "the submission of external relations to internal requirements."[57] In practicable terms, it necessitated the creation of an "auto-centric economy" focused on consumer needs and living standards, especially in food production, education, and technology. In contrast to the emphasis on cash crops inherited from the colonial era, self-reliance suggested a new economy predicated on internal "impulses" rather than profitability. In 1974, Amin wrote that "the struggle for social liberation from class exploitation is indissolubly linked to the national liberation struggle of the people of Asia and Africa."[58] Like Nyerere, who had earlier lamented the limits of "flag independence" – independence in name only – Amin viewed political independence as inadequate for the liberation of newly decolonized nations.[59] Delinking, in radically changing the division of labor and specialization imposed on the South by the capitalist centers, thus marked a more meaningful point of departure in what Amin viewed as a two-step process of decolonization.

Amin's ideas about delinking led to his skepticism toward the NIEO, which he discussed at the Conference on Africa and the Problematics of the Future, cohosted by the IDEP, in the summer of 1977. Conceived as the Third World counterpart to the contemporaneous Club of Rome, the conference was held in order to remedy the absence of Southern

---

[54] Samir Amin, "Accumulation and Development: A Theoretical Model," *Review of African Political Economy* 1 (August–November 1974), 12–13.

[55] Amin, "Accumulation and Development: A Theoretical Model," 12, 13–14. *Italics in original.*

[56] Ibid., 15.

[57] Samir Amin, *Delinking: Towards a Polycentric World* (London: Zed Books, 1990), x.

[58] Samir Amin, *Imperialism and Unequal Development: Essays by Samir Amin* (New York: Monthly Review Press, 1974), 2, quoted in Ng'wanza Kamata, "Samir Amin and Debates at the University of Dar es Salaam in the 1980s," *Agrarian South: Journal of Political Economy* 9, no. 1 (April 2020), 64–77, especially 70.

[59] Nyerere, "Freedom and Unity," 41.

perspectives in envisaging the "scenario-makers" following the UN declaration of an NIEO, which emerged overwhelmingly from the North. The legal scholar Umut Özsu has observed, for instance, the Brandt Commission's role in centering rights discourse and neoliberal capitalism in reconciling the North–South divide.[60] Such prescriptions stemmed from the experiences of industrialized countries and were not necessarily applicable to the African context:

> If . . . we have the ambition to participate in the reconstruction of a world which respects . . . the personality of every nation and the particular contribution of every people, I believe that we cannot but question tirelessly the ultimate purpose of development and consider the impact of possible developments on the autonomy and the contribution of every people and every nation to the universal community.[61]

In urging African intellectuals and diplomats to "present ou[r] own thinking as to the scenarios for the future of our continent," Amin proposed promoting the interlocking aims of national independence and popular development, economic growth and human development.[62]

Amin rightfully feared that the early "cruel failures" of the NIEO appeared to presage its eventual relegation to "the dustbin of history." Rather than focus solely on the "revision" of the current international order, Amin suggested turning to political and economic integration instead. Beyond the mere broadening of markets, Amin envisaged horizontal integration in the vein of African unity. The NIEO, he observed in 1981, simply impelled the "peripheral bourgeoisie [in the Global South to] . . . bec[o]me the subordinate ally of imperialism by joining in the new division of labour."[63] Only by "delinking" from the global capitalist system did the Global South stand a chance of attaining food sovereignty, which Amin saw as crucial for overcoming postcolonial constraints on

[60] Umut Özsu, "Neoliberalism and Human Rights: The Brandt Commission and the Struggle for a New World," *Law and Contemporary Problems* 81 (2018), 139–165.

[61] Opening address by M. Samir Amin on the Occasion of the Conference on Africa and the Problematics of the Future, July 18, 1977, Dakar, United Nations African Institute for Economic Development and Planning, ECA Repository, https://repository.uneca.org/handle/10855/42426.

[62] The scenarios Amin and his fellow conference organizers envisaged fell into three broad categories: the continuation of "dependent" development, the revision of the international division of labor per the NIEO, and the adoption of an "auto-centred, self-reliant development."

[63] Samir Amin, "Some Thoughts on Self-Reliant Development, Collective Self-Reliance and the New International Economic Order," *The World Economic Order: Past and Prospects*, eds. Sven Grassman and Erik Lundberg (New York: Palgrave, 1981), 544.

national independence. Within this framework, food security, land (re) distribution, and egalitarian economic relations took precedence over urban industrialization.

The argument for Africa-centric alternatives to the NIEO extended beyond "revolutionary intellectuals" like Amin and others of his ilk. It was also on the minds of such regional elites as Adebayo Adedeji, who vociferously championed self-reliance during his tenure as the executive secretary of the ECA. An economist who served as Nigeria's erstwhile Minister of Economic Reconstruction and Development in General Yakubu Gowon's military government, Adedeji oversaw the nation's rebuilding efforts following the Nigerian–Biafran War. In the first half of the 1970s, he also played a leading role in establishing the Economic Community of West African States (ECOWAS), which grew out of his 1970 article in the *Journal of Modern African Studies* on regional economic integration.[64] Unlike his predecessor, Gardiner, whose more conservative outlook steered the organization away from Amin's vision, Adedeji – who headed the ECA between 1975 and 1991 – was a vocal proponent of a more radical strategy of delinking. As Amin has noted, the ECA director and his team had "considerable autonomy," since the IDEP's founding document was "a document in the diplomatic and ambiguous style of UN 'resolutions,'" providing the ECA with vast transformative potential depending on its leadership.[65] In Adedeji's mind, the international conferences on fostering the North–South dialogue – UNCTAD IV, the Conference of Economic Cooperation among Developing Countries, the Conference on International Economic Cooperation, and others – had accomplished little in the way of negotiated structural change. The "spirit of confrontation" they did achieve was no match for the persistent deterioration of economic and social conditions in Africa.[66]

While Nyerere harbored a "vision of overcoming dependence ... to be realized domestically through socialist policies and internationally in the New International Economic Order," then, Adedeji questioned the utility

---

[64] Adebayo Adedeji, "Prospects of Regional Economic Cooperation in West Africa," *Journal of Modern African Studies* 8, no. 2 (July 1970), 213–231.

[65] Amin, *A Life Looking Forward*, 153.

[66] "The Crisis of Development and the Challenge of a New Economic Order in Africa," Statement by ECA Executive Secretary Adebayo Adedeji, February 24–March 3, 1977, Thirteenth Session, Fourth Meeting of the Conference of Ministers, Economic Commission for Africa, ECA Repository, https://repository.uneca.org/handle/10855/18020.

of the NIEO for African nations at all: "[A] new international economic order is nothing more than the external expression of a new national (and in Africa, multinational and regional) social and economic order and that without the latter there can be no truly enduring and beneficial new international economic order as far as Africa is concerned."[67] The emphasis on *the* NIEO, he argued, had blinded African political elites – eager to participate in the growing number of international conferences – to the "irrelevance" of most of its principles to the continent's long-term development goals.[68] Even the G-77's prized Integrated Programme for Commodities (IPC) and the Common Fund – a series of arrangements designed to stabilize global markets for such Third World exports as cocoa, coffee, and sugar – would "not lead to the restructuring of the African national economy."[69] Between 1960 and 1975, the continent's annual growth rate was a meager 4.9 percent, while its debt burden skyrocketed from $7 billion to $28 billion.[70] Because of its excessive dependence on external factors, "each time the industrialized market economies sneeze, the African economies catch pneumonia!"[71]

In order to overcome the development crisis engulfing the continent, Adedeji suggested that ECA member states needed to usher in a novel socio-economic regime with national and regional dimensions as well as structural changes in international economic relations. What he called the "Three New Orders" encompassed new national, regional, and international economic orders: "A new international economic order which is not based on the achievement of an increasing measure of national as well as collective self-reliance and self-sustained growth and development in Africa will not provide African countries with maximum benefits."[72] In other words, the NIEO must be accompanied by the (re)deployment of

[67] Getachew, *Worldmaking after Empire*, 154; Adebayo Adedeji, "Africa and the New International Economic Order: A Re-assessment," National Bank of Egypt Diamond Jubilee Commemoration Lecture, Cairo, December 19, 1979," *Towards a Dynamic African Economy: Selected Speeches and Lectures 1975-1986* (London: Frank Cass and Company, 1989), 199.

[68] Adedeji, *Towards a Dynamic African Economy*, 208–209.

[69] "African Position on a Common Fund under the Integrated Programme for Commodities," Arusha, Tanzania, October 6–8, 1977, E/CN.14/VP.1/108, ECA Repository, https://repository.uneca.org/handle/10855/6111.

[70] "Survey of Economic and Social Conditions in Africa for 1976," Economic Commission for Africa, ECA Repository, https://repository.uneca.org/handle/10855/19053.

[71] "The Crisis of Development and the Challenge of a New Economic Order in Africa," 3, ECA Repository.

[72] Ibid., 30.

resources on national and regional levels, including the expansion of welfare services, the development of intra-African development assistance, and the creation of African multinational corporations in mining and industrial fields. Crucially, this imagined new order insisted that development was not merely a question of increased net resource flows but a matter of the distribution of the national product centering on social justice and equity *among* as well as *within* nations.

The ECA, for its part, was committed to "ensuring the direction of resources to productive sectors and to the promotion of structural change" in addition to reducing foreign exchange expenditures.[73] From the mid-1970s onwards, the ECA developed and advocated a host of strategies to supplement the twin guiding principles of self-sustainment and self-reliance. Noting the continent's continued dependence on foreign technology, markets, and skilled personnel, for instance, ECA experts formulated work programs to repair higher education, provide advisory services for negotiating agreements on the extraction of natural resources, strengthen member states' technological capabilities, and develop African-owned multinational shipping companies. They were convinced that "[u]nless inclinations toward innovative thinking and action are built into educational systems ... it is unlikely that the acceleration and diversification sought after ... [and] any meaningful degree of self-reliance can be achieved."[74]

Above all, the ECA under Adedeji drew on Amin's ideas about an "auto-centric economy" to urge African governments to shift "their productive resources to the production of commodities for which there was a growing domestic market both for household consumption and as raw material for manufacturing" rather than expand production for the colonial-era externally oriented market.[75] Chief among these was a renewed focus on improving food production through crop diversification as well as new storage processes and production methods.[76]

Yet the ECA's ability to create meaningful change on a regional or continental level was frustratingly limited. Its strengths – technical expertise, institutional continuity, and quixotic features unmarred by compromise

[73] Ibid.

[74] Revised Framework of Principles for the Implementation of the New International Economic Order in Africa, ECA Executive Committee Meeting, November 17–18, 1975, ECA Repository, https://repository.uneca.org/handle/10855/12705.

[75] Adedeji, *Towards a Dynamic African Economy*, 211–213.

[76] "The Crisis of Development and the Challenge of a New Economic Order in Africa," 14, ECA Repository; Revised Framework of Principles for the Implementation of the New International Economic Order in Africa.

and political calculations – were simultaneously shortcomings. An independent organ with the resources to undertake path-breaking research, the ECA's decision-making abilities nonetheless remained subsidiary to those of sovereign governments. The apolitical nature of the ECA suggested that its bureaucrats "were unlikely to wield influence in the political ranks of the countries from which they had, in effect, defected."[77] The sometimes-fraught relationship between the ECA and African governments was vividly captured by the arbitrary detention of at least four ECA staff members between 1978 and 1979 by the Marxist Derg regime in Ethiopia, who accused them of "anti-government activities."[78] In the same vein, Adedeji bemoaned that "in respect of some of these prerequisites of the growth of intra-African trade, some Governments display less enthusiasm in action than in public declaration."[79] While regional and international organizations "have a critical role to play in supplementing Governments' effort in the achievement of these Three New Orders," he argued, ultimately it was the responsibility of individual governments to take "concrete steps" toward self-reliance.[80] The latter's emphasis on participation in conferences – especially its optics – at the expense of more tangible measures thus troubled Adedeji: "conferences in the African region are generally an end by themselves – forums where words are mistaken for wisdom, resolutions for resolve, activity for action, promise for performance and aspirations for commitments."[81] The failure of the continent's elites to assess conferences and resolutions based on their "quality, realism and relevance to our development needs and the follow-up actions taken" rendered them "counterproductive" and "a waste of scarce resources" over the long haul.[82] Adedeji's concerns echoed those shared by Nkrumah and Nyerere in the early 1960s. Then and now, the hard-won sovereignty of newly independent nations – and its attendant privileges – proved too alluring to cede even in the name of Pan-African solidarity.

---

[77] Isebill Gruhn, *Regionalism Reconsidered: The Economic Commission for Africa* (Boulder: Westview Press, 1979), 31.

[78] Letter from Ali B. Tall to Clayton C. Timbrell, May 5, 1981, File 3, Box 22, Series S-0913, UN Archives in New York.

[79] "The Crisis of Development and the Challenge of a New Economic Order in Africa," ECA Repository.

[80] Programme of Work and Priorities for 1976 and 1977, Economic Commission for Africa, Economic and Social Council, ECA Repository, https://repository.uneca.org/handle/10855/650.

[81] "The Crisis of Development and the Challenge of a New Economic Order in Africa," ECA Repository.

[82] Ibid.

***

In a way, self-reliance reached its apogee in the late 1970s. The 1979 Arusha Programme for Collective Self-Reliance and Framework for Negotiations – concluded at the fourth Ministerial Meeting preliminary to UNCTAD v – sought to enhance South–South cooperation through technical and economic cooperation among developing countries in order to bolster their collective bargaining position in North–South negotiations. The follow-on 1980 Lagos Plan of Action spearheaded by the ECA in conjunction with the OAU aimed, for its part, to achieve economic integration on a continental basis. Yet both initiatives forewent its more utopian aspects in favor of language deemed palatable for African leaders. Between 1964 and 1980, proponents of self-reliance – a loose coalition of intellectuals, bureaucrats, and statesmen – oscillated between the imperative of reforming the existing economic system and the will-o'-the-wisp of subverting it. Ultimately, the prospect of homegrown development through Pan-African unity was not enough to catalyze the political will necessary to attain genuine economic sovereignty.

Self-reliance's moment in the sun was no sooner glimpsed than foreclosed. By the 1980s, the neoliberal counterrevolution – driven, on the one hand, by the elections of conservative leaders in the West who were less sympathetic to Southern perspectives and, on the other hand, debt crises in Latin America and Africa – prompted the Global South in general and Africa in particular to eschew the self-reliance approach in favor of market-oriented interventions put forward by the International Monetary Fund and the World Bank. Meanwhile, the unity among the countries of the Global South fractured in the face of novel and sometimes diverging aims, such as the emergence of newly industrialized countries (NIC) in parts of Southeast Asia and Latin America and their propensity for bilateral economic agreements with the developed world.

Even as the optimism of the postcolonial decade waned, African leaders have continued to invoke the language and logic undergirding "self-reliant" development to frame contemporary discussions about economic, environmental, and technological justice in regional and international forums, including the 2015 African Union assembly in Johannesburg and the 2021 UN Climate Change Conference.[83] The

---

[83] "Declaration on Self-Reliance," Assembly of the Union, Twenty-Fifth Ordinary Session, June 14–15, 2015, http://au.int/sites/default/files/decisions/9664-assembly_au_dec_569_-_587_xxiv_e.pdf.

"polluters-must-pay" attitude the Dakar group of experts led by Amin adopted in the early 1970s, especially, has resurfaced with a vengeance amidst calls for climate reparations.[84] On the flip side, the very persistence of these demands for redress suggests just how little progress has been made. In light of such continuities as a strict pecking order in the international arena, Africa's continued dependence on development finance institutions, and the exclusion of marginalized voices from discourses about sustainable development, Amin's observations ring especially salient. "Development for whom?" he had asked in the mid-1970s.[85] Africa's search for a new international economic order would press on.

[84] "Intelligence Note REC – 11 Prepared by the Bureau of Intelligence of Research," *FRUS*, 1969–1976. Shola Lawal, "The World Needs to Quit Oil and Gas. Africa Has an Idea: Rich Countries First," November 9, 2021, *The New York Times*, www.nytimes.com/2021/11/09/climate/africa-fossil-fuel-gas-cop26.html.

[85] Samir Amin, "Accumulation and Development: A Theoretical Model," 16.

12

Guam's Quest for Indigenous Chamorro Self-Determination in the Age of Pacific Anticolonialism

Kristin Oberiano

When Robert A. Underwood took the stand at the United Nations in New York in 1982, he represented the Indigenous Chamorro people of Guam before the world.[1] Underwood was one of three representatives from the Organization of People for Indigenous Rights (OPI-R), a Guam-based activist group that sought to ensure that the Chamorro people had the right to self-determination and the right to decide the political status of the non-self-governing territory. OPI-R requested that the United Nations' Committee of 24 uphold Chapter XI of the Charter of the United Nations which laid out the rules for decolonization. Underwood testified that the "inalienable right to self-determination has yet to be fully exercised on Guam because the people of Guam (the Chamorro people) have been denied their rights in the past."[2] OPI-R hoped that the UN would compel the United States to carry out the empire's responsibilities to its colonial possessions.

Yet, Underwood's speech on behalf of OPI-R fell short of advocating for a particular UN political status – independence, free association, or

---

[1] I have chosen the widely used spelling of "Chamorro" to describe the Indigenous people, language, and culture of Guam and the Mariana Islands. I do acknowledge that there have been recent changes made by the Kumisión I Fino' CHamoru (Chamorro language Commission) on Guam to decolonize the Chamorro language through revisions in orthography, such as utilizing the spelling "CHamoru" to better fit the sounds of the language. "Guåhan" is also used to refer to Guam.

[2] Parenthesis is original. Organization of People for Indigenous Rights, "Self-Determination: A People's Right," MSS 010, Box 5, Folder #7, the Papers of Congressman Ben Blaz, 1984–1992, the Richard F. Taitano Micronesian Area Research Center, University of Guam, 11. (Hereafter cited as OPI-R, "Self-Determination: A People's Right").

integration into the colonial power – choosing instead to emphasize "the
right to self-determination" for those "who have been denied political
self-fulfillment for over three-hundred years." He emphasized the cultural
legacies of United States colonialism in Guam, such as how the colonial
government had inculcated the Indigenous people to believe that they
were "inferior, ignorant and backward," and at times told them that
"the Chamorro people in fact did not exist." OPI-R believed that an
exercise of Indigenous self-determination would be the first step to alleviate and rectify both the political status of the island and the social and
cultural impact of US colonialism in Guam. Specifically, it would allow
the Indigenous Chamorro people to reclaim the island in the face of
increased US militarization and settler colonialism in Guam since World
War II. For Chamorros, decolonization as a practice had grown beyond
the realm of national and international politics and became a cultural and
social process that contained the potential to validate and recognize the
desires of colonized Indigenous peoples.

The quest for Chamorro self-determination of the 1970s through the
1980s was a pertinent example of how Pacific Indigenous peoples cre-
atively and defiantly re-envisioned the contours of self-determination and
decolonization. OPI-R and the greater Chamorro self-determination
movement were immersed in the larger context of Pacific anticolonialism
and anti-imperial movements.[3] Alongside advocating for political and
cultural decolonization and the demilitarization of the Pacific, these
Pan-Pacific movements such as the Nuclear Free and Independent
Pacific embraced and centered Indigenous identity as a core component
of self-determination. Chamorro leaders and activists from Guam were
involved in and learned from these movements to hone their anticolonial
rhetoric and envision for themselves a self-determined and self-governing
Guam. In order to justify Indigenous self-determination, they underscored
their political existence as both US colonial subjects and, significantly, as
an Indigenous people. The Chamorro self-determination movement arose
alongside and was influenced by the emergence of the global
Indigenous consciousness.

Emboldened by decolonization movements across the Pacific, the
Chamorro self-determination movement embraced Indigenous identity
as integral to the political process of self-determination. It was an

---

[3] The best monograph on Pacific decolonization: Tracey Banivanua Mar, *Decolonisation
and the Pacific: Indigenous Globalisation and the Pacific* (Cambridge: Cambridge
University Press, 2016).

Indigenous cultural self-determination movement steeped in criticism of US imperialism, setter colonialism, and militarism in the Pacific. This chapter shows how Chamorro leaders and activists led rhetorical, political, social, and cultural campaigns via the Guam Commonwealth Movement to validate their existence as an Indigenous people and justify their right to self-determination. Significantly, the movement eschewed the status of independent nationhood for Guam instead advocating for an intermediary political status of Commonwealth, which sought to create a special negotiated status for the island within the US empire. The resulting draft of the Guam Commonwealth Act established Indigenous Chamorro rights and the possibility for Indigenous Chamorros to participate in a future plebiscite for true political self-determination.

The antagonism that Chamorro leaders and activists faced, however, was indicative of how the US used multiculturalism and the Fourteenth and Fifteenth Amendments of the US Constitution to discredit the idea of Indigenous rights, bypass the age of decolonization, and hold onto its Pacific colonies despite the Charter of the United Nations. The self-determination process did not prioritize the political and cultural formations envisioned by Indigenous peoples, instead serving those of the colonial power and immigrant and settler communities.[4] Thus, the history of Chamorro self-determination on Guam is also a history of how the United States continued its formal colonialism in the late twentieth and into the twenty-first century via the structure of settler colonialism. Similarly to Bermuda, which Quito Swan writes about in this volume, Guam remains one of the seventeen United Nations non-self-governing territories nearly eighty years after the signing of the United Nations Charter and the international consensus – at least in rhetoric – toward decolonization.

Despite the political loss, the Chamorro self-determination movement of the 1970s and 1980s catapulted a Chamorro renaissance and an embrace of Indigeneity. The potential for UN self-determination led Pacific Indigenous peoples such as the Chamorro people of Guam to envision a decolonized world of their own through transnationally minded anticolonial and decolonial movements that centered Indigenous identity and culture. After the supposed age of decolonization and well into the twenty-first century, Indigenous rights in places like Guam could

---

[4] S. James Anaya, *Indigenous Peoples in International Law* (Oxford; New York: Oxford University Press, 2004).

no longer be extracted from subsequent articulations of self-determination and decolonization.

GUAM AND THE UNITED STATES' EMPIRE

The Chamorro self-determination movement on Guam arose in the midst of dramatic political, economic, and social changes in the island's landscape after World War II. Chamorro activists and leaders sought to ensure that the Chamorro people maintained cultural and political control in the face of increasing US military involvement, a growing non-Chamorro population, and an emphasis on international investments into the island's economy.

The history of Guam since the Chamorro people first encountered Ferdinand Magellan in 1521 is a history of empire and Indigenous resistance.[5] The island of Guam and the Chamorro people were colonized by Spain in the sixteenth century until the United States annexed the island during the Spanish–American War in 1898. The US and Germany split the Marianas into two separate colonies despite the related Indigenous Chamorro people who inhabited the whole archipelago. From 1899 until the Japanese attack on December 8, 1941, Guam was governed by a US Naval Government which consisted of a presidentially appointed Naval Governor and an advisory Guam Congress comprised of Chamorros. The Naval Government on Guam instituted Americanization projects including education, healthcare, and infrastructure which attempted to rid Chamorros of cultural identity and bring the island into an American modernity. Although it granted an Organic Act to its other colonies of the Philippines, Puerto Rico, and the US Virgin Islands in the early 1900s, the US did not grant Chamorros on Guam an Organic Act until 1950, thus denying US citizenship and a civilian government for the island for fifty years. Despite this, in the years before World War II, Chamorro elites generally felt an affinity toward the United States, sending multiple petitions to the President of the United States as well as US Congress to grant the island's peoples a civilian government and US citizenship.[6] These

---

[5] For general histories of Guam, see Pedro C. Sanchez, *A Complete History of Guam* (Rutland, Vt.: Tuttle, 1964); Robert F. Rogers, *Destiny's Landfall: A History of Guam* (Honolulu: University of Hawai'i Press, 1995); Pedro Sanchez, *Guåhan, Guam: The History of Our Island* (Agaña: Sanchez Publishing House).

[6] For a history of pre–World War II citizenship movement on Guam, read Penelope Bordallo Hofschneider, *A Campaign for Political Rights on the Island of Guam, 1899–1950* (Saipan, CNMI: Division of Historical Preservation, 2001).

petitions were either not heard or were ignored all together. This diplomacy included a historic trip across the Pacific and the North American continent by Baltazar Bordallo and Francisco B. Leon Guerrero to meet with US President Franklin D. Roosevelt in Washington D.C. in 1938. Despite the great lengths Chamorros would go to advocate on behalf of themselves, they were not able to successfully attain US citizenship and a civilian government due to racial prejudice and neglect on the part of the empire.

World War II hindered any chance for US citizenship because the Japanese empire invaded and occupied Guam. After the US recaptured the island from Japanese occupation toward the end of World War II in 1944, Guam became the US's forward military base in the Pacific region.[7] As the Cold War became a possibility and fears of communist aggression grew, the US doubled-down on its military installations on Guam in defense of the Asia-Pacific region, in the process making the issues faced by the Chamorro people secondary to US military policy. The island experienced rapid militarization starting in 1944 through the 1970s that included the building of two massive military installations – Naval Base Guam and Andersen Air Force Base – as well as smaller bases and stations in later decades. At the height of military land annexation in the late 1940s, the US military controlled close to two-thirds of the island, dispossessing Chamorro people of ancestral lands and relocating them to new villages. This land annexation was detrimental to Chamorro life and culture. As Chamorro lawyer and policy-maker Michael Philips wrote in a 1996 article, "Land is the soul of our culture; it, together with the sea, gives life to the Chamorro."[8] Land annexation transformed Chamorro lives. They could no longer depend on the land and ocean to support their subsistence lifestyles, and were forced into a cash economy that was almost completely affiliated with the US military.

---

[7] There are several authors who have written about this pivotal time in Guam's history. They include, Tony Palomo, *An Island in Agony* (Self-published, 1984); James Viernes, "Fånhasso I Taotao Sumay: Displacement, Dispossession, and Survival in Guam" (Master's, University of Hawai'i at Manoa, 2008); and Anne Hattori, "Guardians of Our Soil: Indigenous Responses to Post-World War II Military Land Appropriation on Guam," in *Farms, Firms, and Runways: Perspectives on US Military Bases in the Western Pacific*, ed. L. Eve Armetrout Ma (Chicago: Imprint Publications, 2001), 186–202.

[8] Michael F. Philips, "Land," in *Hale'ta: The Quest for Commonwealth, Issues in Guam's Political Development, The Chamorro Perspective* (Agaña: The Political Status Education Coordinating Commission, 1996), 3.

In order to transform the island into a military base, the United States military needed labor, and its contractors looked toward the Philippines to recruit temporary workers.[9] Filipino workers streamed into the island under the purview of the US Navy and outside US federal immigration law. While many of them were temporary and transient – moving back to the Philippines after earning and saving wages – a good number of them stayed on island, living in the villages that surrounded the labor camps. For some Filipino workers, the US immigration law was adapted to provide a pathway for US citizenship, allowing them to settle permanently on Guam. With US citizenship, these Filipino men petitioned their Filipino wives to the island and raised their children on Guam.

Although Chamorros would receive an Organic Act and US citizenship in 1950, the behemoth of the US military and the growth of the non-Chamorro population on Guam after World War II became concerning to Chamorros who felt that they could no longer control the island's political and cultural future. In the 1920s, Chamorros comprised 92 percent of the island's population, approximately 13,000 people. After World War II and the commencement of the military build-up, Chamorros were 45 percent of the island's population while Filipinos rose to from 3 percent before World War II to 12 percent afterwards.[10] By 1980, the Filipino population doubled in size, garnering 21 percent of the population, while the Chamorro population remained at 45 percent. The total population in Guam in 1980 was approximately 105,000. Within thirty years (1920–1950), Chamorros became a minority in the island they were Indigenous to. Today, there are more Chamorros living in the continental US than in the whole of the Marianas archipelago.

Although they would not use the phrase, Chamorro activists from the 1960s through the 1990s were describing the process of settler

---

[9] A history of Filipino labor migration to Guam can be found in: Vicente Diaz, "Bye Bye Ms. American Pie: The Historical Relations between Chamorros and Filipinos and the American Dream," *ISLA: Journal of Micronesian Studies* 3, no. 1 (1995): 147–60; Alfred Peredo Flores, "'No Walk in the Park': US Empire and the Racialization of Civilian Military Labor in Guam, 1944–1962," *American Quarterly* 67, no. 3 (2015): 813–35; Kristin Oberiano, "Territorial Discontent: Chamorros, Filipinos, and the Making of the United States Empire on Guam," (PhD Dissertation, Harvard University, 2021); Colleen Woods, "Building Empire's Archipelago: The Imperial Politics of Filipino Labor in the Pacific," *Labor* (Durham, N.C.) 13, Nos. 3–4 (2016): 131–52.

[10] Government of Guam, Interagency Committee on Population, "Guam's People, 'A Continuing Heritage': A Statistical Profile of the Territory of Guam, 1920–1980" (June 1988), 134. Copy found at the Pacific Collection, Hamilton Library, University of Hawaiʻi at Mānoa.

colonialism, in which the United States military had dispossessed, displaced, and replaced Chamorro people in order to occupy land and control labor for military purposes.[11] In addition to land dispossession, many Chamorros believed that they were being replaced by a Filipino migrant labor force employed by the US military. For instance, when Chamorro representative to US Congress Antonio B. Won Pat was asked about Filipino labor in Guam in a 1956 US Congressional hearing, he stated that the US military preferred to hire Filipino workers because they were "paid what we call in common terminology coolie wages or slave wages."[12] Chamorros felt they were consistently competing with a migrant labor regime that was transient and cheaper to employ, thus leaving them with limited options in the post–World War II Guam economy. Paired with the status of US territory and Americanization acculturation efforts, the combination of land annexation and the dilution of Chamorro population numbers by immigrants and settlers helped the US military to retain control over the island, pushing Chamorros further away from self-governance.

Until the early 1950s, many Chamorros believed that US citizenship would alleviate their woes and provide a path to air grievances about US military policy on Guam. Yet citizenship did not solve crucial problems. Military land annexation continued to occur, and Chamorros (they referred to themselves as "Guamanians") found structural limitations that prevented local self-governance. For example, the Governor of Guam was appointed by the President of the United States until 1970. In addition, Chamorros on Guam saw how other Pacific colonies, including those in the Trust Territories of the Pacific Islands, were able to negotiate their political status with the US beginning in the 1960s. The Northern Mariana Islands, whose Indigenous peoples are also Chamorro, began negotiations with the US over what form their future political status should take in the early 1970s. At the recommendation of Richard F. Taitano – a Chamorro from Guam and a former presidentially appointed Deputy High Commissioner for the Trust Territories of the Pacific Islands – Chamorro leaders on Guam thought that they too should be able to negotiate a new political status within the United States.

[11] Oberiano, "Territorial Discontent," 35 and 147; PulanSpeaks, "Robert Underwood – Reflections on Chamorro Activism," January 22, 2021, video, 1:05:49, www.youtube.com/watch?v=54A5SQTaZmo&t=23s&ab_channel=PulanSpeaks

[12] US Congress, House, Committee on Education and Labor, *Minimum Wages in Certain Territories, Possessions, and Overseas Areas of the United States*, , 84th Cong., 2nd Sess., 1956, Part Two, 487.

Through a series of acts in the Guam Legislature, Chamorros on Guam commenced two movements that attempted to change the island's territorial status within the US. These were the movements for the Guam Constitution (1970s) and for the Guam Commonwealth (1980–1997).

While the Guam Constitution Movement was conservative in its aims, the Guam Commonwealth Movement was indicative of how Indigenous Chamorros attempted to negotiate with the US empire on their own terms and rethink the United Nations' definition of decolonization in a "postcolonial" world. The Guam Commonwealth Movement was a nearly two-decade-long concerted effort by the local government in Guam and the island's community to craft a political status that would reflect the needs and desires of the whole community.[13] In September of 1982, the Commission on Self-Determination held an island-wide plebiscite to determine which political status the island's residents preferred. Seventy-three percent of the voters chose Commonwealth because it offered the most room for negotiation with the US federal government regarding the island's federal-territorial relationship, and was "promoted as a flexible status which could later lead to Statehood, or even Independence."[14] Rather than directly advocating for independence, which did not suit their desire for more self-governance within the US empire, Chamorros attempted to define for themselves what self-determination and decolonization looked like. Ambiguous by design, Commonwealth seemed to offer more possibilities for representation and negotiation when compared to the status quo under the Guam Organic Act, in which the federal government had unilateral decision-making over issues such as militarization and immigration. Commonwealth also left open the possibility for further revisions, ensuring that those on Guam could continue negotiations with the US federal government in later decades. Subsequently, Chamorro rights activists such as OPI-R attended public government meetings and hearings and influenced government officials – some of whom were also activists – to craft what would become the draft Guam Commonwealth Act.

---

[13] Oberiano, "Territorial Discontent," 321. For more reading on the Guam Constitution and Guam Commonwealth Movement, read Joseph F. Ada, "The Quest for Commonwealth The Quest for Change," in *Kinalamten Pulitikåt: Siñenten I Chamorro: Issues in Guam's Political Development: The Chamorro Perspective, the Hale'ta Series* (Hagåtña: Political Status Education Coordinating Commission, 2002); Robert Rogers, "Guam's Quest for Political Identity," *Pacific Studies* 12, no. 1 (November 1, 1988): 49–70.

[14] Ada, "The Quest for Commonwealth," 161.

As a whole, the Guam Commonwealth Movement attempted to create a new and special political status within the United States' empire, one which the people of the island were able to write themselves. The draft Guam Commonwealth Act expressed "the consensual aspirations of the people of Guam to change the island's political status from that of an unincorporated territory to that of a self-governing Commonwealth, recognizing the sovereignty of the United States of America."[15] Thus, the resulting draft of the Guam Commonwealth Act was an example of how, as Tracey Banivanua Mar describes, "decolonisation in the Pacific has developed as a *post*colonial phenomenon ... where the nation, as the primary formation of decolonised independence, has proven inadequate."[16] The desire for Commonwealth in Guam reflects how Chamorros molded the UN decolonization process in their own way. After several drafts and public hearings, an educational campaign, and island-wide plebiscites, the draft Guam Commonwealth Act was approved locally in 1985 to be presented to US Congress for consideration. To the dismay of Chamorro activists, all Guam residents, regardless of racial or ethnic background, were eligible to vote.

The Chamorro people of Guam were a victim of the UN's "saltwater principle" in, perhaps, an unexpected way. Banivanua Mar shows how Pacific decolonization arose relatively late in the age of decolonization in which the United Nations leveraged the saltwater principle – the notion that "only non-self-governing-territories separated by ocean, or saltwater, from their administering power would be able to evolve toward self-determination and self-government." This principle determined which colonies could and could not participate in a UN-prescribed self-determination and decolonization process.[17] Although the Pacific islands were eligible for self-determination under this rule, the saltwater principle effectively limited the ability for colonized peoples living within continental empires to claim self-determination. It also relinquished the UN's responsibility to curtail internal colonialism or settler colonialism.[18]

---

[15] Guam Commission on Self-Determination, "Guam's Quest for Commonwealth: The Draft Guam Commonwealth Act, June 11, 1986," Mangilao: University of Guam Micronesian Area Research Center, Online publication, 2, www.guampedia.com/wp-content/uploads/2013/08/Guam-Commonwealth-Act.pdf

[16] Banivanua Mar, *Decolonisation and the Pacific*, 14 (emphasis in original).

[17] Ibid., 143.

[18] My definition of settler colonialism is derived from a combination of scholars who theorize the general structure and process as well as those who study specific historical periods and geographies. They include: Patrick Wolfe, "Settler Colonialism and the

Even though Guam was eligible for self-determination as a result of the saltwater principle, all residents of the island could participate in a binding decolonization plebiscite, much to the chagrin of the Chamorro people, who came to represent less than half of the island's total population by the 1950s. Under the UN's rules, non-Indigenous residents of Guam also had a right to self-determination. In addition, the UN limited the options for what decolonization and self-determination entailed – independence, free association, or integration into the colonizing power – thus disallowing Indigenous and colonized peoples to envision other possibilities for their self-government.

Despite the UN's stipulations, Chamorros drafted the Guam Commonwealth Act to include provisions that attempted to curtail ongoing militarization and immigration, a boon for Chamorro rights activists who saw these two issues as the most detrimental to Chamorro people. In regard to the military, the draft act stipulated that the US military and the local Guam government would have to mutually consent to US military operations on the island. Secondly, the draft would provide the territorial government with local control over immigration – something that the Commonwealth of the Northern Mariana Islands was able to negotiate.[19] Most striking was that the Commonwealth attempted to counteract the saltwater principle that undergirded the decolonization process by ensuring that only the Chamorro people would be able to vote in a binding plebiscite for the future political status of Guam. Thus, the draft act was an expression of self-determination that did not necessarily fit the UN's decolonization options. Despite the UN's rules and local and federal opposition, the Chamorro drafters of the Commonwealth Act inscribed Indigenous Chamorro rights into the draft, making it a non-negotiable component in any change to the island's political status.

GUAM AND PACIFIC ANTICOLONIALISM

The confidence with which Chamorro leaders and activists incorporated Indigenous rights into the draft of the Commonwealth Act was due in

Elimination of the Native," *Journal of Genocide Research* 8, no. 4 (December 1, 2006): 387–409, https://doi.org/10.1080/14623520601056240; Lorenzo Veracini, *Settler Colonialism: A Theoretical Overview* (Houndmills, Basingstoke; New York: Palgrave Macmillan, 2010); Juliet Nebolon, "'Life Given Straight from the Heart': Settler Militarism, Biopolitics, and Public Health in Hawai'i during World War II," *American Quarterly* 69, no. 1 (2017): 23–45.
[19] Guam Commission on Self-Determination, "Guam's Quest for Commonwealth."

part to the rhetoric and tactics learned from activism in the US continent and across the Indigenous Pacific. Although they only participated in a small way in many of the international conferences, Chamorros' actions and political movements in Guam were part of the Pacific movement and the larger global Indigenous movement to resist colonialism and exercise self-determination. For Chamorros on Guam, self-determination meant the political exercise of determining a future status for the island as well as the revitalization of Chamorro culture and identity in Guam. When drafting the Guam Commonwealth Act, political leaders such as Guam governors, senators, and appointed officials worked alongside Chamorro rights activists to envision a world in which Chamorro self-determination and self-governance of Guam was a possibility. Many of the OPI-R activists were leaders in the movement to preserve Chamorro culture in Guam's changing social and cultural landscape. Ron Teehan, a Chamorro activist and founder of the Guam Landowners' Association, and Chris Perez Howard, a Chamorro writer and poet, sat next to Robert Underwood at the United Nations in New York in 1982. OPI-R also included Bernadita Camacho-Dungca and Clotilde Gould, two Chamorro women dedicated to the preservation of Chamorro language and story-telling; Benjamin Cruz, a Chamorro lawyer; Laura Souder, a Chamorro feminist scholar; and Hope Cristobal, a community activist. A few Filipino allies were also involved in OPI-R, including Nerissa Lee, Maria Teehan, and William Hernandez. These Chamorro activists and Filipino allies used their diasporic experiences and background in American education systems to criticize the US global empire and formulate a rhetoric of Indigenous Chamorro rights. Chamorro sociologist Michael P. Perez described OPI-R as the "intelligentsia of the Chamorro Movement."[20]

The term "Indigenous," however, was a relatively new rhetorical strategy employed by Chamorro activists in the 1970s and 1980s. The politics of identity formation and naming coincided with how Chamorros on Guam understood their evolving relationship with US empire. In the immediate post–World War II period, the Chamorro people of Guam had adopted the appellation "Guamanian" to distinguish themselves from

---

[20] Michael P. Perez, "Chamorro Resistance and Prospects for Sovereignty in Guam," in *Sovereignty Matters: Locations of Contestations and Possibility in Indigenous Struggles for Self-Determination*, ed. Joanne Barker (Lincoln: University of Nebraska Press, 2006), 177.

Chamorros in the Northern Mariana Islands.[21] "Guamanian" also con-
noted a particular affiliation and affinity for the United States because the
Americans ousted the Japanese from the island in World War II. To some
Chamorros, "Guamanian" sounded more like "American." The self-
determination movement of the 1970s and 1980s, however, brought
"Indigenous Chamorro" into common lingo. As Robert Underwood
writes in a 2015 article, "the use of the term 'indigenous' proved to be a
watershed contribution because the comparisons to other 'indigenous'
peoples became part of the political and social dialogue. This had not
been the case in the past because of the complexity of identity and self-
identification issues historically in Guam."[22] Thus, the Chamorro adoption of "Indigenous" as an identity was also a redefinition of their
relationship with the United States and the rest of the world. No longer
were Chamorros just American colonial subjects, but they became one of
the many Indigenous peoples claiming a specific set of rights globally.

In this way, the Chamorro self-determination movement was part of
the wider Pacific and global zeitgeist to define the Fourth World and
Indigenous anticolonialism. Chamorro activists' participation in international forums in the Pacific helped to shape the rhetoric used to justify
Indigenous rights within the Guam Commonwealth Movement and its
draft act. For instance, the movement for a Nuclear Free Pacific (later also
known as Nuclear Free and Independent Pacific) influenced some of the
rhetoric used by Chamorro activists, particularly around the relationship
between Indigenous rights, self-determination, demilitarization, and anti-
nuclearism.[23] The Nuclear Free Pacific Movement (NFP or NFIP) grew
out of a conference held in Suva, Fiji, in 1975 and continued to meet in
different Pacific nations or colonies every two to three years. In 1975, the
conveners and the delegates came together to discuss the ramifications of
nuclear weapons in the Pacific, especially in the midst of nuclear testing in
Micronesia as well as in French Polynesia. According to Banivanua Mar,

[21] Gina E. Taitano, "Adoption of 'Guamanian'," October 8, 2020, Guampedia, Inc., www
.guampedia.com/adoption-of-guamanian/
[22] Robert Underwood, "Dies Mit: The Origin and End of Chamorro Self-Determination,"
Micronesian Educator, Vol. 22 (Special Edition, November 2015): 107.
[23] For readings on the Nuclear Free and Independent Movement, see Banivanua Mar,
Decolonisation and the Pacific, 1–3, Roy H. Smith, *The Nuclear Free and Independent
Pacific Movement: After Moruroa* (London: Tauris Academic Studies, 1997); Quito
Swan, "Giving Berth: Fiji, Black Women's Internationalism, and the Pacific Women's
Conference of 1975," *Journal of Civil and Human Rights* 4, no. 1 (Spring/Summer 2018):
37–63.

the participants came to "the conclusion that colonialism underpinned nuclear testing."[24] They believed that "if colonized peoples, whose territories were testing grounds for all sorts of external militaries, had the independent capacity to say 'no' to what was done in their lands, nuclear testing might be stopped."[25] Eventually, NFP incorporated independence and decolonization into the movements. If colonization was the foundation for nuclear testing in the Pacific, then decolonization and independence would allow Pacific Indigenous peoples to protect their lands and livelihoods. Decolonization and national independence were intertwined with environmental and ecological movements.

Not only was anti-nuclearism connected to anticolonialism, but anticolonialism in the Pacific was inherently an Indigenous project. In subsequent conferences and meetings, delegates from around the Pacific helped to draft the Charter of the Rights for Indigenous Peoples, declaring that "indigenous people, everywhere, have an incontestable right, surpassing that of any alien occupying power, to determine the future destiny of their own lands."[26] They referred to the "Fourth World" of colonized peoples who faced "subjugation in their own lands."[27] The Charter to establish the Rights of Indigenous Peoples also listed the colonial injustices experienced by Pacific Indigenous peoples including the "immediate or eventual excursion, even genocide," the Christianization efforts, the "confiscation of land, the enslavement of tribes, the trail of dishonoured treaties, the misuse of imported alien laws [read as "settler laws"] that disregarded indigenous rights, and the alternating use of crude military suppression and sophisticated racial institutionalism."[28] Self-determination and decolonization were not just redresses for colonization, but acts of Indigenous cultural revitalization and preservation.

But more than a list of colonial wrongs, the NFP charter's reference of the Fourth World – four years after the publication of George Manuel's seminal work *The Fourth World: An Indian Reality* – demonstrates not

---

[24] Banivanua Mar, *Decolonisation and the Pacific*, 1.   [25] Ibid.

[26] "Charter to Establish Rights of Indigenous Peoples," copy in possession of author.

[27] For further reading about the concept of the Fourth World, see George Manuel and Michael Posluns, *The Fourth World: An Indian Reality* (New York: New York Free Press, 1974); and the new edition with introduction by Glen Cloutard, "Introduction: A Fourth World Resurgent," in *The Fourth World: An Indian Reality* (Minneapolis: University of Minnesota Press, 1974).

[28] "Charter to Establish Rights of Indigenous Peoples," in *Nuclear Free and Independent Pacific Conference Proceedings 1978*, Publications of the Pacific Concerns Resource Center, Nuclear Free and Independent Pacific Movement, and associated organizations Nic Maclellan Collection, Pacific Manuscripts Bureau, Victoria, Australia.

only how Pacific peoples found similarities in the colonial experiences, but also how the Pacific was engaged in a burgeoning dialogue of the global Indigenous. In Glen Cloutard's summary of Manuel's concept, the Fourth World refers to "a process or movement of decolonization grounded in the purposeful revitalization of those relational, land-informed Indigenous practices and modes of life that settler-colonization sought to destroy in its drive to transform Indigenous peoples' lands into the settler-state and capital."[29] NFP's charter was an articulation of this Fourth World with Pacific peoples seeing the ocean as another geographic and ontological space that informed Pacific Indigeneity. Indigenous identity was central to how the NFP envisioned a decolonized Pacific World. And the Chamorro people of Guam, especially with their experience of settler colonialism, participated in this world-making too.

The claim of Indigenous identity played a foundational role in the Chamorro critique of United States settler colonialism in Guam and the rest of the Pacific. This critique was especially seen in a conference held in Guam in November 1982 called the "Micronesian Educational and Solidarity Conference." The objectives of the conference included "the exchange of information, working toward a nuclear-free Pacific, self-determination, liberation, cultural identity, and the rights of indigenous peoples."[30] Delegates from Japan, New Zealand, Hawai'i, New Caledonia, Tahiti, Kiribati, and Palau arrived in Guam to talk about topics including the islands' economic dependence on the military and various political models envisioned by Indigenous peoples. The conference was held at the Guam Legislature building, where the Pacific delegates listened to speeches and lectures about surviving atomic bombs, the continued nuclear testing in French Polynesia, the practice of nuclear waste dumping in Japan and the California coast, as well as listened to Titewhai Harawhira speak about Indigenous Maori resistance to nuclear testing and waste dumping.[31] The conference also included a "die-in" demonstration in Agaña (Hagåtña) – Guam's capital village – that the delegates organized: "The group listened to air raid sirens, a simulated atomic blast and 'fell,' pointing up [*sic*] the mass deaths the atomic bombs cause."[32] Some of the demonstrators "held pictures of bodies from the

[29] Cloutard, "Introduction: A Fourth World Resurgent," xi.
[30] Bart Stinson, "Conference Topics: Nukes, Culture, Rights," *Pacific Daily News* (November 16, 1982), 4.
[31] Paul Borja, "Nuke Bombs, 'Colonialism' Criticized," *Pacific Daily News* (November 18, 1982), 4.
[32] Ibid., 1.

atomic bombs dropped on Hiroshima and Nagasaki."[33] After the demonstration, OPI-R member Benjamin "B. J." Cruz "led them in chanting civil rights song, 'We shall overcome.'"[34] In doing so, Cruz demonstrated how Guam was the nexus that connected Pacific anticolonialism and decolonization movements with the legacy and history of the American Civil Rights movement. This conference shows how Pacific anticolonialism was wrapped up in discourses of decolonization, self-determination, anti-nuclearism, and Indigenous rights. For Chamorros on Guam, it was also about their civil rights within the United States' empire.

Chamorro activists from Guam also joined the NFP conference held in Vanuatu in August 1983 and learned from other Pacific nations about the relationship between anti-nuclearism, anti-militarism, and Indigenous self-determination. Marilyn Manibusan, who had been a core member of PARA y PADA (a predecessor to OPI-R), advocated for Chamorro rights in the Commission on Self-Determination on Guam as well as in conferences around the Pacific. She proclaimed at the conference, "As Pacific Islanders, we must stand true to our principles of peace and freedom. We must resolve never to compromise the lives of our future: OUR CHILDREN!"[35] As their island was transformed into a crucial military base in the midst of the Cold War, Chamorros of Guam shared the sentiment that nuclear weapons were an existential threat to Pacific peoples. Alongside other Pacific nations arguing for the "inalienable right to self-determination," the Chamorro delegates learned about other Pacific decolonization movements, and they, too, shared their own struggles on Guam. Chamorro delegate James Castro, the leader of the Chamorro Grassroots Movement, told a Guam-based newspaper reporter, "'It was an education in itself' ... 'People were sharing what they were struggling with and how they were handling it.'"[36] He further noted that Vanuatu "just went through a big struggle for independence and won so they had a lot to tell us."[37] Additionally, when Chamorro rights activists noted that they were fighting for Chamorro self-determination on Guam, Pacific leaders and activists became intrigued by the possibility. Hope Cristobal, a member of OPI-R, also attended the

---

[33] Ibid.

[34] Paul Borja, "A-bob Survivor Lectures," *Pacific Daily News* (November 18, 1982), 4.

[35] Marilyn Manibusan, "Freedom from Fear," Nuclear Free and Independent Pacific Conference, July 10–20, 1983, 74.

[36] Shannon Babauta, "Guam Grabs Attention at Vanuatu," *Islander Magazine* by the *Pacific Daily News* (August 21, 1983), 5.

[37] Ibid.

conference in Vanuatu and reported that the delegates networked with people across the Pacific and that "many offers of help were made to the people of Guam – legal or otherwise."[38]

Locally, Chamorros expressed their Indigeneity through a movement for language revitalization in schools and called for a greater prominence of Chamorro culture and practices in the public sphere. There was lively debate surrounding the purpose of public education, particularly with regard to whether the curriculum should discuss content that was formulated in the continental US or if it should be Guam-based and Chamorro-centric.[39] Members of OPI-R like Clotilde Gould and Bernadita Camacho-Dungca were ardent supporters of Chamorro language study and preservation.[40] Robert Underwood was a social studies teacher who founded and organized the first Chamorro Week at the George Washington High School in Guam, in which students and teachers delved into the history, culture, language, and arts of the Chamorro people.[41] Since the first iteration in 1974, Chamorro Week has become a cultural institution at all the public schools on the island. These social and cultural movements were not seen as separate from the discourse around self-determination, but were intimately intertwined.

When the organization testified at the United Nations in 1982, OPI-R was in the midst of an unprecedented wave of Pacific Indigenous anticolonialism. OPI-R delegates made four demands at the UN, two of which dealt with Indigenous peoples and self-determination.[42] The first was to remind the US to take the UN Charter on decolonization seriously. OPI-R

---

[38] Ibid.

[39] This debate among Chamorro culture advocates is most apparently seen in an issue of a newspaper magazine called *The Islander* published by *Pacific Daily News* in 1977. Dan Gibson, ed., *The Islander* (January 16, 1977).

[40] Camacho-Dungca co-wrote *Chamorro-English Dictionary* and *Chamorro Reference Grammar*, two books that linguistically explained the Chamorro language and which are used to teach Chamorro language today. Clotilde Gould wrote about the importance of language as fundamental to Chamorro identity in "Uno Dos Tres Kuatro," *Islander Magazine* published by *Pacific Daily News* (January 16, 1977). Donald Topping and Bernadita C. Dungca, *Chamorro-English Dictionary* (Honolulu: University of Hawai'i Press, 1975); Donald Topping and Bernadita C. Dungca, *Chamorro Reference Grammar* (Honolulu: University of Hawai'i Press, 1980).

[41] Phill Mendel, "Chamorro Week: Catching Up on Culture," *Pacific Daily News* (February 24, 1974), C-2. For more reading on the debate, see Oberiano, "The Paradox of Paradise," in "Territorial Discontent."

[42] The other two demands requested that the United Nations fund and assist education campaigns regarding political status and self-determination and that the UN visit Guam and listen to the Chamorro people. OPI-R, "Self-Determination: A People's Right," 15.

asked the Committee of 24 to "authorize and make legal a plebiscite of self-determination in accordance with the treaty obligations of the U.S. by being a signator [*sic*] to the U.N."[43] The second was for the United States to acknowledge the Indigeneity of the Chamorro people and their unique claims to Guam. They hoped that "all binding plebiscites and referendums relative to the question of Guam's ultimate political status must recognize that it is the Chamorro people who have not yet engaged in self-determination and it is only they who shall be allowed to participate."[44] The rise of the non-Chamorro population on Guam and the rhetoric and practice of multiculturalism threatened to dilute Chamorro political power. The central tenet of OPI-R's stance – Indigenous peoples were the only ones who should be able "to decide for themselves, the conditions under which their countries shall be administered" – aligned with the NFP's Charter for Indigenous Peoples and was in response to US colonialism, militarism, and settler colonialism in Guam.

Pacific Indigenous anticolonialism in the age of decolonization had to contend with the ramifications of the saltwater thesis and the waves of settler colonialism that changed the political structures and social demographics of the islands. The legacies of settler colonialism factored into how the Chamorro people of Guam articulated their positions on self-determination. As OPI-R testified at the UN in 1982, "immigrant citizens, U.S. citizens from Wisconsin or Indiana have no right to self-determination of Guam. It is illogical and unfair for them to move to Guam and participate in Guam's self-determination because the Chamorro people have yet to exercise their self-determination."[45] In referencing Wisconsin or Indiana – Midwestern states with stereotypically white populations – OPI-R hinted at the racial composition of settler colonialism in which white statesiders sought to change the political landscape of the island.[46] In another section of their speech, OPI-R referred to the "large numbers of Filipinos and other aliens" who were brought into the island to build the military bases, and whose population "threatens to make Chamorros strangers in their own land."[47]

---

[43] Ibid.   [44] Ibid.   [45] Ibid, 11.

[46] Robert Underwood was more explicit in a piece titled "Chamorro Challenge to Statesiders" in which he argued that white statesiders who had moved to Guam began to change the political and cultural landscape in Guam to mold Guam into a multicultural American paradise. Underwood, "Chamorro Challenge to Statesiders," *Islander Magazine* published by *Pacific Daily News* (October 23, 1977), 8–13.

[47] OPI-R, "Self-Determination: A People's Right," 11.

Furthermore, OPI-R saw how settler colonialism in Guam was connected to Indigenous peoples' experiences globally. In an article titled "Immigration and Guam's Future" published in an educational booklet that argued for Chamorro self-determination, Robert Underwood wrote, "viewed from the Chamorro perspective, the painful lessons of the natives of Hawaii and the Maoris of New Zealand are all too powerful."[48] Not only were they "reduced in size," but "they began to disintegrate as a people, as a collective body."[49] OPI-R wanted to ensure that the Chamorro people had the right to a self-determination plebiscite because they "have been denied their rights in the past."[50] Along with other Chamorro activists and allies, Underwood feared that without intervention and the preservation of Chamorro rights and self-determination in any political status change for the island, the Chamorro people of Guam would become "a permanent underclass in the next century."[51]

Guam was just one example of how the UN's saltwater thesis made it possible for Pacific islands to become independent, but nonetheless made it virtually impossible for Indigenous peoples in settler colonized islands to practice self-determination. As Banivanua Mar wrote in *Decolonisation and the Pacific*, "for the Pacific region, Resolutions 1541's narrow definition of *who* (or *where*) had the right to self-government, and *what* self-government would be, effectively abandoned the majority of native, Indigenous, first and colonised peoples who were minorities in settler states."[52] Thus, the non-self-governing islands in which the Indigenous peoples had now become demographic minorities were subject to the desires of those who had settled the island and who often challenged the views of the Indigenous peoples. In the decades after the age of decolonization, self-determination and decolonization for the Chamorro people seemed to become less of a possibility.

GUAM AND THE PROBLEM OF US MULTICULTURALISM

On Guam, Chamorro rights activists were successful in influencing local politicians to include Chamorro self-determination in the drafting of the

---

[48] Robert Underwood, "Immigration and Guam's Future," in *Chamorro Self-Determination*, eds. Laura Torres Souder and Robert Underwood (Mangilao, Guam: Chamorro Studies Association and the Micronesian Area Research Center University of Guam, 1987), 60.

[49] Ibid.   [50] OPI-R, "Self-Determination: A People's Right," 11.

[51] Underwood, "Immigration and Guam's Future," 60.

[52] Banivanua Mar, *Decolonisation and the Pacific*, 145.

Guam Commonwealth Act. Yet, in the era of multiculturalism dictating the equality of all peoples, the non-Chamorro population of Guam, including Filipinos and white statesiders, did not necessarily agree with Chamorro rights activists, who they often labeled as racist and discriminatory. White statesiders often used multicultural ideals to dismiss Chamorro rights activists.[53] Leader of the Guam chapter of the immigrant advocacy organization Workmen's Circle, Shelby Shapiro, said in one public hearing, "What is unique about the island is that, given a population a bit less than that of a small city (around 100,000) in a relatively small land area (about 210 sq. miles), there is a generally cosmopolitan outlook. Why? Because of the island's multicultural aspects."[54] For Shapiro, the multiculturalism of the island made it a supreme example of American opportunity. He villainized Chamorro activists for advocating for Indigenous rights. For him, Chamorro self-determination was antithetical to American ideals and thus should not be considered for inclusion into any political status change for Guam. Shapiro believed Indigenous rights had no place in the US empire.

Filipinos were also skeptical of Chamorro rights. Because OPI-R and other Chamorro rights advocates often lambasted US immigration policy on Guam and the changes brought on by the overwhelming number of Filipino immigrants, many Filipinos – especially those of the post–World War II migration wave – believed that Chamorro rights were in direct contradiction to their rights as immigrants and naturalized citizens.[55] At one public hearing on the Commonwealth Act in 1985, a Guam-born Filipino resident criticized the goal of Chamorro rights, stating that "the term indigenous person [is] a discriminatory term."[56] In particular, he felt that the label "indigenous" and Chamorro rights interfered with his American right to vote. Other Filipinos felt as if their economic opportunities and their ties to Guam could be jeopardized if the Chamorro

[53] White statesiders often included businessmen and former military affiliates who settled in Guam.

[54] "Public Hearing on the Draft Commonwealth Act Dededo Community Center," July 25, 1985, Box 58, Folder July 16–31, 1985, Papers of Ricardo Jerome Bordallo Second Term, Micronesian Area Research Center, University of Guam. (Hereafter cited as "Public Hearing on Draft Commonwealth Act Dededo Community Center," Papers of Ricardo Jerome Bordallo Second Term).

[55] Those of Filipino heritage whose family migration stories began in pre–World War II were generally supportive of Chamorro rights.

[56] "Third Public Hearing on the Draft Commonwealth Act, July 22, 1985," Papers of Ricardo Bordallo, Second Term, Box 58, Folder August 1–14, 1985, Richard F. Taitano Micronesian Area Research Center, University of Guam Mangilao.

people were to be granted a self-determination plebiscite. Another Filipino man lamented about the potential loss of his property if Chamorros obtained self-determination. He testified, "I can assure that my family and with other peoples in Guam they feel alienated ... Many Filipinos are saying, hey 'time to ship up,' otherwise we will be ... kicked out of this island."[57] Affected by the legacies of US colonialism and the continued military presence in the Philippines, many Filipinos migrated to Guam because it was an American island of economic opportunity, a place where the American Dream was a possibility. Yet, the Guam Commonwealth Act and the practice of Chamorro self-determination seemed to hinder that possibility for Filipino immigrants and their families.

For opponents of Chamorro rights, the presence of Filipinos in Guam represented an embrace of American multiculturalism on the island. Yet the Filipino population was not an equally colonized people in the perspectives of OPI-R, other Chamorro rights advocates, and Filipino allies. While they acknowledged the legacies of US colonialism in the Philippines, Chamorro rights activists saw how, in the context of Guam, Filipinos embodied a settler population that drove US settler colonialism. For them multiculturalism masked the trauma of US colonialism on Guam. In response, Chamorro activists and community members expressed their Indigenous ties in order to claim Guam's political future. For example, Chamorro language educator Bernadita Camacho-Dungca spoke of her family's ties to the village of Dededo, a village that had seen a rapid influx of Filipino immigrants in the years after World War II due to its proximity to US military installations. At a public hearing, she said that "I am a Chamorro born, raised, educated and married in this land that I'm sitting on. The generations of my mother are still sitting here in Dededo."[58] By giving her genealogy, Camacho-Dungca claimed Dededo as a Chamorro village, one that was "the best example of how accommodating a Chamorro is," and she pleaded with the audience to allow Chamorro rights and self-determination. Chamorro senator Marilyn Manibusan fervently defended the notion of Chamorro rights as well. In direct response to the Filipino man who questioned the idea of

---

[57] "Public Hearing on Draft of Commonwealth Act," Papers of Ricardo Bordallo, Second Term, Box 58, Folder July 1–15,1985, Richard F. Taitano Micronesian Area Research Center, University of Guam Mangilao.

[58] "Public Hearing on Draft Commonwealth Act Dededo Community Center," Papers of Ricardo Jerome Bordallo Second Term.

"indigenous," she exclaimed: "They ask me what I am, and I say, I'm Chamorro. I'm from Guam. I'm indigenous. How can anyone find fault with that? How can anyone point at me and tell me I am being discriminatory when I call myself Chamorro?"[59] Through an embrace of Chamorro genealogical ties to Guam and the term "Indigenous," Chamorro rights advocates articulated a criticism of US settler colonialism and imperialism.

Although Chamorro leaders and activists attempted to redefine the contours of what self-determination and decolonization could look like in the 1980s, the influence of multiculturalism, especially as practiced in the United States settler colonial empire, seemed to stymie any chance of Indigenous rights. Despite Chamorro activists' best efforts to leverage Indigenous rights rhetoric in Guam and in the Pacific, the United States federal government saw the draft Commonwealth Act's provision on special rights for Chamorro people as a violation of the US Constitution. If passed, the federal government argued, the Guam Commonwealth Act would place too much power in the territorial government, especially in regard to military operations and federal immigration policy. Significantly, representatives from the Department of the Interior, the Department of Justice, and the US Navy found the vote for self-determination by only the Chamorro people to be in direct contradiction to the US Constitution's Fourteenth and Fifteenth Amendments. These nineteenth-century Reconstruction amendments were crafted after the US Civil War to ensure that birthright and naturalized citizens were treated equally under the US Constitution, and that all US citizens had the right to vote. These laws were enacted in order to protect the constitutional rights of Black Americans' during Reconstruction. One hundred and twenty years later, the representative from the Department of the Interior testified that the clauses for Chamorro rights in the draft Guam Commonwealth Act "could be used to deny some U.S. citizens the right to vote based solely on their ethnic background." They were "unconstitutional."[60] Ironically, perhaps, the US weaponized equality and multiculturalism to deny redress for the specific racialized legacies of US colonialism experienced by the Indigenous Chamorro people. In doing

[59] "Third Public Hearing on the Draft Commonwealth Act, July 22, 1985," Papers of Ricardo Bordallo, Second Term.

[60] US Congress, House, Committee on Interior and Insular Affairs, *Guam Commonwealth: Hearings before the Subcommittee on Insular and International Affairs Part II*, 101st Cong., 1st sess., 1989, 275.

so, the United States federal government stipulated that all residents of the island of Guam, regardless of race, had an equal right to vote in Guam's self-determination and decolonization process. While the Government of Guam and other presidential administrations attempted to revise the act in the following years, activists pushed to keep the cause of Chamorro rights alive in any political status change. Ultimately, the Guam Commonwealth Act was shot down by US Congress in 1997. The inclusion of Indigenous Chamorro rights and self-determination within Guam's political status was determined to be unfeasible within the United States' empire.

"DECOLONIZATION FATIGUE"

The possibility of exercising self-determination and the zeitgeist of Pacific decolonization in the 1970s and 1980s propelled a resurgence of Chamorro political activism, a renaissance of Chamorro culture and language, and a rearticulation of Chamorro identity based in "Indigenousness." Even when the Guam Commonwealth Act died in Congress in 1997, Chamorro activists and leaders sought other ways to practice self-determination.[61] In 1997, the Guam Legislature established the Commission on Decolonization to replace the Commission on Self-Determination.[62] In the next year, the Guam Legislature passed a law to establish and fund a registry for native inhabitants of Guam. The law defined "native inhabitant" as those who received US citizenship as a result of the Guam Organic Act of 1950 and their descendants so that "the qualifications for voting in the political status plebiscite shall not be race-based, but based on a clearly defined political class of people resulting from historical acts of political entities in relation to the people of Guam."[63] The law cited the legacies of Spanish and US colonialism, the

---

[61] For most of the early 2000s, the Commission on Decolonization had been inactive, perhaps due to the exhaustion felt after the failure of the Commonwealth Act.

[62] Guam Legislature, "An Act Relative to Funding the Commission on Decolonization and the Chamorro Registry Advisory Board for the Purpose of Conducting a Decolonization Plebiscite on December 12,1999, for Funding Scove Operations and for Other Related Purposes," Public Law No. 24-296. Passed October 21, 1998.

[63] Guam Legislature, "An Act Relative to the Creation of the Guam Decolonization Registry for Native Inhabitants of Guam Self-Determination, to Appropriate Funding for the Vote on Self-Determination and Other Purposes," Public Law No. 25-106. Passed March 10, 2000.

Treaty of Paris of 1898, and the United Nations Charter, and staunchly made the case that Chamorros were native inhabitants to Guam and were, indeed, the "self" in self-determination.[64] To avoid claims that the law was race-based, legislators centered the year 1950 as the criteria of who was a "native inhabitant," which allowed those without Chamorro heritage and their descendants to vote, including Filipinos who resided in Guam before 1950 and gained US citizenship as a result of the Organic Act. Chamorro activists and leaders once again negotiated Chamorro identity within the United States' legal system in order to protect what they believed was their inalienable right as Indigenous peoples to self-determination.

Nevertheless, Chamorro advocacy for self-determination before the UN in 1982, their activist work in the villages of Guam, and their testimonies in US Congressional hearings reflect the subtle yet important evolution of the notion of "decolonization" as experienced in the Pacific. The Chamorro self-determination movement demonstrated how decolonization in the Pacific emerged, as Banivanua Mar shows, "as an identity, a belief system and a thought process that practiced independence, and injected the spaces that Indigenous peoples occupied with practices of self-determination."[65] In the postcolonial era, the idea of decolonization had evolved to become capacious, referring not solely to the creation of the nation-state, but to the embrace of alternative and often Indigenous-inspired ways of national and international politics, from language revitalization, to the hybridity of colonial and Indigenous religions, to Pacific demilitarization and anti-nuclearism. This transformation is similar to what Quito Swan historicizes in Bermuda, and how Black Reggae sound system culture in the 1990s is indicative of how anticolonial activism and decolonization rhetoric moved beyond the political to encompass cultural expressions. Guam was no different. The Guam Commonwealth Movement should not be taken as an ambivalent acquiescence to the presence of the United States on Guam, but as an envisioning of decolonization that benefited the Chamorro people, even if that vision of decolonization did not fit the prescribed boxes offered to them by the United States and the United Nations. Guam, then, is a site to study how Pacific Indigenous peoples engaged in a transnational movement that was more than anticolonial in its aims, but decolonial in its intellectual, political, and cultural vision of the world.

---

[64] Ibid.   [65] Banivanua Mar, *Decolonisation and the Pacific*, 224.

As of 2023, the island of Guam has not had a self-determination plebiscite and is still on the UN's list of non-self-governing territories. The Chamorro self-determination movement is alive, hoping that one day Chamorros will have the opportunity to practice self-determination even though the age of decolonization has long passed. As Chamorro scholar, lawyer, and writer Julian Aguon poetically wrote in *The Properties of Perpetual Light*, "Guam may have to bear the burden of being a colony in a world suffering from decolonization fatigue, but – to be clear – her people mean to live."[66]

[66] Julian Aguon, *The Properties of Perpetual Light* (Mangilao: University of Guam Press, 2021), 32.

13

Reggae, Sound Systems, and Arrested Decolonization in Bermuda

Quito J. Swan

Lying some 560 nautical miles east of Cape Hatteras, North Carolina, Bermuda is one of fourteen remaining British Overseas Territories. In 1995, Bermuda held a racially charged public referendum in which, out of only 58.8 percent of eligible voters, 73.6 percent voted *against* and 25.7 percent voted *for* independence. Given this status, contemporary observers might incorrectly assume that "arrested decolonization" in Bermuda stems from the absence of anticolonial praxis among its majority Black population. Historically, Bermuda's white oligarchy intensified this issue by popularizing simple *master narratives* that falsely claimed that slavery was *benign*, British colonialism was *good*, and Black radicalism *nonexistent*. The anticolonial insurgency of Black Power dispels such myths. For example, the Movement witnessed the British Government's attack on revolutionary youth groups like the Black Beret Cadre. It was also marked by the assassinations of British Governor to Bermuda Ian Sharples, his Aide-de-Camp, and the British Police Commissioner across the 1970s. In 1977, island-wide uprisings occurred when Erskine "Buck" Burrows and Larry Tacklyn were hung for these and other related murders. Colonialism marginalized the study of Black Power in the public education system and criminalized literature such as the Cadre's *Black Beret*. But these attempts to muzzle the soundscapes of Bermuda's Black Radical Tradition were not entirely successful, and written literature on Black Power arguably remains in a relatively nascent stage.

Even more so, Black Bermuda is a *sonic culture*.[1] As such, this chapter argues that it is critical to explore Black anticolonialism through its

[1] Julian Henriques, *Sonic Bodies: Reggae Sound Systems, Performance Techniques, and Ways of Knowing* (London: Continuum Books, 2011), ix.

cultural *soundscapes*, and not just "ballot politics." It explores how Black youth engaged questions of decolonization through Reggae, Dancehall, and sound system culture in the "global 1990s." Arguably the era's most dominant form of Black popular culture, the epistemologies, pedagogies, and socioeconomics of Bermuda's deep-rooted sound system heritage have not been thoroughly studied as a political "studio" of anticolonial praxis, grassroots organizing, and spatial self-determination. This is important to understand Bermuda's development into a critical Black Atlantic hub of sound system culture, which I would argue was a form of Black internationalism.

Finally, "the global 1990s" refers to a critical but understudied era of Black internationalism that extends both before and beyond the decade. This broad moment includes: Ronald Reagan's domestic and foreign policies in the Americas (US invasion of Grenada and Panama, the Iran-Contra affair, and 'Wars on Drugs'); the Gulf War; the Los Angeles uprisings, police brutality, and Rodney King; the anti-apartheid movement and Nelson Mandela's presidency in South Africa; the O. J. Simpson trial; the Nation of Islam's Million Man March; the deaths of Tupac Shakur and Biggie Smalls; ethnic conflicts across Rwanda, Burundi, Ethiopia, and Eritrea; hurricanes Hugo and Katrina; and Britain's highly publicized withdrawal from Hong Kong. Remarkably, sound system culture documented much of this, and remains an untapped audio archive of the era.

BERMUDA, RASTA, AND REGGAE

According to Julian Henriques, a sound system is a "unique apparatus – a musical medium, technological instrument and a social and cultural institution." The functioning heart of a sound system may be that it juggles music for an audience at a "session" or a "dance," but a sound is much more than the music that it plays. A sound can include a collective of individuals who may serve overlapping roles, like deejays, mike toasters, music selectors, audio engineers, operators, and managers. Sound systems can "perform as sonic war machines, vehicles for cultural expression, vessels for identity and pleasure, economic engines, commercial ventures, instruments for musical production, institutions for artists training, multimedia communication systems [and] test-beds for technical innovation."[2]

---

[2] Ibid., 3; see also Carolyn Cooper's *Sound Clash: Jamaican Dancehall Culture at Large* (New York: Palgrave Macmillan, 2004).

They can be cultural ambassadors for their neighborhoods, communities, countries, and Diasporas.

Sound systems first emerged in Jamaica in the 1950s. Using African Diasporic music like R&B, Boogie Woogie, Merengue, and Calypso, they held musical battles (clashes) with their competitors to determine who played the best records, whose system (box) *sounded* the best, and who could draw the biggest crowds. Sound system culture developed in stride with the growth of Ska, Rocksteady, Reggae, and Dancehall in the 1960–70s. Both a receiver and amplifier of Caribbean ways of knowing, sound system culture includes its international community of artists, sounds, promoters, venues, studios, journalists, labels, vendors, carnivals, fans, and investors. It created its own Diasporas, archives, and historical narratives by globally circulating its clashes, dubplates, albums, and concerts on LPs, cassettes, CDs, and DVDs via record stores, travelers, and radio.

Reggae reached Bermuda by at least 1969, when Ska icon Cecil "Prince Buster" Campbell, Judy Mowatt's Gaylettes, and Hortense Ellis "played to full houses" as part of Reggae'69.[3] Weeks later, Bermuda's Pauulu Kamarakafego chaired the First International Black Power Conference. Reggae intersected with the island's deep-rooted Black musical traditions like Gombey, Calypso, Soul, and Jazz. Kingsley Swan's Calypso Islanders, the Talbot Brothers, and Michael Clarke, and promoters like Olive Trott and Choy Aming are testimony to this heritage.

Reggae's inherently rebellious soundscapes of Rastafari – anticolonialism, Pan-Africanism, concern about state surveillance, and critique of the West as being of a Biblical Babylon – resonated with Black Power. The concept of "Babylon" became an instrumental word and political identifier for capitalism, colonialism, the carceral, European culture, surveillance, police officers, and colonial education. Bermuda's Black Beret Cadre drew up its plans for a political revolution with the music of Peter Tosh and Mighty Sparrow playing in the social backdrop. While the Foreign and Commonwealth Office (FCO) marked the Cadre as its "public enemy no. 1,"[4] it also targeted Bermuda's growing community of Rastafari. In January 1973, Bermuda's Special Branch's "First Basic

---

[3] "Prince Buster to Tour Caribbean," *Daily Gleaner*, June 18, 1969, 7; "Reggae'69 Troupe Has Run-On with police," *Daily Gleaner*, July 11, 1969, 2.

[4] See Quito Swan, *Black Power in Bermuda: The Struggle for Decolonization* (New York: Palgrave Macmillan, 2010) and *Pauulu's Diaspora: Black Internationalism and Environmental Justice* (Gainesville: University Press of Florida, 2020).

Paper on Rastafarians in Bermuda" questioned if the "cult [posed] a threat to internal security." The paper examined Rasta in Jamaica, Marcus Garvey's Universal Negro Improvement Association (UNIA), and the 1930 coronation of Ethiopia's Ras Tafari Makonnen as Haile Selassie. This it found as testimony of Garvey's prophetic calls for Black people in the West to "look to Africa, when a Black king shall be crowned." It saw the basic tenets of Rastafari as being that "Selassie was the living God, Ethiopia was the home of Black man," and that repatriation to Africa was the only path to Black redemption. The document referenced aesthetics, locks, long beards, and the community's debates on the use of ganja (marijuana), referencing Rasta's clashes with police over the trade. It also claimed that "Nya men" were the violent component of Rasta, named after Ethiopian freedom fighters who fought against Italy's invasion of Ethiopia in 1935.[5]

Special Branch claimed that Bermudians had long since frequented Jamaica in search of "narcotics," but noted that in July 1972 numbers of these youths began to "wear plaits in their hair" and "wooly type hats" with the red, green, and gold colors of Ethiopia. Some wore badges with portraits of Selassie. Persons interrogated by the police increasingly "professed association" with Rastafari. As opposed to the Cadre or the local Nation of Islam it could find no single leader or common group among these wearers of Ethiopia's colors. But they alleged that a Michael Ebbin obtained materials from Jamaica that were addressed to an "African Society." Additionally, they periodically gathered at private residencies to smoke herb and hold "desultory discussions" on their faith. The group totaled some fifty individuals between the ages of sixteen and twenty-five who could be seen conversing in three prevalent areas – Devil's Hole, Bailey's Bay Harlem, and St. Monica's Road. According to Special Branch, most of the group had criminal records and convictions for violence and the use of narcotics. "They were extremist in character," but did accept whites who rejected society. The group was united by a "mutual interest in crime" and marijuana, and two members had sought exemption from conscription in Bermuda's regiment. It was not yet known if they sought repatriation to Africa or if the wearing of "wooly caps" was a whim, like the wearing of daishikis in the aftermath of the Black Power Conference.[6]

---

[5] Bermuda Police Special Branch, "First Basic Paper on Rastafarians in Bermuda," January 9, 1973, FCO 63/1099, National Archives of the United Kingdom, London, England.
[6] Ibid.

The state also directed its surveillance of Rastafari's youth through the Government's Race Relations Council.[7] In 1972, Council member Rev. Charles Fubler informed the police that a group of Rastafarians mounted "anti-social and racial" placards in front of City Hall.[8] This was the work of Gershwyn "Rabbonni Shiloh" Smith, who led the Young Progressives; fascinatingly, Smith informed the media that he was protesting the Apollo Mission to the Moon. One of his posters announced an upcoming "Rasta festival."[9] Established in 1969, the culturally based Young Progressives from Spittle Pond's "Mount Paran" were "self-styled on the order of Mahatma Ghandi's peaceful struggles in India."[10]

Of course, one would not need to be a "Black magic man from Amsterdam" or "witch doctor from Brixton" to know that one cannot tally Rastafari by counting dreadlocks or spliffs. But *where one finds Boogie, one usually finds Woogie* – Reggae and Rastafari become part of Black Bermudian popular culture in the 1970s. In 1972, London-based student Anthony Outerbridge informed the *Bermuda Recorder* that he missed Bermuda's Calypso and Reggae.[11] The paper's London correspondent Elaine Ellingham reported how British Black kids were having a great time with Reggae, as artists like Max Romeo "spoke to them in their language"; Trinidad's Steve Bernard played the music on Radio London, and record stalls on Portobello Road sold Reggae records.[12] In his column "Manhattan Chessboard," Warren Allen Smith told the *Recorder* that the Wailers, Johnny Nash, and Jimmy Cliff could be heard on Radio WMRL and Radio WBLS.[13]

In 1973, Bermuda's New Generation band played Reggae, Jazz, Calypso, and R&B at St. George's Barbarella Restaurant and toured New York. By 1974, one could buy Reggae records, 8 tracks, LPs, 45s, speakers, posters, and lights from stores like Family Affairs in Hamilton's

---

[7] George Buchanan, "The Black Beret Cadre and Its Manifesto," 10 August 1971; Minutes of the Race Relations Council Meeting, 1 March 1971, 11 May 1971, Race Relations Council Working Papers, Dec 1970–Dec 1972, Bermuda Government Archives, Hamilton, Bermuda.

[8] Minutes of the Race Relations Council Meeting, 12 December 1972, Race Relations Council Working Papers.

[9] "First Basic Paper on Rastafarians in Bermuda."

[10] Lois Smith, "The Young Progressives," *Fame*, Vol. 1, No. 4 (October 1974): 35.

[11] "Bermudians Training to Further Career Opportunities," *Bermuda Recorder*, April 29, 1972, 5.

[12] Elaine Ellingham, "Letter from London," *Bermuda Recorder*, December 1–8, 1973, 1, 4.

[13] Warren Allen Smith, "Manhattan Chessboard," *Bermuda Recorder*, March 10, 1973, 12.

Cedar Park Arcade and Shelly Bay Plaza and Dub City.[14] In that year, one writer to the *Recorder* pleaded for more Reggae, Calypso, and Rocksteady to be played at the Mangroves. While the best nightclub for playing such music, it had not been doing so of late, and the people wanted "something lively and unique" to dance to like j'ouvert-style, "ole 'mas music."[15]

On July 29, 1977, Peter Tosh performed at Summerfest 77, a three-day music festival held at Bermuda's National Stadium that included guitarist Richie Havens, New York's Funk group Brass Construction, Cape Verdean band Tavares, and Jazz pianist Ramsey Lewis. According to *Billboard*, some 22,000 persons attended the weekend affair which took place during Cup Match, a national holiday founded by Black Bermudians to commemorate the abolition of slavery. Summerfest was organized by Julian Hall, a 27-year-old Black lawyer and Secretary of the conservative United Bermuda Party (UBP), which was the political wing of Bermuda's white oligarchy. He informed journalist Stan Mieses that he was his Party's "link to the disaffected youth of Bermuda," and was "trying to change the image of Bermuda as a sanitorium for second honeymooners." Summerfest's lineup was designed to attract Bermudians between the ages of sixteen and forty-five and its 60 percent Black population.[16] Initially, the police kept a low profile. Herb was smoked openly, and a petition was being handed around for its legalization.[17]

But all was not well. It was a "tumultuous weekend" for the "staid and stodgy paradise." Police constantly harassed the festival. Tavares's musical director was denied entry into the island because of a local drug conviction five years prior. The same issue happened with Brass Construction, until Hall's folks convinced the "airport militia" to release him. Lewis's piano was dropped on stage and destroyed. Havens "fell into some sort of trance on stage and played for hours until he was led away muttering and shaking" while the "anxious crowd shouted for Tosh."[18]

---

[14] "Family Affairs," *Fame*, Vol. 1, No. 3 (September 1974): 7.

[15] "Please More Rock Steady and Reggae at the Mangroves," *Bermuda Recorder*, May 25, 1974, 11.

[16] "22,000 at 3-Day Bermuda Festival," *Billboard*, Vol. 289, No. 32 (August 13, 1977): 32; Stan Mieses, "Paradise Invaded by Pop Music," *Daily News* (Fort Walton), August 12, 1977, 25; "Bermuda Pop Fest Could Turn Into an Annual Affair," *Billboard*, Vol. 287, No. 12 (July 27, 1977): 59.

[17] "Everything Was Smoking at National Stadium," *Royal Gazette*, July 27, 1977, 3.

[18] Stan Mieses, "Breakthrough in Bermuda," *Daily News* (New York), August 1, 1977, 302; Mieses, "Paradise Invaded by Pop Music"; "Festival Group," *Royal Gazette*, July 26, 1977, 1.

Tosh, who had released his distinctly anti-apartheid album *Equal Rights* that year, took the stage by storm. His inspiring and powerfully political set appealed to the nearly 10,000 persons in attendance. His songs "Equal Rights" and "Get Up, Stand Up" struck a deep chord with Bermuda's Black youth. Tosh's band superbly jammed over his "Stepping Razor" and was "clearly right for the climate." Between his singing and speaking, the highlight of Bermuda's largest musical event was that Tosh lit a "Marley" – a large ganja spliff – on stage. The police fruitlessly threatened to remove him from stage after only twenty minutes. Some forty-five minutes later, he ended under more threats, but then returned for an encore. While in Bermuda, he had been very vocal about Bermuda's repressive anti-ganja laws.[19] Interviewed years later in *High Times*, Tosh was asked by journalist Bagga Brown if he had been banned in certain countries. His response was that while he did not know if it was official, in Bermuda he had said "certain things on a TV interview" that displeased the establishment, and thus the interviewer had "not been seen on TV since."[20]

Mieses found the show to be a "victory for the native youths" who were "trying to bring Bermuda up to date in the world of popular culture." Interestingly, Hall was arrested at the end of the show for not abiding by the island's "arbitrary" curfew laws over the three days. Before being taken away by officers, he informed the audience that it was "unfortunate that it [was] still a criminal offense to have too much fun."[21] Writing in the Bermuda's Industrial Union's *Workers' Voice*, Sherol Hunt found this "fussing and confusion" about Summerfest to be the kind of frustration that drove "young people to petty crime."[22]

Reggae was met with some skepticism from certain corners of Black Bermuda. In the aftermath of Summerfest, educator Dale Butler decried how Bermudians who were "weak culturally ... sponged on to Reggae like a suck rock to a damp towel." Writing in the *Workers' Voice*, he argued that they listened to the music as a means of escape. They were so concerned with being "dread" that they missed that Reggae was "message

[19] *Daily News* (New York), August 1, 1977, 302; Mieses, "Paradise Invaded by Pop Music"; Mieses, "Breakthrough in Bermuda"; "Ten Thousand People Attended the Final Night of Summerfest," *Royal Gazette*, August 1, 1977, 3.
[20] Bagga Brown, "Peter Tosh and Bunny Wailer," *High Times*, No. 82, April 1983, 33.
[21] *Daily News* (New York), August 1, 1977, 302; Mieses, "Paradise Invaded by Pop Music"; Mieses, "Breakthrough in Bermuda."
[22] "Finance Dept's Sherol Hunt," *Workers' Voice*, August 26, 1977, 3.

music and message music [was] life." He wanted its fans to apply its words to their lives, as opposed to just moving to its beat.[23]

The *Workers' Voice* "Roots Council" disagreed with Butler. It claimed that, unfortunately for Summerfest's sponsors, "star attraction Tosh" had "spoke all too clearly against the status quo." It called for Bermudians to save their souls by listening to Reggae, arguing that Black American Soul music was escapist and geared toward partying – "Is it mere coincidence that the type of Black music commercially pushed to the forefront in America" had "been largely devoid" of politics, in contrast to the "militant sixties"? In contrast, Reggae threatened "the escapist slumber" that grasped young Black people across the world. It had become the Black youth's "most popular form of music in Bermuda," and deserved this "top-ranking rating," due to its authentic Blackness. As such, "music had again become a potential political force" as the voice of the people and not a tool for the state. Both Bob Marley's 1978 One Love Peace Concert and Steel Pulse's participation in the Anti-Nazi League's carnival march through East London (the social base of the fascist National Front) were examples of this phenomenon. As such, Bermuda's establishment wanted Reggae's social awareness to remain on the "subconscious level," and "When the most popular music for young Black Bermudians was merely non-political soul, the radio stations could never play enough of it." But now that it was Reggae, the music "aired by radio DJs" was "no longer the same as that heard in cars or on portable tape-decks." This demonstrated either an "inexplicable disregard for popular opinion and choice," or a conspiracy to suppress the music. But Reggae *was* Africa, and this was suppressing the "growth of true culture."[24]

Journalist Alvin Williams also saw Reggae as a "unifying force" between Bermuda and other Caribbean peoples. When Cliff's *The Harder They Come* played in the island, a theater manager threatened not to screen any more Reggae-themed movies, under police claims that the movie glorified criminal behavior and gun play. In defense of the movie, Williams invoked Frantz Fanon's argument that there was a "thin line between a criminal and revolutionary," who both attacked the order from outside of the law.[25] This was quite relative for Bermuda.

[23] Dale Butler, "Sponge Brains," *Workers' Voice*, August 26, 1977, 3.
[24] Roots Council, "Save Your Soul … Listen to Reggae," *Workers' Voice*, October 13, 1978, 5.
[25] Alvin Williams, *Workers' Voice*, April 4, 1980, 4; February 6, 1981, 5, 6.

The UBP sponsored the Tosh concert at a moment of intense racial politics, speaking truth to Walter Rodney's charge that petty bourgeois leadership in the Caribbean often attempted to co-opt the popular culture of steel pan, Calypso and Reggae for its own dubious purposes.[26] In 1976, Erskine "Buck" Burrows and Larry Winfield Tacklyn were tried for the aforementioned Governor assassination and related deaths, such as one that occurred during a shopping center robbery that FCO officials claimed was a "fund-raising mission" for the Berets. While Tacklyn was acquitted for the Governor's incident, both men were hung at Casemate's Prison on December 2, 1977; British troops were flown in to suppress the subsequent three days of uprisings.

Local Reggae group Ital Foundation emerged that month "as a group of ghetto youths who first started gathering, reasoning, and playing" music in the "hills overlooking" Victor Scott Primary School in Back-a-Town's Glebe Road. The group's music spoke to the dramatic politics of the moment. Its 1980 Garvey, Rastafari inspired album *Ital Foundation Volume 1* featured tracks like "Repatriation," "Zion Heights," and "Black Man's Redemption." Its "Concrete City" lamented how African people were brought to Bermuda to slave on Bermuda's "concrete plantation." They were now surrounded by Bermuda's 24 miles of concrete ghetto, corruption, confusion, and illusion.[27]

For example, mainstream media and literature mystified Burrows and Tacklyn as "crazed gun men." However, Burrows's confession revealed more clarity about his political consciousness:

I, Erskine Durrant Burrows, as former Commander in Chief of all anti-colonialist forces in the island of Bermuda, wish to willingly reveal the part I played in the assassination and murder of the former Governor of Bermuda Mr. Richard Sharples and his ADC Captain Hugh Sayers ... I wish to state ... that it was upon my direct orders what was done was done, performed with a magnum .357 six-shot handgun. I was not alone when I went up to Government House to kill the Governor, but I shall never reveal who or how many others were with me.[28]

---

[26] Walter Rodney, "Contemporary Political Trends in the English-Speaking Caribbean," *Black Scholar* 7, No. 1 (September 1975): 15–21.

[27] "Local Band to Play at Bermuda Dance in New York," *Bermuda Recorder*, September 9, 1973, 1; Vejay Steede, "Reggae Music in Bermuda," in *Bermuda's Musical Connections* (Washington DC: Smithsonian Institute, 2002), 265; "Reggae Group Breaks Barriers," *Bermuda Times*, October 20, 1989, 14; Ital Foundation, "Concrete City," *Ital Foundation Volume 1*.

[28] TNA: PRO MEPO 26 223 1, June 13, 27, 1976, Note for Mr. Marriage, who is Crown Prosecutor for my case, signed Erskine Burrows.

One of Burrows's motives for killing Sharples was "to make the people, Black people in particular, become aware of the evilness and wickedness in" Bermuda. The other was "to show that these colonialists were just ordinary people like ourselves who eat, sleep, and die just like anybody else and that we need not stand in fear or awe of them." He also sought to "reveal Black people to themselves," as during the Governor's funeral many Black people stood "with tears in their eyes crying for a [white Governor] who when he was alive didn't care if they lived or died ... and yet when many of their own people pass away there is sometimes hardly a tear shed for them." For Burrows, this was the result of colonialist propaganda.[29]

Born on March 15, 1944, in Friswell's Hill, Burrows had lived a troubled life, one that was impacted heavily by the carceral state. The fifth of nine children, his divorced mother, Viola Burrows, died when he was twelve. He became a ward, and, sent to live in the group home Sunshine League, promptly ran away. He lived between Court Street and a wooden shack in Pembroke. In January 1974, Burrows was found guilty on five counts that included armed robbery of the Bank of Bermuda of some 28,000 dollars on September 25, 1973, and a grocery store, with two automatic pistols and rifle. He was captured while riding a moped. Burrows was carrying a sawed-off shotgun during the bank robbery, and evaded police by hiding in a banana patch off Court Street. After distributing monies in the Back-a-Town area, he earned the name of Black Robin Hood. At the time of his arrest, he had 2,000 USD in his possession, and told police that he had given the rest away. The police believed that he lived "an austere life," which included the "non-consumption of meat" and a maximum of physical exercise." Apart from crime, his only vice seemed to be gambling. He did not smoke marijuana or drink alcohol, although he perhaps was "experimenting with marijuana" at the time of his arrest. He had been existing "like a guerilla," heavily armed and evading police. Burrows was clearly training, perhaps exemplifying Ranajit Guha's notion of peasant insurgency.[30]

[29] Ibid.

[30] "Antecedents," November 5, 1973; Supreme Court of Bermuda, Criminal Jurisdiction 1974: No. 4 Judge's Notes; Police Statement, Buck Burrows, October 19, 1973; R-v-Erskine Durrant Burrows, Supreme Count of Bermuda Criminal Jurisdiction 1974:4, Criminal Appeal, National Archives of Bermuda, Hamilton, Bermuda; Ranajit Guha, *Elementary Aspects of Peasant Insurgency in Colonial India* (Durham, NC: Duke University Press, 1999).

He informed police that he was known as "Buck, Dipper, and the Cuba Kid." Since the robberies, he had been living in a cave near Bermuda's Ocean View golf course. He was carrying a note about the "Black man's history," signed "Coba" and a few Molotov cocktails. Another note suggested plans to take a hostage for ransom money, to hijack a plane and to escape to Algeria. Another stated, "the hand of Coba has moved before." Officers pressed him about whether this was a reference to a prior killing.[31]

Tackyln's overt politics are harder to trace. Born on April 1, 1952, he was marked as an "illegitimate child." He was unmarried with no children or job, and had no fixed abode. His mother lived in the United States, his father was deceased, and he was "illiterate" despite having a "token education." According to one detective, he had never held a regular job and "spent most of his time on Court Street." Tacklyn had been arrested in May 1973 for armed robbery of Master's Hardware. He was sentenced to fourteen years in prison for unlawful possession of an offensive weapon, armed robbery, and deprivation of liberty. His several previous convictions include the use of offensive words, escaping lawful custody and resisting arrest (1970). He had two convictions for possession of *Cannabis sativa* (1971) and for offensive behavior (1973).[32]

In 1970, under the advice of the FCO, the UBP had introduced an Offensive Behavior Bill to specifically target the Cadre. It was used to imprison Cadre Chief of Staff John Hilton Bassett after the group burned the Union Jack in 1970 to condemn South Africa's Sharpeville Massacre and Britain's support of apartheid. While incarcerated, Berets met, befriended, and shared with Burrows anticolonial literature like Fanon's *Wretched of the Earth*.

During his interrogation, Tacklyn refused to cooperate with the investigating officer. He declined to sign a transcript of his recorded statement, claiming illiteracy. He shouted obscenities at the officer, stating that the discourse only "made him stronger." After flexing his muscles, he announced that the brothers were not "united but the day was coming."[33] That year, Tacklyn had attempted to travel to Canada and the United States with Beret Ottiwell "Chaka" Simmons. His arrest occurred upon his return to Bermuda. He claimed that he was going to make "strong

---

[31] Police Statement, Buck Burrows, October 21, 1973.
[32] "Larry Winfield Tacklyn," May 19, 1973; "Larry Tacklyn," May 16, 1973, Supreme Court Criminal Larry Winfield Tacklyn Case 49/1973, Bermuda National Archives.
[33] Larry Tacklyn Statement, May 17, 1973, Bermuda Police.

connections" in Halifax, Toronto, New York, and the West Indies. When asked by officers why he was denied entry, he responded, "You know about it – those people had my record waiting for me – they read it off to me, you're responsible for them putting me in that dark hole for five days."[34]

SOUND SYSTEMS AND STAGE SHOWS

In the early 1970s, Kent "Fadda Dub" Outerbridge began traveling to Jamaica to buy records and sell them out of his home. In 1974, he established Dub City Retail (International), which distributed Reggae albums, records, and cassettes via stores in Court Street and Cottage Hill. He and his life partner, Olive-May Smith, built Dub City into a sound system and record label, and it became a haven for Reggae artists, Rastafari faith, and Black Diasporic engagement through its distribution of clothing, material culture, concert tickets, and cassette recordings of clashes and performances. From the counters of Dub City, one could find cassettes from international sounds like Stone Love, Metromedia, Bodyguard, Black Kat, Waggy Tee, Poison Dart, and London's Sir Coxsone.[35]

The session was a semi-autonomous space of Black Bermudian identity formation, Diasporic cultural exchange, and technical innovation, one from which local sound systems instrumentally infused Reggae culture into Bermuda. This included Nuclear Weapon, Diamond Emperor, Playboy International, Magnum Force, Jah Life, Wildfire, Firestone, African Pride, Embassy Crew, Genesis, Rude Boy International, Souljah One, and Spanish Town. Into the 1990s, these sounds held sessions across Pembroke Community Club, Number One Shed, Clayhouse Inn, Devonshire Recreational Club, Bailey's Bay Club, Warwick Secondary, White Hill field, Incubator, and Spinning Wheel. These sounds, which at times had their own record labels, helped produce local artists like Lady Tyson, Daddy Yella, Troyan, Runksie, Corvin Melody, Fat Jaw, Shingae, Sister Carol, and Junior C. The UBP responded to this growth with anxiety. In 1989, it passed a Noise Pollution Act which stated that loud music that was an annoyance between midnight and 6AM could result in a

[34] May 22, 1973, Lois Browne to J. Barrington-Jones; "Larry Tacklyn," May 16, 1973, Larry Winfield Tacklyn Case 49/1973, Bermuda National Archives.
[35] Jonathan Bell, "Community Mourns Reggae Ambassador," *Royal Gazette*, May 31, 2017; "Dub City," *Bermuda Times*, November 21, 1990, 10.

police force issued summons. This was amended in 1994 to be effective twenty-four hours a day.[36]

Bermuda was well on its way to becoming a significant Black Atlantic hub of Reggae. Throughout the long 1990s, it hosted leading artists from Ziggy Marley's Melody Makers to Shabba Ranks. Steel Pulse performed at Clayhouse over three days in 1985. Interviewed by Waheedah Zarif (Gloria Whitter), band leader David Hinds remarked that he had always heard of Bermuda as being commercialized, so he expected to experience "a lot of corruption and negativity." However, he found Bermudians to have a sense of harmony that he hoped to see throughout the Caribbean and Africa.[37]

Bermudians also traveled to Jamaica's annual Reggae Sunsplash, which started in 1978. Former Premier of Bermuda Ewart Brown was a close friend of its founder, Tony Johnson, and served as its first medical technician; according to Brown, the name "Sunsplash" was conceived in his living room. By 1979 he had helped build a "well equipped First Aid Station with volunteer doctors and nurses on call" for the festival. In 1991, Bermuda began to host its own Sunsplash concerts. Its National Stadium lineup included Maxi Priest, Dennis Brown, Shinehead, Andrew Tosh, Carlene Davis, and the A-Team Band. In 1992, it was headlined by South Africa's Lucky Dube, Aswad, Barrington Levy, and Papa San.[38]

From the 1980s into the 1990s, musical feuds between Dancehall artists like Ninja Man and Super Cat and Bounty Killer and Beenie Man drove sound system culture; this was reflected by lyrics of warfare, gun play, and hypermasculinity. Yet, Dancehall continued to grapple with contemporary questions of a decolonizing Caribbean: hard times, hungry children, advocacy of ganja use, gender politics, IMF structural adjustment programs, political economy, the carceral state, back-a-towns, Diasporas, food insecurities, surveillance, fallen soldiers, revolution, and pandemics. However, the mid-1990s witnessed a renaissance of Rastafari consciousness in sound system culture. Led by artists such as Garnett Silk,

---

[36] Winston Lambe, "Bermuda Bubbles with Local Record Labels," *Bermuda Times*, September 4, 1991, 10; "Noise Act Eroding Tourism," February 1, 1994, *Bermuda Times*, March 4, 1994, 2; see also *The Birth of a Trust: Bermuda's History Through Music* (Hamilton, Bermuda: Dread and Baha, 1997).

[37] Lambe, "Bermuda Bubbles," 10; Waheedah Zarif, "David Hines," *Workers' Voice*, April 5, 1985, 6.

[38] "Reggae Sunsplash," *Bermuda Times*, May 5, 1989, 9; "Onions in the News," *Bermuda Times*, May 1, 1992, 14; Franki P, "Reggae Sunsplash'91," *Bermuda Times*, July 10, 1991, 12; "Lucky Dube Headlines Local Sunsplash," *Bermuda Times*, July 10, 1992, 17.

Capleton, Luciano, and Buju Banton, all of whom performed in Bermuda, Dancehall reengaged the ideas of repatriation, African womanhood, spiritual warfare, Black unity, and promised lands in Africa. This moment was patterned by a growth of African-centered political and cultural awareness among Bermuda's Black youth, who engaged both overtly politically *conscious* Reggae and "politically unconscious" *slack* Dancehall for answers to their own political, cultural, and personal struggles. Sound system culture held space for both *slackness* and *culture*, reflected in the curating of popular CD series like VP Records's *Strictly the Best.*[39]

The history of Bermuda's most renowned sound system, Souljah One, reflects this phenomenon. In the 1980s, David "Magixx" Cunningham founded Rudeboy International in the Devil's Hole area. On its way to becoming a leading sound, its clashes with Spanish Town were the stuff of local lore. While attending college in London, Magixx joined and gained experience with veteran sound system Saxon. Upon his return home, he founded Souljah One, with its name being a reference to a "soul servant in Jah's army, one who stands alone" in righteous battle. After traveling to Jamaica to record dubplates with major artists, "little Souljah One" began to represent Bermuda internationally.[40]

Its first clash outside of Bermuda occurred that year against Earth Ruler in New York, where Magixx introduced the audience from Brooklyn, New Lots, Utica Avenue, and 90s crew to "Bermuda juggling." Souljah One's first song that night was a remix of Buju Banton's "Murderer" and Bob Marley's "Crazy Ballheads," followed by Garnett Silk. Its dubplates referenced Bermuda and Devil's Hole.[41]

Souljah One's global acclaim inspired a sense of "national pride" among Bermuda's Black youth. One consistent indictment of colonialism was that it had produced a lack of pride among Black Bermudians about their culture, accomplishments, and belief in their ability to be successful in all areas of life unless sanctioned by white patronage. But Souljah One's significance went beyond "pride": its name, positionality, and music reflected an insurgent soundscape that Bermudian Black youth could rally around, one that intersected with student activism,

[39] VP Records, *Strictly the Best*, Vol. 13, 1994.
[40] "Souljah One Sound," https://chicagopromo.proboards.com/thread/23/souljah-sound-bermuda
[41] "Souljah One vs Earthruler 94 NYC," Hecklers Inc/Di Phoenix, https://soundcloud.com/hecklersphoenix/souljah-one-vs-earthruler-94-nyc-hecklers-remaster?in=hecklersphoenix/sets/soul-jah-1-dances

anticolonialism, Black modernity, transnational politics, Diasporic travel, entertainment, and Rastafari philosophy.

NATIONALIST YOUTH ALLIANCE

Souljah One's base was comprised of teenagers and young adults who were born in Black Power's insurgent 1970s; they carried birth names like Che, Chelito, Makonnen, Fanon, Makeba, Oladapo, Iman, Kenya, Raziyah, Bismallah, Meshach, Zenji, Kashima, and Tafari. They heard the whispers of Black Power through Bermuda's sonic traditions; the Reggae session was an inclusive space that engaged their various cultural, political, and religious orientations as Christian, Muslim, Hebrew Israelite, Seventh Day Adventist, and Rastafari. This group came of political age in "the global 1990s," and collectively raised their own questions about self-determination. In the context of Bermuda, the decade included a shooting at the Spinning Wheel Nightclub, the murder of Rebecca Middleton, and the police force's racialized Operation "Cleansweep." The year 1995 witnessed the suspension of Bermuda's Olympic football team after seven of its members were arrested in Miami for conspiracy to import marijuana, and the closure of US military bases in Bermuda. In 1998, the Progressive Labor Party (PLP), which was supported by Bermuda's Black working class, won its first national election since its 1963 formation. Prior to this, the UBP had dominated party politics. The NOI's Louis Farrakhan visited that year, after having being denied entry previously by the UBP.

This generation included students who attended the Bermuda College, Historically Black Colleges and Universities, and predominantly white institutions across the metropoles of the Americas, Africa, and Europe. They returned home during intense summer and winter breaks transformed by their transnational experiences with racism, Black popular culture, and Black thought. They exchanged these epistemologies with other Bermudians, often at the intersections of sound system venues – sessions, stage shows, weddings, codfish breakfasts, cricket and football games, cookouts, hair salons, church, capoeira *hodas*, dojos, binghis, and bookstores like True Reflections. They returned and left Bermuda with music, locks, tee shirts, VHS cassettes of Haile Gerima's *Sankofa* (which screened at the Liberty Theatre in 1995), Afrocentric lectures, and books like Assata Shakur's *Assata*, Nellie Musson's *Mind the Onion Seed*, Cyril Packwood's *Chained on the Rock*, Marcus Garvey's *Philosophies and Opinions*, George Jackson's *Blood in My Eye*, bell hooks's *Outlaw*

Culture, Rodney's *Groundings with My Brothers*, and Horace Campbell's *Rasta and Resistance*. With the island's voting age set at eighteen, this group reflected a new voting power block. Those born in 1975 would have had the opportunity to have voted in the 1993 general election, which was narrowly won by the UBP.

In 1991, students at the Bermuda College, led by Esan Frederick, claimed that the administration refused to play Reggae in the Student Center. That same year, College students formed the Nationalist Youth Alliance (NYA), a political group which saw itself as acting in the tradition of Bermuda's Black freedom struggles. In the aftermath of the 1993 election, it released its anticolonial newsletter the *Nationalist*. This was as a "result of brainstorming sessions" in which it sought to constructively "articulate its rage and frustrations" at Bermuda's entrenched inequalities. This was part of its political strategy for the next election. Through essays, political satire, poetry, and visual art, the *Nationalist* unflinchingly called for Blacks to unify in a fight against racism, colonialism, and capitalism.[42]

For example, its 1994 political cartoon, "Tea and Crackers," depicted Bermuda's colonial structure as a manifestation of white power. Queen Elizabeth II is depicted at the head of table (Bermuda). To her right is British Governor to Bermuda Lord David Waddington, who is sitting on Bermuda's Black Premier, John Swan. Swan, the current leader of the UBP, is shown as a dog and is fetching a bone of orders. To the Queen's left are white UBP Members of Parliament Dr. Clarence Terceira (of Portuguese descent) and Sir John Sharpe; they have the "UBP Pocket Manual," implying that they and not Swan lead the Party. A Black Regiment Officer is serving tea. Jerome Dill, a Black UBP MP, is referred to as a gnome, suggesting that he was a public figure head. An onlooker is using "offensive" expletives to reference the tea party; he is a stand-in for Black resistance in Bermuda who can see colonialism for what it is.[43] For the NYA, this was a vivid form of political education.[44]

The NYA was alarmed by the criminalization of Black Bermudians, who represented some 90 percent of its prison population. The group identified with "Buck" Burrows and Tacklyn and politicized the

---

[42] "Reggae Returns to Bermuda College," *Bermuda Times*, June 12, 1991, 2; "Youth Alliance Slams Gazette," *Bermuda Times*, January 21, 1994, 8; "Government Panics Over 'Nationalist' Magazine," *Workers' Voice*, January 14, 1994, 1.

[43] Swan, *Back Power in Bermuda*, 188–189.

[44] Ibid.; see also Edwin Smith, "How the People Feel: Visual Art and Socio-political Critique in Bermuda, 1959–2009," Ph.d. Dissertation, 2012.

criminalized memories of both men. This included printing a segment of Burrows's confession in the *Nationalist*. In January 1994, the paper's ten-page issue featured a chained fist and the word "Uprising" on its front cover. It declared: "Our history has shown us that progress is only achieved when we as Black people decide that change is what we must have – by any means necessary." It called for Blacks to break away from slavery and powerlessness and become truly liberated by building a new nation. This, it argued, could only be achieved by "means of a most brutal struggle ... for the redemption, resurrection, and preservation of the Black race" against Bermuda's "evil racist power structure." It read, "P.S. Brother Buck and Brother Larry: They killed the body but the spirit lives on." It called for reparations, denounced the UBP and Black leaders who rejected their community. Attracting significant public attention, it forced Bermuda to reconcile Black Power's anticolonial memories in a moment of critical conversations regarding political independence that perhaps prompted Queen Elizabeth II's visit to Bermuda that March. One page saluted the Mau Mau in Kenya, the Azanian People's Liberation Army (APLA) in South Africa, the Black Panther Party, Haile Selassie, and Black Bermudian political leaders like Eva Hodgson, Walton Brown, E. F. Gordon, Lois Browne Evans, and Walter Robinson as positive examples of leadership in Bermuda.[45]

On January 10, the front page of Bermuda's daily paper, the *Royal Gazette*, read "Youth magazine urges 'fight for change.'" It began, "Killers Buck Burrows and Larry Tacklyn are being remembered in a radical magazine which urges Blacks to fight by any means." On January 11, the paper noted that the Police's Special Branch was probing the magazine, but the writers were yet to be identified even as it was being distributed among Bermuda College students.[46]

The UBP attacked the NYA. Party leader Pamela Gordon was "unconvinced" that young people were behind the *Nationalist*. Acting Premier John Pearman publicly declared: "It is unfortunate that the author of this magazine has seen fit to circulate a document that recommends a violent solution to our lingering racial and other social problems – when the Government has only recently created a new Ministry to seek and

---

[45] "Youth Magazine Urges 'Fight for Change," *Royal Gazette*, January 10, 1994, 1; National Youth Alliance, "Liberation Time Is Now: For We Are Not Yet Free," *Bermuda Times*, January 21, 1994, 4, 6; "MPs Discuss New Youth Magazine," *Royal Gazette*, January 12, 1994, 1.

[46] " 'Fight for Change," *Royal Gazette*, January 10, 1994, 1.

implement solutions to these difficulties." It claimed that these views were "contrary to those of most people on the island."[47]

In response to the *Gazette's* "criminal biased stories," the NYA released a statement, "Liberation Time Is Now: For We Are Not Yet Free," in the *Bermuda Times*, a Black newspaper founded by Ewart Brown. The NYA stressed that its reference to Burrows and Tacklyn was not a "celebration of violence," but a reminder that "the burning desire" to see true freedom, justice, and equality in Bermuda had not been extinguished. While it had "no intention of emulating the revolutionary acts committed by the two brothers in the foreseeable future," it appreciated the "emotion expressed by them."[48]

The NYA argued that "Afrikan people" had historically raised their voices and weapons "in response to the evils committed against them." This included the Mau Mau in Kenya, Bermuda's Progressive Group, and Azanian People's Liberation Army in South Africa. It argued that "violence in pursuit of justice was justified," while physical and social violence to subjugate a people was never acceptable. "Brother Burrows and Brother Tacklyn were simply reacting to the economic, political, cultural, and psychological violence" daily enacted against Bermuda's Black majority. They would not have resorted to violence if Bermuda was an equitable society, as inequality created possibilities for physical eruption. As such, the NYA called for whites to pay Black people reparations for their centuries of free labor. However, as Bermudian whites had displayed an unmatched level of moral corruption, it did "not expect any form of compensation from those who" continued to thrive on Black oppression. Hence, they appealed to Black people – those in the barber shops, the schools, and street corners, to collectively formulate a strategy for self-determination.[49]

Furthermore, Afrikan children needed to be educated about their histories and cultures. Freedom meant engaging in a "brutal struggle" against the island's racist educational and financial establishment. They were insulted by Gordon's assertion that young people were *not* behind the *Nationalist* – several young people recognized the UBP's hypocrisy.

---

[47] "Government Panics Over 'Nationalist' Magazine," *Workers' Voice*, January 14, 1994, 1.

[48] National Youth Alliance, "Liberation Time Is Now," *Bermuda Times*, January 21, 1994, 4, 6.

[49] Ibid.

Quoting the Wailers, the NYA called for Black people, to "GET UP, STAND UP, and FIGHT for what [they] knew to be RIGHT!"[50]

By and large, the Black community supported the NYA. PLP leader Freddy Wade was not surprised and felt that the UBP was not in tune with the people's feelings. Hodgson, who was co-chairperson of the National Association for Reconciliation, found the Government's response to be "deeply disturbing." If the NYA was anti-white, and they might just have been anti-injustice, it was because they were reared in a patently anti-Black society that had ignored recommendations from people like her about how to address racism. The *Workers' Voice* felt that the Government had "panicked," arguing that the *Nationalist* did not call for violence and was only raising concerns that the Bermuda Industrial Union and the PLP had lamented for years. Alvin Williams's "Fear of Youth Magazine" argued that there needed to be no shock at such expressions by Bermuda's college students – the UBP needed to understand young Black rage.[51]

The *Bermuda Times* found that the NYA, the "most talked about organization in Bermuda," was simply calling for "an aggressive approach to eradicating" institutionalized racism. The Government's reaction only showed "just how disconnected" it was from the community and Black youth. As did the *Workers' Voice*, the *Bermuda Times* argued that much of what the *Nationalist* had stated was not new nor marginal – Black people had felt this way for some time. Drawing on the LA uprisings after Rodney King's assault by the police, the paper stressed that the *Nationalist*'s position reflected the long-term alienation and frustration of Bermuda's Black youth about inequalities and was not a spontaneous reaction to a single event. Many Black people agreed with their claim that white supremacy needed to be purged from Bermuda's collective consciousness. If not, a renaissance of Black radicalism would be on the horizon. The *Nationalist*'s use of the words "uprising" and "most brutal struggle" were not incendiary; they were "metaphors in a philosophical" discourse around throwing "off the psychological shackles of white supremacy which [continued] to enslave Black people." Yet, "apologists for institutionalized racism" intentionally interpreted these words to mean advocacy of a "violent physical war against whites; thereby taking this dialogue from the intellectual realm into the physical

[50] Ibid.
[51] "Black Anger Not Surprising, Says Hodgson," *Royal Gazette*, January 17, 1994, 1; Alvin Williams, "Fear of Youth Magazine," *Bermuda Times*, January 21, 1994, 4.

realm – the streets. If their 'warped interpretations' were correct Bermuda would be in flames by now."[52] Such apologists had historically delegitimized Black radicalism in Bermuda by attributing Black insurgency to non-Bermudian West Indian migrants – now they claimed that the *Nationalist* was written by adults.

The NYA was placed under surveillance, phone calls were traced, and the police conducted probes, searched homes, and confiscated materials. Nineteen-year-old John Gibbons was arrested and detained. The Court unsuccessfully attempted to charge him with threatening or insulting the Queen on the eve of her visit to Bermuda on March 8.[53] The *Bermuda Times* felt that the "gestapo-like tactics" used by the police were "repugnant and deplorable" and that it was the police who intimidated the NYA before the visit.[54]

In fact, the *Nationalist* had repeated an insult to the Queen that was made by Kamarakafego in the House of Parliament in 1969. It also called for Bermudians to boycott any "flag waving parade" during her visit to send a clear message to her Majesty that the "sun had set" on the British Empire. It correctly argued that the monarchy was linked to white supremacy, the enslavement and deaths of millions of Black people, and racist education systems:

Every day of our lives as Africans we are threatened with job loss, sexual harassment, economic exploitation, cultural brutalization, Eurocentric miseducation and a biased system of justice by a group of people who have proven over the centuries that our lives mean nothing to them. The most obvious symbols of those threats are visible in the British flag, the police force, the governor and of course the Queen of England.[55]

Writing in the *Workers' Voice*, Duane Dickinson supported the NYA's position about the Queen's visit, and its strong but truthful booklet. Bermuda needed to get out of its "GHETTO MENTALITY." He decried

---

[52] "Government Panics Over 'Nationalist' Magazine," *Workers' Voice*, January 14, 1994, 1; "Police Probe Youth Magazine," *Royal Gazette*, January 11, 1994; "Youth Alliance Slams Gazette," *Bermuda Times*, January 21, 1994, 1; Editorial, "The Nationalist Stirring Black Nationalism," *Bermuda Times*, January 21, 1994, 2.

[53] "Government Panics," *Workers' Voice*, January 14, 1994, 1; Alvin Williams, "A Review of 1994," *Workers' Voice*, December 16, 1994, 2.

[54] "Police Probe New Youth Magazine," *Royal Gazette*, January 11, 1994; "The Empire May Have Disappeared, but the Legacy Lives On," *Bermuda Times*, February 11, 1994, 2; Editorial, "The Nationalist Stirring Black Nationalism," *Bermuda Times*, January 21, 1994, 2.

[55] "National Youth Alliance Protests Queen's Visit," *Bermuda Times*, March 11, 1994, 1, 5.

how Bermudians turned out to see the Queen in new hats, dresses, suits, and shoes. The streets of Hamilton were "jam-packed with school children" and lots of locals waiting for the Queen to pass by. Beyond that, he heard the Queen discuss her trip on the radio, when she commented that since her last visit in 1975 Black people now had higher-paid positions. Dickinson found this to be racist, as she seemed surprised by the abilities of Black people:

"And we must take that from her?" "We give this woman TOO MUCH RESPECT. It seems to me that we give her more respect than we give God ... Bermuda ... What has the Queen done for you? Yes, nothing! As she goes around Bermuda, I guess she says: 'Look at all these Blacks' they have really come along way. BERMUDA, WAKE UP!"[56]

Indeed, in a speech to the annual Speaker's Dinner the Queen claimed that race relations had changed dramatically since the 1970s, as "Black people [had] taken the lead in many areas of national life." At that same dinner, UBP leader Swan stated that it was time for political change in Bermuda, in reference to the independence which was being hotly debated in the house.[57]

Reggae's anticolonial soundscapes enveloped the NYA's calls that March. During the week of the Queen's visit, Bermuda's Tuff Life Productions held Part One of Reggae Fest'94, with Terror Fabulous, Barrington Levy, Jigsy King, Tony Curtis, and the Wailers. Souljah One deejayed for the show. Buju Banton and Wayne Wonder held at concert at Hamilton's Number One Shed. On March 31, Souljah One and Genesis opened for an "Arms House Clash" between New York's Addies and London's Saxon there as well. After acknowledging Bermuda's "sexy body ladies," and its "bad boys" from Devil's Hole, South Side, and 42nd, Addies's Babyface began the clash with a Buju Banton dubplate over Marley's "Zimbabwe," followed by Garnett Silk's "Kingly Character," which rang, "Look to the East, for the coming of a Black king." Ricky Trooper and Killamanjaro performed with Dub City.[58]

[56] Duane Dickinson, "Wake Up Bermuda," *Workers' Voice*, March 25, 1994, 2.
[57] "Queen Tells of Island's Dramatic Change," *Royal Gazette*, March 9, 1994, 1.
[58] Addies vs Saxon, Bermuda, 1994, https://soundcloud.com/hecklersphoenix/king-addies-vs-saxon-94-bda-hecklers-remaster?in=hecklersphoenix/sets/bermuda-audio; "Reggae Fest'94," March 11, 1994, 12; "Around the Community," March 31, 1994, 10; *Bermuda Times*.

BOUNTY KILLER, BERMUDA, AND THE INDEPENDENCE
REFERENDUM OF 1995

Over the next year, as public discourses on independence intensified, anticolonial politics found life in sound system culture. In August 1994, Burning Spear, Mowatt, Louis Culture, and Spragga Benz headlined Bermuda's Reggae Sunsplash at Bermuda's National Stadium. Headliner Burning Spear's canon of music is a tribute to Marcus Garvey and Pan-Africanism. Junior C and Ras Georgis also performed. Georgis, a white "blonde-haired, dreadlocked" Bermudian, acknowledged the suffering of "all of his survivors in the ghetto," across Bermuda's Middletown, Incubator, and the Village. Mowatt exhilarated the crowd by referencing Mandela, the ending of apartheid, and a "free South Africa." She "bigged up the Black women" – "They say that when you train a man, you train an individual. When you train a woman, you train a nation." The crowd joined in as she sang the Wailer's "Lively Up Your Self," and "Get Up, Stand Up."[59]

In September 1994, Keith Simmons's Bermuda Tent Productions held the first Reggae Culture Shock at Somerset Cricket Club. The show featured Tony Rebel, Freddy McGregor, Capleton, and headliner Garnett Silk. With a surreal unique voice, spiritually laced lyrics, and rebel music, Garnett performed songs like "Let Them Talk," "Blessed Be the Almighty God," and "Hello Mama Africa." His "Advantage" called for Jah Jah to "help the underprivileged." In December 1994, a few months after his visit to Bermuda, he died tragically in an explosion in his home in Mandeville, Jamaica, while attempting to save his mother from the burning house. Silk was one of the most significant artists of the era and his dubplates were coveted and embraced by sound systems, including Souljah One.[60]

In 1995, Reggae albums like Buju Banton's *Till Shiloh*, Capleton's *Prophecy*, Beenie Man's *Blessed*, Bounty Killer's *No Argument*, and *Reggae Gold 95* were bursting with political content. This body of music influenced sound clashes, including in Bermuda, where the referendum

---

[59] "Burning Spear Headlines Bermuda Reggae Sunsplash," *Bermuda Times*, August 12, 1994; Gotta Haveit Productions, "Bermuda Reggae Sunsplash 1994," *Bermuda Times*, August 26, 1994, 15.

[60] Sekou Hendrickson, "Culture Shock Dancehall Reggae Returns Tonight," *Royal Gazette*, July 7, 2018, www.royalgazette.com/other/news/article/20180707/culture-shock-dancehall-reggae-returns-tonight/.

bill was closely passed in March 1995. In July 1995, a clash between Souljah One and British DJ David Rodigan invoked decades of racial and colonial tensions. Bass Odyssey, Soul Supreme, and Souljah One held a subsequent session at Ferry Reach, days before the referendum, with Hurricane Felix on the horizon. With selectors of all three sounds chomping at the bit to go to war, promoters stressed that this was not a clash, but an "independence thing." The selectors played *tune* for the people, a heavy dose of Bob Marley, and encouraged Bermudians to "Wake up." During its set, Souljah One remarked, "People, it is up to you and the people you know, you and yourself 'cause tonight is an independence night … a one man you must follow and that is God Almighty and you must know that before you vote … Independence me telling you!" They followed with a dubplate by local artist Corvin Melody, which began, "There will be no sound clash tonight." Souljah One finished by playing a Garnett Silk dubplate as a tribute to the late singer as one of the greatest Reggae artists who died tragically, like Bob Marley, Jacob Miller, and Peter Tosh. They dub played, "They persecute me for things I know not, Oh Jah I promise to serve thee to the end, but my enemies Souljah One I'm asking you to play this song for I, so that my enemies my hear and die. Souljah One bear us a sound and chant them down. ..." Souljah One's toaster finished, "Big up all the independent people … No matter what your country do you must be independent."[61]

Bermuda's referendum on independence was held on August 16, 1995. Called by the UBP's John Swan – who favored independence – the vote was based on the question, "Are you in favor of independence for Bermuda?" Swan's Party was split on the issue, as the UBP had historically relied on the political, military, and logistical support of British colonialism to maintain power over the island's Black majority. PLP leader Freddy Wade called for his Party to boycott the vote, asserting that the community had not been educated enough about independence. He argued that independence needed to be decided via a general election and that the people would have no say in the new constitution under Swan's route. The boycott had a negative impact on the voter turnout.[62] Of the 58.8 percent of eligible voters, 73.6 percent voted against independence, and 25.7 percent voted in favor of it.

---

[61] https://soundcloud.com/soundtapedotcom/odyssey-ssupreme-souljah96.
[62] Alvin Williams, "An Open Plea to My Union Brother and Sisters," *Workers' Voice*, April 14, 1995, 2.

In September 1995, Beenie Man and Bounty Killer performed in Bermuda. Given their past feuds, the audience was surprised to find that it was not a clash. Beenie took the stage first and rinsed his remix of "Crazy Ballheads," which featured Luciano. Bounty Killer, self-identified as the "Poor People's Governor," performed his entire catalogue of music, but also used his time to overtly engage the audience politically. He built community with the audience by giving shout outs to Souljah One and Spanish Town, local Black neighborhoods, "gangs," and other parts of the Black world, "Bermuda, I just gotta say, man from Robert Tree, Lord a Mercy, man from White Wall, Man From 42nd, Lord a Mercy, All the Man from Tivoli, Lawd a mercy. Brooklyn, Devil's Hole, Lawd a mercy...! He then proceeded to sing from one of his more popular songs, "Coppershot," which denounced FBI informants and police surveillance of Black communities.[63]

Bounty asserted that he was "a Rasta in in his heart," and recognized "all the people who loved Emperor Selassie and loved themselves." He then sang his song "Powers Youth," in which he described dreaming about locking his hair about becoming a Rasta. "He decried corrupted people who ceded their sovereignty to the Queen of England but yet believed that "Selassie was dead." He followed this with his song, "Down in the Ghetto," which spoke about crooked politicians who brought guns, crack, and cocaine into the ghetto which supported the killing of the poor. Bounty stopped the song, out of empathy for impoverished Black people suffering in Somalia and South Africa. As such, he called for all people who were proud to be Black to sing along with him, "Bermuda make me hear you!" Bounty himself was "once a ghetto boy" who suffered from "poverty and hunger." He asked all those who knew "their roots, culture and heritage" to raise their hands, and sang his next song for his "suffering Black brothers and sisters," "all Africans," and especially Nelson Mandela, who fought "for the Black nation." He sang his anti-apartheid song "Prophecy Fulfill," which he had released on his 1993 album *Down in the Ghetto*. The song viewed Mandela's release from prison as the "fulfillment of prophecy," and it placed Mandela in the Black Radical Tradition of Martin Luther King, Jr., Malcolm X, Garvey, Paul Bogle, "Lady" Queen Nanny, Tosh, and Marley.

Bounty then set his sights to politics and independence in Bermuda: "Listen . . . Me nah know if politician a try take over Bermuda too, but me

---

[63] Beenie Man vs Bounty Killer, Bermuda 1995, https://www.youtube.com/watch?v=Rjv9KnsCp4Q.

discover say the people them don't get independence." In contrast, Bounty argued, he was from Jamaica where he had "freedom of speech" and would speak his mind. He then launched into his blistering, "Go Now," in a cappella, which lamentes how politicians stacked the people like groceries on a shelf. He questioned if "the guys in Parliament" had a conscience, because they came into the ghetto daily to make "long statements" and promises while exploiting the poor. He asked Bermudians to look into themselves, calling for politicians to "go now!" Over the roaring crowds and the music of his Caution band, he brilliantly continued to sing how it was confusing how politicians could act as if they were not voted in, and as such could be voted *out*. The people needed better education and housing, and he cried to see his Black brothers die. He called for armed struggle against the state, if politicians continued to take the people "for idiot."

Referencing Bermuda's Robert Tree Crew, Frontline, and 42nd crew, Bounty called for Black people not to clash against each other, but to fight against the "system." He was there to clash against the Pope and Queen Elizabeth II, not Beenie Man. He went into his song "Mama" and further decried poverty, religious persecution, the miseducation of children, state violence, and political and economic exploitation. He admitted that he sang a lot of "gun tune" but it was time for culture as the people were looking for direction. Bounty sang his "Roots, Reality, Culture," which, before singing, he exclaimed, that anyone who did not this song did not understand who Bounty Killer really was. "[64]

Bermuda's Kim Dismont Robinson, MA student at the University of Florida, would certainly have agreed with Bounty. Her January 1996 essay, "How Dancehall Saved Bermuda," argued in defense of Reggae's unruly offspring. She noted how the Souljah One–Rodigan clash received front page complaints in the *Gazette* the following day, as sound clashes typically did. Robinson argued that Dancehall did not need to be condemned for its gun lyrics, excessive use of ganja, or misogynistic "slackness lyrics" which were demeaning to women, particularly when critics talked less about the positive lyrics of Capleton and Silk. In identifying with Reggae, she felt that Bermudians were identifying with their "West Indian bredren." This was a positive step, as Bermuda was a part of the West Indian family. Colonialism ensured that Black Bermudians hailed from various Caribbean islands, who were reminded of this while

[64] Ibid.

traveling – "try telling an American or Briton that you're separated from a Bajan, and they will look at you like you are crazy." There were stark economic differences, however, given Bermuda's GDP was higher than most countries in the West Indies. Robinson argued that this resulted in Bermudians becoming more caught up in physical wealth, which led them on a path toward spiritual and cultural bankruptcy, arrogancy, and materialistic "snobiness." But then Dancehall showed up and reminded Bermudians of their cultural and historical relationships with the rest of the region. For Robinson, this was the first time that Bermudians were identifying with West Indians. Bob Marley "began with Babylon System and his descendants in the 1990s continued to keep it real."[65] This, in essence, was a process of decolonization.

Sound system culture could "free decolonization," but it played a critical role in galvanizing the PLP's youth base in its victory over the UBP in the 1998 national elections. According to PLP leader and Premier of Bermuda Jennifer Smith, this monumental occasion ended the rule "of the oligarchy that had controlled this island for more than three decades."[66] Independence, however, was another matter. In 2004, the PLP's controversial Independence Commission (BIC) found that race dominated the discussions – Black Bermudians linked the island's colonial status to slavery, segregation, and racial inequality, and saw independence as necessary for racial unity. In comparison, many whites saw Britain as their "Mother Country" and expressed fears that an independent Bermuda would be compared to the "recently emerged, poor, Black led Caribbean countries."[67]

In 2005, a UN Special Mission to Bermuda also found that racial issues "dominated the discussion" of independence. The "wounds ... of the historic legacy of segregation were very apparent," particularly among older Black Bermudians. In contrast, white Bermudians raised concerns that independence would affect the "stability" of the island and damage the economy. In 2018, current Premier David Burt asserted that the next chapter of Bermuda was independence. He stated in the House of Assembly that it was "unacceptable in a modern democracy" to have "decisions made thousands of miles away that impact our customs, our

---

[65] Kim Dismont Robinson, "How Dancehall Saved Bermuda," *Bermuda Times*, January 5, 1996, 10, 13.

[66] Progressive Labor Party, *A New Bermuda*, 1998, Hamilton: Progressive Labor Party.

[67] BIC, *Report of the Bermuda Independence Commission*, August 2005, 36, Hamilton: Bermuda Independence Commission, Bermuda.

institutions and our livelihoods." While the Party would "serve as a vehicle in moving Bermuda to independence," it was not on the current agenda of the PLP. As such, unless driven from beyond Parliament, decolonization in Bermuda will remain arrested for the foreseeable future.[68]

[68] United Nations, *Report of the United Nations Special Mission to Bermuda*, A/AC.109/ 2005/19, June 21, 2005; David Burt, "Burt: Our Next Chapter Is Independence," *Royal Gazette*, May 24, 2018.

14

Epilogue: The National and the Colonial in the Anticolonial Transnational

Michael Goebel

Puerto Rico, which barring Tony Wood's chapter is mostly absent from the present volume, encapsulates many of the difficulties inherent in understanding colonialism and defining anticolonialism. Although the island's official designation as an unincorporated territory studiously avoids the tainted terminology of colonialism, its relationship to the United States is irrefutably colonial in that Puerto Ricans have neither a sovereign state of their own nor full rights as US citizens. In the sense that both the option of independence and the option of incorporation as the fifty-first state would do away with this intrinsically colonial dimension of the US–Puerto Rican relationship, they can both legitimately claim to be anticolonial. But is the shaky plurality of voters who in past referendums have opted for the maintenance of the status quo therefore pro-colonial? They would likely object to such a characterization. Instead, they view their island's relationship to the United States as insufficiently colonial to require a kind of liberation that entails risks without certain benefits. Insofar as they concede their island's coloniality at all, they apparently see reforms around the edges of the status quo as the most adequate remedy to whatever is still there in terms of vestiges of colonialism. While, if prompted, the vast majority of Puerto Ricans would probably profess to oppose colonialism, without concurring on what it is or where it manifests itself most perniciously, they will necessarily diverge on how to combat it. In other words, they disagree over the most appropriate definitions of colonialism and thus also of anticolonialism.

If Puerto Ricans cannot agree, why expect unanimity from historians? By attempting a collective delineation of the history of "the anticolonial transnational," the present volume invites commentary on how such an attempt amends our understanding of the national and of the colonial. The purpose of the following pages is to raise this question on the basis of the key features that characterize this volume within the larger historiography of anticolonialism and decolonization: first, its particular (spatial) attention to transnational dimensions of anticolonialism that exceeded the binary relationship between colony and metropole; and second, its (temporal) argument that the ideological aim of a new nation-state and the moment of formally reaching that aim are both ill-suited to delimiting the historical contours of anticolonialism. Against this backdrop, the following pages will ask two questions: First, what does the prefix trans-do to our appreciation of the importance of nationalism within anticolonialism? Second, if the nation-state was neither the defining ideological goal nor the temporal endpoint of anticolonial struggles, how do we redraw our definitional boundaries around anticolonialism in a manner that avoids making the phenomenon amorphous?

The groundwork for raising such questions has been laid only in the last two decades or so. Historians writing in the twentieth century barely asked them because, when they wrote about colonial situations and decolonization, they largely, if often implicitly, equated anticolonialism with the goal of achieving sovereign statehood – and thus with "nationalism," if by that term we mean, following Ernest Gellner, "the political principle, which holds that the political and the national unit should be congruent."[1] Scholarly debates in the immediate aftermath of formal decolonization often revolved around the question of whether this principle had been granted by metropolitan policymakers or conquered by anticolonial nationalists.[2] By the 1980s and 90s, historians, inspired or irritated by Benedict Anderson, concentrated on the degree to which anticolonial nationalism should be viewed as a discourse derivative of nationalism in Europe, or rather as something else altogether.[3] More recently, however, a host of scholars – such as Frederick Cooper, Adom Getachew, and Manu Goswami – have rescued from oblivion strands of anticolonial thought that envisioned paths to enfranchisement, self-determination, or sovereignty other than national.[4] The presumably

---

[1] Ernest Gellner, *Nations and Nationalism* (Oxford: Blackwell, 1983), 1.

[2] E.g., Rudolf von Albertini, *Decolonization: The Administration and Future of the Colonies, 1919–1960* (Garden City, NY: Doubleday, 1971).

[3] Partha Chatterjee, *Nationalist Thought and the Colonial World: A Derivative Discourse?* (London: Zed Books, 1986).

[4] Frederick Cooper, *Citizenship between Empire and Nation: Remaking France and French West Africa, 1945–1960* (Princeton: Princeton University Press, 2014); Adom Getachew,

self-explanatory insouciance with which earlier generations of historians equated anticolonialism with nationalism has been shattered. As Erez Manela and Heather Streets-Salter underline in their introduction to this volume, the authors assembled herein contribute their own part to this breakage, cumulatively offering an understanding of anticolonialism in which the nation-state no longer looks "natural and inevitable."

At first sight, the fracture may appear to be a result of inserting the prefix trans- before "national," or of the arrival of the transnational turn in the history of anticolonialism more broadly. After all, transnational history has essentially rested on the, unfortunately often ill-defined, call to go "beyond the nation-state" in historical writing.[5] Such a call was long seen as superfluous to colonial history, which by definition concerned chiefly places that were not nation-states. Even if we portray colonies, through nationalist eyes, as proto-national, their colonial history could never neatly be separated from the metropole, so that Ann Laura Stoler and Frederick Cooper's demand to "treat metropole and colony in a single analytic field" involved an inescapably transnational angle, too.[6] Yet, as the present volume highlights, by exploring the manifold transfers and networks across various parts of the colonial and formally postcolonial world, the transnational lens can still be applied productively, directing our attention away from metropolitan-colonial bilateralism. It is this kind of transnationalism that may at first sight make the constituent parts of empires look less (proto-)national. Choosing the prefix trans- instead of the formerly more common inter-(national), as this volume does, moreover foregrounds non-state actors as well as dimensions of anticolonialism not first and foremost directed toward achieving statehood and participation in international society, or future inter-state relations, for instance through the United Nations.

The contributions to this volume demonstrate how such an approach brings to the fore ingredients of anticolonial struggles worldwide that did not exclusively or primarily serve the pursuit of independent nation-states. One example were visions of ethnocultural belonging not easily

---

Worldmaking after Empire: The Rise and Fall of Self-Determination (Princeton: Princeton University Press, 2019); Manu Goswami, "Imaginary Futures and Colonial Internationalisms," *The American Historical Review* 117, no. 5 (2012): 1461–1485.

[5] See e.g., the "AHR Conversation: On Transnational History," *The American Historical Review* 111, no. 5 (2006): 1441–1464.

[6] Ann Laura Stoler and Frederick Cooper, "Between Metropole and Colony: Rethinking a Research Agenda," in *Tensions of Empire: Colonial Cultures in a Bourgeois World*, eds. Cooper and Stoler (Berkeley: University of California Press, 1997), 1–56, here: 4.

transfigured into the straightjacket of territorially contiguous nation-states, such as the pan-Asianism and the pan-Africanism addressed by Nicole CuUnjieng Aboitiz and Sarah Dunstan in this volume.[7] As shown by Zaib un Nisa Aziz and Tony Wood, the amalgamation of anticolonialism with anti-capitalist ideas and left-wing internationalism, enabled partly by Lenin's characterization of imperialism as the highest stage of capitalism, could likewise demote the nation-state as the most promising vessel for achieving greater rights. White allies, who the chapters by Michele Louro and Lydia Walker reveal to have often been women, also helped tie anticolonialism to a host of causes exceeding questions about the formal juridical-territorial arrangement of national sovereignty. Following Mark Reeves's chapter about the Philippine diplomat Carlos Romulo, we may even wonder if some anticolonialists stood neither on the Left, where historians have long found them, nor on the extreme Right, where they have been excavated more recently,[8] but instead in a socially bourgeois and politically accommodationist, albeit right-leaning, Middle, which was quite comfortable with certain aspects of empire.

The main benefit of this kind of kaleidoscopic and capacious approach is to drive home the multifarious nature of anticolonialism beyond the supposedly unifying objective of sovereign statehood. In fact, characterizing anticolonialism exclusively in terms of this objective, purportedly settled through what David Armitage has called the "contagion of sovereignty,"[9] risks making the entire phenomenon look unsatisfactorily anemic. Anticolonialism was, as this volume reveals, about far more than acquiring a chic palais for an embassy in Paris or Geneva, even if Romulo's case suggests that it could be precisely about that. From Cheikh Anta Diop's academic Africanization of ancient Egypt, treated in Dunstan's chapter, to late-twentieth-century Reggae in Bermuda, explored by Quito Swan, anticolonialism was always also about what both Swan and this volume's editors, borrowing from Charles Taylor, call "the politics of recognition" in a white-dominated world. In its left-wing

---

[7] See also their monographs: Nicole CuUnjieng Aboitiz, *Asian Place, Filipino Nation: A Global Intellectual History of the Philippine Revolution, 1887–1912* (New York: Columbia University Press, 2020) and Sarah C. Dunstan, *Race, Rights, and Reform: Black Activism in the French Empire and the United States from World War I to the Cold War* (Cambridge and New York: Cambridge University Press, 2021).

[8] David Motadel, "The Global Authoritarian Moment and the Revolt Against Empire," *The American Historical Review* 124, no. 3 (2019): 843–877.

[9] David Armitage, "The Contagion of Sovereignty: Declarations of Independence Since 1776," *South African Historical Journal* 52 (2005): 1–18.

iteration, delineated by Zaib un Nisa Aziz and Tony Wood, it was just as much about combating capitalism, the exploitation of labor, and global economic inequality. Above all, and in virtually all cases, it was about remedying the dearth of rights of the colonized that was intrinsic and endemic to colonialism – an issue that became particularly condensed in the figure of citizenship in the globally few cases of republican empires.[10] From this perspective, anticolonialism resembled William Galston's dictum about liberalism: "a basket of ideals," which may well "come into conflict with one another if a serious effort is made to realize any one of them fully, let alone all of them simultaneously."[11]

However, should historians treat all these examples, like the three Puerto Rican options, as equally, albeit *differently*, anticolonial? Or are we allowed, even commissioned, also to canvass them as *more or less* anticolonial, and to determine different degrees of proximity to some sort of ideological core? Discourses and ideologies have fuzzy boundaries, so no one will want to draw too sharp a boundary around them. But the terms we use to designate these discourses or ideologies have their own histories and path dependencies, which limit the plausibility of an all-in approach. It is remarkable in this respect that the authors assembled in this volume appear to feel more or less obligated to justify the treatment of their chosen topics or personalities as instances of "anticolonialism," presumably because they anticipate that doing so will not, across all chapters, be equally intuitive for the imagined reader.

Many chapters touch upon phenomena for which the label of anti-colonialism is both definitionally admissible and heuristically illuminating, but not always the most obvious. The majority of the Latin American activists and intellectuals populating Wood's chapter would never have objected to being called anticolonialists. But, except for the Puerto Ricans, they tended to associate the colonial with the past Spanish Empire, from which most of their countries had long achieved independence, so that they framed their activism in opposition not to colonialism, but to (US) *imperialism*. While Reeves's chapter about Romulo reveals the diplomat's irreproachably anticolonial family tree, reconstructs instances in which he campaigned against specific symptoms of American colonialism, and cites his principled opposition to European colonialism in other Asian countries, his "faith in America" and in its promise of the Philippines' future

---

[10] Cooper, *Citizenship*.

[11] William A. Galston, *Liberal Purposes: Goods, Virtues, and Diversity in the Liberal State* (Cambridge: Cambridge University Press, 1991), 95.

independence diminished his appetite for concrete steps precipitating the archipelago's decolonization. We can call this, following Reeves, a "nonradical vision of anticolonialism," but could we not just as well argue that Romulo's professed "Americanism" whittled away at the anticolonial share within his overall basket of ideals?

Along similar lines: Léopold Sédar Senghor, the later Senegalese president to whom Reeves compares Romulo, accumulated impeccably anticolonial credentials over decades. Though a demonstrably late convert to the nation-state solution, his postwar attempts to reform the French Empire into a less unequal federation likewise qualify as anticolonial insofar as he hoped that such reforms, qua the extension of citizenship to Africans, would flatten the steep rights differentials characteristic of colonialism. But once these reforms turned out to be insufficiently capable of achieving precisely that, he could salvage his anticolonial credentials only by quickly coming around to the nation-state solution already adopted by his more radical Guinean peer, Ahmed Sékou Touré.[12] Yes, Senghor and Sékou Touré were *differently* anticolonial, in that they had different understandings of the colonial that required opposition. But it is also true that Senghor was readier than Sékou Touré to accommodate a range of aspects of colonialism into his political and cultural vision. Can we not therefore call him *less* anticolonial without for that reason buying into Frantz Fanon's denunciation of all those unpersuaded by the nation-state model as "pharisees"?[13]

The problem of defining the boundaries of anticolonialism became only more acute after independence, when freedom fighters turned statesmen became torn between, on the one hand, taking credit for having finished the matter of colonialism altogether through the masterstroke of national sovereignty, and, on the other hand, justifying their policies by citing the need of removing its wreckage. The later chapters of this volume demonstrate that the benchmarks for certifying the anticolonialism of this or that person, movement, idea, or policy only grew wobblier with increasing temporal distance from the fulcrum of independence. For instance, the turn away from the New International Economic Order (NIEO) toward ideas of self-reliance, which Vivien Chang compellingly

---

[12] Janet G. Vaillant, *Black, French, and African: A Life of Léopold Sédar Senghor* (Cambridge, MA: Harvard University Press, 1990) is probably still the best Englishlanguage biography, though the entire political process can be best followed through Cooper, *Citizenship*.

[13] Frantz Fanon, *The Wretched of the Earth* (New York: Grove Press, 1963), 246.

reconstructs, stood in an undeniably anticolonial tradition, evidenced not least in the continuity of personnel. But from another angle, both the NIEO and the rise of self-reliance could just as plausibly be interpreted as attempts to try something new altogether, a result of the realization that anticolonialism had produced no more than a Pyrrhic victory, in the form of independence, especially with respect to the economic goals in the orbit of anticolonialism. If the new arose from the obsoleteness of the old, it may not be best to designate both with the same term. Quite consequently, Chang calls her period "postcolonial" and for the most part reserves the label "anticolonial" for a kind of political kudos that was a spillover from the "colonial era."

This practical use of terms should make us rethink the increasingly common scholarly dissociation between anticolonialism and nationalism. How tangential do we want nationalism to be to our histories of anticolonialism? The transnational perspective adopted in this volume does not, in and of itself, undermine the view, supposedly dominant until recently, that "took the advent of new nation-states as natural and inevitable." Theoretically, as Kiran Patel has argued, transnational perspectives on history should not tempt us into a "wishful thinking that seeks to abolish nationalism and nation-states altogether by denying their importance as subject matters of analysis." On the contrary, "the very logic of the transnational" implies that "the nation-state or an elaborated national consciousness represent a certain point of reference."[14] Practically, the twentieth-century world, with which the chapters of this volume are concerned, saw a massive proliferation of the nation-state as a form of political legitimation – not only, but particularly in the world regions on which this volume concentrates. Widening our lens sideways, beyond the tunnel of a single metropolitan–colonial relationship, casts additional doubts on an understanding of anticolonialism to which the nation-state model was incidental: first, because this kind of transnational perspective reveals the serial repetition of a formally similar outcome across a multitude of cases; second, because it brings into view the transnational circulation of the nation-state model itself.

The ostensibly "anti-teleological approach"[15] to the study of anticolonialism and decolonization, which portrays the nation-state as a

---

[14] Kiran Klaus Patel, "Transatlantische Perspektiven transnationaler Geschichte," *Geschichte und Gesellschaft* 29 (2003): 625–647, here 628 and 629.
[15] I borrow the label from Michael Collins, "Nation, State, and Agency: Evolving Historiographies of African Decolonization," in *Britain, France, and the*

surprising and unforeseeable outcome of anticolonial struggles, often rests on exactly the methodological nationalism that this volume contributes to overcoming: reducing the analysis to a singular colony-then-nation (albeit in its relationship to the metropole), while blinding out what happened in the neighborhood and the wider world. To present Algeria's transformation into a nation-state in 1962 as counterintuitive or startling, for example,[16] means to disregard the independence of Tunisia and Morocco in 1956; events that in light of decades of joint North African anticolonial movements surely increased the imaginability of such an outcome even in the more rugged terrain of Algeria. Likewise, to portray the federalist citizenship of the French Community of 1958, with hindsight, as a generally workable fix to colonial injustices,[17] requires us not only to overestimate the intersection between French largesse and African satisfaction, but also to omit the many parts of the French Empire, such as Indochina, where neither colonizers nor colonized even tried such a solution.

As the present volume impressively shows, the various parts of any given empire, as well as the various parts of the colonized world, were connected in multiple ways, which also facilitated the circulation of the nation-state model as a supposed panacea. The Comintern, a transnational organization par excellence, served as a key vessel during the interwar period. For all its internationalism and anti-capitalism, the Comintern touted the nation-state as a one-size-fits-all cure to the malady of colonialism much more consistently than those its lexicon dubbed as "bourgeois nationalists," who ironically were often less convinced of sovereign statehood, and instead more invested in all things cultural. Tellingly, the full English name of the Comintern-financed organization that emerged at a conference in Brussels in 1927, mentioned in many contributions to this volume, was League against Imperialism and for National Independence.[18] To emphasize this ultimate aim and synchronize the world's miscellaneous anticolonialisms toward this target, the organizers of the Brussels conference, tapping into the transnational

Decolonization of Africa, eds. Andrew W. M. Smith and Chris Jeppesen (London: UCL Press, 2017), 29.

[16] Todd Shepard, *The Invention of Decolonization: The Algerian War and the Remaking of France* (Ithaca, NY: Cornell University Press, 2008).

[17] Cooper, *Citizenship*.

[18] Michele Louro, Carolien Stolte, Heather Streets-Salter, and Sana Tannoury-Karam (eds.), *The League against Imperialism: Lives and Afterlives* (Leiden: Leiden University Press, 2020).

FIGURE 14.1. Participants of the Conference of the League against Imperialism, Brussels, 1927. Messali Hadj is the fifth from the left.

Latin American networks explored by Wood, spotlighted Puerto Rico as the one Latin American example that still required formal independence. Likewise, the organizers elbowed anticolonial activists, such as the Paris-based Algerian Messali Hadj, who did not (yet) have formal independence as their utmost priority, into adopting this watchword and propagating it on the Brussels stage.[19]

After the Second World War, the United Nations accelerated this global streamlining toward the nation-state model. One may quibble over whether that organization should not more appositely have been called United States, had that name not already been taken. But the Universal Declaration of Human Rights passed by the UN General Assembly in 1948 expressly promulgated that "everyone has the right to a nationality." As Cindy Ewing outlines in her chapter, the UN Trusteeship Council

---

[19] Michael Goebel, "Forging a Proto-Third World? Latin America and the League against Imperialism," and Dónal Hassett, "An Independent Path: Algerian Nationalists and the League against Imperialism," both in *The League against Imperialism*, eds. Louro et al., 53–105.

became a forum of international solidarity, in which newly independent member states relayed petitions from "non-white peoples and non-Western nations, many still under colonial occupation" (p. 167). Not unlike the League of Nations' earlier Mandates Commission examined by Susan Pedersen,[20] this internationalization was simultaneously a process of nationalization. As Eva-Maria Muschik has recently argued, the UN played a key role "in the transition from a world of empires to one of nominal nation-states in the 1950s and 1960s."[21]

The pan-visions of shared civilizational spheres, explored by CuUnjieng Aboitiz and Dunstan in this volume, were fundamentally different, but they could also work as vehicles for the spread of anticolonialism *and* nationalism. Unlike the Comintern, stingy in supplying the cultural raw material from which to build nations, the pan-visions offered rich understandings of ethnocultural belonging. Insofar as the material they provided, and the demographic units they imagined, did not match (that is, usually exceeded) the national units that eventually became encased in nation-states, they are often seen as alternatives or competitors to the nation-state model. However, different spheres of imagined belonging can be complementary, even mutually supportive, especially if the various spheres in play are not equally national. As exemplified by the centrality of Catholicism for Irishness or of Orthodoxy for Greekness, unmistakably non-national, for instance religious, signifiers can bolster national consciousness instead of undermining them. And as the evocative title of CuUnjieng Aboitiz's book, *Asian Place, Filipino Nation*, suggests, Asianism may well have buttressed Filipino nationhood; at least until its instrumentalization by Japanese imperialists diminished its appeal for anticolonialists and nationalists outside of Japan.[22] As Cemil Aydin has shown, the rise and decline of pan-Islamic and pan-Asian thought more broadly paralleled its usefulness as a cultural tool of opposition to the force (the West) perceived as most threatening to Asian nations. In this constellation, pan-visions coexisted happily with, and occasionally reinforced, the smaller constituent nationalisms.[23]

[20] Susan Pedersen, *The Guardians: The League of Nations and the Crisis of Empire* (Oxford and New York: Oxford University Press, 2015).

[21] Eva-Maria Muschik, *Building States: The United Nations, Development, and Decolonization, 1945–1965* (New York: Columbia University Press, 2022), 2.

[22] CuUnjieng Aboitiz, *Asian Place, Filipino Nation*. On its imperialist use and subsequent denouement: Jeremy Yellen, *The Greater East Asia Co-Prosperity Sphere: When Total Empire Met Total War* (Ithaca, NY: Cornell University Press, 2019).

[23] Cemil Aydin, *The Politics of Anti-Westernism in Asia: Visions of World Order in Pan-Islamic and Pan-Asian Thought* (New York: Columbia University Press, 2007).

This was also true of pan-Arabism and pan-Africanism, although the demographic units they denoted were less clearly non-national from the get-go: In the absence of state monopolies on the signifier "nation," the Jamaican-born Marcus Garvey could evoke an "African nation" in the singular, while the Geneva-based Syrian activist Shakib Arslan could publish a journal titled *La Nation Arabe*. If Africans and Arabs were nations, then pan-Africanism and pan-Arabism were non-nationalist ideologies only in the sense that their imagined reference nations could not easily be trimmed into a territorially contiguous state, making the fulfilment of Gellner's principle of congruency all but impossible. What was possible, however, was to transfigure "African" from a national into a racial and/or geographic demonym, made up by multiple constituent African nations in the plural. The presence of that plural in the title of Cheikh Anta Diop's 1954 book, *Nations nègres et culture*, the content of which Dunstan examines in some depth, betrayed how far pan-Africanists had advanced in this conceptual operation prior to the independence of most of sub-Saharan Africa. This multiplication and re-localization of the national prepared the ground for the attempts of postcolonial leaders, such as Ghana's Kwame Nkrumah, to fold pan-Africanism into the legitimation of new postcolonial states that were invariably "sub-African."[24] As a Google Ngram of "pan-Africanism" reveals, the very prefix pan- truly began to make sense only once judged against the emerging backdrop of multiple African nation-states.[25]

None of the above means that the nation-state as a remedy to the injustices of colonialism appeared equally conceivable and advisable to all historical actors, everywhere, at all times. The political benefit expectable from evoking Gellner's principle of congruency between state and nation varied between people, places, and over time. So did what Benedict Anderson termed the emotional plausibility of nationhood – which in many cases would follow from, not precede, the evocation of the nation-state principle.[26] Nor does any of the above mean that the nation-state

---

[24] Matteo Grilli, *Nkrumaism and African Nationalism: Ghana's Pan-African Foreign Policy in the Age of Decolonization* (Cham: Palgrave Macmillan, 2020). On the role of the Trinidadian pan-Africanist George Padmore in these attempts: Leslie James, *George Padmore and Decolonization: Pan-Africanism, the Cold War, and the End of Empire* (New York: Palgrave Macmillan, 2015), 143–190.

[25] https://books.google.com/ngrams/graph?content=Pan+-+Africanism&year_start=1950&year_end=1970&corpus=26&smoothing=0

[26] Benedict Anderson, *Imagined Communities: Reflections on the Origins and Spread of Nationalism*, 2nd edition (London: Verso, 1993), 47–66.

was implemented in a uniform, let alone "successful," manner. The question of who or what, in the eyes of today's historian, truly deserves the label of the nation-state is an ill-advised starting point for histories of anticolonialism. Elevating real and complete congruency between the political and the national unit into the threshold of what counts as a nation-state would end up defining nation-states out of existence. Real-life congruency to everyone's satisfaction would also render the invocation of the nation-state principle – that is, nationalism – superfluous for the purposes of political legitimation. The narrower and more productive question is therefore about when, where, and why this principle gained traction.

We need not turn to the recent historiography's counterfactuals, such as Algeria or French West Africa, in order to see that the nation-state was, indeed, "not inevitable" everywhere. It truly has been avoided (so far) in some places. Guam and Bermuda, with which this volume's last two chapters are concerned, are cases in point. There are demographically larger examples too, such as Puerto Rico or New Caledonia. More broadly still, there are forms of governance, usually monarchies, in which political power is not even legitimized as flowing from the people/nation. As Manela and Streets-Salter point out, decolonization was clearly incomplete, or "arrested," by the late 1960s, and it still is today. The UN gained no fewer than thirty-four newly decolonized member states between 1968 and 1990 alone, followed by a new wave of admissions in the wake of the breakups of Yugoslavia and the Soviet Union. Even as we may not want to call the latter postcolonial, another six countries from the Pacific, which fit that designation more unequivocally, have been added since 1994. If this list shows "arrested" decolonization after 1960, it equally reveals the incompleteness of nationalization.

It is not impossible to identify broad patterns in this incomplete global history of when, where, and why the national dimension was more or less central to anticolonialism, and of when, where, and why the nation-state solution was therefore a more or less likely outcome of anticolonial struggles. For one, the willingness of metropolitan actors to extend forms of political-juridical integration capable of *both* flattening colonial hierarchies *and* forestalling the alternative of national independence hinged in good part on demography. The infamous warning by former French prime minister Édouard Herriot that the French Union of 1946 might turn France into "the colony of its former colonies" was less plausible for Martinique or Réunion, whose inhabitants had in any event held French citizenship since 1848, than it was in relation to West Africa,

Madagascar, or Indochina.[27] In many demographically small islands, such as Bermuda or Guam, the absence of indigenous majorities, extreme economic dependence on the motherland, and the longevity of colonialism conspired to encumber the evocation of a pre-colonial past to undergird Gellner's nationalist principle. It is no surprise that this volume's chapters on "arrested" decolonization disproportionately concern the kinds of places that in French used to be belittled as the "confetti of empire," or that, in more recent American diction, have been called the "pointillist empire."[28]

But even in this realm, examples such as Kiribati and Vanuatu, quite conceivably followed at some point soon by New Caledonia, should alert us to the ongoing imaginability of sovereign nationhood. Nor should the seemingly perpetual delay of a national outcome in some places be historically severed from its earlier arrival elsewhere. The prospects of fighting colonialism through integrationist (or federalist) reforms in one corner of an empire often hinged on the exclusion of another such corner. If the Jones Act of 1916 provided the legal justification of Romulo's confidence in the Philippines' future independence, another Jones Act, passed the following year, extended US citizenship, albeit of a second-class nature, to Puerto Ricans and thus undermined the option of independence. As Mary Lewis has pointed out, "although the creation of the French Union [of 1946] offered some colonial subjects a greater stake in associating with France, in Tunisia, it in some ways achieved the opposite effect, by underscoring Tunisia's sovereign status under international law."[29] The British Nationality Act of 1948, which created the legal figure of the "Citizen of the United Kingdom and Colonies," was precipitated by an independent Canadian citizenship in 1946 and eventually passed once India's independence in 1947 appeared to have taken the demographically most significant question concerning its applicability out of the equation.[30]

---

[27] Cooper, *Citizenship*, 105.

[28] Robert Aldrich and John Connell, *France's Overseas Frontier: Départements et territoires d'outre-mer* (Cambridge: Cambridge University Press, 1992), 16 and 243; Daniel Immerwahr, *How to Hide an Empire: A History of the Greater United States* (New York: Farrar, Straus, and Giroux, 2019).

[29] Mary D. Lewis, *Divided Rule: Sovereignty and Empire in French Tunisia, 1881–1938* (Berkeley: University of California Press, 2014), 170.

[30] Matters of course turned out far more complicated in practice: Sarah Ansari and William Gould, *Boundaries of Belonging: Localities, Citizenship and Rights in India and Pakistan* (Cambridge: Cambridge University Press, 2019).

It is certainly true that, as Cooper writes, the nation-state "has not proven itself to be such a clear route to human progress," or even to be the most persuasive antidote to colonialism.[31] Making Puerto Rico the fifty-first state may indeed be a more plausible path to "human progress" than the island's national sovereignty.[32] But the extent to which the solution of incorporation will, after the fact, qualify as equally anti-colonial as the national alternative will depend on its proponents' future ability to convince Puerto Ricans that their remedy to colonialism was more than homeopathic. Incorporation may, in this respect, require an ongoing effort at persuasion that the nation-state solution, from which it is harder to walk back into incorporation, does not. That this volume's latter chapters on "arrested" decolonization disproportionately focus on places that never adopted the nation-state as a form of political legitim-ation only goes to confirm the extent to which the national and the colonial continue to be juxtaposed in a conceptual dichotomy. Unlocking it, for better or for worse, is more difficult than the historians who wish to dissociate anticolonialism from nationalism appear to imagine.

[31] Frederick Cooper, *Africa and the World: Capitalism, Empire, Nation-State* (Cambridge, MA: Harvard University Press, 2014), 68.

[32] Alberto C. Medina, "Let Puerto Ricans Choose Their Fate – and Give the U.S. Congress a Deadline to Accept It," *The New Republic*, July 22, 2022.

Index

For EU product safety concerns, contact us at Calle de José Abascal, 56–1°, 28003 Madrid, Spain or eugpsr@cambridge.org.